AF709084

The Unexplored Keynes and Other Essays

Anand Chandavarkar is graduate of the University of Bombay and the London School of Economics. He has served as an academic in India: Research Economist, Bank Award Commission, India; Director in the Reserve Bank of India; Assistant Director, the International Monetary Fund; Economic Adviser, Bank of Libya; Consultant to the Organization for Economic Cooperation and Development (Paris), the World Bank, and the Presidential Commission on Finance and Banking, Sri Lanka. He is the author of *Keynes and India* (Macmillan Press, 1989) and *Central Banking in Developing Countries* (Macmillan Press and St. Martin Press, 1996). He has published widely in leading academic and professional journals, including *The Economic Journal, The Oxford Economic Papers, The Quarterly Journal of Economics* and the *Economic and Political Weekly*, and also contributed to *The Cambridge Economic History of India*. He was an invited speaker at the Tenth Keynes Seminar at the University of Kent, Canterbury, England (1991) and the One Hundredth Annual Meeting of the American Philosophical Association, (Eastern Division), Washington D.C., 2003.

The Unexplored Keynes and Other Essays

A Socio-Economic Miscellany

ANAND CHANDAVARKAR

ACADEMIC FOUNDATION
NEW DELHI

First published in 2009
by

ACADEMIC FOUNDATION
4772-73 / 23 Bharat Ram Road, (23 Ansari Road),
Darya Ganj, New Delhi - 110 002 (India).
Phones : 23245001 / 02 / 03 / 04.
Fax : +91-11-23245005.
E-mail : books@academicfoundation.com
www. academicfoundation.com

© 2009
Copyright: Academic Foundation.

ALL RIGHTS RESERVED.
No part of this book shall be reproduced, stored in a retrieval system, or transmitted by any means, electronic, mechanical, photocopying, recording, or otherwise, without the prior written permission of the copyright holder(s) and/or the publishers.

Cataloging in Publication Data--DK
Courtesy: D.K. Agencies (P) Ltd. <docinfo@dkagencies.com>

Chandavarkar, Anand G., 1925-
The unexplored Keynes and other essays : a socio-economic miscellany / Anand Chandavarkar.
p. cm.
On John Maynard Keynes, 1883-1946, British economist.
ISBN 13: 9788171887361
ISBN 10: 8171887368

1. Keynes, John Maynard, 1883-1946. 2. Keynesian economics. I. Title.

DDC 330.156 22

Typeset by Italics India, New Delhi.
Printed and bound in India.

In loving memory of

Gopalkrishna Chandavarkar and Surendranath Chandavarkar

for debts that can never be repaid

For Marilda Chandavarkar

Contents

II A Post-Keynesian Miscellany

Acknowledgements

My grateful thanks to:

Deena Khatkhate for invaluable assistance.

Dedicated staff of the Joint Bank-Fund Library, Washington DC, particularly Ms. Southamini Borlo and Chet Nunoo-Quarco for highly competent and ungrudging bibliographic assistance and helpful arrangements.

Patricia McGuire, Archivist, King's College, Cambridge for very professional and courteous assistance in accessing the Keynes's papers, fully in keeping with the best traditions of that august foundation.

Professor Kenneth Arrow and Professor Robert Solow for helpful comments on Chapter 25 (Economics and Philosophy: Interface and Agenda).

Syed Ali Akbar (Director of Public Instruction, Hyderabad, Dn) unstinting family friend and well-wisher.

Arthur Monteiro for meticulous and expeditious word processing.

COPYRIGHT ACKNOWLEDGEMENTS

Blackwell Publishing for the following articles: 'Saving Potential of Disguised Unemployment' in *The Economic Journal*, June 1957 and 'The Nature and Effects of Gold Hoarding in Underdeveloped Economies', *Oxford Economic Papers*, June 1961.

David Papineau (King's College, London) for citations from the Richard Kahn Papers in the King's College Library, Cambridge, England.

Economia Internazionale, Genoa, Italy, for article on 'Money and Economic Growth', XVIII(3), February 1965.

Elsevier Science and Technology Journals for articles on 'Keynes and the International Monetary System Revisited: A Contextual and Conjectural Essay' (*World Development*, December 1987) and 'Of Finance and Development: Neglected and Unsettled Questions' (*World Development*, January 1992).

MIT Press Journals for 'The Premium for Risk as a Determinant of Interest Rates in Underdeveloped Rural Areas', *Quarterly Journal of Economics*, May 1965.

Palgrave Macmillan for 'Keynes and the Role of the State in Developing Countries' in *Keynes and the Role of the State* (edited by Derek Crabtree and A.P. Thirlwall), The Macmillan Press, 1989.

Chapter 16, 'Legal Tender Currency and Public Debt' (*Public Finance*, XVII(1), 1962) is reprinted with the permission of the original publisher, Public Finance/Finances Publiques.

Unpublished writings of J.M. Keynes, copyright The Provost and Scholars of King's College, Cambridge, 2008 located in King's College Library.

Every effort has been made to trace all copyright holders, but if any have been inadvertently overlooked, the publisher will be pleased to make the necessary arrangements at the first opportunity.

I

The Unexplored Keynes

1 An Archival Pilgrimage to King's College, Cambridge*

John Maynard Keynes is by far the most written-about economist. Yet there always seems to be some unexplored facet of this many-splendoured polymath and leading intellectual progenitor of the International Monetary Fund. One such aspect is the supreme paradox that Keynes, who never visited India and had no personal or family links with the country, made major contributions to economics through his analysis of Indian monetary problems. India loomed large in the life and work of Keynes, the economist, statesman, and teacher.

This fascinating, but little researched, theme in Keynes's life occurred to me while I was preparing the chapter 'Money and Credit' for Volume 2 of *The Cambridge Economic History of India*, published in 1983. I followed this with an article, "Keynes and India", in the *Economic and Political Weekly* in June 1983, to commemorate the Keynes Centennial. Still the theme seemed to cry out for much fuller treatment, and this led me to undertake a book on Keynes and India (The Macmillan Press, 1989).

What drew Keynes to India? It was the sheer intellectual challenge of the uniqueness and complexity of India's monetary system. As he put it, "Indian currency can always find something new with which to instruct the student. More numerous and skilled commissions have sat over it than any other currency in the world. Yet no sooner does a Commission rise than this currency presents some further problem...to perplex its official custodians."

Inevitably, the trails pointed to the source—the Keynes papers at King's College, Cambridge, in the loving care of Dr. Michael Halls, its dedicated modern archivist. I was permitted, by courtesy of (then) Provost Bernard Williams, to consult the Keynes Papers in November 1985 as the very last visitor prior to their closure for cataloguing. This was a delightfully rewarding week's archival pilgrimage to King's, the most photogenic of all the Cambridge colleges, and home of a long line of distinguished economists (Pigou, Keynes, Kahn, Ramsey, Shove, Kaldor, Stone and Passinetti) and savants like Forster and Lowes Dickinson.

* Reprinted, with minor revisions, from *IMF Staff News*, September 1987.

The Keynes Papers are housed in the King's College Library, which is reached by the same staircase that leads to the suite of Keynes's life-long friend and collaborator, Lord Khan—a charming misspelling with an Indian Muslim twist on the entrance board, noticed by everyone except his Lordship! My window seat in the Library overlooked the rooms occupied Keynes as a Fellow. Truly, a room with a view, and in Forster's College, too! There are, unfortunately, no Keynes memorabilia, except possibly for his small chest of drawers in Dr. Halls' office.

Keynes's unpublished papers reflect his sustained interest in India. He corresponded more with Indian students than with any other student group. A good example is his sustained relationship with a favourite pupil, B.P. Adarkar, the distinguished Indian economist (Chapter 12). The papers also illumine many an episode in his eventful life. For instance, Harrod's biography of Keynes suggests that Keynes's withdrawal from the Vice-Chairmanship of the Indian Fiscal Commission (1922) was because of his involvement with the ballerina Lydia Lopokova (the future Lady Keynes) around that time. But these two events were quite unrelated. Keynes had, in fact, booked his passage from Venice to Bombay on 2 February 1922, but at the eleventh hour the Government of India changed his agreed schedule of stay in India for the Commission. This was unacceptable to Keynes because of his prior commitments in England. This seems a more plausible explanation than Keynes's involvement with Lydia Lopokova, which went back to 10 October 1918, when he first met her at the Sitwells. Lydia's first letter to Keynes is dated 28 December 1918 (Hill and Keynes, 1989). If his inamorata was the real factor, Keynes would not have agreed in the first place to be considered for the Indian Fiscal Commission. Interestingly, Keynes recommended the published report of the Commission as required reading to his students, as recalled by one of them, Harold Dunkerley (c. 1942, King's College). But Keynes's failure to visit India was, arguably, a loss to development economics, as perceptively observed by Polly Hill to the author (1 May 1987). "Like an anthropologist, Maynard was a field worker; to be chairman of an insurance company was necessary for his theoretical work. The pity of it is that he was never a fieldworker in India. Would he have become a development economist had he set eyes on rural India? After all, he loved farming." But Keynes will always be gratefully remembered for his unhesitating willingness to serve under an Indian Chairman, Sir Ibrahim Rahimtoola, in the heyday of the Raj, an unprecedented gesture.

Keynes, after graduating in Mathematics at Cambridge in 1905, served in the India Office from 1906 to 1908, spending the first five months in the Military department and the remainder in the Revenue, Statistics, and Commerce department. Amidst his official work, Keynes found time to work on his King's College fellowship dissertation on Probability, and to amuse himself by copying select quotations from the picturesque 'Ind-lish' articles in Indian newspapers, such as the following: "Mr. Morley [the Secretary of State for India] is a mountain in labour which has produced a huge monstrosity, a thing of shreds and patches. He has brought out only a small rat by boring a hill." (*Akhber* (sic)-*e-Soudagar*, which translates as *Trader's Journal*).

These two years in a Byzantine bureaucracy were an invaluable apprenticeship for Keynes, the future economic policymaker and statesman. Equally, they made him sensitive to the *amour propre* of a subject nation, as in the memorable episode when Indian students were the subject of a scurrilous anonymous article in the *Cambridge Review* of 13 May 1909, referring to the "numerous 'bounders' among them...who are not prepared or fitted intellectually for the University." This provoked a spirited riposte—the only one from a don—from Keynes on 20 May 1909, who "regretted...an article so lacking in discernment and feeling" and "the commonplaces of prejudice, which should not have been brought forward anonymously and unsubstantiated."

Keynes's first publication, *Indian Currency and Finance* (1913), which established him as a monetary economist, is an original and elegant statement of the gold exchange standard and a pioneering formulation of the developmental rationale of central banking (written without the benefit of a 'mission' to India and discussions with the Ministry of Finance). Keynes regarded the Bank of England as too orthodox and therefore an unsuitable model for India. Instead, he commended the examples of the state banks of Germany and Russia in providing for direct credit and rediscount facilities to promote industry and agriculture and recommended the rapid expansion of the bank network of the proposed State Bank of India. Keynes's developmental agenda for India's central bank came to belated fruition in the 1950s. *Indian Currency and Finance*, among others, led to Keynes's membership of the Royal Commission (Chamberlain) on Indian Currency and Finance from 1913 to 1914. Subsequently he figured as an expert witness to two official inquiries on Indian monetary affairs—the Babington Smith Committee in 1919 and the Hilton Young Commission in 1926.

Later, at the Bretton Woods Conference of 1944, Keynes emerged as a persuasive advocate of an appropriate quota for India and a permanent seat for it on the Executive Board of the IMF. What made Keynes espouse India's case? Undoubtedly, he sensed India's 'economic significance' and potential importance in Fund-Bank membership. More than that, it reflected his characteristic concern for the underprivileged. Equally, as an eminent economist he was struck by the highly competent and persuasive presentation of India's case by a high-powered delegation, which included Sir Chintaman Deshmukh (the first Indian Governor of the Reserve Bank of India) and two non-official financial experts, Sir Shanmukham Chetty and A.D. Shroff. They were ably assisted by the meticulous staff work of Dr. B.K. Madan, the Secretary of the Indian delegation (and later an Executive Director of the Fund).

Doubtless, the patrician 'gravitas' and awesome versatility of Sir Chintamani (brilliant civil servant, prize-winning botanist at Cambridge, and Sanskrit poet) must have also struck a responsive chord in Keynes, the Renaissance man. No wonder Keynes remarked: "The excellence and closeness of our relations with the Indian delegation deserves special comment. Sir Chintaman Deshmukh handled his case with high dignity, ability, and reasonableness." The Indian delegation was the only one of the 44 delegations to be so singled out by Keynes, which is all the more remarkable considering that it was also the only delegation representing a dependent country without any political status or influence.

Keynes would have been delighted that the US idea of a full-time Executive Director devoting his whole attention to Fund affairs was, reportedly, fulfilled most completely by one of his most brilliant pupils, J.V. Joshi, the first Indian Executive Director of the Fund from 1946 to 1948. Much later, another distinguished Indian, I.G. Patel, Director of the London School of Economics (and former Governor of the Reserve Bank of India and Honorary Fellow of King's) also served on the Executive Board of the Fund (1958–1961). I.G. Patel knew Keynes from Patel's days as student secretary of the Political Economy Club at Cambridge.

Judging alike by his published and unpublished work and activities, India was the one country other than Britain that figured most prominently in Keynes's life. Keynes's India Connection was, arguably, the longest saga for any economist in time and space—from the spirited defence of Indian students in 1908 to the principled support for India at Bretton Woods in 1944: a glorious epitaph to 'Keynes Indophilus.'

Finally, Keynes's role in the foundation of the Fund prompts some interesting speculations. How would Keynes have fared with a latter-day Fund? The young Keynes would have assuredly been turned down for the Fund's Economist Programme (No degree in Economics and irrelevant work experience—shipping pedigree bulls to Bombay while at India Office). Likewise, the Staff Papers would have rejected his articles unread (No equations or regressions—the only 'model' he ever understood was the ballerina Lydia Lopokova). The older Keynes would not have been invited as a Visiting Scholar to the Fund (Never held a professorial chair). The Bretton Woods Center would surely have blackballed him as well ("...the worst player of golf I have known", commented C.R. Fay, historian and Keynes's contemporary as an undergraduate). Just as well. It enabled Keynes to design the source of our pensionable livelihood! R.I.P.

A posthumous India connection: in one Hindi film of relatively recent vintage (*Chashm-e-Buddoor* (God Save You from the Envious), the elegant heroine is shown, between two soulful lyrics, totally absorbed in Keynes's *The General Theory of Employment, Interest, and Money* (what else!), oblivious of the doting grandmother trying to catch her eye! Is there another economic classic thus cited outside a footnote? This charming scene in celluloid (and Indian, too) would have tickled Keynes, patron of the Cambridge Arts Theatre.

An Inquisitorial Postscript

There is still one abiding mystery of King's College. Why King's, the acclaimed Vatican of economics, has yet to elect an economist as its Pope. Keynes and his acolyte Richard Kahn were both successful Bursars, but no economist has made it to the ranks of Provost, an office which has been filled by historians, scientists, classicists and even an engineer turned social anthropologist, Sir Edmund Leach. Other Cambridge colleges have had economists as their heads: Trinity (Amartya Sen); Queens' (John Eatwell); and Clare (R.C.O. Mathews). According to a former Provost, Noel Annan, Keynes, "who at that time had been living openly with the ballerina Lydia Lopokova, withdrew from the contest" to succeed Provost Durnford when he died (Annan, 1999: 116).

Surprisingly, the Green Ties Party of dons led by Sheppard and Keynes, who stood for 'the virtues of intellectual adventure, gaiety, pleasure, vitality; they also stood for sexual disreputability' (ibid: 114), declared "that at no price could they consent to Clapham moving from the tutorship to the Lodge" (ibid: 116). 'Honest John' Clapham, the economic historian, was the leader of the Black Ties Party, who were "respectable, *bien-pensant* and the guardians of orthodox scholarship" (ibid: 114). When, however, the tertium quid resigned in 1933, Sheppard was elected, marking the triumph of the Green Ties. This, certainly, was not Keynes's finest hour, a blot on his escutcheon. For once, the icon had stooped to conquer. Regrettably, Annan's fascinating study of the Oxbridge intellectual aristocracy throws no light on the omission of King's to elect an economist as Provost. Is it that economists do not qualify either as Mentors, Eccentrics, or Geniuses, the provocative subtitle of his study? But the whole episode reads like a real-life precursor of C.P. Snow's classic, *The Masters*, set in another Cambridge college.

References

Annan, Noel (1999). *The Dons (Mentors, Eccentrics and Geniuses)*. London: HarperCollins.

Hill, Polly and Richard Keynes (1989). *Lydia and Maynard: Letters Between Lydia Lopokova and Maynard Keynes*. London: Andre Deutsch.

2 Keynes Eponymous: A Reappraisal

Yet one more book about John Maynard Keynes, the most discussed and documented economist of all times, might justifiably prompt the type of question Quentin Bell, an artistic contemporary of Keynes, was moved to ask in the preface to an exhibition devoted to Bloomsbury: "Haven't you had enough?" The massive literature on Keynes and Keynesian economics is an exponential growth industry now firmly based, among others, on the monumental biographical trilogy of Robert Skidelsky and the latest evaluation of Keynes by Paul Davidson (2007) which would seem to suggest that we have reached saturation levels. Yet no matter how much has been said or written, there seems to be always room for exploring yet another new or neglected facet of a many-splendoured genius like Keynes. Truly, Keynes's life and work are a cornucopia for the diligent author or editor. No wonder Keynesian scholarship tends to partake of the inexhaustible quality of the proverbial Widow's Cruse.

But, as so memorably stated by Austin Robinson, a close acolyte of Keynes: "I want to see Keynes reassessed by another generation. For *reassessed he must be*" (emphasis provided) (1975: 9). "If in the process of reappraisal Keynes does not emerge as a truly great man (and economist), something, let me repeat, will have gone sadly wrong with the criteria of greatness" (1972: 545–6). It is in this spirit of reappraisal that this present work attempts to review and analyse some of the least known and the least researched aspects of Keynes's persona, writings and activities in Part I, followed by a post-Keynesian miscellany in Part II. The fact that there are still unexplored aspects of Keynes is more a tribute to his awesome versatility and fecundity than a stricture on contemporary scholarship. Equally, Keynes comes across as an eternal contemporary whose writings in the dim distant part seem so uncannily relevant to ever emergent unforeseen and unintended consequences of policy imperatives.

However, Keynesian scholarship has also to contend with a uniquely daunting hurdle that to date only about one-third of Keynes's papers have been published in the thirty-volume edition of the *Collected Writings of John Maynard Keynes*. The magnitude of what still awaits the analysts of Keynes may be gauged from the exhaustive review of the unwritten books and papers of J.M. Keynes by Rod O'Donnell (1992) and the authoritative observation of the then modern archivist of King's College that "despite the variety of interest shown in the Keynes papers, there remain several areas of research comparatively unexplored" like Keynes the scholarly polemicist.(Cox, 1995: 173) What surprises will Keynes's still unpublished economic and philosophical papers have for posterity? As Keynes himself famously remarked, "The inevitable never happens. It is the unexpected always."

The basic concepts and tenets of Keynesianism have been authoritatively rated as 'irreversible' (Samuelson [1971], 1986: 867) and have achieved a certain kind of permanent revolution as well supported by a comprehensive survey of references to various schools of thought as cited in the top ten Economics textbooks in 1990.

References in Economics Schools in Top Ten Textbooks

School	Index frequency
Keynes and Keynesianism	442
Friedman and Monetarism	252
Marx and Marxism	131
Rational Expectations	119
Laffer and Supply-side	95
Austrianism	67
Galbraith and Institutionalism	53

Note: This table is based on the combined references to specific theories and their expounders found in the name and subject indices. The top ten textbooks, selected according to a survey of publishers at the 1990 annual meeting of the American Economic Association, are McConnell and Brue; Baumol and Blinder; Lipsey, Steiner, and Purvis; Ruffin and Gregory; Miller; Samuelson and Nordhaus; Dolan and Lindsey; Byrns and Stone; Qwartney and Stroup; and Bronfenbrenner, Sichel, and Gardner. Keynesian influence may be even greater than this table indicates, since elements of Keynesian macroeconomic modelling may be integrated into other schools.

Source: Mark Skousen (ed.) (1992). *Dissent on Keynes*, New York: Praeger.

More important, Keynes provided the basic building blocks of macroeconomics as they affect average or total activity—employment, output, price level, liquidity preference, interest rate, consumption function, marginal efficiency of capital, and aggregate effective demand. The very grammar, vocabulary, and idiom of economics show the pervasiveness of Keynes, Keynesian, Keynesianism, as a substantive and as a modifier, which make Keynes the only truly eponymous economist.

Concomitantly, there has been a pervasive diffusion of the Keynesian revolution at the pedagogic, literary and institutional levels in graduate schools (Moggridge, 1995: 223–42) including the incorporation of Keynesian components in the hydraulic and mechanical models of economic dynamics developed by Walter Newlyn and A.W. Phillips. There have been ten Keynes seminars, a college named after Keynes in the University of Kent, Canterbury, and an *Encyclopaedia of Keynesian Economics* (Cate, Harcourt and Colander, 1997). No other economist has been thus commemorated. But the "Keynesian revolution was not just a revolution in economic theory. Keynes was a prophet, or propagandist... He was selling his policy to politicians and public, by essays in persuasion and by newspaper articles galore. *The General Theory* was his way of selling his policy to professional economists" (Hicks, 1977: 147). Keynes was not only a seminal economist but the great persuader who mobilised the English language in the service of economics even as Churchill mobilised it in the defence of Britain. His wondrously aphoristic phrases have an eternal resonance. As the distinguished Indian historian-diplomat, K.M. Panikkar, wrote to Joan Robinson, the distinguished British economist: "Why the best prose writers in English—I am not thinking of the Ivory Tower prose writer like Virginia Woolf but of those who use prose as it should be used as a weapon of offence and defence, of great polemics, and fine descriptions—why is it that the two best prose writers have been economists, Keynes and Tawney. *Economic Consequences* and the *Tract* to me are great examples of prose: the first on a level with *Burke's Letter to a New Whig* and the *Tract* as good as Berkeley —both being theological" (JVR/51/270/5). The famous aphorism "We are all Keynesians now", commonly attributed to President Richard Nixon has, in fact, a much wider conceptual connotation than its provenance as a fiscal stimulus in the early 1970s. As Skidelsky well put it: "Although there are Keynesian, anti-Keynesian and non-Keynesian economists, there are no pre-Keynesian economists. That is a crucial measure of his contribution" (communication to the author). One could add post-Keynesian, neo Keynesian, synthetic and bastard Keynesianism to complete the Keynesian bestiary.

However, the very stature of Keynes and the magnitude of his contributions poses the critical question: do Keynes's contributions represent a scientific revolution in terms of the criteria formulated by recognised philosophers of scientific method like Thomas Kuhn and Karl Popper? In a basic sense the very notion of a scientific revolution as formulated by Kuhn (1996) to mean displacement of an overarching disciplinary matrix of four main components of symbolic generalisations, metaphysical or heuristic commitments, values, and examples by another matrix is not really applicable to economics. None of the recognised conceptual revolutions in economics associated with David

Hume's *Political Discourses* (1752), Adam Smith's *Wealth of Nations* (1776), the Neo-Classical School of Ricardo and John Stuart Mill, the marginal revolution of Walras, Menger, Jevons, the neoclassical Cambridge School of Marshall and Pigou, and Keynes's *General Theory* are really comparable in their scope and impact with the Copernican, Newtonian, Einsteinian, and Darwinian revolutions in astronomy, physics and biology. Economic doctrines are relative to their assumptions and the social milieu and are never displaced to be cast in the dustbin like Ptolemaic astronomy. Each revolution in economics serves to enlarge its explanatory and heuristic value. As argued by Karl Popper, "The advance of knowledge consists, mainly, in the modification of earlier knowledge" (2002: 37) and "the criterion of the scientific status of a theory is its falsifiability, or refutability, or testability" (ibid.: 48). Even more important is that "there are degrees of testability: some theories expose themselves to possible refutations more boldly than others" (ibid.: 346). All these criteria are amply satisfied by the *General Theory*, which has emerged as the prime matrix of testable hypotheses, the defining achievement of the Keynesian Revolution.

For instance, the key concepts of the *General Theory* like unemployment, liquidity preference, propensity to consume, and the multiplier, are all amenable to different degrees of testability, except for the 'animal spirits of entrepreneurs to invest or to innovate' which just defy modelling. Consequently, Keynesian economics is a prime candidate for fuzzy subset analysis in terms of the theory of fuzzy sets initiated by Zadeh. A good example of the econometric substantiation of the *General Theory* is the masterful path-breaking article on the US consumption and investment functions by T.C. Liu and C.G. Chang (1951). "If the main task of the theoretical social sciences is to trace the unintended social repercussions of intentional human actions" (Popper, 2002: 460) this properly belongs to the realm of the wider economics of welfare which was beyond the Keynesian remit.

Keynes's epistemology is best explained in his letter to R.F. Harrod, 4 July 1938, which is far more insightful than any commentaries by others:

> It seems to me that economics is a branch of logic, a way of thinking; ...But one cannot get very far except by devising new and improved models....Progress in economics consists almost entirely in a progressive improvement in the choice of models.... But it is of the essence of a model that one does not fill in real values for the variable functions. To do so would make it useless as a model. For as soon as this is done, the model loses its generality and its value as a mode of thought.... The object of statistical study is not so much to fill in missing variables with a view to prediction, as to test the relevance and validity of the model. Economics is a science of thinking in terms of models joined to the art of choosing models which are relevant to the contemporary world. It is com-

pelled to be this, because, unlike the typical natural science, the material to which it is applied is, in too many respects, not homogeneous through time. The object of a model is to segregate the semi-permanent or relatively constant factors from those which are transitory or fluctuating so as to develop a logical way of thinking about the latter, and of understanding the time sequences to which they give rise in particular cases. Good economists are scarce because the gift for using 'vigilant observation' to choose good models, ...appears to be a very rare one. In the second place, as against Robbins, economics is essentially a moral science and not a natural science. That is to say, it employs introspection and judgements of value.' (*Collected Writings*, vol. 14, 1973: 246–7)

Thus, for Keynes, economics was a 'technique of analysis' and a moral science, which he deployed to make the world a more civilised place in which to live. This defined Keynes's intellectual stance as issue-oriented and problem-solving, which explains why every one of Keynes's books, except the first volume of the *Treatise on Money*—a conspicuous outlier in the Keynesian canon—was a search for a solution to a problem or a crisis, whether it was the *Economic Consequences of the Peace*, and of Mr Churchill, reform of the Indian monetary system and the gold standard, the causes and cure of the Great Depression, *How to Pay for the War*, and the creation of a new international monetary and economic order after World War II. Consequently, abstract themes in economics or the magnificent dynamics of economic history like the exploitation of colonies never attracted Keynes. Reforming the Indian Rupee and the creation of a central bank of India was far more important for him than analysing the economic drain from India—the theme of a classic book by Dadabhai Naoroji, the Indian economist and a Liberal MP of the House of Commons. Keynes emphatically rejected the favourite Indian nationalist charge that by forcing India to keep its gold reserves in London, Britain was appropriating India's export surplus. A letter in his papers, dated 25 January 1924, to two Indian economists, P.A. Wadia and G.N. Joshi, sums up his attitude to the 'exploitation' issue:

I do not understand the train of thoughts which leads you to suppose that the gold exchange standard has been introduced in British interests...this is totally untrue. The suggestion that it has involved India in advancing money to Great Britain loses its force when it is remembered that during the period in question Great Britain has loaned to India, against long-dated securities, far more than the aggregate of the floating reserve which the India Office maintains in London...the resources of the gold standard reserve, which now amount to more than forty million pounds, wholly represent profits of the present currency arrangements as compared with a gold standard; so that if a gold standard had been enforced India would have been by now just that much poorer...you say that this policy has 'deprived India of millions of worth of gold which might have flowed into the country, diffusing prosperity and stimulating her industries' [which] suggests that you allow to gold magical properties which it is no longer usual to attribute. (MR/1/2/44-46)

In one material respect even Keynes never broke free of the Oxbridge corset of a somewhat superior disdain of the scholarly apparatus in his writings, more particularly in the *General Theory*, where he found room for monetary cranks like Major Douglas and Silvio Gessell but overlooked the contributions of Swedish and American economists. As Jacob Viner, while leafing through Kenneth Boulding's B. Litt. thesis remarked scathingly, "Huh, Oxford, no footnotes" (Boulding, 1992: 8). Keynes's forte, however, was his uncanny intuitionism which he shared with much of Cambridge philosophy (Whewell, Sidgwick, Moore and others), which conceived intuition as a form of visual intellectual perception. Thus, Keynes referred to 'the gaze of intuition', 'the peering eye of philosophy', the 'eyes of common sense', and 'the mind's eye' (O'Donnell, 1991: 339) and allied his superb intuition to stylised facts in the *General Theory*. He ascribed Newton's pre-eminence to his "muscles of intuition being the strongest and most enduring with which a man has ever been gifted" (CW X: 365). Was it his intuitionism that found a curious affinity with the untutored virgin minds of the monetary underworld? Small wonder that Ernest Bevin, the uneducated trade unionist member of the Macmillan Committee (1930-31) impressed Keynes as the one "member who understood his unorthodox ideas better than any of the others" (Bullock, 1983: 85).

It has been rightly said that Keynes started life "as a philosopher" (O'Donnell, 1989: 11) and "philosophy provided the foundation of Keynes's life and came before economics; and the philosophy of ends came before the philosophy of means" (Skidelsky, 1983: 133). Undoubtedly, the theme of Keynes the philosopher has been extensively covered in the literature beginning with O'Donnell's pioneering monograph (1989) and thereafter by the Ninth Keynes Seminar (1989) followed by Bateman and Davis (1991), Davis (1994), Backhouse and Bateman in the *Cambridge Companion to Keynes* (2006). These authoritative contributions, however, concentrate almost exclusively on Keynes the mature philosopher, and his work on probability and expectations, which explains why this book (Chapter 10) explores the remarkable philosophic output of the young Keynes as an Etonian and later as a Cambridge undergraduate member of the then secret intellectual fraternity of the Apostles. These papers show a wide range covering metaphysics, epistemology and ethics but this chapter concentrates on themes which show the young Keynes as a precocious embryonic social philosopher, a rare example of the philosopher as an infant prodigy as it were, a syndrome more associated with mathematics, music and chess. Apart from their intrinsic interest, these early philosophic forays are equally significant since "early influences remained of great importance throughout Keynes's life" (Harrod, 1951: vii).

The roots of economics go back to philosophy and the great economic thinkers have been rightly acclaimed as worldly philosophers. How would Keynes have responded to the question posed by latter-day economists, which is discussed at length in Chapter 25, since economics raises serious philosophic issues? Can economics, a subject of cognitive dissonance with no predictive power, claim to be a science? Economic laws are at best the statements of tendencies which make it 'a discipline, not a science', for it 'deals with the ever changing and subtle forces of human nature'. Keynes would assuredly have endorsed the timely warning of Robert Shiller against the 'physics envy' malady of economists and his plea for a 'higher fraction of the economics profession' to more interest in 'history, psychology, institutions and economic policy'. But economics does adhere to the scientific method and the criteria of falsifiability. Paradoxically, despite its deficiencies, economics has emerged as the imperial social science and economists function as imperial advisors to government and civil society. Keynes would have emphasised that both economics and philosophy are techniques of analysis rather than bodies of doctrine. The approach to the interface between economics and philosophy through the relevant subdisciplines of philosophy, *viz.*, epistemology, religion, ethics, psychology as well as rhetoric, would have been most congenial to his mindset as the quintessential fox who did not hesitate to morph into a hedgehog when it came to support causes of reason and conscience, whether it was a just peace for Germany, women's suffrage, conscientious objectors, monetary reform, or a viable and equitable post-war economic order.

Chapter 24 critically reviews the economic philosophy of Joan Robinson, the distinguished acolyte of Keynes, selecting the many issues and arguments in her book which are relevant to developing economies, including the need for greater focus on the allocation of the national surplus between immediate versus future beneficiaries. For her the operative criterion is: 'What is investment for?' She shows the relationship of ideology with theory and history and the advancement of Keynesian theory over *laissez faire* on grounds of logical consistency and relevance and observes that Keynes brought history back to economics (communication from Prue Kerr).

Keynes wrote famously about *The End of Laissez Faire* (1926). Although he never formulated a systematic theory of state intervention, it is possible to develop a meaningful state-theoretic approach to the economics of developing countries drawing on his writings and policy experience (Chapter 8). In fact, Chapter 27 explodes the myth of *laissez faire* in colonial India, first identified by the economic historian Eric Hobsbawm, and reviews the specifics of state intervention in British India. In all this Keynes, the applied economist, drew on his rich formative experience as a creative civil servant in the India Office and the British Treasury (Chapter 3). As a perceptive institutional architect who drew up a scheme for a State Bank of India, Keynes's writings on central banking (Chapter 6) offer many valuable insights, particularly the case for the independence of central banks, which has many resonances in the Indian context (Chapter 21).

How would Keynes have viewed and reacted to the principal contemporary international monetary issues, namely, the framework of management, liquidity, the exchange rate regime, the adjustment mechanisms, and the problem of developing countries (Chapter 9)? Keynes would, arguably, have favoured a variant of crawling pegs rather than free floats for exchange rates, and a symmetrical (compulsory) adjustment mechanism for surplus as well as debtor countries, but would have been averse to the SDR link while welcoming the flexibility of the International Monetary Fund in meeting the requirements of developing countries consistently with the uniform treatment of all members.

The international grants economy is an adjunct to the international exchange economy, which was Keynes's primary concern, but he would have viewed post-war international aid as wholly congruent with his worldview, which was high-minded enough even to espouse the case for a defeated Germany. Chapter 26 evaluates the authoritative study of the history and politics of United Nations Development Aid by a former UN executive, Digambar Bhouraskar, and his agenda for its rationalisation to make it selective and targeted. But aid donation is not necessarily a developed-country prerogative but can be equally the subject of fruitful technical cooperation with the Third World itself, as substantiated by the UNDP's programme of TCDC (Technical Cooperation among Developing Countries).

But was Keynes a development economist in any meaningful sense? Chapter 7, which seeks to answer this question, concludes that Keynes was not directly concerned with growth and development, although he was the first to formulate the developmental role of a central bank in the context of India. However, Keynes did contribute to the apparatus of growth economics, as pointed out by Thirlwall, of the concepts of natural and warranted rates of growth and the application of his ideas by Roy Harrod (dynamic economics), Joan Robinson (disguised unemployment) and Nicholas Kaldor (growth models). The most influential paradigms of development economics, such as increasing returns, cumulative causation, backwash and spread effects, balanced growth and human capital hardly owe any debt to Keynes. For the mainsprings of economic growth one turns to Arthur Lewis, who typifies the taxonomic approach to growth, by providing 'not a theory but a map', given the sheer multiplicity of the determinants of growth (Chapter 18). But by far the most challenging problem for developing countries is the critical trade-off between more growth and more employment.

These aspects are supplemented by an overview of the varied issues relating to finance and development (Chapters 19 and 20); notably, the implications of the dichotomy of formal and informal finance; the modalities and sequencing of financial reform; the challenge of maintaining competition in oligopolistic systems; the scope for market-related monetary policy instruments; the case for autonomy of central banks and divestiture of their developmental role and revamping of their prudential functions. This calls for a sharply focused, country-specific, issues-oriented research agenda.

Keynes, the quintessential applied economist and a policy adviser conceived economics as much a normative as a positive science. Although Keynes inspired the choice of an economist, G.F. Shirras as India's first Director of Statistics (1914–1921), he never contemplated the appointment of an Economic Adviser to the Government of India even though the East India Company as early as 1772 had James Steuart, author of *An Inquiry into the Principles of Political Economy* (1767) as its economic adviser. The pioneer economic adviser of modern India was a little-known Ivy League American economist, Ralph Whitenack, who served the princely ruler of Baroda state with distinction during 1906–1909 and 1918–19 (Chapter 22). A star Indian pupil of Keynes, I.G. Patel, who served as India's Economic Adviser, and later as Director of the London School of Economics, offers an insider's view into the making of economic policy in the largest democracy in his memoirs (Chapter 23).The persona and activities of the distinguished economic historian, Dharma Kumar, are reviewed in Chapter 28.

The Keynesian canon, like any other, has had its due share of exegesis as in respect of one of its core concepts of liquidity preference which, because of its complex motivation renders the Keynesian analysis largely inapplicable to gold hoarding in underdeveloped economies (Chapter 5). India's demand for gold (1925–1940), as analysed in a pioneering study by I.G. Patel, seems to be more responsive to the relative price of gold than to income (Chapter 15).Likewise, given the highly aggregative character of liquidity preference as a portmanteau concept, it has to be disaggregated by motivation and the type of economy and extent of financial intermediation (Chapter 19). In fact, the institutional factors such as monopoly, risk and administrative charges seem to be more influential than liquidity preference as determinants of interest rates in less developed countries (Chapter 17). The concept of disguised unemployment, formulated by Joan Robinson, and its putative saving potential (Ragnar Nurkse) is an important offshoot of Keynesian economics, whose significance depends on empirical data, such as whether the marginal productivity of labour in agriculture is zero, negative or positive (Chapter 4). But the phenomenon also extends to the urban sector of developing economies, as well substantiated by the pioneering study of Joshi and Joshi (1976), for Bombay, India and even the G7 industrial countries (Eatwell, 1995). The history of the concept and measurement of disguised unemployment is a striking example of the outreach of the Keynesian revolution and the testability criteria of Karl Popper as supportive of it.

Like all high priests, Keynes too had his Levite, Richard Kahn, whose path-breaking contributions have been, ironically, overshadowed by his more publicised role as the intimate collaborator and sounding-board of Keynes. Although even the Kahn Memorial Issue of the *Cambridge Journal of Economics* (February 1994) does justice to his varied theoretical contributions, it overlooks some of his little noticed but significant writings and activities, most notably his views on the pedagogics of economics, his experiences as a national and international civil servant, his tenure as an influential member of the House of Lords, his perceptive analysis of post-full employment inflationary pressures, the rationale for an income and prices policy, and his formulation of a post-Keynesian approach to planning and development in the less developed countries. All these aspects of Kahn's contributions are evaluated in Chapter 14.

What, then, is our final evaluation of Keynes? Typically, genius is monolithic, associated with one big idea or one collateral sphere of activity, like Copernicus, Newton, Einstein, Bohr, Spinoza, whereas Keynes was a polycentric genius, a profoundly multi-cameral mind, a rare combination of genius allied to a dauntingly diverse talent, heroic and prudential, who straddled with effortless ease the disparate worlds of ideas and affairs—Cambridge, the City, Whitehall, and Bloomsbury. He stands *sui generis* in intellectual and cultural history. But genius too has an all too human face, and a downside with feet of clay. Keynes too had his fill of flaws and foibles as was so well exposed by Toye (2000). A liberal at home, he was a Social Darwinist abroad, who advocated coercive negative eugenics for Asians and Africans. He even thought it was foolish to guarantee investment loans to countries where 'Black Africans' live (Toye: 151). He adored the genetic aristocracy of England, the Great Villiers Connection, while he scorned the proletariat as the "great unwashed." He shared many of the prejudices of his class and age like his attitudinal anti-semitism, albeit redeemed by his philo-semitism in practice (Chapter 11). Arguably, his anti-semitism could be better regarded as a peripheral fringe of an inherently compassionate *pro bono* personality than a fatal flaw of character. In the midst of an arduously busy life he always found time for the needy and deserving, whether it was women's suffrage, conscientious objectors, a vanquished Germany, milk for the starving children of Austria, and as a guarantor as in 1925 of the London Artists' Association to provide financial support for artists of merit and to organise exhibitions of their work. His 'noblesse oblige' was equally matched by a rare strain of humility and gratitude to his two most notable mentors, Alfred Marshall, the economist and Edwin Montagu (1879–1924), the Liberal politician and Secretary of State for India to whom, as he confessed to his wife Lydia, he "owed nearly all [his] steps up in life." Which other genius has so ever expressed his debt to mentors? But then, is there any *a priori* reason to expect a genius to be also a paragon of virtue—an improbable blend of Aristotle and Francis of Assisi—when, as Immanuel Kant said, "Out of the crooked timber of humanity, no straight thing was ever made?" Rather, genius, too, is susceptible to the binary category of Chinese philosophy—Yin and Yang—the sunny and shady side of men and things.

The book concludes with a review of a unique crime novel authored by an economist and a historian that features the contending Keynesian chairman of the Council of Economic Advisors and a Chicago Monetarist chairman of the Federal Reserve System. Who is the culprit in this suspenseful whodunit? Even crime fiction has succumbed to the Keynesian revolution. A fitting coda to a Keynesian miscellany.

References

Boulding, Kenneth E. (1992). *Towards a New Economics (Critical Essays on Ecology, Distribution and Other Themes)*. Aldershot: Edward Elgar.

Bullock, Alan (1983). *Ernest Bevin: Foreign Secretary, 1945-1951*. New York: W.W. Norton.

Cate, Thomas, Geoff Harcourt and David C. Colanders (eds.) (1997). *An Encyclopaedia of Keynesian Economics*. Cheltenham, UK: Edward Elgar.

Cox, Jaqueline, (1995). "Keynes, an Archivist's View", in Alwin F. Cottrell and Michael S. Lawcor (eds.), *New Perspective on Keynes, Annual Supplement to Volume 27, History of Political Economy*. Durham: Duke University Press.

Davidson, Paul (2007). *John Maynard Keynes*. Basingstoke: Palgrave Macmillan.

Eatwell, John (1995). *Disguised Unemployment: The G7 Experience*. No. 106, UNCTAD/OSG/DP 106.

Harrod, R.F. (1951). *The Life of John Maynard Keynes*. London, Macmillan.

Hicks, John (1977). *Economic Perspectives (Further Essays on Money and Growth)*. Oxford: Clarendon Press.

Joshi, Heather and Vijay Joshi (1976). *Surplus Labour and the City (A Study of Bombay)*. New Delhi: Oxford University Press.

Kuhn, Thomas (1996). *The Structure of Scientific Revolutions*. Chicago, Ill.: The University of Chicago Press.

Liu, Ta-Chung and C.G. Chang (1951). "US Consumption and Investment Propensities: Prewar and Postwar", *American Economic Review* 4(4): 565–82, September.

O' Donnell, R.M. (1989). *Keynes: Philosophy, Economics and Politics*. New York: St Martin's Press.

————. (1991). *Keynes as Philosopher-Economist*. New York: St Martin's Press.

O'Donnell, Rod (1992). "The Unwritten Books and Papers of J.M. Keynes", *History of Political Economy* 24(2): 767–87.

Popper, Karl (2002 [1963]). *Conjectures and Refutations*. Abingdon, Oxford: Routledge Classics.

Robinson, Austin (1975). "A Personal View", in Milo Keynes (ed.), *Essays on John Maynard Keynes*. Cambridge: Cambridge University Press.

————. (1972). "John Maynard Keynes: Economist, Author, Statesman", *The Economic Journal* 82(326): 531–46, (June).

Samuelson, Paul (1986 [1971]). "Liberalism at Bay", *Collected Scientific Papers of Paul A. Samuelson*. Cambridge, Mass.: MIT Press.

Skidelsky, Robert (1983). *John Maynard Keynes: Hopes Betrayed*, Vol. 1, 1883-1920. London: Macmillan.

Skousen, Mark (ed.) (1992). *Dissent on Keynes (A Critical Appraisal of Keynesian Economics)*. New York: Praeger.

Toye, John (2000). *Keynes on Population*. Oxford: Oxford University Press.

3 Civil Servant Extraordinaire

"What made Keynes an extraordinary civil servant was the same mixture of qualities which made him an extraordinary economist; his life-enhancing vitality and optimism, like Churchill's; his conviction that to every problem there was a solution" (Skidelsky, 2001:154). His life and activities exemplified this stance, which was so well manifested in his distinctive tenure in the India Office (1907–08) and the British Treasury (1915–1919) where he served as Secretary of the Wheat Committee to organise government purchases of Indian wheat and subsequently as Principal Representative of the Treasury at the Paris Peace Conference in 1919. He was awarded the title of Companion of the Order of the Bath (CBE), a rare honour for a temporary member of the civil service, and a signal recognition of his distinguished service. During World War II, he worked as an unpaid Advisor to the Chancellor of Exchequer (Kingsley Ward, John Anderson, Hugh Dalton) with special authority on India's financial questions. Even when he ceased to be a civil servant, Keynes was a very proactive member of two Royal Commissions of Inquiry on Currency and Finance, *viz.*, the Austen Chamberlain Commission on Indian Currency and Finance (1913–14) and the Macmillan Committee on Finance and Industry (1929–1931).

In 1921 (7 October) Keynes was appointed Vice-Chairman of the Indian Fiscal Commission but resigned on 2 February 1922 within a week of booking his passage from Venice to Bombay, ostensibly on grounds of incompatibility of the timing of the Commission's schedule with his pressing academic and other commitments but really on account of his close involvement with the ballerina Lydia Lopokova whom he eventually married (1925).He served as member of the British Economic Advisory Council (1930–1939). Keynes also figured prominently as an expert lead witness who gave extensive evidence to the Indian Exchange and Currency Committee (Chairman, Sir Henry Babington Smith), 1919 and the Royal Commission on Indian Currency and Finance (Chairman, Hilton Young), 1926.

Paradoxically, Keynes, although later a successful and effective civil servant, was also by any reckoning an improbable civil servant. His pre-entry credentials were rather unconventional and he joined the civil service almost by default. He graduated in the Mathematical Tripos (Part I) at Cambridge as

Twelfth Wrangler (1905) in a vintage year in which the legendary mathematician J.E. Littlewood, collaborator of G.H. Hardy and Srinivasa Ramanujam, stood first. This was a satisfactory result but a little disappointing to Keynes himself who realised that he was not in the Littlewood league, which confirmed his decision not to proceed to Part II of the Mathematical Tripos. Keynes stayed on a fourth year to prepare himself for the civil service examination and also attended Alfred Marshall's lectures on economics and read widely in economics without, however, completing the Economics Tripos. Thus, Keynes entered the civil service without any formal training in economics. But his decision to appear for the civil service examination was taken with almost total nonchalance, which even provoked his London hostess Philippa Strachey, Lytton Strachey's sister, to ask: "Really, Mr Keynes, is this a pose or do you care whether you get into the civil service or not?" As it turned out, Keynes stood second out of 104 candidates, obtaining 3498 marks (out of a maximum possible of 6000 marks) and the top candidate, with 3917 marks, was Otto Niemeyer, a classical scholar of Balliol College, Oxford, who later made his mark as a successful financier and administrator. Ironically, Keynes scored his worst marks in the subject in which he possessed a solid knowledge, namely, Mathematics (256 marks out of a possible 600 and seventh in order of merit) whereas he was placed first in Political Science, Logic, Psychology, and in Essay (*Oxford Magazine*, Supplement, November 1906, Civil Service Competition). Even more galling to him was his performance in Economics (356 marks as against Niemeyer's 370) which provoked him to say, "I evidently knew more about Economics than my examiners" (Chandavarkar, 1989: 9). This outcome prompted the rather sardonic comment that "Niemeyer was to spend the rest of his career illustrating his superiority as an examinee" (Sayers, 1972: 591).

Keynes's subsequent fortuitous entry into the India Office was albeit a very fortunate event alike for his career and for monetary economics. Successful candidates were allowed, in order of their examination marks, to choose a department in which a vacancy was available; if there was a Treasury vacancy the top candidate usually took it. "Niemeyer decided to be unorthodox, preferring the India Office, which would have left the Treasury open to Keynes." But at the last minute Niemeyer changed his mind and went to the Treasury. Keynes thereupon took the India Office (ibid.: 591–2). He entered the India Office on 16 October 1906 as a junior clerk at a salary of £200 a year in the Military Department where he was required to assist R.M. Stewart. In addition to book-keeping, his assignment covered matters such as leave and pay, the Indian Medical Board, medals, decorations, pensions and prize money. But after barely four months service in the Military Department, Keynes was transferred at the beginning of March 1907 to the Revenue, Statistics, and Commerce Department, a move which was congenial to him in every way. Throughout his India Office tenure, Keynes discharged his duties very conscientiously and even perceptively. His minutes covered a bewildering variety of subjects and problems, as, for instance, the shipment of young pedigree stud Ayrshire bulls from Hull to Bombay; dating of commissions in the India Medical Service; the proposed grant of a monopoly of bonded warehouses in Cyprus; the prevention of liquor smuggling from Portuguese India into British India; the combating of illicit distillation of country liquor in the Punjab; the Indian jute trade; the appointment of an economist to the post of Director of Statistics. Paradoxically, Keynes's work at the India Office concerned virtually all subjects except monetary affairs. All his official memoranda are notable for their shrewd eye for detail, a rare feel for the subtle interplay of economic and social factors and, above all, an uncanny instinct for the practical solution. But Keynes was never the meek deferential clerk. He always stood up to anyone whenever he felt that his facts and figures were right, as when he clashed with a superior official who had questioned his figures. Keynes was, however, vindicated by higher authority. Equally, for a civil servant Keynes displayed his deep compassion for the aggrieved victims of official high-handedness, as when he prepared a lengthy memorandum on what he thought was the unwarranted censure of an official in charge of the stamp office in Rangoon, Burma. This was an early manifestation of an exquisite sensibility, which surfaced spectacularly when he resigned from the Treasury over the inequities and flaws of the Carthaginian Peace Treaty with a defeated Germany (1919). In sum, Keynes's India Office spell was a necessary apprenticeship in the political economy of the possible and to his memorable career as an economic statesman. His experience at the India Office and his extensive networking with senior officials like Sir Robert Chalmers and Basil Blackett at the India Office and on the Royal Commission on Indian Currency and Finance (1913–14) proved invaluable when he joined the Treasury in January 1915 as assistant to Sir George Paish, Special Advisor to the Chancellor of the Exchequer.

Keynes always remained a zealous guardian of the rights of aggrieved civil servants against the aspersions of politicians and even prime ministers, as when he took issue with Lloyd George who, in the second volume of his 'War Memoirs' criticised opinions alleged to have been expressed by Keynes, as a Treasury Official, in a secret memorandum to the Chancellor of the Exchequer in September 1915. Keynes wrote as follows to the Editor of *The Times*, 23 November 1933:

"Mr. Lloyd George has...on the basis of a few sentences of a lengthy document, detached from their context and from the setting of the facts to which they were directed, ...has criticised opinions alleged to be mine.

The object of this letter is not to debate what I may have advised in 1915, but to explain how it lies beyond my power to do so. An ex-civil servant is not free either to publish or to defend what he wrote in his official capacity. The present permanent head of the Treasury has confirmed this ruling to me as being applicable even to a paper from which an ex-Prime Minister has publicly quoted extracts. I do not question this ruling, which I accept as being in the interests of the Civil Service. But since the comments which Mr. Lloyd George has based on the extracts in question have received a wide publicity, I am entitled to have it known how the matter stands.

In his address on the Civil Service delivered before the Institute of Public Administration last Mr. Baldwin regretted the publication in the Foreign Office Archives of memoranda over the signatures of civil servants, even though in extenso and without comment. The publication, however, by an ex-Prime Minister with abusive comment of a selected extract from official advice given by a civil servant to another Minister seems to carry the doubtful precedent somewhat farther.

Mr. Lloyd George would, perhaps, defend his action on the ground that I had recently made so bold as to publish a character sketch of him. Regarded thus as a competition in personalities, I make no complaint of what, indeed, any prudent person would have expected from the subject in question. But I hope that the history and criticism of our financial policy during the War, a chronicle of high interest which still remains to be written, will not be confused by these polite exchanges, perhaps as inexcusable on the one side as on the other." (Keynes, 1989: 19–20).

Keynes always remained the very epitome of the creative and ethical mandarin.

References

Chandavarkar, Anand (1989). *Keynes and India (A Study in Economics and Biography)*. Basingstoke: Macmillan Press.

Keynes , J.M. (1989). "Letter to the Editor, *The Times*", *Bibliography and Index: Collected Writings of Keynes,* Vol. XXX. pp.18-19. London: Macmillan.

Sayers, R.S. (1972). "The Young Keynes", *The Economic Journal* 82(326): 591–9, June.

Skidelsky, Robert (2001). *John Maynard Keynes: Fighting for Britain, 1937–46.* London: Macmillan.

4 The Saving Potential of Disguised Unemployment

This note attempts to analyse some of the assumptions and limitations of the proposition advanced by Professor Ragnar Nurkse (in *Problems of Capital Formation in Underdeveloped Countries*, Oxford: Basil Blackwell, 1953) that "the state of disguised unemployment implies to some extent a disguised saving potential as well" (ibid: 37). The reasoning underlying the proposition is briefly as follows. The saving potential is the difference between the output and the consumption of the productive labour on land which, under conditions of disguised unemployment, is offset by the unproductive consumption of the surplus labour. This could be converted into effective saving by transferring the surplus labour to alternative occupations and utilising the resultant food surplus to feed the transferred labour in its new occupation, provided that the marginal propensity to consume of both the retained and transferred labour remains constant.

Some of the limitations on the effective mobilisation of the saving potential of disguised unemployment are no doubt recognised by Professor Nurkse, such as the possibility of leakages in the subsistence fund through increased consumption by the retained and/or the transferred labour and through costs of transport of food to the place of work of transferred labour. He also makes the important qualification that

> the formation of capital through the use of surplus labour is self-financing only if the mobilisation of the concealed saving potential is 100 per cent successful. If it is less than completely successful the scheme seems to break down; the amount of saving, or in real terms the subsistence fund available to support the workers engaged on real capital accumulation proves insufficient.... It seems to be a question of all or nothing. Either the whole of the food surplus that becomes available on the land through the withdrawal of the surplus labourers is mopped up to feed them in their new occupations, or nothing can be done at all. (ibid.: 39–40).

This in itself is an important factor limiting the practical significance of the proposition. But there are other important limitations arising from the nature of the saving potential and its real magnitude and the additional costs of mobilising it.

First, the real magnitude of the saving potential is much smaller than it appears to be if elements which do not constitute genuine saving are excluded from it. The size of the savings fund embodied in disguised unemployment is inflated partly because of abstraction from the implications of the existence of large-scale indebtedness which is a common feature of agriculture in underdeveloped areas. To the extent that the food consumption of surplus labour, and often enough that of productive labour, is financed by borrowing, there is no saving potential in the strict sense. That the magnitude of unproductive borrowing by cultivators is considerable is amply borne out by available data for at least some underdeveloped countries.* Thus, this part of the saving potential of disguised unemployment is not genuine saving.

The magnitude of the saving potential also appears to be larger than what it is partly on account of 'economies of joint consumption' in the family farm arising from the common use of accommodation and household goods. Thus, this constituent of the saving potential exists merely because of the 'joint household', which is an institutional feature of disguised unemployment and would naturally disappear with the transfer of labour; and the other part, which is sustained by borrowing, is not genuine saving.

Secondly, the proposition is valid only in real physical terms and on the assumption that the supply of food produced by the retained labour does not decline in response to price changes. This, no doubt, to a limited extent approximates the conditions in the non-monetised subsistence sector of an underdeveloped economy. But it may not necessarily hold good when the effects of price variation on production of food are considered.

The influence of price changes on food output may be illustrated with reference to the alternative uses of food produce, namely, customary payments in kind, which are usually in the nature of fixed costs, seed for the next season, consumption on the farm and sale in the market. It is obvious that the last three decisions are interdependent among themselves and are together influenced by current and expected prices. And since 'saving potential' in the sense in which it is used by Professor Nurkse refers to the food consumption of unproductive labour, on the farm, it is not an independent variable, but depends upon the marketable surplus and also provision for seed and through

* According to the Report of the All-India Rural Credit Survey, considering for instance, the proportion to total borrowings of borrowing for 'family expenditure', most of which is generally considered non-productive, we find the proportion to be quite considerable, being about 47 per cent for the average cultivator. Even for the big and large cultivators, it is as high as 37 per cent and 41 per cent respectively; the proportion of such borrowing is still higher for the medium cultivator (about 49 per cent) and highest of all for the small cultivator (about 60 per cent) (Vol. II: 338).

them on the level of prices. The interdependence of the saving potential and the price level renders it an unstable quantity, and consequently the assumption of an invariant saving potential in the form of a constant supply of food is not valid. Since food output is partly consumed by food producers, their reserve demand has to be taken into account. Any constellation of prices which results in a reduction of the supply of food would mean a reduction of the saving potential, as would happen if the productive labour which stays back on land has a 'backward rising' supply schedule, in which case the savings fund may be wiped out before mobilisation. It is, of course, not suggested that the backward rising supply schedule is typical of producers' reactions in underdeveloped areas. Even if it were, the schedule would have this shape only for a part of its length and the mobilisation of the saving potential of disguised unemployment could conceivably be completed before the point where the supply schedule becomes backward-rising. But income effects of price changes on the supply of food are particularly relevant wherever the family farm is the predominant unit of production, as is generally the case under conditions of disguised unemployment. These income effects might so operate as to produce a backward-rising supply curve. Professor Nurkse's analysis implicitly assumes that variations in price data are of no significance for food production. This follows from the static character of his model, but as he interprets the subsistence-fund as 'a flow rather than a stock' (ibid.: 44), a certain dynamic element is introduced into the model in so far as the 'flow' is not constant and may vary under the influence of current and expected prices. Consequently, it would be difficult to isolate the saving potential from the effects of price fluctuations.

In addition to the limitations arising from the instability of the saving potential and the existence of certain constituents which are not genuine savings, there are others arising from the fact that the costs of mobilising the savings potential, even if it is assumed to be stable, would be probably greater than its real magnitude. According to Professor Nurkse, the leakage in the subsistence fund through costs of transport of food 'can be reduced by scattering the projects in rural areas, but in practice it can probably never be entirely suppressed' (ibid.: 39). There are, however, distinct limits to decentralisation of those types of capital projects whose location is determined primarily by technical considerations. The mobilisation of the savings potential at relatively low costs may, however, be made possible through development of cottage industries and such other occupations which do not create costs of transfer and housing of surplus farm labour and which involve minimum possible use of additional complementary resources. This line of approach constitutes an important part of the economic case for cottage industries under conditions of disguised unemployment.

Thus, the saving potential of disguised unemployment—in itself somewhat exaggerated by the economies of joint consumption—is largely a conceptual magnitude which could be said to exist only under the highly restrictive assumptions of constant population, constant marginal propensity to consume of the retained and transferred farm labour, abstraction from the income effects of price changes on food production, and from the implications of large-scale agricultural indebtedness. Furthermore, in practice the costs of mobilising the saving potential of disguised unemployment, to the extent that it exists, would probably be greater than the magnitude of such saving.

Professor Nurkse's analysis is theoretically significant insofar as it points to the existence of 'a relationship between consumption and investment, which stands midway between the classical and Keynesian approach' (ibid.: 38), namely, the possibility of increasing capital formation without reducing current levels of consumption. But even this relationship is subject to several limitations, as shown in the present note, which have not been brought out by Professor Nurkse's analysis. There is also the important consideration that it would be unrealistic, even if it were practicable, to posit plans of economic development on the basis of current levels of consumption in underdeveloped countries, when these levels are recognised to be both low and even declining.

5 The Nature and Effects of Gold Hoarding in Underdeveloped Economies*

The hoarding of gold is often regarded as a major source of the misdirection of resources in underdeveloped economies and hence one of the root causes of their economic backwardness. It is commonly held as the leading species of a widespread genus of socially unproductive investment in these economies, which includes some traditional asset preferences such as the hoarding of currency, commodities, and the excessive accumulation of wealth in the form of land and luxury real estate. The theory of the baneful effects of the hoarding of gold and other precious metals, which was originally propagated in modern economics in the works of Lord Keynes[1], has persisted with remarkable tenacity in much of the literature on the economics of underdevelopment[2] without any systematic analysis of its real nature and economic effects. It is, however, necessary to know whether the causes and consequences of the hoarding of gold in underdeveloped countries really conform to received doctrine. In the present paper it will be argued that its motivation is of a character that renders the Keynesian analysis of liquidity preference largely inapplicable to it, and further, that the actual extent of misdirection of resources involved is much less than commonly supposed, and even where there is such misdirection its mechanics are also different from those posited in the Keynesian framework. The irrelevance of monetary conditions, such as the state of credit and the structure and level of interest rates and hence of monetary policy to the phenomenon of gold hoarding also emerges from the analysis. To the extent that the accumulation of private wealth in the form of gold does involve some economic waste the relevant implications for policy are also indicated, notably the rationale and possible methods of gold mobilisation.

I

It is useful to have some idea of the order of magnitude of the hoarding of gold before analysing its nature and effects as this would indicate, *prima*

* *Source*: *Oxford Economic Papers*, New Series, 13(2): 137-48. June 1961.

facie, whether the problem is of a sufficiently serious magnitude. Though comparative estimates of private holdings of gold in different underdeveloped countries are not available, it would suffice for purposes of the present analysis to refer to some estimates for India, which is regarded as the classic example of a country with an insatiable appetite for the precious metals.[3] These estimates show that the total private stocks of gold in India would be around 105 million ounces, i.e., of the value of about $3675 million on the basis of the US Treasury's buying price of $35 per ounce.[4] This is a large amount in absolute terms, being the historical accumulation of stocks, but new hoarding is small in relation to the household sector's savings and the national income. Recent studies of the savings pattern in India show that during the years 1950-1958 gold as a proportion of the household sector's savings averaged around 3·6 per cent and 0·2 per cent of national income and its average rate of growth was 1·7 per cent.[5] These orders of magnitude dispel the notion of excessive 'thesaurisation' of the Indian economy, particularly in recent years. Thus, the role of gold as a savings medium in India is comparatively insignificant and it is unlikely to be more important in the case of other underdeveloped economics.

There is, equally, a good deal of misconception concerning the real nature and motivation of gold hoarding in underdeveloped economies. Hoarding can be attributed to three conceptually distinct motives, namely, precautionary purposes, the psychic income accruing from jewellery and ornaments, and expectation of capital appreciation, corresponding to which gold can be regarded as a liquid asset and a store of value, as a durable consumer good and as a hedge. Such hoarding is largely a non-monetary phenomenon notwithstanding some formal similarities of gold and money such as liquidity, non-interest yielding character, etc. The differences in the underlying motives for holding cash balances and for hoarding gold render the Keynesian analysis of liquidity preference largely inapplicable to the case of hoarding of precious metals in underdeveloped countries. Thus, the transaction motive is obviously not relevant since gold is not a medium of internal exchange. The hoarding of gold is no doubt partially actuated by the precautionary motive and a fairly useful index of this would be the volume of gold sales by agriculturists to meet either such fixed monetary costs like taxes, interest and rent as cannot be met out of income, or else to maintain customary levels of consumption. But distress sales of gold are not normally of an appreciable magnitude because the esteem value attached to gold, particularly ornaments, being very high, its outright sale to meet current or capital outlays is only resorted to in exceptional circumstances such as acute depression. This is also evidenced by the comparatively negligible role of gold and silver (bullion and ornaments) as security for institutional and non-institutional credit.[6] The normal hoarding of gold cannot be regarded as a form of 'hump saving' because it is not actuated mainly by the desire to "provide for the saver's needs during his own lifetime, saving destined to be subsequently dissipated in dis-saving."[7]

Though gold functions as a store of value its specific role in underdeveloped countries, as a hedge against currency instability and inflation is questionable.[8] First, the underdeveloped economies are better cushioned against instability than advanced economies in so far as a substantial portion of their income is derived from the non-monetised sector,[9] and to this extent the need or desire for a 'hedge' is attenuated. Secondly, some of them, like India, have had a measure of monetary stability over the last half century and more to an extent not enjoyed by even some European countries such as France, Greece, and Italy where there is consequently a distinct demand for hoarding of gold as a hedge against currency instability. It is also doubtful how far the economic sophistication of the average individual in the underdeveloped economies, unlike in advanced countries, extends to the notion of holding an asset which will not depreciate in terms of his currency. Besides, gold is subject to some disadvantages as a hedge against inflation. Its value has no relation to the growth and development of the economy and consequently it does not, like equities and real assets, share in the fruits of economic progress.[10] It could, of course, also be maintained that gold functions as a hedge precisely because of the absence of a unique organic or functional relationship between gold prices and the growth of the economy which renders gold comparatively immune to price fluctuations affecting other assets. Gold in the form of ornaments in countries like India cannot be a good hedge because of a peculiarity of the ornaments market: their sale usually involves a capital loss in so far as the seller cannot get value for the cost of workmanship. This means that gold, apart from being a non-income-yielding asset in all forms, is subject in its most important form (ornaments) to a capital loss in the event of sale. The internal price of gold being much higher in most underdeveloped countries than its international price, its utility as a hedge has to depend exclusively on the internal market, quite apart from any statutory restrictions on export. Though the balance of the argument on the effectiveness of gold as a hedge against inflation in underdeveloped economies is somewhat indeterminate, the fact remains that the role of gold as a hedge is distinctly subsidiary.

The speculative motive also does not operate in the case of the large mass of gold hoarders, since it is only the dealers and middlemen in gold who are chiefly concerned with making estimates of future prices of gold and to take up 'positions' thereof with a view to profitable sale subsequently. This shows that Kahn's description of 'speculative indulgence' is inapplicable to the major part of the hoarding demand for gold in underdeveloped economies. By far the larger proportion of the stock of hoarded gold in underdeveloped economies consists of jewellery and ornaments, which means that gold in these countries is really more akin to a durable consumer good than to cash balances and its use value and esteem value is more important than the precautionary and speculative motives. The hoarding of gold is primarily motivated by the psychic income accruing from possession and use of ornaments and this in turn is largely a reflection of the sociological and historical milieu of countries which have underdeveloped economies as well as traditional societies such as those in the Middle East and South-East Asia. It is the role of gold as a durable consumer good that affords the real clue to the phenomenon of gold hoarding in these areas.

II

The demand schedules for money (cash balances) and for gold are largely independent of each other and, therefore, changes in the cost and availability of money as reflected in interest rates and money-market conditions have no effect in either direction on the demand for gold. The steadiness of demand for gold in these economies shows that investment in gold does not depend, as argued by Kahn, on "among other things, the general state of credit and on levels of rates of interest."[11] In fact, it is the "other things", comprising largely of non-monetary factors which really determine the level of demand for gold. The demand for gold being interest-inelastic no practicable rise in rates of interest is likely to divert gold from private hoards into the banking system or into interest-bearing securities[12] or prevent further hoarding.

The demand for gold is also, over a considerable range, largely independent of its price because of the esteem value being the primary motive for it. In other words, the hoarding of gold is undertaken for reasons unconnected with the price of gold. In point of fact, the demand for gold in underdeveloped economies is determined largely by variations in the level of incomes. An increase in incomes is likely to lead to an increase in the offtake of gold even as, under exceptional circumstances, a fall in incomes to levels insufficient to maintain the customary standard of living and/or to meet fixed money costs such as taxes, rent, and interest may result in liquidation of gold hoards. It is, however, difficult to say to what extent gold hoards represent reductions in consumption—in which case they would be genuine net saving—or are merely a substitute for other forms of saving. In the case of lower-income groups whose marginal propensity to consume is normally very high, the purchase of gold would more probably be at the expense of consumption whereas in respect of the higher income groups whose marginal propensity is low, it would represent savings which would have been made in one form or another. The insensitivity of gold hoarding to gold prices is also evidenced by the comparative absence of self-correcting price expectations in the gold market and, consequently, it cannot be maintained that "every rise in gold price will diminish the desire to hoard gold as the risk of a subsequent fall in the price of gold becomes greater."[13] On the contrary, the strength of demand for gold is such as to generate perverse expectations so that a rise in the price of gold may even increase the demand. The lack of any consistent and determinate relationship between the hoarding of gold and the price of gold means that a rise in the price of gold would be ineffective as a means of preventing gold hoarding or of mobilising existing hoards.[14]

But a high or rising level of gold prices has hardly any significant economic consequences. It reflects the strong normal propensity to hoard gold relatively to a fixed supply of gold in underdeveloped economies with a free internal market for gold since in most of these communities there is neither new production nor fresh imports. A rise in gold price leaves the total quantum of hoarded gold unaffected because the economy as a whole cannot hoard more gold than the fixed existing supply, nor does it raise the general price level or affect the productive potential and real capital formation in the economy.

A rise in the internal price of gold in terms of the local currency cannot be regarded as an operative causal factor in inflation, which is basically a reflection of the excess of monetary demand over available real output in the economy. It is really a symptom and cannot be regarded as a cause of inflation even under conditions of hyper-inflation, which may persist as long as the underlying causes of inflationary pressure are operative.[15] In point of fact, it is difficult to posit any systematic relationship between gold prices and commodity prices and one cannot, therefore, attribute any primacy to gold prices as a causal factor, whatever the degree of inflation. Besides, a rise in the price of gold has hardly any deleterious effects on the general cost price structure even remotely comparable to those associated with a rise in prices of wage goods which are really the key prices in an underdeveloped economy. A diversion of demand to gold from other commodities would actually be anti-inflationary and permit an increase in development expenditure with a smaller degree of rise in general prices. A rise in the internal price of gold does not stimulate the consumption of holders even if it increases their net worth, since gold being largely held for its psychic income it is unlikely to be dehoarded from time to time for purchase of goods and services. Consequently, hoards of gold cannot be regarded as a pocket of latent inflation. In so far as they represent forgone consumption they have a net anti-inflationary impact and as such, far from being anti-social, they act as a safety valve for the inflationary pressures to which most underdeveloped countries are at present subject in their attempts at accelerated development.[16] The deflationary effects of gold hoarding can always be offset, if necessary, by government creation of purchasing power in excess of current receipts from taxes and borrowing from genuine savings. The extent of such hoarding indicates one of the safe limits to possible deficit financing by public authorities, though it is conceivable that under certain circumstances such deficit financing itself may stimulate gold hoarding through adverse expectations regarding the future course of money values. But more hoarding of gold need not be a bar to development expenditure by government. The rise in internal prices of existing gold stocks does not, by and large, amount to a diversion of real resources from productive channels except perhaps for the wastage of entrepreneurial talent in gold transactions, which anyhow is likely to be of the second order of smalls. Sales and purchases of existing gold do not also affect the magnitude of total real savings since they merely represent asset transfers within the economy.

III

It is only if the assumption of a fixed supply of gold is invalid that the hoarding of gold has a bearing on economic development, namely through absorption of real resources which could have been utilised in productive investment as, for instance, when precious metals are imported (including illicit imports) and, therefore, have to be paid for ultimately by exports of goods and services or else, in the case of hoarding, of locally produced gold through diversion of domestic factors of production from more productive activities. It is, however, arguable whether the direct or indirect absorption of real resources by gold production and imports has been of such a magnitude as to create any special problems. Since domestic production of gold in most underdeveloped countries has been negligible, their demand for precious metals has been met by imports financed out of their real export surpluses and to that extent they have no doubt constituted a misdirection of resources which could have been better utilised for imports of capital or consumer goods. Though the import of gold has a wholly anti-inflationary effect, it is less productive than the use of an equivalent amount of foreign exchange for imports of useful goods and services. This is because the effect of gold imports is largely limited to the resultant absorption of purchasing power whereas the import of other durable consumer goods and capital goods, in addition, also enhances productivity in the economy. But even with regard to the historical imports of gold and the precious metals in underdeveloped countries, it would be misleading to regard them as purely a net leakage of resources. It can be maintained that precious metals have played the role of 'inducement goods' for producers of agricultural commodities and thereby helped to maintain and even increase their marketed surplus.[17] This was, in fact, partly the rationale of official gold sales during World War II in India and the Middle East.[18] The role of precious metals as an inducement good and, consequently, as an instrument of monetisation and development of subsistence economies is overlooked in historical and contemporary discussions of the problem. It arises partly on account of the implicit assumption of Keynesian analysis that all imports represent net leakages from the income stream, whereas imports are often complementary to domestic investment not only for technical reasons, as in the case of capital goods and raw materials, but also because of the incentive effect of consumer goods on domestic producers operating through 'straightening' of backward-sloping supply curves of effort in the economy.[19] There is, however, the possibility of the incentive effect of gold import being swamped by the loss of productive potential represented by forgone imports of producer goods.

Thus, the hoarding of imported or domestically produced gold cannot necessarily be regarded as a drag on economic development and historically even when it has so acted it has hardly operated along the Keynesian chain of causation, namely, through the action of the liquidity trap in preventing the fall of "the rate of interest to a level which was more compatible with the growth of real wealth";[20] it has no bearing on the direction or pace of development unless it involves absorption of real resources and even such absorption may not always be of an appreciable magnitude. It, therefore, follows that the importance assigned in the Keynesian scheme of ideas to the role of gold hoarding as a case of excessive liquidity preference holding up real investment is misplaced.

IV

The foregoing analysis shows that in the absence of domestic production and import of gold there is no absorption of real resources through gold hoarding and there is, therefore, no policy problem involved so long as the stock of gold in the community as a whole is constant because under these conditions only its ownership pattern changes and there are no positive economic effects associated with this. The real objective of policy, so long as gold remains an important medium of international payments, should be the mobilisation of gold hoards to cover part of the foreign exchange gap of the economy though the release of gold hoards, will not mean a corresponding release of internal real resources for capital formation; and unless the gold is used to finance imports of real goods and services its continued hoarding is of no consequence. In this respect gold constitutes an important exception to the fact that the real problem of underdeveloped economies is not one of mobilising the 'fund' of idle savings but of increasing the 'flow' of saving because in so far as it is capable of being mobilised as foreign exchange the magnitude of the stock of gold is certainly relevant.[21] Though the utilisation of hoarded gold as foreign exchange would be in the nature of a once-for-all operation even if its actual mobilisation, which represents drawing down of a stock, is phased over a period of time, it would still constitute a vital accession of resources to an underdeveloped economy in crossing the crucial foreign exchange 'hump' in the pre-take-off period.[22] This is the only economic justification for mobilising gold hoards in underdeveloped economies. But any scheme for the mobilisation of gold hoards will always encounter the fundamental objection that so long as the major portion of hoarding demand emanates from non-monetary motives, it is idle to expect any substantial response to such schemes, however, attractive the terms of assets in which gold is to be converted. Even so, it would be pertinent to examine the feasibility of schemes aimed at mobilising gold hoards.

The government could acquire gold from private hoards in the country to meet the foreign exchange liabilities of the public sector even though such purchases at open market prices, which are very much higher than the international parity prescribed by the International Monetary Fund, might appear highly uneconomic since their valuation for finance of any imports will necessarily have to be in terms of the very much lower international parity price.[23] Similarly, such open market purchases, which are meaningful on the assumption that they absorb only the existing internal stocks of gold, might also seem to run the risk of encouraging illicit imports so that the eventual accretion to official foreign exchange reserves of gold would be more than offset by the indirect loss of foreign exchange as measured by the excess price of illicit imports of gold over its international price. However, the direct and indirect losses as a result of official purchases of gold at the higher internal prices would be justifiable in real terms if the higher productivity of the domestic real assets made possible by the imported goods can more than offset this initial loss. This also follows from the fact that owing to the existence of an indispensable import content in development programmes domestic saving is no substitute in real terms for the goods and services that cannot be produced at home and which have therefore to be necessarily imported. Official purchases of gold at internal market prices would not raise any insuperable problems arising from the disposal of the premium gains of private sellers of gold, on the reasonable assumption that they would anyhow be retained within the economy. Their inflationary potential could be adequately controlled by monetary, fiscal, and other instruments of policy. If the money received in exchange for gold is saved in other forms or invested in new assets, it does not obviously create any problem and even if it is used to buy existing assets the resultant rise in prices of such assets would not have any deleterious consequences. In the event of its being diverted to luxury expenditure, it should be possible to levy indirect taxes on items of luxury consumption. Indirect taxation of the probable avenues of expenditure of these proceeds would be more practicable than direct taxation of such gains, since apart from the possibility of evasion, they might deter hoarders from selling any gold even if the marginal rates of direct taxes on gold sales are well below unity whereas indirect taxes are less likely to act as deterrents.

One possible scheme of gold mobilisation would be the issue of government securities to be subscribed and also redeemed in gold after a specified period of time, since *prima facie* there would be no point in the issue of securities which are subscribable in gold but redeemable in domestic currency because the possibility of selling gold and investing the proceeds in government securities is always there. But the issue of government securities, subscribable and redeemable in gold, whether they are of the 'income type', i.e., yielding a periodic interest income, or of the 'appreciation type', i.e., yielding accumulated interest on maturity, would raise difficult organisational problems such as calculation of interest, etc. Actually, only that portion of gold held as a convenient medium for concealment of taxable income and wealth might be attracted into gold bonds if these are issued in the form of bearer securities.

In view of the difficulties inherent in mobilising private gold hoards for the use of the public sector, a more promising approach would be to attempt to mobilise these hoards to raise the foreign exchange required for the indispensable import content of the private sector itself but through the mediation of the government. This could take the form of issue of import licences for capital or essential consumer goods to such private importers as are able to produce the requisite amount of gold from sources known or accessible to them. Such a scheme will be aimed naturally at those producers who expect that any loss that they might incur through export of gold at the international parity price will be more than offset by the prospective profit on their projects financed by the imported materials and equipment. Import licensing to the private sector merely on production of the requisite amount of gold has, of course, the risk that importers' scales of priority may differ from those of government and, consequently, the requisite amount of gold may not be forthcoming. Besides, the major portion of hoarded gold being in the form of jewellery and ornaments, it is not available in an easily disposable and exportable form.

It is conceivable that unorthodox schemes of gold mobilisation in the form of bearer gold bonds or the issue of import licences on production of gold may put a premium on illicit imports of gold and tax evasion and create difficult problems of choice between economic 'realpolitik' and social ethics. The balancing of the economic and social costs of such schemes against the gains of acquiring much-needed foreign exchange will challenge the resources of economic statesmanship and administration in the underdeveloped economies.

NOTES

1. It is interesting to note the continuity of ideas on this subject in Keynes's writings. Thus, in Indian Currency and Finance (London: Macmillan, 1913) it is said, "India, as we all know, already wastes far too high a proportion of her resources in the needless accumulation of the precious metals.... It is interesting to reflect that India's love of the precious metals ruinous though it has been to her development, has flourished in the past to the great advantage of the Western nations" (p.99). This was further refined in The General Theory of Employment, Interest and Money (London: Macmillan, 1936) to bring out its mechanics of operation in the framework of the analysis of liquidity preference and its effects on investment. "The history of India at all times has provided an example of a country impoverished by a preference for liquidity amounting to so

strong a passion that even an enormous and chronic influx of the precious metals has been insufficient to bring down the rate of interest to a level which was compatible with the growth of real wealth" (p.337).

2. The following references are typical of the earlier and recent contributions to the subject.

   Even in some very poor countries savings are more than negligible (as an aggregate) but they are either standing idle as hoards or move into unproductive capital formation. In the Balkans, for example, the hoarding of currency notes is stated to be perhaps as much as 25 per cent of the total circulation. Gold coins and foreign currency are also hoarded. Similarly, hoarding has also gone on for generations in the Orient. But such hoarding means that what is saved is not made available for industrial equipment or for agricultural improvements. (Norman S. Buchanan (1946). "Deliberate Industrialisation for Higher Incomes", Economic Journal: 541, December).

   "...in underdeveloped countries, the speculative indulgence in hoarding of commodities and gold and in wasteful forms of building leads to misdirection of resources. These anti-social methods of holding private wealth call for strict controls and stringent penal measures. Their extent does also depend, among other things, on the general state of credit and on levels of rates of interest. This is a sense in which monetary policy is very important." (R.F. Kahn (1958). "The Pace of Development", The Challenge of Development. Jerusalem: Hebrew University. p.185).

3. Keynes, The General Theory ..., p.337.

4. "Estimates of Gold and Silver Stocks in India", Reserve Bank of India Bulletin, April 1958, pp.3 and 4.

5. "Savings in the Indian Economy", Reserve Bank of India Bulletin, March 1960. See also an earlier study by V.V. Bhatt on "Savings and Capital Formation in India", Economic Development and Cultural Change. Chicago, Ill.: University of Chicago, April 1959, p. 336.

6. The relevant data for India bear this out. Thus, the advances against bullion (gold and silver) as at the end of the years 1956-1959 were less than 1 per cent of total bank credit. The proportion, inclusive of advances against ornaments, for which data are available only from 1960, is also very small (2·4 per cent). (Source: Report on Trend and Progress of Banking in India and other Reserve Bank data.) The All India Rural Credit Survey's intensive inquiry in 1951-52 based on a stratified random sample survey of 75 districts showed that borrowings per cultivating family for 'all strata' which were secured by pledge of bullion and ornaments amounted to 2·5 per cent of its total borrowings. (Source: This is derived from the tables on pp. 591–5 of the Technical Report of the Rural Credit Survey, vol. III, Reserve Bank of India, 1956, which gives the strata-wise magnitudes of total borrowings and borrowings pledged by bullion and ornaments per cultivating family).

7. As defined by R.F. Harrod in Towards a Dynamic Economics. London: Macmillan, 1948, p.49.

8. For instance, P.T. Bauer and B.S. Yamey, The Economics of Underdeveloped Countries (Nisbet: Cambridge University Press, 1957), p.134, refer to the role of trinkets, precious stones, and metals "as insurance against currency inflation".

9. For instance, the non-monetised sector in India is estimated at about one-third of the economy as a whole. An important index of this is the proportion of imputed value of consumption in kind to the value of total consumption of households in India, which is placed at 36·8 per cent for rural and urban areas. The proportions for rural and urban areas separately are estimated at 44·3 per cent and 11·4 per cent, respectively (The National Sample Survey, Fourth Round, April-September 1952, No. 18, p.13, issued by Cabinet Secretariat, Government of India, 1959).

10. Even in regard to equities, doubts have been expressed about their efficacy as a 'hedge'. Thus, T. Wilson, in his article on "Equities and Growth" (London: Lloyds Bank Review, October 1959), while not denying that equities have offered some protection against inflation, also adduces evidence in support of the thesis that "it would not be true to say that equities have offered adequate security against inflation" (p.16).

11. Monetary experience in Greece after World War II has been invoked to show that a rise in interest rates could lead to dishoarding of gold. Thus, according to Sir Theodore Gregory ("Minutes of Evidence", Committee on the Working of the Monetary System. London: H.M.S.O., 1960), "the rise in bank deposit rates in Greece did induce people to hold currency instead of sovereigns. That is very significant; it overcame not a liquidity preference but a gold preference" (Q. 10788, p.727). "...in countries in which there is a gold market in which holders of gold are not very certain of their legal position, they hold sovereigns just because there is nothing else to hold, and the mere fact that they are offered a higher rate of interest is a sufficient inducement to switch from one to the other. I do not think that (in underdeveloped countries particularly) people have clear ideas about liquidity preference" (Q. 10789).

    This line of reasoning overlooks that, assuming gold hoarding to be sensitive to interest rate changes, an increase in bank deposit rates should have really led to a switch of sovereigns into deposits rather than currency. Besides, the very fact that notions of liquidity preference—which is rightly distinguished from gold preference—are amorphous in underdeveloped countries should make one chary of attributing any impact on gold hoards from changes in interest rates.

    In this context it is interesting to recall Goschen's address to the London Chamber of Commerce in 1891, "you may raise your rate of interest to 6 per cent but the bulk of the people will not carry less gold in their pockets than they did before, and I doubt whether from other quarters you would be able to get much addition to your central store" (quoted by J.M. Keynes, Indian Currency and Finance, p.73). Though Goschen had in mind, primarily, the insensitivity of the transactions circulation of gold to interest rate changes, he was also sceptical of their efficacy in mobilising non-transaction stocks of gold. This would be even more so where the non-monetary demand for gold is stronger, as in the underdeveloped countries.

12. This was proved by the poor response to the Government of India's 3½ per cent National Plan Loan 1964 issued in 1954, which allowed the facility of tendering subscriptions in jewellery and ornaments. Such subscriptions amounted to only Rs. 85,000 out of a total subscription of Rs. 1300 million (see "Statement of Parliamentary Secretary to Finance Minister", Government of India, 12 September 1954).

13. N. Kaldor (1956). Indian Tax Reform. New Delhi: Ministry of Finance, Government of India, p.118.

14. Thus, R.F. Harrod argues ("The Role of Gold Today", South African Journal of Economics, March 1958, p.10) that "a stiff increase in the price of gold would relieve the situation, not only by increasing the value of world stocks in relation to international trade but also by stimulating new output in the long run and by reducing the very large seepage of gold into private hoards."

    Though there has been a continuous rise in the price of gold in India since 1956-57, the first year of the Second Five Year Plan (see table), it has not curbed gold hoarding in the country.

Spot Price per Tola of Gold in Bombay (in Rs.)*

Year	*Highest*	*Lowest*	*Average*
1956-57	109·62	98·94	104·52
1957-58	114·37	104·50	108·46
1958-59	120·50	104·19	112·08
1959-60	134·62	116·50	124·40

* Tola = Three-eighths of an ounce.

Source: Reserve Bank of India Bulletins.

15 According to Kaldor (Indian Tax Reform, p.119), in a state of hyper-inflation "it may be quite true that an enhanced rate of increase in the price of gold will cause an enhanced rate of increase in the price of wheat or rice, or other staple foods."

16 The anti-inflationary significance of gold absorption by the public is well brought out by war-time experience of gold sales in India and the Middle East. "Even when the peasant has been ready to take paper money he liked the paper money so little that he was ready to spend it at the first opportunity, whereas the gold round his wife's neck would be wrung from him only under the duress of depression. The brake which the gold sales put upon the inflation of the paper currency thus gave the situation some stability, it reduced the element of 'repressed inflation'" (R.S. Sayers (1956). Financial Policy, 1939-1945. London: H.M.S.O. p.284).

17 According to Bauer and Yamey (The Economics of Underdeveloped Countries, pp. 140-141), "the importance of new or improved consumer goods in inducing producers to join the exchange economy is implicit in the term 'inducement goods' often rightly applied to these commodities." But this is unduly restrictive since a good need not necessarily be new or improved for it to act as an inducement good. Rather this description is applicable to any good which has the effect of evoking an increased supply of effort to the exchange sector. In fact, familiar but scarce and intensely desired goods qualify especially for this role. One might, therefore, legitimately extend the concept of inducement goods to precious metals which have also been instrumental in extending the exchange economy and the magnitude of the marketed surplus in underdeveloped economies. Gold can function as an inducement good not only through an increase in its supply and availability, but also through a rise in its price, because the demand for gold being price-inelastic over a considerable range an increase in its price could also have an incentive effect since buyers are thereby induced to earn higher incomes to acquire gold.

18 "...[a] large share of the success of the cereals collection campaign of 1943 in the Levant States was due to the availability of relatively cheap gold. This readiness of the peasant to part with grain in exchange for gold – a perfectly normal phenomenon of Eastern prosperity – was immensely important" (Sayers, Financial Policy, 1939-1945, p.284). Much the same point is also made in his analysis of wartime sales of gold in India, which were justified on the ground that "availability of gold for hoarding purposes should tend to lessen the hoarding of commodities: by bringing supplies of foodstuffs on the market, the gold sales would put a brake on the inflation of commodity prices" (p.268).

But Chinese experience in the final years of World War II has been apparently different: "Aircraft loads of gold were imported as a means of fighting famine conditions, though with doubtful effect" (Kaldor, Indian Tax Reform, p.119).

19 All this reflects the neglect in the General Theory of 'complementarity' in the capital structure and investment pattern.

20 Keynes, The General Theory ..., p.337.

21 For instance, the fund of idle savings in the form of hoards of currency or time and savings deposits with banks does not create any problem of mobilisation since it has already been 'invested' during the income period in which it was 'saved' and in the event of these idle savings being mobilised and spent their expansionary effect is the same as that of a corresponding increase in spending financed with newly created money.

22 The estimated stock of hoarded gold in India at around $3,675 million may be compared to the estimated deficit in the balance of payments during the Second Five Year Plan of about $4400 million. It would, however, be rather unrealistic to assume maximum mobilisation of gold hoards.

23 This should be possible consistently with the obligations of member countries of the International Monetary Fund, which while it "strongly deprecates international transactions in gold at premium prices and recommends that all its members take effective action to prevent such transactions in gold with other countries or with the nationals of other countries" would not object to domestic transactions in gold at prices above parity "unless they have the effect of establishing new rates of exchange or undermining existing rates of other members, or unless they result in a significant weakening of international financial position of a member which might affect its utilisation of the Fund's resources" (Report of External Transactions in Gold at Premium Prices, Washington DC: International Monetary Fund, 1950, p.6).

6 Keynes and Central Banking*

Keynes's many-sided contributions to economic thought and policy have been exhaustively reviewed but his contributions to the theory and practice of central banking have hardly received any attention in the literature.[1] This paper attempts to fill this gap by a review and appraisal of Keynes's ideas and activities in the sphere of central banking under the following categories: (i) the rationale of central banking; (ii) the instruments of central banking; (iii) the Bank of England; (iv) internal bank cooperation; and (v) an overall appraisal.

Rationale of Central Banking

Keynes based the rationale of a central bank not only on its regulatory functions, i.e., as the controller of the monetary system, but even more on its developmental role as an agency to promote financial intermediation in an emergent economy. Long before the recommendation of the Brussels Conference of 1920 for establishing a central bank in countries where there is no central bank, Keynes had presented the most detailed schemes for establishing a central bank in India although it was still a British dependency. This is particularly noteworthy considering that half a century later it was still being debated "whether a central bank should be established in every independent political unit is very much an open question."[2] Keynes, very significantly, noted that successive proposals for a state bank in India were so often "smothered in the magnificent and empty maxims of political wisdom", which clearly implied that there were no valid economic arguments against the creation of a central bank. Initially, Keynes argued the case for a state bank for India on the ground that the divorce between the responsibility for the note issue and that for banking generally lead to the keeping of two separate reserves, the government's and the bankers', and the reserves of the latter were insufficient without the assumption of responsibility by the former. This dual reserve system created rigidity in the note issue. The absence of a state bank also made it difficult for the government to centralise its cash balances to the

* *Source: Indian Economic Review* XX(2): 283–97, July-December 1985.

best advantage and also deprived it of a source of continuous financial advice and experience—always a valuable argument for a new central bank. It could not also prudently place all its free reserves in a private institution.

Keynes in his 'Memorandum on Proposals for the Establishment of a State Bank in India' (6 October 1913) to the Royal (Chamberlain) Commission on Indian currency and finance[3] rejected the Bank of England as an unsuitable model for India because being, essentially a product of history, it had a strictly conventional role as the Government's bank of issue, and a lender of last resort operating through just two departments of Issue and Banking respectively.[4] Instead, he commended the examples of the European state banks, which were based on conscious design, had more flexible currency issue systems than the Bank of England, and developmental objectives, such as the provision of direct credit and rediscount facilities to promote industry and agriculture. The state banks of Germany and Russia had several novel features which were missing in the Bank of England but which were thought more appropriate to Indian conditions and requirements. For instance, the German Reichsbank was authorised to exceed the statutory limit of note issue without metallic backing, upon the payment of a tax at the rate of 5 per cent per year on the excess. This ruse proved helpful in averting monetary stringency of the type experienced in England under the Bank Act of 1844, while keeping the monetary circulation within the limits set by the needs of business. The Reichsbank had facilities for quick transfer of deposits at no charge from any one of its 486 branches to another branch without recourse to cheques or clearing systems. Thereby it economised the use of specie, which fell from 39.5 per cent of total monetary circulation (1876) to 16.15 per cent (1900). Similarly, the revised statute of the Bank of Russia (1894) provided for direct financing of industry, commerce and agriculture by authorising it to extend credit up to three years and to take loans against bills secured by hypothecation or guarantee, or any other securities deemed adequate by the Minister of Finance. Its rediscount facilities (up to eight months) for commercial paper were extended to private banks on loans on securities which were not acceptable directly by the state bank, with the risk being divided between the two institutions.

Keynes's memorandum covered the proposed state bank's constitution, capitalisation, and functions such as management of note issue, government balances, public debt, and centralisation of reserves. It had several novel features which went beyond those of the European State Banks. First, there was the emphasis on professional management insulated from political interference and on discretionary control of the monetary system.'[5] Secondly, Keynes stressed the primacy of the promotional role of a central bank in an underbanked country like India.[6] His agenda for the proposed state bank of India (c.1913) stated that it should open branches as rapidly as possible at most places with a district treasury without, however, jeopardising the bank's profitability. His proposals, therefore, aimed at a virtually guaranteed dividend to shareholders, which he thought was both just and politic. Keynes was also innovative in advocating appropriate rediscount facilities to Indian banking on the most desirable lines of European experience. But he deprecated any notion of direct competition of the state bank with exchange banks in attracting deposits in London or in the trade remittance business. Subsequently, in his evidence to the Royal Commission (Hilton Young) on *Indian Currency and Finance* (1926) Keynes reaffirmed the role of a central bank in developing commercial banking.[7]

Keynes was, however, equally conscious of the need to regulate commercial banks in India, many of which suffered from under-capitalisation, mismanagement and conduct of non-banking activities. He was concerned that although the growth of banking in India was of utmost importance "a startling series of failures will do much to retard it."[8] He was thus cognisant of the prudential aspects of central banking when it hardly figured in public policy. It is, however, a revealing commentary on the time-lag between ideas and implementation in India's monetary history that it was not until late in the 1940s that the Reserve Bank of India established Departments of Banking Inspection and Development and not until the 1960s and 70s that the State Bank of India (the former Imperial Bank) and the nationalised commercial banks embarked on a planned expansion of branches in under-banked areas.

For all his innovativeness in other respects, Keynes was surprisingly conventional on the disposal of central bank profits.[9] Commenting on the State Bank Memorandum (1913) of Lionel Abrahams (Financial Secretary and later Under-Secretary of State for India) Keynes argued that it would not be easy to determine the net profits of the note issue and thought that the shareholders should have the profits up to a certain percentage, with the surplus being divided between them and the government, subject to decennial revision. Keynes's own scheme for a State Bank for India provided for a division of the annual net profits after due allowance for depreciation and preference dividends (if any), between shareholders, reserves and the government. But the scheme did not address the policy issue of a productive use of currency profits.[10] Thus, even Keynes was no exception to the supposition that the analysis of central bank profits has hardly evoked any attention from economists or practising central bankers.[11] Keynes, however, was positive that even a privately owned central bank like the then Bank of England "should feel quite free not to be influenced in the slightest degree by the necessity of earning a given income", in discharging its monetary policy obligations.[12] But Keynes also recognised that the Bank of England's freedom from political pressure, like that of any other central bank, does not depend on the mere fact that it has private shareholders.

Instruments of Central Banking Policy

Keynes's ideas on this aspect of central banking, which are contained in his evidence to the Macmillan Committee and more systematically developed in his *Treatise on Money*, may be analysed in terms of the three basic instruments: (a) the bank rate, (b) open market policy, and (c) variation of reserve requirements.

The Bank Rate and Credit Rationing

Keynes gave possibly the first systematic exposition of the mechanics of the bank rate as the official published rate of a central bank.[13] Keynes was, perhaps, original only in his attempt to link the Bank Rate of the quantity equation since his Bank Rate doctrine was largely derived from the Cunliffe Committee in Britain (1919). In a free loan market, Keynes argued, a given level of bank rate must be uniquely correlated, if it is to be effective, with a given quantity of money. However, Keynes's quantity equations were subsequently left out of his theoretical system.

Keynes's real originality lay in formulating the concept of "the fringe of unsatisfied borrowers", i.e., who are not considered to have first claims on a bank's funds, but to whom the bank would be quite ready to lend if it "were to find itself in a position to lend more."[14] This leads to the rationing of credit because the demand for credit exceeds its supply at the ruling rate of interest. The amount of bank credit to any borrower is governed not solely by the rate of interest but also by the purpose of borrowing, collateral, and his general credit rating. The existence of this unsatisfied fringe, and of the variability in the standards of credit eligibility, enables banks to influence demand for credit through changes other than the rate of interest. Consequently, this supposes a constraint on the efficacy of bank rate. But Keynes noted that credit rationing cannot be continued beyond the point at which the unsatisfied fringe begins to include borrowers so influential that they can circumvent bank constraints by issuing bills of first class quality or by borrowing direct from the banks' depositors.

Keynes's concept of the fringe of unsatisfied borrowers could be rightly regarded as the genesis of subsequent discussions of credit rationing in the loan market.[15] The concept of credit rationing explains the varied behaviour of the loan market, ranging from (at the macroeconomic level) how credit policy can influence the economy even if demand for money is relatively interest-elastic, to sectoral issues such as urban bias in credit allocation and the denial of credit to weaker sectors. Generally, most models attempt to specify a set of sufficient conditions for credit rationing to occur. But there is no unique set of necessary or sufficient conditions for credit rationing. Although Keynes did not formalise credit rationing in a model, his concept is eclectic enough to include both its quantitative and qualitative aspects, which have been analysed in subsequent discussions. The basic conclusion, as first noted by Keynes and confirmed by subsequent discussions, is that even in the absence of interest rate ceilings and oligopoly the interest rate does not clear the loan market because of lenders' reliance on non-interest rate criteria such as collateral, the purpose of borrowing, borrowers equity, and central bank directives. Thus, the rationing of credit determines the availability of credit as distinct from its cost (i.e., rates of interest).

Open Market Policy

Keynes defined 'open-market policy' as action to vary the amount of a central bank's investments (other than gold) through purchases and sales on it own initiative rather than that of its customers.[16] The exclusion of gold could be explained by the fact that operations in gold were not strictly of the nature of conventional open-market operations.[17]

Keynes's analysis of open-market policy in the British and the US systems showed that the genesis of open-market operations by the US Federal Reserve (c. 1922) was not so much the control of member banks' behaviour, as in England, but the prevention of any further decline in the earning assets of the Reserve Banks. He demonstrated that open market policy and bank rate have different but reinforcing effects. Changes in bank rate may affect central bank advances as an uncertain incidental result of a much wider complex of consequences which a change in bank rate initiates, whereas open market operations have a direct and immediate impact on bank reserves and hence on credit. Bank rate changes primarily affect the short-term rate of interest, whereas open market operations can also influence the long-term rate of interest if the central bank also operates in long-dated securities. Consequently, Keynes regarded the bank rate as more suitable for use to preserve international equilibrium, while open market operations were more effective in influencing investment. Keynes also noted the asymmetry in the relative efficacy of purchases and sales of government securities by the Bank of England. The direct effect of an increase in the reserves of banks as a result of purchases of securities by the Bank of England was a corresponding increase in their credit. But the banks may be able to increase their credit without a significant reduction in the rates of interest charged. The efficacy of the sale of securities in decreasing bank reserves was also likely to be equally unqualified so long as market rates were below bank rate. But if the banks' resistance to credit restriction caused market rates to approach bank rate, it could offset the open market sales by increased discounting by the money market, which cannot be checked except by raising the bank rate.[18]

Keynes believed that a central bank should not hesitate to carry its open market operations to the point of saturation. Therefore, their efficacy depends on the central bank always having an adequate stock of securities. While Keynes also recognised the constraints on such a policy because of 'insufficient ammunition' in a central bank's portfolio, he did not conceive of the possibility of a central bank issuing its own securities independently of the government on the lines of the provision in the statutes of several post-World War II central banks (e.g., Ceylon, the Philippines). Keynes also argued that it may not be possible to equalise the market and the natural rates of long-term interest unless the central bank is required to purchase bonds up to a price far beyond the long-period norm. But these purchases may, if they have to be reversed later by sales, show a serious financial loss.[19] Subsequently, Keynes advocated the extension of open market operations to all maturities as the most important improvement which could be made in the technique of monetary management. He recognised that "owing to the unwillingness of most monetary authorities to deal boldly in debts of long-term, there has not been much opportunity for a test", but he did not analyse the reasons for the reluctance of central banks to deal in long-term securities.[20] The main justification is that trading in short-term securities is the most active and continuous and, consequently, this sector is the most sensitive and effective channel for the conduct of open market operations. This was the rationale underlying the 'bills preferably' doctrine of the US Federal Reserve for a long time.

Variation of Reserve Ratios of Commercial Banks

The apprehension of insufficient securities with central banks led Keynes to investigate the potentiality of an alternative technique, namely, the power to vary with due notice and by small degrees the proportion of legal reserves of commercial banks.[21] Keynes thought that such a provision should be added to 'the powers of the ideal central bank of the future' because the variation in reserve proportions of banks puts on them the most direct possible pressure to move in the desired direction.[22] Keynes proposed that the Bank of England should have the power to vary the 300-day-notice cash ratios of banks (based on daily averages over monthly periods), between 10 and 20 per cent against demand deposits and between 0 and 6 per cent against time deposits. Curiously, despite his familiarity with the German economy, Keynes never referred to an important variant of the reserve ratio technique of 'Einlagenpolitik' used in Germany, namely, the shifting of government balances from the central bank to the commercial banks and vice versa, so as to achieve the same effects on bank liquidity as the direct variation of reserve ratios. There is only a bare reference in Keynes's works to the efficacy of moral suasion by the central bank as a supplement to formal instruments of credit policy.[23]

Keynes was a Director of the Bank of England from 1941 till his death in 1946. Having been one of the foremost critics of the Bank in the inter-war years, his appointment to the Court of the Bank to fill the vacancy caused by the death of Lord Stamp, the only economist on the Court, "created quite a stir".[24] In keeping with the tradition whereby new Directors served on the Staff Committee, Keynes concerned himself with service conditions of the junior staff and the investment policy of the superannuation fund, and also closely scrutinised the implementation of policy decisions. But in assessing Keynes's modest role as a Director of the Bank of England, it has to be borne in mind that a Director as such played little part in those days in shaping Bank policy, which was done mainly by the staff, and by one or two Directors. More importantly, the war had put most normal issues of central banking policy in abeyance, and Keynes was more preoccupied as an Adviser to the Chancellor of the Exchequer, especially on Bretton Woods and the 1945 American Loan. In a war economy, economic debate is rightly subordinated to the needs of pragmatic consensus and immediate action, which was reflected most notably in the "wondrous alliance of Norman [Governor of the Bank of England] and Keynes, unthinkable 10 or 15 years earlier" and the commonality of "attitudes on exchange control between Keynes and the Bank."[25]

However, Keynes's most perceptive observations on the Bank of England predated his service as Director of the Bank. Thus, he was always mindful of the vital distinction between the fleeting policies of Governors and the Bank as an institution. But he never articulated his views on the role of the Court or the Bank except for endorsement of Walter Bagehot's remarks that "The directors of the Bank of England are neither acquainted with right principles, nor were they protected by judicious routines."[26] He also echoed Bagehot's sentiment that "the directors were self-elected from amongst the younger members of a limited range of old established firms, none of them professional bankers."[27] But he recognised the compensating advantages of the prevailing traditions insofar as "steady merchants collected in council are an admirable judge of bills and securities." Even more pertinent is his citation of Bagehot's perceptive analysis of the hypersensitivity of Bank Directors to public criticism and the disadvantages of such an attitude.[28]

Keynes, in his evidence to the Macmillan Committee, suggested the amalgamation of the Issue and Banking Department so that the Bank could have unfettered control over all its assets, with the sole objective of prudent monetary management without having to earn revenue for the Treasury.[29] Although this radical suggestion was not accepted, it was the first explicit recognition of the purely historical character of the dichotomy between the Issue and Banking Departments, an organisational curiosity with no economic rationale, which has been replicated in several newer central banks.

Keynes's ideas on the research and advisory functions and the proper public relations stance for the Bank of England were also well in advance of the contemporary climate of thought and opinion.[30] He thought that the Governor of the Bank should give a comprehensive economic review, say, twice a year, which would come to be regarded as an authoritative exposition of the state of affairs. Equally, he cautioned against too much expression of opinion. Keynes also recognised that the Bank of England was itself seriously hampered by lack of information on basic items such as the active note circulation, the balance of payments, the national balance sheet, output, investment, inventories, and profits. Keynes strongly favoured sampling techniques since they enabled a quicker and better approximation to percentage fluctuations, which are more important than absolute figures as a data base for policy. Keynes thought that the Bank had distinct advantages over government departments for building up a complete statistical service because "it would be more trusted than almost any other collecting agency by those people, particularly in the early days of this system, who fear that the information they were giving might be used to their disadvantage."[31] Keynes wanted the Bank of England to be the centre of knowledge on all matters necessary for monetary management, and felt that if economic life is to be regulated at the source, "there can be no possible instrument of this except the Bank of England ..."[32] This is a most cogent expression of the latter-day concept of the macroeconomic role of a central bank.

International Cooperation among Central Banks

Keynes's evidence to the Macmillan Committee shows that he was among the first to stress the need for cooperation between central banks to promote international economic recovery and to economise the use of gold. He proposed collective measures beginning with the Bank of England, the Federal Reserve System and the Bank of France, to be followed by the central banks of Germany, Holland, Sweden, Switzerland, Spain, Italy, Argentina, and Japan.[33] He advocated a concerted lowering of central bank rates until the price level rose materially and a reduction of legal reserves of central banks to a minimum ratio of 10 per cent below the conventional ratio of about 40 per cent. Accordingly, he outlined a minimum feasible and maximum desirable agenda of 'Methods of Supernational Management' between central banks.[34]

The minimal solution was broadly as follows. All countries must agree not to admit gold into their active circulation and to retain it solely as reserve money for central banks, who must agree to accept some substitute for gold as a part of their own reserve money. All central banks should be allowed the discretion to hold at least a half of their legal reserves as balances with other central banks, or preferably, with the Bank for International Settlements. The legal reserves should be subject to variation by an amount not exceeding 20 per cent of the normal variation, on the recommendation of a committee of central banks. In all countries a 2 per cent margin between the minimum buying and maximum selling price for gold would allow central banks sufficient latitude to handle their short-period domestic credit situations.

Keynes envisaged the ideal arrangement as a supranational central bank without any initial capital but with its liabilities guaranteed by adherent central banks. Its principal objectives would be to maintain the stability or the value of gold (supranational bank money or SBM) in terms of a tabular standard of value based on the principal articles of international commerce and to avoid international profit inflations or deflations. Its assets would comprise gold, securities and advances to central banks and its liabilities would be the deposits by central banks (SBM). Its gold reserves were to be determined at its own discretion and not be required to exceed any fixed minimum percentage of its liabilities. The SBM would be purchasable for gold and encashable for gold at fixed prices with a margin of 2 per cent.

Its technique of attaining these objectives would be partly its bank rate, its discount quota, and discretion to conduct open market operations on its own initiative with the assent, in the case of a purchase, though not necessarily in the case of a sale, of the central bank in whose national currency the securities in question were payable. Keynes thought it would be desirable for central banks to be normally borrowers from the supranational bank at an established rate for periods not exceeding three months at a time, subject to a variable borrowing limit, in consonance with the requirements of the total quantity of SBM. But he did not explain the response of the supranational bank if the central banks preferred to deal with it only as a lender of last resort and the techniques which would ensure regular borrowing by central banks. However, he believed that more than conventional instruments the supranational central bank would have to rely on consultation and joint action at monthly meetings of the board.

Keynes also recognised that "one can ensure nothing by the terms of a paper constitution" and that "the desirable objectives can only be attained through the exercise of daily wisdom by the monetary authorities of the world."[35] Furthermore, it was not realistic to expect of central banks a degree of international disinterestedness far in advance of national sentiment.[36] Keynes thought that the two major obstacles to international cooperation were the tendency of the Federal Reserve System's policies to be dominated by domestic considerations and the lack of familiarity in France with the whole order of ideas.[37] He also speculated that the Bank for International Settlements could well be the nucleus of a supranational bank, but that its future usefulness would largely depend on the support it received from the United States.[38] Keynes, thus, very perceptively sensed the emerging role of the United States as a 'price' leader in an increasingly oligopolistic world economy and of the dollar as the major key currency of the future. Although it remained a paper scheme, Keynes's proposed supranational bank must rank high as an intellectual precursor of post-World War II schemes of international monetary cooperation.

Keynes played a prominent role in the Bretton Woods Conference (1944-45) but the International Monetary Fund as it emerged finally was based more on the White Plan rather than on his own Proposals for an International Currency (Clearing) Union. Keynes conceived the Union primarily as a central bank for central banks based on an international currency ('bancor'), overdrafts (not loans), interest charges on creditor as well as debtor positions, and exchange rates fixed in terms of the bancor. None of these features survived in the IMF's Articles of Agreement. Nevertheless, Keynes's basic ideas of inter-central bank cooperation found institutional and operational expression even if not in the form he desired. His Clearing Union also contemplated a number of parallel supportive organisations for commodity control, a Board for International Investment, and an International Economic Board for controlling the trade cycle. This attests to his growing awareness of the limitations of purely monetary and banking initiatives in the international sphere in contrast to his habitual tendency to neglect the real sector in domestic policies.

Keynes and Central Banking—An Overall Appraisal

The inherent problems of establishing intellectual provenance are further compounded in evaluating Keynes's contributions to central banking, which is a uniquely complex amalgam of ideas, institutions, and operational experience unlike any other branch of macroeconomics. Moreover, there was an impressive body of central banking doctrine in England, Europe, and India preceding Keynes's work.[39] Bagehot's *Lombard Street* (1873) had clearly laid the foundations of modern central banking theory. India, too, was the scene of central banking schemes since Sir James Steuart's writings on Indian monetary problems (1772) and Warren Hasting's 'Plan' for a General Bank in Bengal and Bihar (1773).[40] But these forerunners do not detract from Keynes's contributions to central banking, which are all the more remarkable considering that he had no experience of central banking except for his short and somewhat peripheral spell as a Director of the Bank of England. Nor did he function as a consultant to any central bank except when he served on a committee (1920) to select the Governor for the new South African Reserve Bank.

Keynes's *Indian Currency and Finance* has been rightly accorded "a permanent niche in the history of thought on central banking",[41] a statement which could justifiably be extended to many other writings of Keynes. He consistently demonstrated the regulatory and developmental rationale of a central bank in a dependency like India, often in the teeth of official opposition or indifference. Keynes's originality extended far beyond an eclectic synthesis of central banking doctrine from English, European and US sources to an innovative adaptation to the Indian environment. Yet, it is one of the more glaring ironies of Indian economic history that Keynes, for all his extensive knowledge of and exposure to Indian monetary affairs, was never called upon to advise on the establishment of the Reserve Bank of India in 1935, which also turned out to be a faithful replica of the Bank of England, in perverse contradiction of his considered views and visions. He was alone among contemporary economists in working out organisational details of central banking such as the Board of Directors and the disposition of central bank profits except for an inexplicable omission to provide for their productive use. Keynes also did not give much thought to the implications of the indigenous banking sector in India, an issue which rightly engaged the concern of the Indian Central Banking Inquiry Committee.

Keynes presented the first systematic comparative discussion of central banking techniques, notably the complementarity of bank rate, open market policy, and the variation of reserve ratios. But he did not envisage the possibility of a direct issue of a central bank's own securities to overcome the shortage of 'ammunition' for open market operations; nor did he explore the scope for manipulating government cash balances and for moral suasion as instruments of credit policy. Keynes's omission of the role of qualitative controls on the end-use of credit could perhaps be attributed to the fact that it was not a major contemporary policy issue, being more of a post-World War II phenomenon. Keynes's most notable contribution, however, was the formulation of the concept of the 'unsatisfied fringe of borrowers', which encapsulates the imperfections of financial markets as a constraint on interest rate policies. It is the genesis of the modern concept of credit rationing which has stimulated such a considerable volume of analytic and policy debate. Keynes was always consistently ahead of his times in emphasising the importance of discretionary central banking as against rule-based monetary management. He was perhaps the first analyst to question the economic logic of the purely historical dichotomy between the Issue and Banking Departments of a central bank. His evidence to the Macmillan Committee (1929-1931) on the research and public relations aspects of the Bank of England is an uncanny anticipation of the recommendations of the Radcliffe Committee (1959). Keynes was also prescient in regard to both the scope and limitations of inter-central bank action in a world of economic nationalism.

In sum, Keynes's impressive contributions to the theory and organisation of central banking, as an innovative thinker and as an institutional architect, epitomise the classical and institutionalist Keynes of the *Treatise* and the Committees as against the revolutionary Keynes of the *General Theory*.

NOTES

The author wishes to thank an anonymous referee for helpful suggestions.

1 Cf. R.F. Harrod, The Life of John Maynard Keynes, London: Macmillan, 1951; the series of Keynes Seminars organised by the University of Kent in the 1970s as also the following symposia: Keynes: Aspects of the Man and His Work, D.E. Moggridge (ed.), New York: St. Martins Press, 1974; Essays on John Maynard Keynes, Milo Keynes (ed.), London: Cambridge University Press, 1975; Robert Skidelsky, John Maynard Keynes (Hopes Betrayed, 1883-1920), Vol. I, London: Macmillan, 1983; the Keynes centennial essays by Milton Friedman, F.A. Hayek, Sir John Hicks, and Paul Samuelson in The Economist (London), June (4, 11, 18, 25) 1983; Keynes and the Modern World (Proceedings of the Keynes Centenary Conference), David Worswick and James Trevithick (eds.), Cambridge: Cambridge University Press, 1983 (July).

2 "Are Central Banks Universally Necessary?". In R.S. Sayers, Central Banking after Bagehot, Oxford: Clarendon Press, 1957, p.105.

3 The Collected Writings of John Maynard Keynes (henceforth CW), Vol. XV, Activities 1906-1914, India and Cambridge, Elizabeth Johnson (ed.). London: Macmillan, 1971, pp. 151-219.

4 Keynes exhorted "the framers of the new bank's constitution" to "put far from their minds all thoughts of the Bank of England." "It is in the state banks of Europe, especially in that of Germany, or in those perhaps of Holland or Russia that the proper model is to be found." CW, I, Indian Currency and Finance. London: Macmillan, 1971, p.168.

5 Sayers, n. 2, p.l.

6 As Sayers remarks, in the early days of a central bank the emphasis "must be on the development of a banking system to control. This is not only a logical order; it is also the historical order of events in the underdeveloped country I have most studied; the England of earlier centuries ..." (ibid.: 115).

7 (Sir Henry Strakosch) "Would you not rather say that a central bank would be helpful in expanding the commercial banking organization? Yes, I should (Keynes)." CW, XIX, Activities 1922-1929, The Return to Gold and Industrial Policy, Part II, Donald Moggridge (ed.). London: Macmillan, 1981, p.524.

8 CW, I, p.159.

9 "With regard to the profits of coinage, the Government have announced that they will divert half of the future profits to capital expenditure on railways. But it is to be

hoped that this decision will be reconsidered before the time comes." CW, XV, "Recent Developments of the Indian Currency Question", p. 275.

10 "What is the good of an economical currency if the fruits of economy are to be put in a sarcophagus? The economic error of India tends to be to hoard wealth instead of using it." Abrahams to Keynes, CW, XV, p.215.

11 Even the standard work of M.H. de Kock on Central Banking (4th edn., New York: St. Martin's Press, 1974) has only a brief descriptive subsection on "Distribution of Profits", pp. 307-309.

12 CW, XX, Activities 1929-1931: Rethinking Employment and Unemployment, Donald Moggridge (ed.). London: Macmillan, 1981, p.244.

13 "No systematic treatment of the subject exists in the English language. You will see in vain the works of Marshall, Pigou, Taussig or Irving Fisher. Even Cassel's treatment, which is somewhat fuller, does not examine the train of causation in any detail. Mr. Hawtrey has a little more to say: but he is somewhat unorthodox on this matter, and cannot be quoted as an exponent of the accepted doctrine. There remains one outstanding attempt at a systematic treatment, namely, Knut Wicksell's Geldzins und Guterpreise, published in German in 1898 ...Wicksell's theory is closely akin ...to the theory of the treatise, though he was not successful ...in linking up his theory of bank rate to the quantity equation." "The Pure Theory of Money". In CW, V, A Treatise on Money. London: Macmillan, 1971, pp.166-167.

14 "The Applied Theory of Money". In CW, VI, A Treatise on Money. London: Macmillan, 1971, pp.326-327.

15 Cf. Donald R. Hodgman, "Credit Risk and Credit Rationing", The Quarterly Journal of Economics" 74(2) (May 1960); Edward J. Kane and Burton A. Malkiel, "Bank Portfolio Allocation, Deposit Variability, and the Availability Doctrine", The Quarterly Journal of Economics. 79(1) (February 1965); D.M. Jaffee and Thomas Russell, "Imperfect Information, Uncertainty, and Credit Rationing", The Quarterly Journal of Economics. 90(4) (November 1976); Ernest Baltensperger, "Credit Rationing: Issues and Questions", Journal of Money, Credit and Banking. 10(2) (May 1978); J. Stiglitz and Andrew Weiss, "Credit Rationing in Markets with Imperfect Information", American Economic Review 71(3) (June 1981); Kerry D. Vandell, James D. Hess, Dwight M. Jaffee and Thomas Russell, "Imperfect Information, Uncertainty and Credit Rationing", The Quarterly Journal of Economics 119(4) (November 1984): 841-72.

16 See CW, VI, p.202.

17 "The amount of gold is in a "convertible" international system, one stage further removed from its control; for, directly, it depends on whether the nationals' claims on other banking systems exceed or fall short of foreign claims on them." ibid.: 202.

18 "A considerable part of the value of open-market operations delicately handled may be in its tacit influence on the member banks to move a step in the desired direction ... a progressive series of small inflationary open-market purchases ...are potently, and almost

invariably, effective in inducing the member banks to follow suit." CW, VI, pp. 227-8.

19 "But the choice may conceivably be between assuming the burden of a prospective loss, allowing the slump to continue, and socialistic action by which some official body steps into the shoes which the entrepreneurs are too cold to occupy." Ibid.: 332-335. This last possibility is an uncanny anticipation of the widespread contemporary tendency toward socialization of private risks through official bailouts of troubled industrial and financial units in the USA and Europe.

20 CW, VII, The General Theory of Employment, Interest and Money [1936], London: Macmillan, 1971, p.207.

21 CW, VI, pp.232–3.

22 "In Germany the reserve ratios are much lower and more variable, with the result that the Reiehsbank's control over its member banks' credit policy is far less secure." CW, XI, Economic Articles and Correspondence: Academic, Donald Moggridge (ed.), London: Macmillan, 1983, p.426. For a contemporary evaluation, see A.G. Chandavarkar, "Government Balances as a Monetary Policy Instrument in the Less Developed Countries", Economic and Political Weekly, VII(35) (26 August 1972).

23 "There are ...various other methods of action which are theoretically open to the central bank. In practice, however, the central bank of today – apart from psychological pressure, veiled in the case of the Bank of England, open in the case of the Federal Reserve Bank, by advice, exhortations or threats –has limited itself to these two, namely 'open-market policy" and "bank rate." CW, VI, p.203.

24 Harrod, The Life of John Maynard Keynes, n. 1, p.517.

25 R.S. Sayers, Bank of England, 1891-1944, Vol. 2. Cambridge: Cambridge University Press, 1976, p.591.

26 Review of Reginald McKenna's "The Post-War Banking Policy", CW, XIX, Part II, Activities 1922-1929, Donald Moggridge (ed.). London: Macmillan, 1981, p.773.

27 Centennial appreciation of Bagehot's "Lombard Street", (published in The Banker, March 1926), CW, XIX, Part II, p.468.

28 "...our statesmen...have generally served a long apprenticeship to sharp criticism...But a Bank Director undergoes no similar training and hardening. I am not sure if this sensitiveness is beneficial." Ibid.: 471-2.

29 See CW, XX, Keynes's replies to questions by Mr. Tulloch (p.202) and Mr. Brand (p. 241).

30 "Greater publicity of all kinds will lead to better understanding by the market of what the Bank's intentions are and that will facilitate those intentions being carried into effect and with more certainty. It nearly always pays the market to adapt itself to the real intentions of the Bank. So that the easier it is to interpret those, the quicker in effect will be the methods of control which the Bank uses. Publicity will also help to educate the public and the world and bring much nearer the day ...when the principles

of central banking will be utterly removed from popular controversy and will be regarded as a kind of beneficent technique of scientific control ..." Ibid.: 262-3.

31 Ibid.: 266.

32 Ibid.: 265.

33 Ibid.: 151.

34 CW, VI, pp. 354-367.

35 Ibid.: 360.

36 Ibid.: 257.

37 "...in France...economic science is non-existent. French thought on these matters is two generations out-of-date. Then on top of this we have the gold hoarding propensities of the Bank of France." CW, XX, p.154.

38 CW, VI, p. 363.

39 Cf. Elmer Wood (1939), English Theories of Central Banking Control. Cambridge, Mass.: Harvard University Press; E. Victor Morgan (1943), The Theory and Practice of Central Banking. Cambridge: Cambridge University Press; Vera Smith (1936), The Rationale of Central Banking. London: P.S. King and Son.

40 See A.G. Chandavarkar (1970), "Money and Credit, 1858–1941", Chapter IX, The Cambridge Economic History of India, 2: c. 1757–c., Dharma Kumar and Meghnad Desai (1933) (eds.). Cambridge: Cambridge University Press, pp. 784-789.

41 R.S. Sayer (1972), "The Young Keynes", The Economic Journal, June, p.593.

7 Was Keynes a Development Economist?*

It is pertinent, for a variety of reasons, to raise the questions: could Keynes be regarded as a development economist? Is there anything like a Keynesian theory of development? First, Keynes is widely regarded as "essentially a monetary economist" whose "writings are an intellectual counterpart to the monetary revolution of our time" (Hicks, 1983). Secondly, it has been pointedly said that Keynes "was not concerned with either growth (indeed in 1937 he delivered a lecture on 'some consequences of a declining population ...') or the underdeveloped countries" (Patinkin, 1984). Thirdly, a more eclectic point of view is that although "Keynes himself was little concerned with the problem of economic development, Keynesian economics has had a great deal to do with the emergence of development economics" (Johnson, 1978). Altogether, this theme merits much closer review and analysis than it has received in the literature to date, which either overlooks or deals only peripherally with Keynes's contributions in relation to development economics. This is as true of Harrod's pioneering biography of Keynes as of the series of Keynes seminars organised by the university of Kent in the 1970s, which have covered virtually all aspects of his work except in relation to economic development (Moggridge, 1974; Thirlwall, 1978; Crabtree and Thirlwall, 1980). Similarly, the authoritative articles on the Keynes Centenary by Milton Friedman, Von Hayek, Sir John Hicks and Paul Samuelson (*The Economist*, June 1983) do not touch on this aspect of Keynes's life and work. In view of the comparative neglect of the developmental aspects of Keynes's work, this article attempts to analyse the bearing of the economics of Keynes and Keynesian economics on the economics of development.

Keynes and Developing Countries—India

It is of interest to establish the genesis of Keynes's exposure to developing countries. Keynes never visited any developing country except for holidays in Morocco and Alexandria, Egypt; nor was he interested, as an economist, in any

* *Source*: *Economic and Political Weekly*, XXI(7) (15 February 1986): 304-307.

developing country *per se*, including even India, which is surprising considering the seminal role of the Indian connection in his life and work. Keynes's profound contributions to the theory and practice of the gold exchange standard and of central banking owed a lot to his service at the Indian Office (1906-1908) and his work for successive Indian Currency Commissions and Committees from 1913 to 1926 (Chandavarkar, 1983). Of course, Keynes's interest in India was limited strictly to monetary matters. It was in the nature of a response to the sheer intellectual and institutional challenge posed by the complexities of India's monetary evolution from a silver to a gold exchange standard and the development of a rationale for creating a central bank in an emergent economy and a political dependency. As Keynes himself remarked, "apart from the practical side of the matter, India's intricate and highly artificial system presents problems of special interest to the student of the theory of currency" (Keynes, 1983: i). But issues relating to the economic development of India seldom excited Keynes' interest and attention except marginally. A good example of this is his opposition to India's industrialisation, on the basis of a static concept of the comparative cost advantage of India in agriculture, which is surprising considering that the infant industry argument on the basis of a dynamic comparative cost advantage had been propagated much earlier by Friedrich List (*National System of Political Economy*, 1841) in Germany and others like Alexander Hamilton (*Report on the Subject of Manufactures*, 1791 in USA).[1]

It is well known that Keynes chose the India Office not because of any interest in India but only because it was then one of the two top home departments of the British government. The happy accident of a timely transfer from the Military Affairs Section of the India Office to its economic and commercial side was also a material factor in stimulating his lifelong interest in Indian economics. Keynes's attitude to British rule in India was wholly conventional. Keynes believed that the regime protected the poor against the rapacious moneylenders, brought moral and material progress to India, a sound monetary system and, in short, introduced good government. He never considered the "human and moral implications of imperial rule or whether the British were exploiting the Indians" (Skidelsky, 1983: 176), a stance which was in striking contrast to the two other members of the Bloomsbury Group, Leonard Woolf and E.M. Forster, with their strong empathy for Ceylon and India, respectively. On the other hand, it deserves to be better known that Keynes recommended the abolition of the salt tax in India, which was a major demand of Indian nationalism (Chandavarkar, 1989:42). Keynes noted that the reduction of the salt tax by successive stages had benefited the Indian consumer to its full extent and had led to an increase of 20 per cent in its consumption. But his somewhat naïve faith in the efficacy of cooperative credit societies in India as "a principal agency for the emancipation of the peasant from the village moneylender and for the much-needed direction of new capital into agriculture" (ibid, 41) has not been fulfilled to date. Altogether, the Indian connection further demonstrates the "paradox that Keynes the cosmopolitan was at the same time the most provincial of British patriots" (Samuelson, 1983: 21). The polymath of Bloomsbury and the connoisseur of the civilising arts of life was also totally oblivious of the rich artistic and cultural heritage of India.

Keynes's attitude to India during World War II underwent a radical transformation by the time of the Bretton Woods Conference. At the height of the wartime famine in India, particularly in Bengal, Keynes was unusually caustic and cynical about India and Indians.[2] But later, he emerged as a very conscientious and consistent supporter of India's case on major issues at the International Monetary and Financial Conference at Bretton Woods, New Hampshire, USA (c. 1944). The principal issues which concerned the Indian delegation were the size of India's proposed quota in the prospective International Monetary Fund and the status of India's sterling balances since India was the largest holder of these balances.[3] Keynes was emphatic that it would be out of the question to suggest to India that the price of a further advance towards complete self-government should be a concession by the new Indian administration in the matter of Britain's wartime debt to India which was the major source of India's massive post-war accumulation of sterling balances.

Keynes and the Developmental Role of a Central Bank

Keynes's first publication, *Indian Currency and Finance*, has been described as his "only major work in what would now be called 'development economics'" (Johnson, 1978: 227). This is a misleading statement. The book certainly ranks as a major work on a developing country and has been rightly accorded a "permanent niche in the history of thought on central banking" (Sayers, 1972: 493). But it cannot even remotely be regarded as a contribution to development economics as it does not deal with either the determinants or the policies of economic development in India. This work, like almost all of Keynes's major contributions to economic doctrine, neglects the real sector.

However, in one respect Keynes's *Indian Currency and Finance*, as also his subsequent writings and works on this subject, contain a major, albeit indirect, contribution to development economics. Keynes was the first to present the economic rationale for a central bank as a developmental agency to promote financial intermediation and finance economic development in an emergent economy, instead of being merely a controller of the monetary system as in more developed economies like England. In fact, Keynes explicitly rejected the Bank of England as an unsuitable model for India because, being essentially a product of history, it was a strictly conventional central bank playing the role of a bank of issue, the government's banker, and a lender of last resort but with no developmental role unlike the state banks of Europe, especially Germany, Holland, and Russia which had explicit provision for direct credit, remittances and rediscount facilities to promote industry and agriculture (Keynes, 1971a: 168). Keynes's agenda for the proposed state bank of India (c. 1913) included a programme of rapid opening of branches at most places with a district treasury, a notion which well accords with both economic history and doctrine. As Sayers remarks, in the early days of a central bank the emphasis "must be on the development of a banking system to control. This is not only a logical order; it is also the historical order of events in the underdeveloped country I have most studied: the England of earlier centuries ..." (Sayers, 1957: 115). But Keynes, despite his heterodox approach to the developmental role of a central bank, was surprisingly conventional on the question of disposal of central bank and seigniorage profits and, in fact, deprecated their use for developmental expenditure.[4] On the whole, Keynes's ideas on the developmental role of a central bank have a pioneering and permanent place in the history of central banking. They are all the more remarkable since the role of a central bank in emergent economies, even in contemporary times, has focused almost wholly on monetary policy aspects.

Keynes and Development Economics

Keynes's 'general theory' is basically the economics of the short-run, which addresses the problem of mass involuntary cyclical unemployment in a typical industrial economy on the assumption of given fixed capital equipment. In contrast, the basic problem of underdevelopment is the long-run one of increasing capital accumulation to cure structural unemployment, i.e., too few machines to employ available labour. There is, of course, no systematic discussion of the basic determinants of economic development in any of Keynes's *Collected Writings*, although there are numerous scattered insights, particularly in his celebrated essay on "Economic Possibilities for our Grandchildren". This essay lists the basic determinants of the future rate of economic progress as: (a) "our power to control population", (b) "our determination to avoid wars and civil dissensions", (c) our willingness to entrust to science the direction of those matters "which are properly the concern of science", and (d) "the rate of accumulation as fixed by the margin between our production and our consumption" (Keynes, 1932: 373). The last condition, which makes prior saving a determinant of investment, has a wholly classical flavour. This was superseded by Keynes's later formulation in the *General Theory* of the equality of savings and investment and the doctrine that since investment creates its own saving the latter is not in effect a constraint on development—a doctrine whose uncritical application has provided the theoretical rationale for deficit financing of development programmes in many developing countries. Admittedly, this line of thought has to be appropriately qualified. It does not imply that Keynes always believed that savings was not a resource constraint on development. This was true for periods of involuntary unemployment—but at full employment, as Keynes always argued, the classical conditions still applied and the lack of savings (idle resources) could hamper economic development. The question then is whether underdeveloped countries are constrained in their growth by a lack of savings at full employment or an excessive liquidity preference for unproductive assets such as gold or commodity hoards which creates (disguised) involuntary unemployment.

Keynes's intellectual influence on development economics was indirect through the use made by others of the various testable and measurable concepts derived largely from the *General Theory*, and partly from the *Treatise*, notably: (1) liquidity preference and credit rationing, (2) the multiplier, (3) disguised unemployment (formulated by Joan Robinson), and (4) growth models of the Harrod-Domar type.

Keynes made liquidity preference the main causal factor in the stagnation of an underdeveloped economy. According to Keynes:

> The history of India at all times has provided an example of a country impoverished by a preference for liquidity amounting to so strong a passion that even an enormous and chronic influx of the precious metals has been insufficient to bring down the rate of interest to a level which was compatible with the growth of real wealth. (Keynes, 1936: 337)

This passage is the only reference in the *General Theory* to the problems of an underdeveloped economy. However, Keynesian doctrine on this subject has to be appropriately qualified. For one thing, the motivation of gold hoarding in developing countries is of a character that renders the Keynesian analysis of liquidity preference largely inapplicable. Furthermore, the actual extent of misdirection of resources in gold hoarding is much less than commonly supposed and even where there is such misdirection its mechanics are also different from those posited in the Keynesian framework (Chandavarkar, 1961: 137-148). Gold hoarding in underdeveloped economies is largely a non-monetary phenomenon notwithstanding some formal similarities between money and gold such as their liquidity and non-interest yielding character. Gold hoarding is actuated by a combination of three conceptually distinct motives, namely, precautionary purposes, the psychic income accruing from jewellery and ornaments, and expectation of capital appreciation. Corresponding to these motives gold can be regarded as a liquid asset, a store of value, as a durable consumer good (not mentioned by Keynes) and a hedge. The bulk of gold stocks in India and other developing countries is in the form of jewellery and ornaments, unlike in countries like France where gold is held in the form of bullion or coins. Gold in developing countries is held principally for its use value and esteem value, which, therefore, makes its stocks insensitive to change in the rate of interest and monetary conditions. Historically, the import of gold into the underdeveloped countries has not been monetised because its virtually once-and-for-all absorption (the perennial sink theory) into ornamental hoards has acted as a permanent leakage from the monetary stream. Similarly, gold ornaments play a negligible role as bank collateral. On the other hand, gold arguably has played the role of an incentive good for the primary producer in developing countries and to that extent it may even have been instrumental in maintaining an adequate export surplus. Of course, since hoarded gold also represents potential foreign exchange which can be mobilised for productive investment, it imposes considerable social opportunity costs on developing economies which are subject to foreign exchange constraints. Studies of savings in India show that the proportion of gold has averaged around 3.6 per cent of household savings and 0.2 per cent (1950–1968) of national income, which should dispel the traditional notion of the historical 'thesaurisation' of the Indian economy. All these nuances are missing from the standard Keynesian analysis of liquidity preference. Consequently, the importance assigned in the Keynesian scheme of ideas to gold hoarding as a case of excessive liquidity preference holding up real investment has to be substantially qualified. Interestingly, the proposal for the sale of gold in India and the Middle East during World War II as an anti-inflationary measure did not emanate from Keynes, who was one of the two wartime advisors to the

British Chancellor of the Exchequer (the other was Lord Catto) but from R.A. Harari, Chief Economic Advisor, General Headquarters, Middle East. Richard Kahn conveyed this proposal to Keynes (Moggridge, 1992: 757). The Keynesian analysis of liquidity preference as a determinant of interest rates has also to be drastically qualified in relation to developing countries, wherein institutional and social factors are more influential than behavioural factors. Thus, interest rates in developing countries are, conceptually, an aggregate of (a) liquidity premium, i.e., the pure Keynesian rate of interest; (b) the risk premium, i.e., the risk of default on principal; (c) costs of administration (transaction and information costs); and (d) market imperfections because of monopolistic and oligopolistic lenders who also function as oligopsonistic buyers of rural produce. The aggregate of the risk premium, the costs of administration and market imperfections is more important than liquidity premium—the main element of the Keynesian analysis—in determining the overall height of interest rates in developing countries.

It is, however, pertinent to note that Keynes did recognise that "there is clearly no absolute standard of 'liquidity'...The conception of what contributes to 'liquidity' is a partly vague one, changing from time to time and depending on social practices and institutions" (Keynes, 1973: 240). In the same context, Keynes also noted that the competition of a high interest rate on mortgages may well have had the same effect in retarding investment in new capital assets as high interest rates on long-term debts. Thus, different degrees of liquidity preference are associated with different types of assets. However, these aspects are overlooked by most Keynesians, except for Joan Robinson who rightly observed that "the most important influences on interest rates—which account for, say, the difference between 30 per cent in an Indian village and three per cent in London—are social, legal and institutional" (Robinson, 1965: 246). Consequently, the fantastic levels of nominal interest rates prevailing in the disorganised rural financial markets of developing countries are essentially a mechanism to keep peasants permanently in the debt cycle; the actual payments of interest cannot exceed the margin between subsistence and income.

But more than liquidity preference and its consequences for the rate of interest, investment and hence development, it is the availability of credit which is significant in the developing countries, where because of market imperfections the clearing mechanism in the credit market operates not so much through price adjustments (i.e., movements of rates of interest) as through quantity adjustments. Here Keynes's concept (in his *Treatise on Money*)—missing from the *General Theory*—of the fringe of unsatisfied borrowers, i.e., who are not considered to have first claims on a bank's funds, but to whom the bank would be quite ready to lend if it was to find itself in a position to lend more, is more relevant (Keynes, 1971b: 326-327). In fact, the importance of non-institutional finance in developing countries generally suggests that the rationing and availability of credit rather than interest are the more influential factors.

The Keynesian concept of the multiplier was formulated in the context of an industrial economy with mass involuntary unemployment and idle productive capacity, and an elastic supply of working capital so that when it operates, the supply curve of aggregate output slopes upward towards the right, albeit with breaks because of bottlenecks, and results in semi-inflation. It becomes vertical only after reaching the point of full utilisation of capacity and full employment, resulting in price inflation thereafter. These assumptions do not hold good in underdeveloped economies with their predominance of household enterprises and family farms. The greater recourse in a developing economy to debits in cash from bank deposits in successive rounds erodes the credit-creating capacity of the financial system, leading to progressive disintermediation. There is, consequently, a dampening of the investment as well as of the credit multiplier due to supply bottlenecks as well as the greater possibility of leakages into imports and cash transactions.

Keynes's *General Theory* addressed the problem of cyclical involuntary unemployment whereas the underdeveloped countries typically suffer from rural underemployment, a phenomenon for which the concept of disguised unemployment, first formulated by Joan Robinson (1973: 199-211) in more relevant but in a modified version. The original concept referred to the diversion of wage labour as a result of a decline in aggregate demand, and in the absence of unemployment assistance and social security, to occupations of lower productivity. But as Joan Robinson pointed out pertinently, "disguised unemployment, as I conceived it, had nothing to do with the question of surplus labour in what is nowadays called an underdeveloped economy. At that time (c. 1937), there were no ex-colonial nations clamouring for 'development'" (ibid.: 175). Subsequently, this concept has been transmogrified into an amorphous bundle of description, analysis, and policy prescriptions and applied uncritically to underdeveloped economies. It has generated a voluminous and controversial literature, beginning with Rosenstein-Rodan's pioneering work on *Problems of Industrialisation of Eastern and South Eastern Europe* (1943), which was possibly the first time the term 'underdeveloped countries' was used. The controversy has ranged around the issue: whether disguised unemployment, in the sense of agricultural labour with zero marginal productivity, is economic reality or else a fallacious proposition insofar as it is only symptomatic of low-productivity technology and farmers in underdeveloped countries and rational in exploiting available technology (Schultz, 1964). The merits of this debate are, however, not germane to the present essay. Suffice it to say that the concept of disguised unemployment is a testable hypothesis which did not originate with Keynes but with Joan Robinson. Its subsequent applications to underdeveloped countries are due to others. Thus, Nurkse developed the concept of the saving potential of disguised unemployment (Nurkse, 1953: 37). This, however, is subject to major limitations (Chandavarkar, 1957).

Similarly, the familiar Harrod-Domar models are an extension of the Keynesian system to 'growth' defined as increase in investment capacity and income of advanced economies rather than the structural transformation of underdeveloped economies. However, these models, which demonstrate that a country's growth is determined by the propensity to save and the capital-output ratio, have been used as the basis for planning models for developing countries. But, as Hirschman rightly points out, "growth economics had evolved independently from development economics as a direct offshoot of the Keynesian system and its macroeconomic concepts" (Hirschman, 1981: 12).

Perhaps, the most significant intellectual contribution of Keynes to development policy, as distinct from development economics, was his abortive wartime scheme (1942) for a separate post-war international General Council for Commodity Controls for stabilisation of commodity prices, whose primary beneficiaries would have been the developing countries (Keynes, 1974: 279-315). This, significantly, was envisaged by Keynes as a contributory measure to the prevention of the trade cycle of development support for the World Bank scheme as a manifestation of the principle of using savings surpluses of the developed countries for the underdeveloped countries – the forerunner of global Keynesianism.

Keynes and Development Economics—An Appraisal

In the light of the foregoing, it could be said that Keynes's original contributions to development economics consist in his demonstration of the developmental role of a central bank in an emergent economy and the applicability of his concepts like the fringe of unsatisfied borrowers, liquidity preference, and the multiplier. But Keynes himself did not explore the linkages between money, economic growth and development, which was done subsequently by James Tobin, McKinnon, and Shaw. It could also be conceded that the concept of disguised unemployment and the Harrod-Domar growth models, "while not of Keynes's own conceiving, are essentially Keynesian both by direct discipleship and by intellectual affinity with the concentration on fixed capital investment as the prime economic mover in *The General Theory* (Johnson, 1978: 232). Nevertheless, the most influential paradigms of modern development economics seem to owe very little directly to Keynes or his leading disciples. Thus, one could list concepts like cumulative causation, backwash and spread effects (Gunnar Myrdal), centre and periphery (Raul Prebisch and the structuralists), balanced growth (Nurkse, Hirschman), big push (Rosenstein-Rodan), take-off (Rostow), human capital (Schultz), unlimited labour (Arthur Lewis) and choice of techniques (Amartya Sen). It is, therefore, somewhat farfetched to talk of the *Keynesian Theory of Development* (Kurihara, 1959). Perhaps, a more judicious appraisal would be that although Keynes himself was not directly concerned with the problem of economic development, "the claim of development economics to stand as a separate body of economic analysis and policy derived intellectual legitimacy and nurture from the prior success and parallel features of the Keynesian revolution" (Hirschman, 1981: 7). Nor should it be overlooked that during Keynes's lifetime the principal problem was depression and unemployment and not the development of poor and backward regions. Even Keynes could not have been expected to evolve a conceptual apparatus for application to unforeseen problems. After all, the philosophic basis for his classic analysis of long-term expectations and uncertainty was not—as he himself remarked—that the inevitable happens. It is only the unexpected!

NOTES

1 Keynes in his review of Theodore Morison's book on The Economic Transition of India (1911) was critical of Morison's "agreement with much current opinion in India, where a considerable part of the educated class seem to desire, with patriotic fervour, the industrialisation of their country...such a change is not, in the future, which none can foresee, either desirable or likely. It is an unfortunate consequence of the English connection, that industrialism should present itself to India as the royal road to prosperity and to a dignified position among nations...every diversion of indigenous capital from agriculture, where her relative advantage is great to industries, where...the

relative positions of coal, iron and the sea place her at a disadvantage, will be to the detriment of her economic prosperity" (Keynes, 1983: 27–9).

2 "Heaven knows that few can have a lower opinion of the Government of India today than I have, nor is there anyone more conscious of how it has muddled this [famine policy] and most other matters...since the Indianisation of the Viceroy's Council, the once prized efficiency of the Indian Civil Service and the government, at any rate on the administrative side, has largely disappeared, which is a sad forecast of what will happen when we have entirely withdrawn our hands. Personally, I am so fed up with India, that I should like to clear out on any terms and at the earliest possible moment" (Keynes, 1982: 188).

3 "...India is much more concerned with equality, a near equality with China than with the absolute amount, though they would like something extra...I am going to see White [the US delegate] privately again shortly and put up to him a solution which I have reason to believe will satisfy India and help Australia a little...I am hopeful that I have persuaded him [White] to make a sufficient concession to India to keep them moderately satisfied..." (Keynes, 1980: 79).

4 "With regard to the profits of coinage, the government has announced that it will direct half of the future profits to capital expenditure on railways. But it is to be hoped that this decision will be reconsidered before the time comes" (Keynes, 1971c: 275).

References

Chandavarkar, Anand G. (1957). "The Saving Potential of Disguised Unemployment", *The Economic Journal* 67(266): 335–8, June.

———. (1961). "The Nature and Effects of Gold Hoarding in Underdeveloped Economies", *Oxford Economic Papers* 13(2): 137–48, June.

———. (1983). "Keynes and India: A Centennial Review and Appraisal", *Economic and Political Weekly* 28(18): 1233–37, 9 July.

———. (1989). *Keynes and India: A Study in Economics and Biography.* London: Macmillan

Crabtree, Derek and Anthony P. Thirlwall (eds.) (1980). *Keynes and the Bloomsbury Group.* The Fourth Keynes Seminar, Canterbury, 1978. London: Macmillan.

Friedman, Milton (1983). "A Monetarist Reflects", *The Economist*, 287(7292): 17–19, 4 June.

Harrod, Roy F. (1951). *The Life of John Maynard Keynes.* New York: Harcourt, Brace, Jovanovich.

Hayek, Friedrich V. (1983). "The Austrian Critique", *The Economist*, 287(7293): 39–41, 11 June.

Hicks, John R. (1983). "A Sceptical Follower", *The Economist*, 287(7294): 17–19, 18 June.

Hirschman, Albert O. (1981). "The Rise and Decline of Development Economics", in *Essays in Trespassing.* Cambridge: Cambridge University Press, pp. 1–24.

Johnson, Harry G. (1978). "Keynes and Economic Development", in *The Shadow of Keynes.* Oxford: Basil Blackwell, pp. 227–33.

Keynes, John M. (1932). *Essays in Persuasion.* New York: Harcourt, Brace, Jovanovich.

———. (1971a). "Indian Currency and Finance [1913]", *The Collected Writings of John Maynard Keynes (henceforth CW)*. London: Macmillan.

———. (1971b). "A Treatise on Money: The Applied Theory of Money [1930]", CW-VI. London: Macmillan.

———. (1971c). "Activities 1906–14: India and Cambridge", CW- XV. London: Macmillan.

———. (1973). "The General Theory of Employment, Interest and Money [1936]", CW- VII. London: Macmillan.

———. (1974). "The International Control of Raw Materials", *Journal of International Economics* 4: 299–315, August.

———. (1980). "Activities 1941–6: Shaping the Post-War World: Bretton Woods and Reparations", CW,-XXVI. London: Macmillan.

———. (1982). "Social, Political and Literary Writings", CW-XXVIII. London: Macmillan.

———. (1983). "Economic Articles and Correspondence: Academic", CW-XI. London: Macmillan.

Kurihara, Kenneth K. (1959). *The Keynesian Theory of Development.* New York: Columbia University Press.

Moggridge, Donald E. (ed.) (1974). *Keynes: Aspects of the Man and His Work* (The First Keynes Seminar, Canterbury, 1972). New York: St Martin's Press.

Nurkse, Ragnar (1953). *Problems of Capital Formation in Underdeveloped Countries.* Oxford: Basil Blackwell.

Patinkin, Don (1984). "Keynes and Economics Today", *American Economic Review* 74(2) (May).

Robinson, Joan V. (1965). *The Accumulation of Capital.* London: Macmillan.

———. (1973). "Disguised Unemployment", in *Collected Economic Papers*, Vol. 4. Oxford: Basil Blackwell, pp. 199–211.

Rosenstein-Rodan, Paul N. (1943). "Problems of Industrialisation of Eastern and South Eastern Europe", *Economic Journal* 53: 202–11, June–September.

Samuelson, Paul A. (1983). "Sympathy from the Other Cambridge", *The Economist*, 287(7295): 19–21, 25 June.

Sayers, Richard S. (1957). *Central Banking after Bagehot.* Oxford: Clarendon Press.

———. (1972). "The Young Keynes", *Economic Journal* 82(326): 591–9, June.

Schultz, Theodore W. (1964). *Transforming Traditional Agriculture.* New Haven: Yale University Press.

Skidelsky, Robert (1983). *John Maynard Keynes: Hopes Betrayed*, Vol. 1, 1883–1920. London: Macmillan.

Thirlwall, Anthony P. (ed.) (1978). *Keynes and International Monetary Relations* (The Second Keynes Seminar, Canterbury, 1974). London: Macmillan.

8 Keynes and the Role of the State in Developing Countries*

...it is of the essence of state planning to do those things which...lie outside the scope of the individual.

—Keynes, *State Planning*, 1932.

[Keynes] wanted governments to have discretion and...economists to come to their assistance...But he certainly had no exalted view of the wisdom of governments or the virtues of economic science.

—Sir Alec Cairncross, *Keynes and Laissez-Faire*.

Introduction

Although Keynes did not formulate a systematic theory of the role of the State in either developed or developing countries he had, nevertheless, a remarkably consistent vision of the State in both his writings and activities. On the other hand, he did not specifically address the problems of developing countries as a group, an essentially post-World War II preoccupation. It is, however, possible to develop a meaningful Keynesian state theoretic approach to the economics of developing countries by drawing generally on his *Collected Writings* (CW) as well as unpublished material, and specifically on his analysis and policy prescriptions for India as the only developing country with which he was professionally concerned—as civil servant, economist, commissioner and witness for Royal Commissions of Inquiry, war-time adviser to the British Cabinet and co-architect of the Bretton Woods institutions—the IMF and the World Bank.

Keynes's observations on the economic role of the State in India, as a large and complex developing country, are no less relevant to developing countries in general, bearing in mind Joan Robinson's celebrated epigram, "Human nature is the same everywhere, but in India it is more so...whatever you say about India the opposite is equally true." More importantly, India, as "the only part of the British Empire to which *laissez faire* never applied" (Hobsbawm, 1969) served as a vast and highly congenial social laboratory for applied utilitarianism. But

* *Source*: Derek Crabtree and A.P. Thirlwall (eds.) (1993). *Keynes and the Role of the State* (The Tenth Keynes Seminar held at the University of Kent at Canterbury, 1991). London: Macmillan, pp. 126-160.

Keynes himself was acutely mindful of the country-specific nuances of even his *General Theory*, much of which, as he said, "is illustrated and expounded mainly with reference to the conditions existing in the Anglo-Saxon countries" (CW, VII: xxvi).

Perhaps the nearest Keynes came to a 'world view' of the East (developing countries) was in a youthfully exuberant and provocative yet remarkably percipient essay at Eton:

> In the West it is the individual that is all important; in the East the mass; and from this text it is possible to trace more than one noticeable difference. Most obviously democracy as opposed to autocracy or despotism must be prevalent in Europe, and similarly in Asia absolute despotism must be not only prevalent but preferable and necessary. The East formed the great civilisations of the past...but it is altogether lacking in that initiative and invention which can emanate only from individuals and without which further progress is impossible. (Keynes, 1900).

It may not be always sensible to invoke the youthful forays even of genius. Nevertheless, it is significant that for the young as for the mature Keynes, the mainspring of economic progress was essentially individual initiative and enterprise in a democratic environment—the celebrated 'animal spirits' of the *General Theory*. Clearly, the Keynesian canon is not relevant to the role of the all-embracing authoritarian State, which still seems the predominant political form in the contemporary developing world. On the other hand, the Third World, along with the industrial democracies and socialist Eastern Europe, is today in the throes of a massive deregulation and liberalisation, which makes an appraisal of Keynes's ideas on the economic role of the State in the developing countries singularly topical. Accordingly, this paper attempts to develop a Keynesian paradigm of the scope and rationale of the State's role in developing countries which rely largely on private enterprise and the price mechanism while employing a varying mix of control and competition. Such an approach also accommodates the category of developing countries which may be politically authoritarian while practising economic liberalism. But the Third World is far from being "a form of bloodless universality that robs individuals and societies of their particularity" (Naipaul, 1988: 34). It is defiantly diverse compared with the industrial countries and Keynesian recipes have, therefore, to be appropriately modified to suit the specifics of developing countries.

Keynes had no fixed policy stances on the role of the State. As he once remarked piquantly: "The peculiarity of my position lies, perhaps, in the fact that I am in favour of practically all the remedies which have been suggested in any quarter.... We have to invent a new wisdom for a new age." (Letter to Ramsay Macdonald, 1932, in Duff 1984).

Keynes's mind-set was essentially that of a pluralist Fox—to use Isaiah Berlin's (1984) expressive dichotomy of intellectuals and artists into Foxes ('who pursue many ends...and entertain ideas that are centrifugal rather than centripetal') and Hedgehogs ('who relate everything to a single central vision'). Likewise, his policy prescriptions could well be described as a pragmatic and eclectic application of Karl Popper's 'piecemeal social engineering'.

Toward a Keynesian State: Theoretic Paradigm for Developing Countries

It has been rightly said that "the most important questions about the role of the State are not How Big? or How Much? but What Kind? What Comparative Advantage? (Killick, 1989: 8). But Keynes was more concerned about the kind of State intervention rather than about its comparative advantages over private enterprise. His core propositions, which are all equally applicable to the developing countries, may be summarised as follows.

For Keynes the political problem was to combine economic efficiency, social justice and individual liberty (*Liberalism and Labour*, 1926, CW, IX: 311). The most important agenda for the government in a democracy "is not to do things which individuals are doing already, and to do them a little better or a little worse; *but to do those things which at present are not done at all*" (emphasis provided) (*End of Laissez-Faire*, 1926, CW, IX: 291). Later, Keynes defined the essence of State planning as doing "things which lie outside the scope of the individual" (e.g., mitigation of cyclical fluctuations and unemployment, industrial and town planning, rural preservation, control of population, migration and immigration), and "not seek to aggrandise the province of the State for its own sake." For him, State planning would not be administered or supervised in detail by democratically elected bodies, who "would be judges not of first, but of final instance, reserve forces to effect a change when grave mistakes had been made" (State Planning, 1932, CW, XXI: 88-92). Most significantly, Keynes was emphatic that "it is not the ownership of the instruments of production which is important for the State to assume" and "apart from the necessity of central controls to bring about an adjustment between the propensity to consume and the inducement to invest, there is no more reason to socialise economic life than there was before" (*General Theory*, 1936, CW, VII: 378–9). According to him, the "whole purpose of nationalisation is to allow considerations of general and social advantage to take their proper place in price policy" and no industry should be "nationalised if it ought to be run solely or primarily on commercial considerations" (*Report of Official Committee on Public Utility Corporations*, 1944, CW, XXIII: 465, 467). Consequently, while he supported the nationalisation of the Bank of England he did not favour nationalisation of joint-stock banks on the ground that the "control of the Big Five, otherwise than through the Bank of England, is not necessary for handling the vital controls" (*The Monetary Policy of the Labour Party*, 1932, CW, XXI: 130). Keynes, in *How to Pay for War* (1940), also showed how the State through compulsory deferred savings under working-class control, and through a combination of universal family allowances, subsidised rationing of necessities, and a post-war capital levy or tax could reconcile the new macroeconomics with social welfare. In sum, for Keynes the proper role for the State was macroeconomic management to achieve economic efficiency and social justice while preserving individual liberty and democracy.

Since Keynes's ideas and insights on the role of the State in the developing countries are scattered throughout his writings and over the entire span of his working life, they are best organised in terms of the contemporary dichotomy of targets (objectives) and instruments of State policy, subject to the caveat that it is not always possible to assign one instrument to one target. Moreover, instruments are operable only through and by institutions, an aspect all too neglected in analytic policy economics. Also, instruments can have multiple targets and, therefore, pose difficult problems of trade-offs and unintended consequences. Since the civil service is the prime institutional instrument of the State it would be appropriate to examine its economic role in the developing countries as envisaged by Keynes before formulating a more detailed agenda of the State (institutional, conjunctural, developmental, and welfare) in terms of the taxonomy of targets, institutions and instruments as suggested by Keynes's writings (see Appendix).

The Economic Role of the Civil Service: Turning Mandarins into Managers

Keynes, being only too mindful of the limitations of the typical 'generalist' civil service in tackling economic issues, was particularly concerned to stress that the efficacy of state intervention in the economy depends on the training and quality of civil servants engaged in economic planning and management. Nowhere is this better illustrated than in his refinement and endorsement of the Government of India's proposal in the 1930s to recruit candidates with a good economics background to staff key positions in its Finance and

Commerce Department, which, in the event, was smothered by the somewhat mindless animus and opposition of the Finance Member, James Grigg, and other British Indian officials who regarded a Cambridge economics education as 'dangerous'.[1] Sir Otto Niemeyer, then an adviser to the Bank of England, believed that "Civil Service candidates could learn finance in India much better than through King's College, Cambridge."[2] Nevertheless, Keynes's elaboration of the economic role of the Indian Civil Service is of abiding interest and significance. He saw the "future salvation [of India] not in restricting private enterprise...but in bringing it under socialised control through the state", and recommended that "the civil service should be reorganised to handle this control effectively" through policies relating to finance, currency and banking. Clearly, Keynes envisaged essentially a macroeconomic role for the Indian Civil Service, rather than the microeconomic one as public enterprise managers, etc. Hence his emphatic supposition that for the most part 'private enterprise' would be unconscious of it, i.e., socialised control through the State (Darling, 1934).

Keynes's innovative suggestions for economic reorientation of the Indian Civil Service went far beyond the subsequent formation of the Finance and Commerce Pool of the Government of India. Its full fruition, as with Keynes's design for a developmentally oriented central bank for India, had to await the creation of the Indian Economic Service after Independence. But Keynes would have been hardly sympathetic to the omniscient economic role of the Indian Administrative and Economic Services in the operational management of all manner of public enterprises, ranging from heavy industry and financial institutions to public utilities, hotels and airlines! In fact, India is a classic example of the slippage of Keynesian 'socialized control' into uncritical nationalisation.

While Keynes's vision of a macroeconomic role for the Indian Civil Service was wholly congruent with his views on the duties of the proposed Economic General Staff for Britain, he did not elaborate on whether he also advocated for India his other proposal that appointments to the Staff "should not necessarily be of the same permanent character as in the regular Civil Service." He favoured "a considerable amount of interchange between the Staff, economic appointments in the outside academic world, and the chief technical economic posts in regular Government Departments" (CW, XX: 26). Keynes's proposals were aimed at obtaining the services for a limited period of economists in the "prime of their powers...whose bent and desire is to devote their lives to scientific research and to guiding from the centre the evolution of the economic structure, rather than to administration or to politics" (ibid.). Keynes stressed the strictly technical role of the economic staff, whose "advice...should not have the last word or the power, but must be a necessary ingredient in the decisions of those who have been entrusted with the last word and with the power" (ibid.: 27). But in developing countries the government economist is more often than not a permanent member of the civil service, with hardly any interchange—only unilateral transfers—of economists between governments and academia as in the West.

Keynes's concerns about tenured economists in the civil service were not unconnected with his lively awareness of the perils of bureaucratic senescence, inertia and formalism whether in developed Britain ('The thing [the India Office] is simply government by dotardry') or in underdeveloped Imperial China. Keynes even cites approvingly a Chinese scholar who found the chief cause of the weakness of China in the requirement of the modern essay in civil service examinations (Class I). "The modern essay was of no practical use and its mastery required long practice. Instituted in 1370, in 1902 it was abolished" (CW, XI: 527). This citation was clearly meant as a message that civil servants should concern themselves with problem solving and crisis management rather than with the mandarin niceties of form and style—a characteristic failing of civil servants in developing countries who, like the 'Bloomsbury' Apostle Saxon Sydney-Turner (of His Majesty's Treasury), seem to produce the perfect minute but no decision!

The State and the Data Base for Economic Policy

Alongside his recognition of the economic role of the civil service, Keynes stressed the importance of timely and adequate data on the key economic aggregates for policymaking, as well as for ensuring due transparency of public policy, through professional compilation and analysis of data on basic economic indicators like national income, money supply, foreign trade, crop forecasts, production, inventories and prices. This dates back to the historic episode when he excoriated the India Office, "who do not realise to what an extent an accurate and easily accessible information oils the wheels of commerce" (CW, XV: 34), and for its startlingly insouciant proposal for filling the post of a Director of Statistics in the Government of India by a chartered accountant! Keynes rightly pointed out that it was no longer possible to collect and present statistics without special knowledge of mathematics and economics and also emphasised the distinction between commercial intelligence and statistics, both of which required government initiative (Chandavarkar, 1989: 17-18). He was only too aware that private enterprise would not have either the incentive or the resources to compile and analyse macroeconomic data.

Fortunately for India, Keynes's advice was eventually accepted with the appointment of a highly qualified economist-statistician (Findlay Shirras) to head the newly created Directorate of Statistics, which helped to give India an economic database far superior to that of many developing countries and even comparable to those of the developed countries. Keynes's support for a single separate department of statistics to serve all government departments was consistent with his plea to the then British government that in setting up an Economic General Staff, "it is not desirable that they should attempt to create *a separate statistical department* (emphasis provided). It should rather be their duty to suggest to the appropriate government departments (including the Government Actuary) ways of improving and extending their existing statistical work" (CW, XX: 24). The message, briefly, was a clear division of labour between economists and statisticians. But then, this also poses an unresolved enigma: Why Keynes, having lobbied so assiduously for a professional Director of Statistics for India, did not also advocate, as its corollary, an Economic Advisor for the Government of India?

The Central Bank: Its Developmental, Monetary and Prudential Roles

Keynes's ideas on the organisation and functions of a central bank are especially significant as his nearest approach to a systematic formulation of the economic role of the State in a developing country (Chandavarkar, 1985b, 1989).

Although Keynes's 1913 scheme provided for a private shareholder's state bank for India (CW, XV: 165–6), he was later (1926) quite categorical that under the prevailing circumstances, the proposed central bank for India "should be a government concern, certainly subject in the last resort to the ...Viceroy Council", while enjoying "a high degree of independence from the Secretariat of Finance and from the Bureaucracy" (Keynes to C.H. Kisch, 1926). While Keynes sought to reconcile the autonomy and accountability of a government-owned central bank in India, he also believed, like many a British official in India, that the interests of the farming masses would be better served by an alien bureaucracy than by a board of directors representing predominantly landlords and urban business. But his shrewd reminder that "we must distinguish between the fleeting policies of governors and the Bank [of England] as an institution" (CW, XX: 154) is even more pertinent to the developing countries, where personalities tend to be so much more influential than rules and institutions.

Most remarkably, Keynes stressed the primacy of the developmental role of a central bank in a developing country like India, whereas the rationale of central banking has been argued almost exclusively in terms of its conventional functions of note issue, government's banker, bankers' bank, lender of last resort, and controller of credit. Keynes envisaged that his proposed central bank for India (1913) would have a developmental agenda of extension of cooperative credit, the improvement and extension of sound banking facilities. Keynes also sought to give an added developmental dimension to the state bank through provision of appropriate rediscount facilities to the maximum extent possible for eligible, medium- and long-term, agricultural, commercial and industrial paper to supplement the normal discount of approved internal bills of exchange to provide the requisite elasticity of note circulation in the busy season. To fulfil developmental objectives, the state bank proposed by Keynes would have combined central and commercial banking (CW, XV: 149, 171, 193, 270). But surprisingly Keynes, without assigning any reasons, disapproved of the Government of India's later proposal to use half of central bank and seigniorage profits for developmental expenditure on projects like railways (CW, I: 159). Arguably, in retrospect, Keynes's inexplicable conservatism on the use of seigniorage profits for developmental finance, instead of the genuine savings of the public, seems justifiable judging by the sizeable losses incurred during the 1980s by central banks in South America and Africa as a result of, among other things, participation in subsidised credit and developmental finance.

Keynes's emphasis on the developmental role of a central bank in its early stages was both logical and historically valid in so far as questions of monetary and credit policy arise only after an adequate banking system has been developed. He was equally cognisant of the prudential role of a central bank and was particularly concerned that "although the growth of banking habits in India" was of utmost importance for economic development, "a startling series of [bank] failures will do much to retard it" (ibid.). He was, therefore, strongly supportive of the need to regulate commercial banks in India with "enormous nominal capital and high sounding titles", many of whom were plagued by serious problems like wide gaps between nominal and paid-up capital, inadequate cash balances, mismanagement, and the combination of non-banking business (coach building and medical attendance) (ibid.: 162-163). Keynes thus visualised the banking and financial system as a public good, which merits state supervision but which does not need to be publicly owned, a nuance all too often overlooked in the developing countries which have proliferated government-owned financial institutions.

As regards monetary policy, Keynes generally favoured discretionary management as opposed to fixed rules, but did not provide any guidelines for internal monetary management in India; nor did he discuss the practical aspects of managing the exchange rate to maintain price stability, which, according to him, should be the principal target of monetary and exchange rate policy in India. Nor did he enquire into whether price stability would give the right price signals to the Indian peasant. His analysis of the instruments of monetary policy (evidence to the Macmillan Committee and in the *Treatise on Money*, Vol. II), namely, bank rate, open market operations and reserve requirements, is also relevant to developing countries, particularly the variation of reserve requirements, which is arguably the most potent monetary policy instrument in the absence of a wide and active securities market so necessary for effective open market operations. However, Keynes did not anticipate the direct issue of securities by a central bank (e.g., as in Indonesia, the Philippines and Sri Lanka) to overcome his feared 'shortage of ammunition' for open market operations.

In contrast, Keynes was ahead of his times in advocating that India's foreign reserves policy should be geared not to the cover requirements of the domestic currency circulation, but to the finance of external trade and payments. He argued that for a country such as India, "where all available reserves are required for capital expansion", it was "not sound or humane policy to burden the present as much for the sake of the future" and "it was nearly as important to avoid extravagance in the reserve policy as to avoid parsimony" (CW, I: 120). Thus, Keynes showed explicit awareness of the role of the State as an arbiter of intergenerational equity.

Keynes, however, did not analyse the scope for state or central bank action to ease the developmental constraints of the excessively high liquidity premium on land and the precious metals in India and to convert the latter into foreign exchange through incentive schemes and open market operations. As regards state initiatives to scale down rural debt in India, Keynes approvingly cited President Roosevelt's programme "to offer all mortgagers state bonds for the value of their debts up to about 60 per cent of the present value of the mortgaged property, in return for which the mortgager was required to forgo all claims on the balance. If he refused the offer, he was left to recover what he could from the debts through courts" (Darling, 1934: 1-2). Surprisingly, Keynes even favoured reviving "usury laws which were operative through the western world till about a hundred years ago." He plainly overestimated the deterrent effects of legal penalties on usurers and the administrative problems of monitoring compliance with usury laws and overlooked that British India did have a Usurious Loans Act (1918) and several Moneylenders Acts (1930 onwards) as well as Debt Relief and Land Alienation Acts, which were never too easy to implement and monitor.

Fiscal Policy

Fiscal policy is a major instrument of state intervention, but Keynes never made public his highly original and constructive proposals for a drastic reorientation of fiscal policy in India, which he thought "was dominated by Gladstonian finance" and "by what financiers had learnt forty years ago!" (Darling, 1934). Most remarkably, his proposal of two budgets in India, ordinary for administrative expenditure and the other for capital works, clearly anticipated his much later (c. 1942-43) recommendation of a current and a capital budget for Britain with the former, i.e., "the ordinary budget", to be "balanced at all times" (CW, XXVII: 325). He thought that in India too large an amount of capital works had been financed from current revenue, "which was unsound." This emphasis on government-financed capital works in India was the nearest Keynes came to a developmental item on the agenda of the State. Even more significant was his endorsement of government borrowing for 'productive objects even if they are not directly productive', like cooperatives. Education, he thought, was more doubtful but it would also depend upon the nature of education. Keynes was also highly critical of the 'old economics', which held that "there was something immoral in borrowing for a purpose which was not directly remunerative." He saw no objection to Darling's proposals that the Government of India should borrow to develop cooperatives and also raise a 25-year loan of around £100 million for rural reconstruction. Furthermore, Keynes believed that "much less objection could be taken to a proposal of this kind now that it was evident that internal loans (i.e., rupee loans) could be raised" in India itself. Thus, he favoured domestic borrowing in India as against the traditional external sterling loans. It is, however, difficult to fathom the Darling-Keynes rationale for government borrowing to develop cooperatives, a movement which is supposed to rely wholly on members' subscriptions and deposits! It certainly did not jive with Keynes's earlier Panglossian faith in Indian rural cooperatives as "a principal agency for the emancipation of the peasant from the village moneylender and for much-needed direction of new capital into agriculture" (CW, XV: 35).

But on the whole, Keynesian fiscal policy has little bearing on the stabilisation and developmental objectives of the State in developing countries, whose problem is one not of contra-cyclical demand management but of promoting structural growth and development, while restraining the growing budget deficits, which seem to be the largest single source of macroeconomic imbalances, judging by the key role of fiscal ceilings in the IMF's adjustment programmes. Moreover, Keynes did not subscribe to fiscal fine-tuning even for developed countries. For him the onus of stabilisation rested primarily on a politically independent monetary policy implemented through an autonomous central bank. The *General Theory* only envisaged a "guiding influence" for the State "on the propensity to consume, partly through its scheme of taxation, partly by fixing the rate of interest, and partly perhaps, in other ways" (CW, VII: 378). Even in regard to India, it has been rightly said, by a former senior official of the Planning Commission, that by the time its economic administrators "were ready to accept Keynesianism, it was already losing its separate identity in a variety of policy frameworks intended to meet the requirements of 'stagflation', unsettled trade and payments situations, and a perceptible decline in the acceptance of the State as an engine of development" (Krishnaswamy, 1991).

Commodity Problems and Buffer Stock Mechanisms

Outside of monetary and banking issues, Keynes's most direct concern with the role of the State in developing countries was through his involvement in commodity problems, commencing with his analysis at the India Office (1907) of the Indian jute trade, particularly on the consequences of adulteration—a classic case of the prisoner's dilemma—and the threat of growing competition from foreign jute as well as substitutes (flax).

Although Keynes overlooked the complications posed by the highly competitive nature (in Bengal) of jute (a cash crop) and rice (a cash-cum-subsistence crop) and the cobweb type cyclical fluctuations of both jute and rice prices, his memorandum is noteworthy for its recommendation for some form of state inspection and legislative regulation of the export trade.

Much later, Keynes was deeply concerned to mitigate the macroeconomic effects of the greater cyclical volatility as well as the secular deterioration of the terms of trade of primary producing countries before and during World War II. Countries whose income depends largely on exports of primary commodities experience undesirable income instability owing to wide and rapid commodity price fluctuations, which Keynes blamed on inadequate incentives for individual enterprises under competitive conditions to store surplus stocks of commodities "so as to maintain continuity of output and to average, as far as possible, periods of high and low demand" (Keynes, 1938: 449). He attributed the inadequacy of private holding of commodity stocks to the negative own-rate of return on such stocks, the carrying costs for insurance, interest and warehousing and the backwardation of forward prices below spot prices, which implies a substantial private risk premium for storage. As a corrective Keynes proposed government storage, which would be cheaper because of government's ability to borrow at lower costs, economies of scale in warehouse costs, and much lower social risk aversion by spreading risks over the whole population. Government storage thus acts as a cheaper form of risk insurance policy, and as an integral part of the infrastructure, a woefully neglected theme in development economics. This mechanism is highly relevant to the contemporary concerns of developing countries, who are typically short of adequate storage facilities to cope with famines as well as sudden excesses of stocks. The Government of India has often requisitioned schools to store excess harvests! Moreover, even in normal times government storage facilities can help to facilitate orderly marketing by generating warehouse receipts which can serve as bank collateral. However, Keynes was categorical that his buffer stock scheme, while "a new and useful instrument for the control (which will need more than one instrument) of the trade cycle" was inadequate because "no radical remedy for fluctuations is possible except through measures to stabilise aggregate effective demand" (CW, XXI: 460), for which he later (1942) proposed his famous (abortive) commodity control scheme (commodity control) to be financed through his proposed International Clearing Union (a world central bank) with commodities stored as widely as possible across producing and consuming countries, embodying the concept of the "ever normal granary." But Keynes's persistent belief that his schemes would also stabilise producer incomes (CW, XXVII: 109, 116, 143, 179) is more applicable to demand shocks than to supply shocks such as harvest fluctuations due to weather variations, which are of as much concern to developing countries (Dimand and Dimand, 1990: 121), or to problems posed by the competition of cash and subsistence crops in developing countries.

Development: A Non-Agenda for the State?

Although Keynesian economics is of considerable relevance to developing countries (see Thirlwall, 1987), Keynes himself was not a development economist, nor did he ever directly address developmental issues. It is, therefore, not surprising that his agenda did not extend to the role of the State in the planned development and diversification of underdeveloped agricultural countries through industrialisation (Chandavarkar, 1985a). Thus, he had a strange, almost Physiocratic scepticism of India's industrial potential, believing that "her future prosperity is to be sought almost entirely in the application of more capital to methods of agriculture" (CW, XI: 28–9), and, almost like a Gandhian, he did not find it "easy to believe that India will find in mills and factories the non-economic goods, which make up along with wealth, the dignity of a nation" (ibid.: 29). Perhaps, in keeping with his agrarian bias, Keynes was fully supportive of—not least because of their political popularity—the Government of India's rural reconstruction schemes in the 1930s (Chandavarkar, 1989: 119).

Keynes's advocacy of free trade for India was based on a wholly static concept of the comparative cost advantage of India in agriculture. His decision to accept the vice-presidency of the Indian Fiscal Commission (1921)—he resigned subsequently—represented, if anything, a "last effort to save India for modified free trade" (CW, XVII: 319). But he never elaborated on what he meant by 'modified free trade'. Keynes, while willing to concede the short-term advantages of tariffs for improving the terms of trade, the foreign balance and government revenues, remained strangely impervious to the infant-industry argument for protection, even when he became a "reluctant protectionist" (Kaldor, 1983: 12), and despite his subsequent support (1933) for "national self-sufficiency" ("let goods be homespun whenever it is reasonably and conveniently possible; and, above all, let finance be primarily national"—CW, XX: ch. 3). Admittedly, effective rates of protection (ERPs) in developing countries often tend to be much higher than warranted on infant-industry grounds. Thus, in Turkey ERPs of well over 200 per cent were common 20 years after start-up of infant industries and in India at least 39 industries enjoyed ERPs in excess of cent per cent in 1968-69 (Krueger, 1990: 14). However, this does not detract from the intrinsic validity of the infant-industry argument for protection.

The most important reason why Keynes's analysis in the *General Theory* does not accommodate the State's role in the economics of development is its "failure to realise the importance of increasing returns in manufacturing industry...and the importance of export-led growth...by state intervention for encouragement of [the development] of industries with a high export potential (as was done in Japan and also in post-war France)" (Kaldor, 1983: 12).

Although Keynes never pronounced publicly on the State's role in promoting human capital formation through education and training, he —writing to Malcolm Darling in the 1930s—sought to justify government borrowing in India for education of the right variety, a stance eminently in consonance with his belief that "economic prosperity depends not on how brilliant a few people are but on how large a scale you are able to produce competent people in all walks of life" (Chandavarkar, 1989: 142). Clearly, for Keynes the key to development lay in the creation of a society based on mass competence, like the USA, in contrast to the 'Oxbridge Rampant' elitist credentialism which Thomas Balogh regarded as the peculiar affliction of ex-colonial societies.

Given the far greater environmental degradation in the Third World, the protection of the environment would have assuredly figured high in Keynes's putative agenda for the State, relying as usual on a judicious combination of controls and incentives. He regarded "town planning and rural preservation" as a good case for "strong powers of central direction" by the state (CW, XXI: 89).

Population: Chaining the Malthusian Devil

Keynes was acutely conscious of both the quantitative and qualitative aspects of population as the central economic and political problem meriting concerted State action.

"Indeed, the problem of population is going to be not merely an economist's problem, but in the near future the greatest of all political questions...which will arouse some of the deepest instincts and emotions of men, and feeling may run as passionately as in earlier struggles between religions...when the instability of modern society forces the issue, a great transition in human history will have begun, with the endeavour by civilised man to assume conscious control in his own hands away from the blind instinct of mere predominant survival" (CW, XVII: 443, 448).

Keynes always regarded the Malthusian as one of the two 'fierce devils' haunting society—the other being the "devil of unemployment escaping through the breakdown of effective demand" (Keynes, 1937: 16). While he analysed the economic consequences of a declining population in the industrial West, he addressed the problem of overpopulation in the context of three typical developing countries, *viz.*, Czarist Russia, British India, and Imperial China, without, however, differentiating between the pressure of absolute numbers and the trend of the net reproduction rate.

Overpopulation was regarded by Keynes as the single most important cause of poverty in Czarist Russia, which was then as much an underdeveloped country as any in the contemporary Third World (CW, XIX: 437). Likewise, he claimed that the greatest failure of British rule in India was that it did not restrain population growth and cited data to show that real wages had risen in the Punjab between 1901 and 1911 when a proportion of the population was wiped out by bubonic plague (Skidelsky, 1990: 1332). In China, as elsewhere, Keynes noted perceptively that "the forces of religion have been powerfully on the side of numerous offspring and it is difficult to believe that the golden age can be recovered while those to enjoy it are so many" (CW, XI: 1527). He would, therefore, have heartily endorsed the jettisoning of Marxist dogma by Communist China in its efforts to control population. But Keynes overlooked that in traditional societies, even more than religion, dire poverty itself operates as a philo-progenitive factor by casting offspring in the role of investment goods and also the principal support for retired, infirm, or elderly parents and dependants in the absence of state-sponsored social security.

Keynes's diagnoses of the population problem led to his prescription of a conscious national policy to "pay attention to the innate quality as well as to the mere numbers of its future members" (CW, IX: 292) and to matters of emigration and immigration (CW, XXI: 89). Nor did he overlook the implications of family planning or women's emancipation and divorce reform for individual liberty and the difficult trade-off problems they pose for society at large, in so far as "birth control touches on one side the liberties of women and on the other side the duty of the state to concern itself with the size of the population just as much as with the size of the army or the amount of the budget" (CW, IX: 303).

Although Keynes was fully supportive of State action to control the size and quality of population through birth control and regulation of migration, he did not address the specifics of State action in the delicate sphere of family planning, which in any democratic society has to rely on voluntary action in response to incentives such as free or subsidised contraceptive services and fiscal and social benefits targeted toward smaller families (e.g., in regard to taxation, housing and schooling facilities as in Singapore). But did Keynes, realistically, expect the British government to control the growth of population in a poverty-stricken, backward, tradition-bound dependency like India without rousing violent political reaction? Even our vastly more scientific and technological age seems to have no answers to the Malthusian Devil, as has been so candidly admitted by the President of the World Bank:

> Given the magnitude and severity of [the population problem], it is alarming that many governments are failing to implement sensible population policies. It is also distressing that international assistance for population activities has declined. These trends must be reversed. A vital part of the Bank's work involves development activities that have a strong impact on population...population issues will be prominent in our dialogue with governments. (Barber B. Conable, President's Address to the Board of Governors of the World Bank Group, Berlin, 27 September 1988).

Arguably, Keynes also underestimated the possibilities of government failures in population policies, but then population, like environment, poses the most complex and difficult trade-off situations for developing countries. It is relatively easy for the State to foster the necessary conditions for population control, but far more difficult to create sufficient conditions, which involve religion, tradition, the gender gap, individual liberty and the sheer constraints of absolute poverty and illiteracy.

Salus Populi

Disaster Relief and Basic Needs

Third World countries are, typically, more prone and less equipped to cope with disasters like famine and flood than developed countries. The inadequacy of *laissez-faire* during catastrophic scarcities strongly suggests that alterations in exchange entitlement alone cannot account for extreme privation, as argued by Sen (1977), and therefore "direct state intervention—not State ownership, which is a different question—is a 'rational' economic policy for such [underdeveloped] countries until such time as starvation ceases" (Rashid, 1980: 502-503).

The only occasion on which Keynes addressed the disaster problem was in his rather uncritical analysis of the great Bengal Famine (c. 1943) as a hoarding phenomenon (CW, XXVIII: 188), whereas, in fact, it was caused by a combination of factors, including some egregious bureaucratic failures which led to a cumulative decline in exchange entitlements (market access and purchasing power) of the most vulnerable classes like landless labour, marginal farmers, rural artisans and craftsmen. Recent research also confirms that an increased dependence on the market economy, and hence greater exposure to its vagaries may, in the absence of countervailing action by the State, accentuate famine distress and mortality (Ravallion, 1987). This suggests that while state intervention is necessary and desirable in famine situations—*'salus populi suprema lex'*, the Roman maxim that no law is above the subsistence and welfare of the people—equally the wrong type of state intervention can accentuate shortages. Although Keynes did not draw any inferences on the type and scope of State action to cope with famines and the like in developing countries, he showed constant awareness of the 'condition-of-the-people' problem during his service in the India Office (1906-1908) and even more during the course of his work for successive Indian Currency Committees. His radical suggestion for the abolition of the salt tax in India (c. 1907), which was so far ahead of Indian nationalist sentiment, was based on the welfare argument that it was not necessary to tax an essential item of mass consumption like salt in a poor country. Keynes was always more solicitous about the interests of the Indian peasant as against those of the urban or exporting classes. His classic evidence to the Indian Exchange and Currency Committee (Babington Smith, 1919), when he argued for a 'high rupee' as enabling the Indian *'ryot'* (farmer) to clothe and feed himself cheaply' (CW, XX: 289), is also an interesting demonstration of the role of exchange rate management as an instrument of a basic needs strategy.

In the same vein, Keynes's support for the National Housing Board (proposed by Sir Raymond Unwin) as a means of meeting "the outstanding capital requirement of today—the provision of houses available to be let at modest rentals", and complementing the "great work of the building societies in meeting the demand for owner-occupied housing" (CW, XXI: 158) is no less relevant for developing countries which suffer from chronic shortages of rental housing. Such shortages, of course, also reflect an archaic system of misconceived rent controls, as in urban India.

Bread, Circuses and 'Permitted Saturnalia'

Keynes was also an ardent advocate of a positive role for the State in promoting the 'non-economic purposes', which for him covered not only education and public health but also the arts, entertainment and protection of the environment through instrumentalities like the Commission of Public Places, the Arts Council and the National Theatre (CW, XXVIII: 335-349). As he so eloquently reasoned, "the ancient world knew that the public needed circuses as well as bread" (ibid.: 349), but "without patrons art cannot easily flourish." He, therefore, welcomed that "at last the public exchequer has recognised [through the establishment of the Arts Council] the support and encouragement of the civilising arts as part of their duty" (ibid.: 368). Keynes was also mindful of the problems of 'optimal taxation' of the arts and cited the BBC "as only the extreme example of the general principle that we penalise music, opera, all the arts of the theatre with a heavy indeed a crushing tax" (ibid.: 345).

Keynes would have argued even more strongly for State support of the arts in developing countries, many of which have a rich artistic and cultural heritage but suffer from the even greater dearth of voluntary non-official endowments for the arts. For instance, the disappearance of princes and landlords in India has also diminished patronage of the arts, literature and sports. But given the perennial claims of satisfying 'basic human needs' in the poorer countries, how far would Keynes have saddled the State with obligations to support the arts? The targeting of art subsidies, too, apart from the problem of coping with the so-called cost (Baumol's) disease of the arts (i.e., prices in the arts rise faster than other prices), is no easy task, even in developed countries, as is borne out by the often acrimonious controversies surrounding the disbursements of the Arts Council in Britain.

While Keynes the Idealist wanted the State to be a patron of the arts, Keynes the Realist also faced up to its role in tackling the even more difficult sumptuary problem of 'permissible saturnalia'.

> How far is bored and suffering humanity to be allowed from time to time, an escape, an excitement, a stimulus, a possibility of change? – that is the important problem. Is it possible to allow reasonable licence, permitted saturnalia, sanctified carnival, in conditions which need ruin neither the health nor the pockets of the roisterers and will shelter from irresistible temptation the unhappy class who, in America, are called addicts? (CW, IX: 303)

Interestingly, some of Keynes's earliest memoranda in the India Office dealt with the prevention of liquor smuggling from Portuguese India into British India and the illicit distillation of country liquor in the Punjab in response to the increase in drinking, particularly among the youth and the lower classes, due partly to higher wages and the fear of the plague. He strongly advocated a low, fixed licence fee to combat illicit distillation and cautioned against any ill-advised attempts at direct prevention of private distillation which might also "stimulate immensely the odious trade of the informer" and only accentuate police corruption and oppression (India Office Minute R and S. No. 3659, 21 December 1907, *Keynes Papers*, King's College Library). The practical good sense of this minute, based on a judicious use of the fiscal apparatus, was characteristic of Keynes's conception of the sumptuary role of the State, which was to resurface in his evidence to the Royal Commission on Lotteries and Betting (1932). Keynes recognised that "the vast majority of the population indulge in greater or lesser degree in some form or another of gambling and betting" (CW, XXVIII: 405) and, therefore, favoured monopolistic state lotteries (as in most Latin countries) as against betting, which would be difficult to prohibit (CW, XXVIII: 401-405). He believed that "economic evils are at a minimum when you put games of pure chance in the hands of the State and control betting on the course, but put great obstacles in the way of other forms of betting" (ibid.: 402). Keynes's suggestions were aimed to "minimise the evils of gambling and the economic waste to the community as a whole, while...maximising such legitimate enjoyment as it can provide" (ibid.: 413). At least in this sphere, the developing countries seem to have applied Keynes's wise prescriptions, judging by their higher median ratio of lottery revenue to the central government's current revenue (1.5 per cent) relative to that in the developed countries (0.7 per cent) (Amatong, 1968: 5).

Developing Countries and International Organisations

In the Keynesian canon the State has also a positive role to play in the international sphere through membership of specialised international organisations such as the IMF and the World Bank, whose primary beneficiaries have been the developing countries as recipients of concessional financial and technical assistance[3] (see also Gold, 1971). Keynes was also perceptive in recognising the benefits for the developing countries of learning the techniques of international economic cooperation through participation in international organisations.[4] On the other hand, the international community's failure to implement Keynes's 'Commod Control' scheme (1942) has meant that there is still no international mechanism to stabilise primary product prices, just as the failure to adopt Keynes's International Clearing Union (functioning as a world Central Bank) has denied developing countries access to a true international reserve money for which the SDRs—frozen at a meagre SDR 21.4 billion since 1981 owing to lack of agreement among the major quota holders—have proved a woefully inadequate substitute.

Redefining the Post-Keynesian Role of the State

Keynes's conception of the role of the State in developing countries was essentially that of a macroeconomic controller in a democracy, which did not involve ownership or micro-level operation of enterprises and institutions. His agenda was much more positive in respect of monetary and fiscal systems and policies than in regard to developmental and structural issues, which he never really addressed. His pioneering formulation of the developmental and prudential role of the central bank in India is still relevant for developing countries. The industrialisation of developing countries remained a surprising blind spot in his mind-set, which never seemed to accommodate infant industry protection or offer any other developmental menu for the State, whereas he was fully supportive of positive state action in regard to population, environment, commodity prices and public welfare.

Keynes's vision of the role of the State in developing countries, generalising from his Indian experience, was understandably circumscribed by the scope of State action in an imperial dependency. The role of the State in developing countries, therefore, needs to be redefined in an age when virtually all of them are sovereign entities coping with the challenges of deregulation and economic liberalisation. Does this necessarily betoken a diminution in the role of the State or a change in the nature and scope of State intervention? Such a reformulation of the rationale and scope of State action in the Third World would, if anything, be wholly in keeping with the spirit of Keynes's celebrated dictum—to 'invent a new wisdom for a new age'.

The following observations are therefore offered as possible building-blocks towards a more realistic formulation of the post-Keynesian role of the State in developing countries, taking account of the mainstream economics case for state intervention, based on correction of market and information failures, incomplete markets, monopoly power, pure public goods, merit goods, externalities, macroeconomic disequilibria, poverty and inequality.

First, and foremost, it is important to specify the nature of the State (unitary or federal, democratic or authoritarian, or a mixture of economic liberalism and political autocracy), which is a major determinant of the scope and efficacy of State action. For instance, fiscal balance is much more difficult to achieve in federal than in unitary states, as is borne out by Indian and Nigerian experience. Although currently most developing country states are non-democratic, and there is no one-to-one relationship between the political character of the State and its economic performance, nevertheless, a convincing case for democracy in the less developed countries can be made based on the prisoner's dilemma and Coase's theorem (Lipton, 1985). In the same vein, it is interesting to note that the single most important indicator of variations in economic growth and performance among less developed countries (1850-1980) is said to be "political organisation and the administrative competence of government" (Reynolds, 1983: 976). Even if it is not the single most important indicator, it could certainly be regarded as a major, albeit much neglected, factor in growth and performance accounting. For instance, the World Bank's annual *Development Reports* find large differences among countries in growth rates and responses to adjustment problems which are related to the efficiency and quality of governmental policy responses. But such responses depend as much on the quality of politicians as on the quality of the civil servants and technocrats. Unfortunately, the Third World is even more deficient in the numbers and quality of its politicians. As Keynes remarked perceptively, "there is no room for the expert, the technician, the scientist, until the politicians have come down to something that can really happen" (CW, XVIII: 19).

Secondly, it is misleading to analyse the role of the State in the less developed countries in terms of a rigid, Manichaean polarity of 'State versus markets'. It has to be refined to accommodate the third sector, neither public nor private, of civil society comprising voluntary non-governmental and non-profit organisations that can contribute to the efficacy of both the State and market sector and serve as a vital countervailing power, but which are conspicuously lacking or weak in the less developed countries. Moreover, the State-market relationship has strong elements of complementarity, most notably in regard to the positive role of the State in improving market efficiency—as so well brought out in the Fundamental Non-Decentralisability Theorem (Greenwald and Stiglitz, 1986), which shows that, in general, efficient market allocations cannot be attained without government intervention. State intervention can contribute to more efficient markets by encouraging competition, e.g., through reduction of transactions and information costs, and correction of imperfect and incomplete markets, spot, forward and futures. This is a constructive role for the State, which is often hampered by the uncritical distrust of the market mechanism on the part of Third World academics and civil servants.

It is even more important to recognise that there is no a priori optimal mix of State intervention, which can only be determined on a pragmatic, case-by-ease, country-specific basis. The empirical evidence for the relative magnitudes of government and market failure is, therefore, necessarily inconclusive despite the claims that government failure necessarily outweighs market failure (World Bank, 1983; Srinivasan, 1985). "In sum, no one has yet shown that the failure of government intervention necessarily outweighs market failure" (Fishlow, 1990: 66). The nature and quality of State intervention is a crucial factor in determining its net outcome, as shown by its success in the East Asian states (Korea and Taiwan) based on the State's prescriptions, in contrast to its failures in South Asia deriving from proscriptions (Bhagwati, 1988: 85). This also shows up a fundamental limitation of the strict Keynesian formulation of the role of the State as doing "things which at present are not done at all" or "lie outside the scope of the individual." This would confine the State to the provision of pure public goods, whereas club goods (whose benefits are excludable and partially non-rival) and private goods offer scope for choice between the government and private sector, both of which would also share 'principal-agent' problems of appropriate managerial incentives.

Thirdly, the role of the State in the less developed countries in the context of privatisation, deregulation and liberalisation will alter, but not diminish, in both the transitional and the post-liberalisation phases. The sequencing and implementation of economic liberalisation and financial reform is an integral part of the State's agenda, as borne out by the experience of Latin America (Argentina, Chile and Uruguay) and South East Asia (Korea, Indonesia, Thailand, Malaysia). But a major obstacle to liberalisation in the less developed countries is the often overlooked collusive coalition of rent-seeking civil servants, private sector beneficiaries of protection, and trade unions, which imposes considerable demands on the soft State's capabilities. Likewise, in the post-liberalisation phase, the State's role would shift from ownership and micro-management to macroeconomic control and prudential surveillance. Thus, the central bank would shed credit subsidies and participation in development finance and limit itself to monetary policy and prudential supervision of the financial system.

Finally, can the State really be neutral in regard to the different trade-offs between growth, efficiency and equity, intergenerational as well as interclass, which are even more pressing problems in the developing countries, given their greater degree of economic and social inequalities? Inevitably, the question arises: Growth, development and economic efficiency, but for whom? A particularly difficult problem is the formulation of a coherent incomes policy and the maintenance of stable efficiency wages given the conflicts of business oligopolies and powerful trade unions and the prevalence of misplaced economic populism. The provision of a social safety net would also be an important responsibility of even the 'minimalist' State in the developing countries, which can ill afford the social costs of unmitigated free markets as manifested in, among others, the homelessness engendered by high and variable mortgage rates in the industrial democracies. A recent World Bank study well substantiates the "urgent need to provide an effective safety net for the poorest in societies ranging from socialist countries undergoing reform to sub-Saharan African economies" (Ahmad, 1991: 105).

Keynes, who uniquely among economists, was as conscious of the failings of economic science as he was of both market and governmental failures, would have been the first to reformulate his agenda for the State in the fast-changing contemporary developing world. For him, as for Alexander Herzen, there were no final solutions.

NOTES

The author gratefully acknowledges the assistance of the British Academy towards his participation in this seminar.

1 "...Sir Eric Coates, who as Finance Secretary along with the Auditor-General, the Commerce Secretary and the Chairman, Central Board of Revenue, had the responsibility of selecting officers for the [Finance Commerce] Pool, had reservations about taking me on the ground that I had studied Economics in Cambridge and might have imbibed dangerous theoretical ideas which might prevent me from learning from experience." (Jha, 1987: 141).

2 Letter to Sir James Grigg, 17 July 1936, 2,3/4/25 (6), *Grigg Collection*, Churchill College, Cambridge (copyright D. C. Grigg and the Master, Fellows and Scholars of Churchill College).

3 The IMF's policies have gone well beyond Keynes's ICU provisions in major respects like the concessionality in charges on the use of the General Resources Account, and the creation of special facilities such as compensatory and contingency financing facility, buffer stock financing facility, the trust fund, subsidy accounts, structural adjustment and enhanced structural adjustment facilities. The addition (of section 2(b) to Article V of the Articles of Agreement of the IMF (Second Amendment) 1973 gives the Fund explicit and very flexible powers to meet the special requirements of members outside the General Resources Account ('If requested the Fund may decide to perform financial and technical services...that are consistent with the purposes of the Fund ...').

4 Responding to a criticism of the *Keynes and White Currency Plans*, Keynes wrote to A.K. Datta, an Indian economist: "India has, surely, as much to gain from this [i.e., benefits of participation in the Currency Plan] as to learn the technique of international co-operation in the economic field" (*Keynes Papers*, King's College Library. Cambridge, 30 December 1943).

REFERENCES

Ahmad, Ehtisham (1991). 'Social Security and the Poor: Choices for Developing Countries', *The World Bank Research Observer*, 6(1) (January): 105–27.

Amatong, Juanita D. (1968). 'The Revenue Importance of Government Lotteries' (unpublished), DM/68/21, International Monetary Fund.

Berlin, Isaiah (1984). 'The Hedgehog and the Fox'. In Russian Thinkers, Harmondsworth: Penguin.

Bhagwati, Jagdish (1988). *Protectionism, Cambridge*, Mass.: MIT Press.

Chandavarkar, Anand (1985a). 'Was Keynes a Development Economist?' *Economic and Political Weekly*, XXI(7) (15 February): 304–7.

————. (1985b). 'Keynes and Central Banking', *Indian Economic Review*, XX(2) (July–December): 283–97.

————. (1989). *Keynes and India (A Study in Economics and Biography)*, London: Macmillan.

Darling, Malcolm (1934). 'Memo of Talk with Keynes', 8 February, Darling Papers, Box 121-46, Centre of South Asian Studies, Cambridge.

Dimand, Robert W. and Mary Ann Dimand, 1990. 'J. M. Keynes on Buffer Stocks and Commodity Stabilization', History of Political Economy, 22(1): 113–22.

Duff, Andrew (ed.) (1984). *John Maynard Keynes (New Wisdom for a New Age)*, Cambridge: Cambridge Liberal Association.

Fishlow, Albert (1990). 'The Latin American State', *The Journal of Economic Perspectives*, 4(3) (Summer).

Gold, Sir Joseph (1971). 'To Contribute Thereby to...Development...Aspects of the Relations of the International Monetary Fund with its Developing Members', *Columbia Journal of Transnational Law*, 10(21) (Fall): 267–302.

Greenwald, Bruce C. and Joseph E. Stiglitz (1986). 'Externalities in Economies with Imperfect Information and Incomplete Markets,' *Quarterly Journal of Economics*, CI(2): 229–64.

Hobsbawm, E.J. (1969). *Industry and Empire, Harmondsworth: Pelican Books*, p. 123.

IMF (1987). *International Financial Statistics, Supplement on Public Sector Institutions*, No. 13, Washington, DC: International Monetary Fund.

Jha, L.K. (1987). *Mr Red Tape*, New Delhi: Allied.

Kaldor, N. (1983). *Limitations of the 'General Theory'. Keynes Lecture in Economics,* London: The British Academy.

Keynes, J.M. (1900). 'The Differences Between East and West: Will They Ever Disappear?', Early Composition, Eton College, in JMK/pp/34/4, November, , King's College Library, Unpublished Writings of J.M. Keynes, Copyright, Provost and Scholars of King's College, Cambridge.

————. (1926). Letter to C. H. Kisch, 22 December, Keynes Papers, King's College Library, Unpublished Writings of J.M. Keynes, Copyright, Provost and Scholars of King's College, Cambridge.

————. (1937). 'Some Economic Consequences of a Declining Population', Eugenics Review, vol. XXIX (April): 14.

————. (1938). 'The Policy of Government Storage of Foodstuffs and Raw Materials', *Economic Journal*, 48(191) (September): 449–60.

————. (1971–89). *The Collected Writings of John Maynard Keynes (henceforth* CW*)*, vols. I–XXX, editors Austin Robinson, Donald Moggridge, Elizabeth Johnson, London: Macmillan.

————. (1971, 1913). CW, *I, Indian Currency and Finance.*

————. (1971, 1930). CW, *VI, A Treatise on Money: The Applied Theory of Money* (includes special prefaces for the German and Japanese translations).

———. (1972, 1931). CW, IX, Essays in Persuasion (includes his 'Means to Prosperity') (1933) and 'How to Pay for the War' (1940).

———. (1972, 1933). CW, X, Essays in Biography.

———. (1973, 1936). CW, *VII, The General Theory of Employment, Interest and Money* (includes special prefaces for the German, Japanese and French translations).

———. (1976). CW, *XV, Activities*: India and Cambridge.

———. (1977). CW, XVII, Activities 1920–2: Treaty Revision and Reconstruction.

———. (1978). CW, XVIII, Activities 1922–1932: The End of Reparations.

———. (1978). CW, XXII, Activities 1939–45: Internal War Finance.

———. (1980). CW, XXVII, Activities 1940–6: Shaping the Post-War World: *Employment and Commodities.*

———. (1981). CW,XIX, Activities 1922-1929: The Return to Gold and Industrial Policy, I

———. (1981). CW, XX, Activities 1929–31: Rethinking Employment and Unemployment Policies.

———. (1982). CW, XXI, Activities 1931–9: World Crises and Policies in Britain and America.

———. (1982). CW, XXVIII, Social, *Political and Literary Writings.*

———. (1983). CW, XI, *Economic Articles and Correspondence: Academic.*

Killick, Tony (1989). *A Reaction Too Far: Economic Theory and the Role of the State in Developing Countries*, London: Overseas Development Institute. p. 8.

Krishnaswamy, K.S. (1991). 'Keynes and the Indian Connection' (Review of Anand Chandavarkar, Keynes and India, 1989), *The Economic Times*, Bangalore (31 January).

Krueger, Ann O. (1990). 'Government Failures in Development', *The Journal of Economic Perspectives*, 4(3) (Summer).

Lipton, Michael (1985). 'Prisoner's Dilemma and Coase's Theorem: A Case for Democracy in Less Developed Countries?', in R.C.O. Matthews (ed.), *Economy and Democracy*, New York: St Martin's Press; London: Macmillan).

Naipaul, Shiva (1988). 'The Illusion of the Third World'. In An Unfinished Journey, Harmondsworth: Penguin.

Rashid, Salim (1980). 'The Policy of Laissez-Faire and Scarcity', *Economic Journal* 90(359) (September): 493–503.

Ravallion, Martin (1987). *Markets and Famines*, Oxford: Clarendon Press.

Reynolds, L.G. (1983). 'The Spread of Economic Growth to the Third World: 1850–1980', *Journal of Economic Literature*, XXI (3): 941–80.

Sen, Amartya (1977). 'Starvation and Exchange, A General Approach and its Application to the Great Bengal Famine', *Cambridge Journal of Economics*, 1(1) (March): 33–59.

Skidelsky, Robert (1990). *Review of Keynes and India: A Study in Economics and Biography by Anand Chandavarkar*, 1989 in The Economic Journal 100(403) (December): 1330–2.

Srinivasan, T.N. (1985). 'Neoclassical Political Economy, the State and Economic Development', *Asian Development Review*, vol. 3: 93–160.

Thirlwall, A. (ed.) (1987). *Keynes and Economic Development (The Seventh Keynes Seminar, University of Kent*, Canterbury, 1985), London: Macmillan.

World Bank (1983). *Accelerated Development in Sub-Saharan Africa: An Agenda for Action*, Washington, DC: The World Bank.

Appendix A-8.1

A Keynesian State-Theoretic Taxonomy for Developing Countries•

Targets	*Institutions*	*Instruments*
(A) Conjunctural	'Economic' civil service, economic general staff, department of statistics, government actuary	Macroeconomic controls, managed exchange rate
Commodity stabilisation	Marketing boards	Government storage and buffer stocks
Saving investment	National investment board	
Money supply, interest rates	Government-owned but autonomous central bank (with accountability and transparency)	Reserve ratios, open market operations, usury laws
Reduction of (i) hoarding; (ii) liquidity premium on land and precious metals, rural debt	Cooperatives	Usury laws
Budget surplus/deficit	Treasury (a) administrative/current budget (b) capital budget	Taxes, expenditure, borrowing, deferred compulsory savings
Balance of payments, external account, foreign assistance	Central bank and membership of international organisations	Exchange rate and reserve management
(B) Structural		
Reduction of population pressure		Family planning, women's rights, divorce reform
Environment	Commission of public places	Public acquisition
Financial development	Central bank	Preferential rediscount facilities, expansion of banking, prudential control
Rural development		Public works
Human capital		Government borrowing (if necessary) for right type of education (vocational)

contd...

...contd...

Targets	*Institutions*	*Instruments*
(C) Welfare		
(i) Disaster relief and basic needs		Government storage of food
(ii) Housing	National housing board (emphasis on low income rental housing)	
(iii) Support of arts	Arts council	Subsidies
(iv) Gambling/alcohol, betting		Sumptuary taxation, licensing and regulation of state lotteries

• This draws on Keynes's prescriptions in the Indian context but also includes instruments and institutions which Keynes proposed for Britain.

9 Keynes and the International Monetary System Revisited*

...there is no doubt where Keynes stood. He trusted to human intelligence. He hated enslavement by rules.

— Sir Alec Cairncross

The person that Keynes was really gunning for...was Keynes himself.

— Sir Austin Robinson

Introduction

This essay attempts to answer the question: How would Keynes as the foremost monetary economist, policy adviser extraordinaire, and prime intellectual progenitor of the post-World War II international monetary arrangements, have viewed and reacted to the principal problems and issues of the contemporary international monetary system? Such an exercise has to be approached with due circumspection for Keynes combined with his intense intellectual curiosity and innovativeness an equally self-critical habit of mind, which was never the slave of any 'foolish consistency of views' that is so often 'the hobgoblin of small minds'. Consequently, the economic ideas of Keynes—as distinct from Keynesian economics—at any point of time are best assessed in their historical and institutional context, drawing on the entire corpus of his writings from his days at India Office (1905–06) to his role as a leading protagonist at Bretton Woods (1944) and Savannah (1946). Such an endeavour carries the all too familiar hazard pinpointed by the Editor of his *Collected Writings* that "one can find more than enough ammunition in Keynes for many points of view, especially if...[one] wishes to lift it out of context" (Moggridge, 1977). It can only lead the unwary to the sterile *cul de sac* of what Keynes really meant. Hence the protective stratagem of the contextual approach of viewing Keynes in the context of time. But a contextual approach is uninteresting except for the historian of thought. It has to be supplemented by the conjectural approach. However, any analyst of Keynes following the conjectural path does well to bear in mind the sage cautionary words of Lord Kahn, his lifelong intellectual collaborator, against any overzealous pursuit of counterfactuals.

* *Source*: *World Development*, 15(12) (1987): 1395-1405.

> The question of what Keynes would be advocating today is, of course, a nonsense question. Were he alive today...his own ideas would have developed enormously; under his influence the ideas of others would have developed on different lines; and the economic situation of the country and of the world would be different. Keynes often used to remark to me that he enjoyed the advantage of waking up every morning like a new-born babe, entirely uncommitted to what he had thought or advocated previously. This is why he has so often been charged with inconsistency. The fact is that he did not resist a change in the situation, or to the development of his own thinking, partly under the influence of other economists. (Kahn, 1975: 32)

It is admittedly impossible to provide an adequately scientific answer to any hypothetical questions and there will always be legitimate doubts about how Keynes's ideas would have actually worked. Nevertheless, an extrapolation of Keynes's ideas using a combination of the contextual and conjectural approaches provides useful insights into present-day problems and policies. These necessary caveats apart, there is another important preliminary question which also affects the application of Keynes's ideas to contemporary issues. Is the term 'system' a valid description of international monetary arrangements since the breakdown of the par value regime and the consequent absence of generally accepted and enforceable rules and conventions governing the conduct of national monetary and exchange rate policies? Some commentators even call it a non-system because there are no unambiguous and accepted 'rules of the game' or objective indicators to resolve the basic problems of adjustment, liquidity and confidence. On the other hand, the International Monetary Fund with its financing, adjustment and surveillance machinery provides a forum for the rule of law in international monetary affairs.

The sheer wealth of historical material on Keynes's ideas on the international monetary system requires a meaningful taxonomy as an organising principle to assess the adequacy of prevailing international monetary arrangements to address the basic problems of decision-making and management: adjustment; provision of liquidity; and the anchorage of the system, the so-called N-I problem in a world of three key or pivotal currencies, the US dollar, the German mark, and the Japanese yen. Accordingly, the following taxonomy is used in the subsequent analysis:

(2) the institutional framework;

(3) international liquidity and convertibility;

(4) the exchange rate regime;

(5) the adjustment mechanism;

(6) the developing countries problem.

The subsequent discussion will not, however, follow the *ad variorum* historical approach, so well presented by Moggridge (1986). It will, while drawing on Keynes's published and unpublished writings, concentrate on those elements of Keynes's thought which have a direct bearing on contemporary international monetary problems and issues.

The Institutional and Management Framework

Keynes's first essay in international monetary cooperation was his scheme of a Supranational Central Bank without any initial capital but with its liabilities guaranteed by adherent central banks (CW, VI: 354-367). Its principal objectives were to maintain the stability of the value of gold in terms of a tabular standard of value based on the principal commodities of international trade and to avoid international inflation or deflation. While Keynes outlined a minimum and maximum agenda of Methods of Supranational Management between central banks, he did not work out the technical and administrative details of management as distinct from the instruments of policy like bank rate, discount quotas, and the power to conduct open market operations in any member country, requiring the approval of the country's central bank in the case of purchases but not in the case of sales. This innovative proposal did not find a place in Keynes's Proposal for an International Clearing Union (April 1943). On the other hand, Keynes's Supranational Bank made no provisions for adjustment of exchange rates, presumably because he felt that an international creditor and banker country like Britain might be compensated for the cost of returning to the gold standard (1925) by the maintenance of exchange rate stability, an argument which was reaffirmed later in the Addendum to the Report of the Macmillan Committee on Industry and Trade (1931) written by Keynes and others. ('For a country in the special circumstances of Great Britain the disadvantages [of devaluation] would greatly outweigh the advantages'. June 1931, p.199.)

In between his Supranational Bank and the ICU, Keynes had advocated the creation of an international note-issuing authority to provide "not a permanent addition to the world's monetary supply, but as a balancing factor to be released when prices are abnormally high as at present and to be withdrawn again if prices were to be rising too much" (CW, IX: 354-355, 358). It was designed to free the hands of central banks to promote loan expenditure and restore employment. This notion of injection and withdrawal of money supply may well have been the genesis of his later concept of deferred compulsory savings in *How to Pay for the War*. The authority would issue gold notes (with face value expressed in terms of the gold content of the US dollar) to a maximum of $5000 million obtainable by the participating countries against an equal face value of the gold bonds of their countries, up to a maximum quota for each country, to be based on an agreed formula (e.g., the amount of gold held in reserves at some recent normal date like end of 1928), provided that no individual quota should exceed $450 million. Under this plan, seven countries would qualify for the maximum quota of $450 million each (Great Britain, United States, France, Germany, Spain, Argentina, and Japan) with others ranging from Italy (266) to Estonia (2). India (i.e., undivided India) would have qualified for a quota of 124, which was lower than those for Holland (175), Brazil (149), and Belgium (126) but higher than for Canada (114), Australia (108), South Africa (39) and New Zealand (35). Thus, unlike the Supranational Bank, this scheme provided for the participation of the non-industrial countries.

The statement that Keynes "in devising all of his schemes...did not give much thought to the technical details of organization and management" of institutions (Moggridge, 1986: 77) has one striking exception. One only has to recall the meticulous attention given to organisational details in Keynes's scheme for the Indian State Bank, which covered details such as the Board of Directors, operational management, and the disposition of central bank profits (CW, XV: 153-202). Keynes also recognised, however, that "one can ensure nothing by the terms of a paper constitution" and that "the desirable objectives can only be attained through the exercise of daily wisdom by the monetary authorities of the world" (CW, VI: 360). Keynes envisaged the role of discretion to comprehend international cooperation between the major central banks, including the type of intimate bilateral contacts like those between Benjamin Strong of the Federal Reserve and Montague Norman of the Bank of England. He also speculated that the Bank for International Settlements (BIS) could well be the nucleus of a supranational bank but that its future usefulness would depend largely on the support it received from the United States (ibid.: 257). Keynes thus very perceptively sensed the emerging role of the United States as a 'price' leader in an increasingly oligopolistic world economy and of the dollar as the major key currency of the future. Keynes also suggested that the governing board of the expanded BIS would be elected by the participating governments, each of whose votes would be proportional to its quota (CW, IX: 28). But after his ICU scheme had been published Keynes remarked: "It is depressing that so much attention has been concentrated on voting; it never crossed my mind that we were under an accusation of having tried to rig this.

Indeed, so little attention was paid to it that we had not even examined how it would work out in practice" (CW, XXV: 241).

His ICU was designed "to secure as much prior certainty as possible concerning the methods of those responsible for daily management, and to limit their initiative and discretion to cases where the rules and purposes of the institution are in risk of infringement, thus keeping them as an instrument entirely passive in all normal circumstances" (ibid.: 404). Keynes's conception of the Fund was essentially technocratic, with civil servants reporting to the Managing Director but with no day-to-day role for the Executive Directors, and he would have found that the present-day Fund with its Executive Board, composed of technocrats, as well as political nominees, and permanently in session, had assumed a totally different character than envisaged by him.

Liquidity and Convertibility

Keynes was concerned with questions of international liquidity (supply and convertibility of reserve assets) in the course of his search for 'the ideal currency of the future' since his *Indian Currency and Finance* (CW, I: 25) and even earlier writings (CW, XV). But it was not until around 1928-1930 that Keynes began to think, in the course of his evidence to the Macmillan Committee and in his *Treatise on Money*, of a shortage of international liquidity as a problem arising because of continued gold accumulation by the Bank of France, the Wall Street boom and the large flows of reserve assets from the rest of the world to the United States.

His projected international central bank was designed to increase world liquidity by lending to countries in balance of payments difficulties and through open market operations in securities denominated in national currencies, or in supranational bank money (SBM). These operations were to aim at maintaining the value of SBM in terms of a tabular standard of the major commodities in international trade (CW, VI: 358-361). This notion of an international monetary authority approximating more to a central bank than a pool of reserve assets was carried over to Keynes's ICU with its Bancor overdraft facilities which, however, also provided for reduction of overdraft limits in the event of threats of inflation (paragraph 6(13)). This points to two interconnected ideas of Keynes, namely, an international central bank able to cope alike with deflation and inflation and thereby designed to play a counter-cyclical role in the world economy. In addition, the ICU's proposals for an automatic increase in members' quotas (overdraft limits) in accordance with the growth in the nominal value of world trade were not matched either in the American (White) plan or the Bretton Woods system. "If they had been the history of post-war international liquidity would undoubtedly have been different" (Moggridge, 1986: 77).

While Keynes's long-term goal was market convertibility for current account transactions he perceptively qualified this by providing for a virtually indefinite period of transition (the present Article XIV) and for the control of capital movements (paragraph VII). Keynes cogently argued that

> there is no country which can, in future, safely allow the flight of funds for political reasons or to evade domestic taxation or in anticipation of the owner turning refugee. Equally there is no country that can safely receive fugitive funds, which constitute an unwanted import of capital, yet cannot, safely be used for fixed investment. (CW, VII: 32)

However, the object was not to hamper international investment but to have a means of controlling short-term speculative movements or flights of capital and of "distinguishing long-term loans by creditor countries which help to maintain equilibrium and develop the world's resources, from movements of funds out of debtor countries which lack the means to finance them" (ibid.: 35). This, according to Keynes, would require "another complementary institution." Nonetheless, the ICU scheme would have required a country with a debit balance in excess of 50 per cent of quota to introduce "the control of outward capital transactions if not already in place" (Paragraph 8(b)(ii)).

Since the IMF does not require the liberalisation of capital account transactions, and the convertibility requirements in its articles are explicitly limited to current account transactions, it is meaningful to speculate on the possible outcome had the Keynesian type of capital controls been in place since 1945-46. They would "have prevented the growth of a Eurodollar market [and one may add the massive explosion of financial innovations] and thus limited how much developing countries could borrow, but that would after all have avoided the debt crisis" (Williamson, 1987: 102). Keynes's proposal for centralisation of all foreign exchange transactions through central banks followed by the clearing of their net balances with the ICU would have facilitated the operation of capital controls and also reduced the excessive absorption of resources into overgrown financial markets and their social diseconomies (Tobin, 1984). Equally, given his consistent stand on the relation between balance of payments financing and development finance, Keynes would not have been too enthusiastic about the SDR link.

In this context it is also interesting to conjecture: How would Keynes have interpreted the role of the Fund's still remaining stock of 103 million fine ounces and the lack of the requisite 85 per cent majority of the Fund's total voting power on the disposal of gold despite the earlier consensus on 'demonetising' gold through the first and second amendment of the Articles. No doubt Keynes's lifelong mission was to de-emphasise gold and to activate it, whether it was held in the sterile hoards of Indian peasants or in the reserves of sophisticated central banks. In line with this Keynes would have been supportive of the Fund's auction sales of gold to constitute the Trust Fund. The status of the remaining gold as a legally liquid but operationally illiquid asset valued on the balance sheet of the Fund at a historical price (SDR 35 per ounce) expressed in terms of a fiduciary reserve asset (SDR) would have struck Keynes. The answer is best left to Keynes, who wrote on 'The Position of Gold Under the Plan' (ICU Paragraph VI):

> Gold still possesses great psychological value which is not being diminished by current events; and the desire to possess a gold reserve against unforeseen contingencies is likely to remain. Gold also has the merit of providing in point of form (whatever the underlying realities may be) an uncontroversial standard of value for international purposes, for which it would not yet be easy to find a serviceable substitute. Moreover, by supplying an automatic means for settling some part of the favourable balances of the creditor countries, the current gold production of the world and the remnant of gold reserves held outside the United States may still have a useful part to play. Nor is it reasonable to ask the United States to demonetise the stock of gold which is the basis of its impregnable liquidity. What, in the long run, the world may decide to do with gold is another matter. The purpose of the Clearing Union is to supplant gold as a governing factor, but not to dispense with it.

In the light of this passage, which has an uncanny contemporary tone, it is plausible to argue that Keynes might not have found the present position of gold held by the IMF altogether paradoxical pending the emergence of an 85 public enterprise cent majority on its ultimate disposal. On the other hand, he would have been intrigued by the lack of sufficient support for the resumption of SDR allocations, considering that his ICU provided for a quantum of international currency, which is "governed by the actual requirements of world commerce, and is also capable of deliberate expansion and contraction to offset deflationary and inflationary tendencies in effective world demand" (Paragraph 1(c)). Any interruption of the supply of Bancors would have been beyond his ken.

The Exchange Rate Regime

Keynes's views on the appropriate exchange rate regime fluctuated more than on any other monetary topic and by the time he drafted his post-World War II monetary reform schemes he had at one time or another studied and recommended virtually every exchange rate regime known to modern economists except the completely free floating exchange rates (Moggridge, 1986). It is, therefore, pertinent to recall that around the time of the Genoa Conference (10 April 1922) when all the European currencies were floating freely at substantial discounts from their pre-war parities, Keynes advocated not a continuance of the float but a series of stabilisations at or near existing market rates, including the possibility of gradual appreciation by 0.5 per cent per month for currencies near their former parities (CW, XVII: 356, 369). Despite the fluctuations in his pre-ICU thinking, Keynes seems to have been broadly in favour of what in contemporary parlance might be called variants of a crawling peg. However, Keynes's ICU provided for an adjustable peg par value system in which all countries declared par values in terms of the Bancor, and undertook to convert balances of their currency needed to make current account payments into the currency of any other member at parity with presumably a modest spread between the buying and the selling rate (paragraphs 6(3), 6(8)).

As for the means of defending exchange rates, Keynes was consistent in all his proposals that national authorities should stand ready to buy and sell reserve assets and that national holdings of reserve assets should be primarily earmarked for external use and not sterilised unproductively as backing for domestic legal tender currency or wasted in public circulation. The real economic rationale of foreign exchange reserves was first enunciated by Keynes in his *Indian Currency and Finance* (CW, I: Chap. 6) to support his case for a gold exchange rather than a gold bullion standard for India and repeated in his subsequent writings (CW, XI: 312-319; CW, XXV: 677-686). Interestingly, the international monetary system, too, had witnessed deviations from the norms and obligations of the Bretton Woods regime even before its formal abandonment in 1971, like: the French devaluation of 1948 as part of the attempt to establish a free market for gold and convertible currencies; the flotation of the Canadian dollar (1950-May 1962); the circumstances of the appreciation of the German mark (1961); and the institution of the two-tier price system for gold (1968). The dialectic of post-war international monetary history and policy seems to have followed the pattern of thesis and antithesis without producing a synthesis.

Keynes was remarkably consistent, whether in the context of Indian discussions or later in the international sphere, in according primacy to domestic price stability as a policy objective and to give exchange stability the second order of importance. The par value system of the ICU was predicated on the availability of an alternative reserve asset (Bancor) and the maintenance of exchange controls over capital transactions. This would have benefited the developing countries by: limiting protectionism generated by currency misalignments; preventing magnification of dollar-denominated external debt relative to their export earnings consequent upon the substantial appreciation of the US dollar (as in 1980-1985); avoiding the dilemma of choice between jeopardising their macroeconomic policy by a movement of the peg currency or losing any prior anchorage to an international currency for invoicing, borrowing and holding assets by pegging to a currency composite (Williamson, 1987: 94). This line of argument would have to be qualified insofar as the growth of protectionism in industrial countries can be largely attributed to factors other than currency misalignment.

Keynes advocated limited exchange rate flexibility with elements of a wider band (5 per cent between the buying and selling prices of gold—see CW, XVIII: 365; CW, IX: 362) and a crawling peg, as identified by John Williamson (CW, XVII: 364), which would have been moved just like the bank rate 'though by small degrees' (CW, IX: 362). Later, during the World Economic Conference, Keynes proposed the linkage of the dollar/sterling exchange rate to differential inflation (CW, XXI: 261–2). Keynes, given his classic indictment of the other much-touted perfectly competitive market—the stock exchange—would not have accorded his imprimatur to its fraternal twin of freely floating exchange markets. One has only to recall his oft-quoted statement: "If the capital development of a country becomes a by-product of the activities of a casino" and "when enterprise [forecasting the yield of assets over their whole life] becomes the bubble on a whirlpool of speculation...[forecasting the psychology of the market] the job is likely to be ill-done" (CW, VII: 158-159).

There is no warrant in the Keynesian schema to believe that free floats of exchange rates and the concomitant speculation would better reflect economic fundamentals than the adjustable par value system. The limitations of speculation would have also emerged given the probabilities of undershooting and overshooting any exchange rate target. As for target zones, is it purely coincidental that an authoritative state-of-the-art survey has citations from all the literature except Keynes's writings (Frenkel and Goldstein, 1986)? Similarly, the replacement of the N-1 (gold or US dollar) currency system by an N-3 pivotal currency system (dollar, mark and yen) would not have been explicable within the framework of the ICU.

THE ADJUSTMENT MECHANISM

Keynes, when he first addressed the adjustment problem as in the ICU, recognised that the burden of adjustment in the historical fixed rate regimes had normally fallen on the deficit (read developing!) countries. Keynes summed up the historical experience of the adjustment process as follows:

> It is characteristic of a freely convertible international standard that it throws the main burden of adjustment on the country which is in the debtor position on the international balance of payments...Thus, it has been an inherent characteristic of the automatic international metallic currency (apart from special circumstances) to force adjustments in the direction most disruptive of social order, and to throw the burden on the countries least able to support it, making the poor poorer. (CW, XXVII: 123)

Consequently, he set out to devise a symmetrical adjustment mechanism designed to divide the burden equitably between the deficit and surplus countries. The process of adjustment as Keynes was at pains to point out, is compulsory for the debtor country and voluntary for the creditor country. Therefore, the object of the new system must be to require the chief initiative from the creditor countries, whilst maintaining enough discipline in the debtor countries to prevent them from exploiting the new ease allowed in living profligately beyond their means (CW, XXV: 27-29, 30). At the same time, Keynes, in his proposals for an ICU wanted institutional remedies for situations where any country whose own affairs are conducted with due prudence is relieved of anxiety for causes which are not of its own making, concerning its ability to meet its international liabilities. This distinction between the endogenous and exogenous sources of balance of payments imbalance found partial recognition in the IMF Compensatory Financing Facility.

It is noteworthy, however, that the net effect of the successive redrafts of the ICU scheme was, in fact, to attenuate the sanctions on surplus countries and strengthen them somewhat as regards the deficit countries. The final Keynes Plan did not contain any sanction stronger than the final 'scarce currency clause', which in the event became virtually a dead letter. In the ICU the maximum liability of a creditor country would lie within its own control since "no more is asked of it than that it should hold in Bancor such surplus of its favourable balance of payments as it does not itself choose to employ in any other way, and only for so long as does not so choose" (paragraph IV-9). Keynes's perceptive anticipation of the oligopolistic role of the United States in world economy would have accommodated the contemporary situation of the United States as the largest debtor country being able to circumvent the burden of adjustment – that normally falls on a deficit country—by virtue of its unique role as the issuer of the premier reserve currency, which thereby enables it to avoid recourse to balance of payments financing from the Fund.

Keynes's ICU had both important similarities and differences as compared with the operation of conditionality in the contemporary IMF. It stated explicitly the rationale of conditionality:

> the overdraft facilities...will be mainly useful...to allow time and method for necessary adjustments and a comfortable safeguard behind which the unforeseen and the unexpected can be faced with equanimity...But if the purpose of the overdraft facilities is mainly to give time for adjustments, we have to make sure, so far as possible, that they will be made. We must have, therefore, some rules and some machinery to secure that equilibrium has been restored. (paragraph 16)

Thus, conditionality, as a necessary condition for any cooperative international monetary institution, was embedded in the ICU as much as in the IMF. The major difference would have been the much larger scale of unconditional drawing rights in the ICU (first half of a member's quota) after which the ICU would have obtained the right to require collateral, reimbursement, exchange rate action, or to recommend further internal adjustment measures. The ICU would have required more stringent measures (conditionality) when an overdraft exceeded 75 per cent of quota, with the penalty of being declared in default. The standard Keynesian doctrine, as refined and synthesised by Meade, identifies two major types of instruments, namely, aggregate expenditure reduction (e.g., fiscal restraint and monetary contraction) and expenditure switching (e.g., devaluation after 50 per cent of quota), which are very much a feature of IMF adjustment programmes. There could, of course, be differences in the assessment of the operation of conditionality between Keynes's ICU and the IMF today, depending upon the mix of expenditure reduction and expenditure switching policies.

Developing Countries

The grand theme of development and the concomitant dichotomy of developed and developing countries are essentially post-World War II phenomena. Keynes, while conscious of the importance of these issues, was unambiguous and consistent on the point that the promotion and finance of development could not be regarded as a direct purpose of international monetary arrangements as the latter were primarily concerned with the efficient functioning of the international adjustment mechanism. When Keynes first drafted his Currency Scheme before the Bretton Woods Conference, he wrote in response to the criticism of the Keynes and White Plans by an Indian economist, A.K. Datta:

> Thank you very much for sending me [your] two very interesting and excellently written articles for the *Eastern Economist*. [New Delhi, 'Lord Keynes and Equilibrium,' 1 October 1943, and 'British and U.S. Currency Plans,' 9 July 1943.] It is not the purpose of the Currency Schemes to deal with different rates of capital expansion causing some countries to be long-term borrowers from the rest of the world and others to be long-term lenders. When you say that 'neither the Keynes Plan nor the White Plan touches this' you are entirely right. They do not pretend to and in the Keynes Plan at any rate this is clearly stated. To deal with that problem requires another type of institution. White's Reconstruction Bank tries to fill that bill ... The Currency Plan aims at providing reserves to tide over short-term fluctuations and an orderly method for altering exchange rates when necessary, and for ensuring multilateral clearing of current trade transactions. *No currency plan can properly attempt to do more than this* (emphasis provided). But they are important objects, and India has, surely, as much to gain from this as to learn the technique of international cooperation in the economic field. (*Keynes Papers*, King's College, 30 December 1943)

This is the earliest and possibly one of the most unequivocal statements of Keynes distinguishing between the purpose of an international monetary institution for balance of payments financing and adjustment (subsequently the IMF) and that of an institution for reconstruction and development finance (the World Bank). This communication is also of historic interest in highlighting the advantages to emergent nations like India of learning the techniques of international economic cooperation through membership in international organisations. Keynes was perceptive in recognising the benefits of 'learning participation' for developing countries as distinct from the financial advantages. India, certainly, is an apt example of a prime beneficiary of this aspect of international organisation. Indian delegations cut their negotiating teeth in forums related to the Fund and Bank long before India used the financial resources of these institutions.

Keynes's subsequent position was wholly consistent with this stand. During the Bretton Woods conference the Indian delegation proposed a major revision of Article I (ii) on Purposes of the Fund, which called for "the development of the resources and productive power of all member countries with due regard to the needs of economically backward countries" (*Proceedings*, Vol. I, Document 162, p.184). The Indian delegation (Sir Shanmukham Chetty) argued that though an increase in the volume of exports and imports was an important aspect of balanced growth, the economically backward countries attached "great importance also to the balanced character and composition of international trade" since "a predominant flow of raw material and foodstuffs in one direction and highly manufactured goods in the other direction is not a really balanced international trade...It is only by greater attention to the industrial needs of countries like India that you achieve a real and rational balance." For this reason the Indian delegation wanted specific mention of "the needs of economically backward countries in the description of objectives of economic policy, which the Fund cannot directly assist but may indirectly facilitate" (*Proceedings*, Vol. II, 1944. Document 383, pp. 1180-1181). Keynes was the Chairman of the Second Commission of the Bank but did not take any position on these proposals of the Indian delegation although he was in close contact with them. The Indian delegates (Sir Chintaman Deshmukh, Sir Jeremy Raisman and Sir Theodore Gregory) were present at the second informal meeting with Dominion and Indian representatives, which was held in Keynes's room, Atlantic City, on Sunday, 25 June 1944. This meeting was convened to enable Keynes to report on his discussions with Dr. White, the US delegate, which, however, did not cover the broad objectives or the Fund. Keynes's silence on this proposal of the Indian delegation could more properly be interpreted as an implicit acknowledgement that the developmental role properly belonged to the proposed Bank for Reconstruction and Development (IBRD). Eventually, Commission I (Fund) agreed to the present wording of Article I (ii), which refers to "...the development of the productive resources of *all members* as primary objectives of economic policy" (emphasis provided).

Keynes's position on development activities as being beyond the purview of an international monetary institution, in a sense was not unconnected with his earlier somewhat negative attitude to tariff protection and the industrialisation of India from his early days in India Office and even thereafter, which reflected his strong free trade convictions, a phase which lasted till his final conversion to protection during his oral evidence to the Macmillan Committee. Keynes then argued his case for protection on the ground that free trade is premised on full employment equilibrium; that protection will yield additional budget revenue; improve the foreign balance in the shortest and easiest way; turn the terms of trade in Britain's favour; and generally revive business confidence. Although Keynes always remained a 'reluctant protectionist' as described by Kaldor, it is noteworthy that despite his long involvement with the economic affairs of a large developing country like India, Keynes remained strangely oblivious of the infant-industry argument for protection—a perennial blind spot in his mind-set. On the other hand, the advocates of infant-industry protection—Frederick List and Alexander Hamilton, among others—too, never extended the infant-industry argument for protection to the equally valid case for development of an infant country (economy), which might have also transformed economics from a science of allocation of resources to an analysis of growth and development. The economics of protection would then have been the true forerunner of the modern economics of development, and this would not have been without its impact on international monetary arrangements.

The consideration of these issues raises a kindred counterfactual question: Would Keynes have favoured the use of international seigniorage and the profits of an international monetary institution to promote development? In this respect, too, Keynes might have tended to be conventional and even orthodox, judging by the only recorded instance of his views on the use of the profits of domestic central banking. Commenting on the State Bank Memorandum of Lionel Abrahams (Financial Secretary and later Under-Secretary of State for India), Keynes argued (1913) that it would not be easy to determine the net profits of the note issue and thought that the shareholders should have the profits up to a certain percentage, with the surplus being divided between them and the government, subject to decennial revision. Keynes's own scheme for a state bank for India provided for a division of the annual net profits after due allowance for depreciation and preference dividends (if any), between shareholders, reserves and the government. But the scheme did not address the policy issue of a productive use of currency profits. Without giving reasons, Keynes, in fact, argued against the use of the profits of coinage for capital expenditure like railway construction (CW, XV: 275).

Nevertheless, there is a valid distinction between Keynes's views on development as an objective of an international monetary institution and the needs and requirements of developing members of such an institution. For instance, while the IMF does not directly promote development, many of its financial policies and facilities are of particular benefit to developing members. Keynes would have heartily approved of the commodity-oriented financial facilities of the Fund as being in accord with his Clearing Union provision for setting up an account in favour of international bodies charged with the management of commodity control and for financing stocks of commodities held by such bodies through agreed maximum overdraft facilities (IX(3), 1943). "By this means, the financial problem of buffer stocks and ever-normal granaries could be effectively attacked."

Keynes's interest in this problem dated back to his famous article in the *Economic Journal* in 1938 on the case for government subsidisation of buffer stocks of food and raw material on strategic and stabilisation grounds (CW, XXVII: 115-120). He returned to this issue in 1942 in the course of a memorandum to the British Treasury with a plan for 'Commod Control' by an independent international body holding buffer stocks of the main traded primary commodities in order to stabilise prices within a range of 20 per cent around a base value that could be adjusted gradually at a rate not normally exceeding 4 per cent per annum (ibid.). This scheme aimed at providing a stimulus to primary production and incomes and thereby to the demand for industrial goods, so that the pace of industrial growth would be stepped up to the limits set by the supply of primary commodities, instead of the latter being circumscribed by the growth of demand from the industrial countries.

Keynes's advocacy of international buffer stocks was based on the reduction of risks, and thereby the stimulation of investment in the primary sector and to the maintenance of a sustainable relationship with the secondary sector of the international economy. A noteworthy feature of Keynes's proposal was his express stipulation that the basic price set by these schemes should take into account "the requirements of a suitable standard of life for the majority of producers concerned... The desire to maintain adequate standards of living has been the mainspring of the movement towards commodity regulation schemes in recent years, and this is a purpose which the buffer stock controls must be prepared to take over" (ibid.: 123). To this end Keynes invoked the concept of 'a reasonable international economic price'; in fixing which

> the Executive shall have primary regard to the level which would provide the average (not marginal) producers of, say, two-thirds or three quarters of the exporting countries, weighted according to their standard tonnages, with a standard of life in reasonable relation to the general standards of the country in which they live, and when these standards have been low, shall err in the generous direction with a view to their gradual improvement. (ibid.: 124)

In his concern for protecting the standard of living of the primary producers, Keynes's thinking shows a remarkable consistency dating back to his classic evidence to the Indian Exchange and Currency Committee (Babington Smith) in 1919, wherein he argued for a high-rupee as 'enabling the "*ryot*" (Indian farmer) to clothe and feed himself "more cheaply" ' (CW, XV: 289).

Keynes's commodity scheme, which has the merit of aiming simultaneously at stabilisation, developmental and welfare objectives, was never institutionalised. Admittedly, Keynes did not inquire too closely into the policy and administrative problems of buffer stocks, notably that stabilising prices would not necessarily stabilise incomes of producers and may even destabilise them, depending on whether the instability of prices originates from supply or demand side factors. Moreover, buffer stock intervention may itself induce price distortions and compound the problem of distinguishing secular, cyclical, structural, and random price changes. Nevertheless, Keynes's commodity schemes might have admirably complemented the Bretton Woods and other multilateral financial institutions. But then, what would Keynes have thought of the rather chequered experience and even failures of post-war commodity schemes like tin?

The post-Keynesian developments in the structure and policies of the IMF in relation to developing countries have gone beyond Keynes's ICU provisions in major respects, like the concesssionality in the charges on the use of the General Resources Account and the creation of special facilities, in addition to the compensatory and buffer stock financing facilities, such as the Extended Fund Facility, the Trust Fund, Subsidy Accounts, and the Structural Adjustment Facility. Before the second amendment of the Articles of Agreement (1978) the Fund had relied on the doctrine of implied powers to assist developing countries, but since then the addition of section 2(b) to Article V ('If requested, the Fund may decide to perform financial and technical services, including the administration of resources contributed by members, that are consistent with the purposes of the Fund ...') gives the Fund explicit and very flexible powers to meet the special requirements of member countries outside the General Resources Account. The developing countries have been the prime beneficiaries of this section.

Concluding Remarks

In retrospect, it may be conceded that Keynes lost the argument for creating the nucleus of a super-central bank in the Fund but it is arguable whether the loss of his long-term goal was "more to do with the way the institution has evolved since 1946 than with the designs of the founders" (Moggridge, 1986: 80). But the one feature of Keynes's thinking, which is so often overlooked today by even knowledgeable commentators, is the fact that his ICU was predicated on the operation of parallel supportive international organisations like the scheme for commodity controls, an International Investment or Development Corporation, a Board for International Investment, and an International Economic Board which was expected to work in close collaboration with the ICU to their mutual advantage (paragraph 5). These were the various modalities by which the ICU could use its influence and powers to 'maintain stability of prices and to control the Trade Cycle'. Keynes was acutely conscious of the limitations of purely monetary cooperation in the international sphere. He did not believe that the ICU would be viable on its own without a supportive network of other economic organisations. This was an institutional recognition of the global interdependence of the monetary and real sectors, a dichotomy which Keynes did not endeavour to bridge, at least to the same extent in his domestic policy schemes. He visualised the ICU as

> the instrument and the support of international policies in addition to those which is its primary purpose to promote. This deserves the greatest possible emphasis. The Union might become the pivot of the future economic government of the world. Without it, other more desirable developments will find themselves impeded and unsupported. (IX-9-The Use of the Clearing Union for other International Purposes)

However, Keynes would have had to allow for an increasingly oligopolistic world economy and a polycentric currency system, which today replicates uncannily the period between the 1922 Genoa Conference and the 1936 Tripartite Agreement (United Kingdom, United States and France) with each of the principal players unwilling to be a leader. The sheer variety of exchange arrangements—single pegs, currency composites, *inter alia*, almost suggests the reincarnation of currency areas around each peg. All these developments highlight the difficult problems of administering an international collective good (the international monetary system) by a Club (a voluntary cooperative association, i.e., the IMF) influenced in varying degrees by coalitions (Summits and Groups 10 and 24). The economic theory of oligopoly, clubs, and coalitions illumines contemporary international monetary problems more than the conventional approach in terms of competitive markets to the international monetary system as a public or collective good. The international monetary system, perhaps, merits a new political economy to enlarge Keynes's vision "of a central institution of a purely technical and non-political character" (paragraph 1 (b)).

The rapid growth of financial innovation and the globalisation of money and the financial system would have engaged Keynes's concerns not only in regard to the difficult questions of coordination of sovereign national monetary and economic policies but also the prudential implications of over-rapid financial development, to which he had drawn pointed attention in his *Indian Currency and Finance*. But it would be a signal disservice to Keynes to even attempt to claim any prescience on his part for subsequent developments. Despite his towering genius he was, perhaps, one of the very few in the history of the subject who was ever mindful of not only governmental and market failures but even more of academic failures. His overriding concern was not to arrive at any settled conclusions but to use and refine economics as a technique of analysis to solve problems and issues of the moment, whether it was Indian currency reform, reparations, gold standard in exchange rates, war finance, or post-war monetary plans. But even Keynes could not have been expected to evolve a conceptual apparatus for unforeseen problems. After all, the philosophic basis for his classic analysis of long-term expectations (not necessarily rational!) and uncertainty was not, as he remarked, that the inevitable happens. It is only the unexpected. As Lord Kahn reminds us: "Keynes was in the habit of saying that if anything was certain, it was that the future would not resemble the past" (Kahn, 1975: 32). It would, perhaps, be appropriate to recall the magisterial message of Keynes's last (posthumous) article.

> No one can be certain of anything in this age of flux and change... [if our] plans palpably fail, then, of course, we and every one else will try something different...We shall do well not to fear the future too much...we shall run more risk of jeopardising the future if we are influenced by indefinite fears based on trying to look ahead further than any one can see. (Keynes, 1946).

It would, however, be permissible to add that the statesman who was so concerned about ensuring symmetry between debtors and creditors in the adjustment process in the ICU would have been equally sensitive today to the other and growing asymmetry of income, development and welfare, and of the gap between the developed and developing countries in the international economic order. Keynes would have been led ineluctably to designing the framework for an orderly International Grants Economy to supplement the International Monetary and Exchange economy to arrive at the optimal policy mix of adjustment-cum-liquidity-cum-aid. There was no disjunction between efficiency, equity and ethics in Keynes's scheme of thought and values, which always strove to escape from "the Benthamite worm [over-valuation of the economic criterion] which has been gnawing at the insides of modern civilisation and is responsible for its present moral decay" (*My Early Beliefs*, 1938).

References

Frenkel, Jacob A. and Morris Goldstein (1986). "A Guide to Target Zones", IMF *Staff Papers* 33(4): 633–73, December.

Kahn, Lord Richard (1975). "On Re-reading Keynes", Fourth Keynes Lecture in Economics from *The Proceedings of the British Academy*, Vol. LX. London: Oxford University Press.

Keynes, John Maynard (1946). "The Balance of Payments of the United States", *The Economic Journal* 16(222) (June).

————. (1971–89). *The Collected Writings of John Maynard Keynes* (henceforth CW). Vols. I–XXX. Editors Austin Robinson, Donald Moggridge, Elizabeth Johnson, London: Macmillan.

————. (1971, 1913). , "Indian Currency and Finance", CW-I.

————. (1971, 1930). "A Treatisc on Money: Th e Applied Theory of Money", CW-VI.

————. (1973, 1936). "The General Theory of Employment, Interest and Money", CW-VII.

————. (1972, 1931). "Essays in Persuasion", CW-IX.

————. (1972, 1933). "Essays in Biography", CW-X.

————. (1976). "Activities: India and Cambridge", CW-XV.

————. (1978). "Activities 1920–2: Treaty Revision and Reconstruction", CW-XVII.

————. (1978). "Activities 1922–1932: The End of Reparations", CW-XVIII.

————. (1980). "Activities 1940–44: Shaping the Post-War World: The Clearing Union", CW-XXV.

————. (1980). "Activities 1940–46: Shaping the Post-War World: Employment and Commodities", CW-XXVII.

Keynes Papers (n.d.). "Keynes Proposals for an International Clearing Union", Command No. 6437. London: H.M.S.O. Copyright Cambridge, King's College Library.

Moggridge, Donald (1977). *Letter Commenting on an Article by Tim Congdon, Encounter,* September 1975, p.89. Cited by Lord Kahn, "A Comment", in T.W. Hutchinson (ed.), *Keynes v. the Keynesians...* London: The Institute of Economic Affairs. p.48.

————. (1986). "Keynés and the International Monetary System 1909–46", in Jon S. Cohen and G.C. Harcourt (eds.), *International Monetary Problems and Supply-Side Economics (Essays in Honour of Lorie Tarshish)*. New York: St. Martin's Press, pp.56–83.

Report of Committee on Industry and Trade (1931). Command No. 3897. London: H.M.S.O., p. 199.

Tobin, James (1984). "On the Efficiency of the Financial System", *Lloyd's Bank Review* (July).

Williamson, John (1983). "Keynes and the International Economic Order", in David Worswick and James Trevithick (eds.), *Keynes and the Modern World*. Cambridge: Cambridge University Press.

————. (1987). "Bancor and the Developing Countries: How Much Difference Would it Have Made?", in A.P. Thirlwall (ed.), *Keynes and Economic Development.* Basingstoke: Macmillan Press.

10 The Young Keynes as a Social Philosopher (1900–1909)

Keynes always regarded economics as a moral science and he was a philosopher by instinct and upbringing long before he turned to professional economics after working in India Office (1906-1908). During his youthful and formative years as a student at Eton and later when he read for the Mathematics Tripos at King's College, Cambridge (1902-1905) his primary intellectual interests were in ethics, logic and probability. Doubtless, his birth and upbringing in a strong non-conformist family generated and nourished a questioning mind, which never accepted truth but rather sought to arrive at it through writing and discourse in high-powered affinity groups, as evidenced by his impressive list of unpublished papers, which covered a variety of striking themes in ethics, metaphysics, aesthetics, social and political philosophy (Table 10.1).

A formative influence on Keynes's early thinking was his membership of the selective secret Cambridge Conversazione Society, better known as The Apostles, founded in 1820, which Keynes joined in 1903 as Apostle number 243. Its objectives were summed up by a prominent Apostle, Sidgwick, as "the pursuit of truth in absolute devotion and unreserved by a group of intimate friends...absolute candour was the only duty that the tradition of the society enforced" (Moggridge, 1992: 66). It comprised Cambridge University students and alumni, a truly distinguished roster which included names like A.N. Whitehead, Bertrand Russell, G.E. Moore, Henry Sidgwick, Lytton Strachey, Leonard Woolf, E.M. Forster, and the economist Treasury civil servant Ralph Hawtrey. But the moving spirit of the Apostles after Keynes's initiation was G.E. Moore and his classic *Principia Ethica*, which explains why a large number of Keynes's papers were addressed to issues raised by Moore. These fall into three groups: early papers written before graduation in June 1905; those written during the year after graduation in the first class, as Twelfth Wrangler in the Mathematics Tripos, Cambridge; and a mixed series of papers written after his return to Cambridge to teach in 1908. The papers most critical of *Principia Ethica* are in the undated second group of Table 10.1. In addition to the Apostles, Keynes was also an active participant in the Philosophical Society moderated by the pacifist social philosopher, Galsworthy Lowes Dickinson, a Fellow of King's College, and the intellectual architect of the League of Nations. This period also saw the early drafts of what eventually became a *Treatise on Probability* (1921).

Table 10.1

John Maynard Keynes: Unpublished Papers, 1904–1909

Dated Papers
The Differences Between East and West: Will They Ever Disappear? – Essay written at Eton College, November 1900
Beauty, 30 April 1904
The Political Doctrines of Edmund Burke, 2 October 1904 – Members' Prize for an English Essay
Truth, October 1904 (12 November 1904)
Toleration, November 1904
Virtue and Happiness (6 May 1905)
Miscellanea Ethica, July-September 1905
Society on 25 May 1912 (Read to Lowes Dickinson's Philosophical Society on 1 November 1905)
Modern Civilisation (28 October 1905)
Paradise (1905)
Shall We Write Melodramas? (3 February 1906)
Egoism, 24 February 1906
Obligation, 2 April 1906
Posterior Analytics (19 May 1906)
Appearances, 8 February 1908 (re-read 19 November 1910)
Prince Henry on Prince Rupert, 28 November 1908
Science and Art, 20 February 1909
The Present Position of Metaphysics in the Society, 29 May 1909
Can We Consume our Surplus? Or the Influence of Furniture on Love (13 November 1909)
Undated Papers
Shall We Write Filth Packets?
Proposition 93 of *Principia Ethica*, 'Ethics in Relation to Conduct'
Have We a Panacea?
On Art Criticism
The Principle of Organic Unity, read again 22 January 1921
British Achievements under Queen Victoria

Source: This is a modified version of the original in D.E. Moggridge.

Dates in parentheses are as ascertained by Moggridge from Keynes's correspondence or in consultation with Professor G.E.R. Lloyd and refer to the date of their discussion—normally at a meeting of Dickinson's Philosophical Society.

If Moore domesticated Keynes's ethical thinking, it was Edmund Burke who was, arguably, the single most formative influence of Keynes's political philosophy, as testified by his masterly essay on 'The Political Doctrines of Edmund Burke' (JMK/UA/20/3), which won him the Members' Prize (so called because it was a gift of the Members of Parliament) and Declamation Prize at Cambridge. It is notable alike for its elaborate scholarly apparatus, somewhat exceptional in Keynes's writings, as well as its substance. Keynes regarded Burke as "perhaps the only political writer, the direct bearing of whose works is wholly topical and contemporary, who could be approached as the source of a consistent and coherent body of political theory" (UA/20/3/4, p. 1) "... Next to India and her affairs, all matters concerning the theory and practice of finance and commerce engaged his deepest attention throughout his career" (ibid.: 29). His essay is a most admiring and circumspect evaluation of Burke's views on *laissez faire*, individualism, property, prescriptive rights, economics, civil liberty, democracy, Empire, the Church establishment, self-government, and the French Revolution.

Keynes stressed that Burke was inclined in his doctrines to "extravagance of their enunciations" (ibid.: 35) and was equally critical of his "dream of a representative class [which] can never be fulfilled...all experience goes to show that no one class can adequately represent either the feelings or the interest of the whole" (ibid.: 58). This latter statement is of particular interest insofar as it tends to rebut the generally elitist stance of Keynes in his obsessive concern with the qualitative eugenics of population and admiration for the Great Villiers Connection in Britain – ability and character run in intergenerational stocks and "that certain small "connections" have produced eminent characters out of all proportion to their size" (1972: 62).

To conclude, Keynes divided Burke's precepts into four main classes: "the science of politics is concerned with means and not ends" (ibid.: 81).

First, "it is not wise to look too far ahead; our powers of prediction are slight, our command over remote results infinitesimal."

Secondly, "there are precepts which are of a negative character...matters affecting persons in their individual capacities should be left alone."

Third are "those rules of a legal nature which shall be with the greatest rigorousness...and only infringed in moments of national crisis and emergency like the sanctity of property and prescription."

In the fourth class "come those rules dealing with the special modes and contrivances of government...which vary with locality and time...corruption, the most dangerous foe of good government be combated by every means; this is the one real and legitimate object of reform. Statesmen must learn wisdom in the school of Burke."

For all his admiration for Burke, Keynes, oddly, overlooked his magisterial indictment of the maladministration of the East India Company in his impeachment of Warren Hastings, the Governor General, in the House of Commons. Keynes would have had a less anodyne view of the *Raj* in India if he had absorbed fully the gravamen of Burke's charges.

The subsequent sections evaluate selected essays that collectively convey the flavour of his overall social and political philosophy of scepticism based on an enduring faith in the powers of reason over passion.

Untitled Essay on British Achievements under Queen Victoria[1]

In this synoptic essay, possibly his first recorded writing at Eton, Keynes strikes a balance sheet of the more notable achievements of Victorian Britain, which also gives us glimpses into the young Keynes's worldview. He notes the "wonderful strides parliamentary reform has made" and cites the repeal of the Corn Laws, abolition of Test Acts, the passage of the Reform Bills, election by ballot, and "a system of public finance sounder than in any other country in the world, where the capitalist bears the heavier burden." He notes that "it is no longer necessary for a member of Parliament to distribute wholesale bribes among his constituents" but adds shrewdly, "it is thought sufficient if he subscribes to all local charities deserving or otherwise." For all that "the country is not yet as tolerant as might be desired but a great advance has been made in this direction. The non-conformists have a far better position than ever before and it was a great step when the universities were opened to them." Concurrently, the "advance in morality and in the influence of the Church has been little short of marvellous...the Oxford movement though it went too far in some cases has awakened the Church from a torpor into which it was beginning to fall." Likewise, Keynes observed: "Humanitarianism is one of the products of the nineteenth century." We have

> societies for the protection of every thing from children to commons; women have entered almost every walk of life except the law and the Church; the philanthropist is more rampant than ever before...well organised charity has to a large extent taken the place of promiscuous doles; the Imperial Penny postage has done much to knit the country and the colonies; the standard of comfort is higher than before...we have outstripped other nations...Liberty, equality and fraternity cried the French; with liberty, equality and morality England has won her way.

Keynes also took a somewhat Panglossian view of British imperialism and of having "perforce taken up the "white man's burden" under which we must endeavour to wield the powers of Empire with more lasting effect and to greater good than the mighty empires...of history." Keynes has, of course, been rightly censured for his overly conventional posture on British imperialism but no historian will deny the comparative beneficence of British as against other European imperialisms when one thinks of its contributions to education, infrastructure, meritocratic civil service, rule of law, creation of self-governing institutions in its colonies and dependencies, most notably in India. On the other hand, there was a glaring economic downside to British imperialism as in the unilateral drain of wealth and income from India, coupled with the unequal and unfair terms of trade (Dirks, 2006). Modern Britain was heavily dependent on the colonial state for its sustenance.

Keynes, however, was more acute in evaluating the aftermath of British colonialism in America. Thus, in a perceptive review of the Seventh Volume of the *Cambridge Modern History* (in the *Cambridge Review*, September 1903) he pinpointed the core weakness of the politics of the newly liberated American colonies:

> While the question of State Rights, with that of slavery interwoven with it, was to the fore, there was a real and fundamental cleavage in political parties; but the absence, with this exception, of any clear or abiding distinction has been the bane of American politics; it is a condition that necessarily encourages an opportunism of the basest kind; and where there is nothing at stake but office the country is captured by the cleverest catch-word. Of course, on any given question parties ranged themselves on opposite sides, but in the absence of traditional principles the side chosen is more a question of opportunity than of conviction. (UA/18/3/5).

The uncanny insights into American politics are still pertinent and on par with those of specialist commentators on US affairs and society like De Tocqueville and Denis Brogan.

Toleration[2]

The theme of this paper in a sense flows from the preceding essay, where Keynes recognises that Victorian Britain is "not yet a country as tolerant as might be desired", but more importantly, it touches on the core values of a liberal democracy, namely, the extent of tolerance of dissent, a question which was revived in political discourse in England in the context of the 'controversy over the French Congregations'. Keynes starkly posed the central question: is it a universal precept or only a useful rule to be practised "according to circumstances and the nature of each individual case...when it suits our purposes" (p. 2). If 'tolerant' is defined to mean "tolerant in action rather than in sentiment or opinion" and if one considers "the actions of individuals in groups, rather than private capacities" then "belief in any doctrine of universal toleration is comparatively new" (pp.1-2). It certainly did not enter the minds of some of the most eminent preachers of toleration in the history of opinion. Thus, Milton denied it to Papists on the ground that they were idolaters. Locke argued that the State could not tolerate Papists because they could not be relied on to keep faith with heretics and atheists "were not at all to be tolerated." Rousseau did not admit atheists in his *Social Contract* and Burke described them as outlaws of the constitution not only the human race. They all believed in toleration "but within limits" (p.3)

Intolerance is "more likely to be used on the side of old falsehoods than on that of the new truths" (p.5). But Keynes is extremely circumspect on the implications of the use of intolerance and considers possible alternatives. We may, following Burke, regard "it as a thing which we have no right to use under any circumstances" (p.6). This Keynes rejects because "there is no action whatever, of which it may be said without reservations and qualifications, that it ought always to be performed." We may regard it "as a good general rule not to be broken lightly, but sometimes to be cast aside after the most careful deliberation" based "on probabilities that must guide our actions" (p.7). This is "true so far as it goes but does it go far enough?" There are "considerable difficulties in communicating doctrine of toleration in any absolute form...are we to allow free propagation of all opinions, however disastrous we may believe such opinions to be?" It "is , in no sense, a universal doctrine but that it would be a good thing for the world if we always treat it as if it were" (p.10).

Remarkably, Keynes, always the gentle sceptic, ends on a very judicious note: "but the object of these scattered remarks has been rather to open discussion than to conclude it."

A necessary concomitant of toleration, according to Keynes, would be:

> The liberty not to be impartial is one of the few liberties still left to us, and you must not try to take it away...the young should be made aware of the existence of two points of view and of the warmth and quality of feeling attached to it; and it is unavoidable that warm-hearted authors should see some facts through coloured spectacles. (CW, XXVII: 43).

This was in response to a leading article on 'Complete Impartiality' in the *New Statesmen and Nation*, 21 January 1935, on a controversy on the choice of school textbooks in London, which arose with the appointment of the Tawney Committee to examine and report on the matter. It is interesting to compare Keynes on toleration with the sentiments of E.M. Forster, a fellow Bloomsbury Apostle, on his plea for Tolerance (1951), who persuasively argued:

> Love is a great force in private life...but love in public affairs does not work. It has been tried again and again by Christian civilisations of the Middle Ages and also by the French Revolution, a secular movement which reasserted the Brotherhood of Man. It has always failed...we can love what we know personally. And we cannot know much. In public affairs...

> something much less dramatic and emotional is needed, namely, tolerance...a very dull virtue. It is negative. It is the only force which will enable different races and classes and interests to settle down together to the work of reconstruction ... tolerance is not the same as weakness. (pp. 59-63)

Surely, the most positive statement ever in support of a negative virtue. That Forster should echo the theme of the young Keynes on toleration after five decades is truly remarkable. Equally, it shows up the inadequacies of the Apostles' commitment to absolute truth or even absolute beliefs, a nuance well elucidated in Keynes's provocative paper on Paradise (JMK/UA/34) where he draws a distinction between the Christian religion which "it is impossible" for him "to believe in any unqualified or unvarnished shape" while clinging with whole tenacity of our natures to Christian doctrine, a doctrine which raised the British and ruined the Roman Empires." To this he added, for good measure, an idiosyncratic list of his beliefs, which included "women's suffrage, the new Mathematical Tripos, abolition of the House of Lords and the Sodomy Acts, cheap weekend tickets, in Heaven and Hell and the Tories Book Club." Keynes, however, never cared in his lifetime to explain or comment on the strange counter-intuitive phenomenon of female Anti-Suffragism in Victorian Britain headed by Mrs Humphrey Ward and others.

Have We a Panacea?[3]

In this essay Keynes raises a series of questions on the futility of utopianism and bemoans the "great lack of moral enthusiasm in the most respectable political theories of today" like Comte's worship of the Great Being, and those of Bentham, and the Utilitarianism of the doctrinaire liberals. "We are even working towards evolution...and believe in nothing whatever" (p.1). He cites Burke as probably the "first to voice the modern feeling of helplessness and worthlessness of panaceas." He emphasised

> the slightness of our power over the future, the inutility of attempting means to ends remote...and we cannot set before ourselves anything more particular than general welfare... political utopias compete with the last popular mood and not with the parliamentary reports. (ibid.: 3).

Keynes concludes that "mankind is to be saved by thought and not love... but how is intellect ever to hold its own against the force or fury of those who think they have a panacea?" (p.4). Keynes's pessimism has been proved more than right by the subsequent depredations of Fascism, Nazism, consumerism and now, more recently, by the onset of Islamist fundamentalism. The essay is a cautionary tale against the ever-present perils of utopianism and by inference an endorsement of what much later Karl Popper called "piecemeal social engineering" as opposed to holistic social engineering.

Modern Civilisation[4]

Keynes addresses the "real as opposed to the phenomenal meaning of modern civilisation...whose fabric is being shaken...whose duties are changing... our ultimate goods are eternal and unchanged" [Moore]. He argued that "metaphysically we can give no rules" with "a wide and general validity that they ought to be obeyed as if they were universal" but "we shall do well to avail ourselves of the general bank and capital of nations and of ages" [Burke] (p.1-2). From this, he deduced, arises that class of actions, commonly known as duties that are generally recognised to be useful to claim our performance irrespective of particular circumstance like the Ten Commandments type of duties, family duties, social duties, public duties. But we are in labour over changes in the sheer scale of the social organisation which will revolutionise our concept of duty into "new duties between buyers and sellers, whether of labour or commodity" (p.5)...."all duties are with respect to time and place" (p.9). Men may not read *Principia Ethica* but "good is changeless and apart, the ought shifts and fades and grows new shapes and forms" (p.10). Keynes thus proclaimed the centrality of obligation as against rights and goods.

'The Differences between East and West: Will They Ever Disappear?'[5]

In this remarkably precocious and richly suggestive essay written at the age of 17 while a student at Eton, Keynes offers daring insights, worthy of a Toynbee or a Spengler, into the eternally controversial theme of the contrasts between Eastern and Western civilisations and the question whether they will ever disappear. A Manichaean divide on which the jury will always be out.

Keynes defines East and West as broadly cultural categories rather than ethnic entities. The West is defined by him as Western Europe encompassing Switzerland, Germany and France beyond which is the East:

> the habitation genie of spirits...chiefly evil...the home of mystery...a new world...in which time is nothing and humanity is nothing; their counter-influences first came into contact in the struggle between Persia and Greece [which embody] one of the root distinctions unchanged to our own times. (p.1).

Keynes then formulates a most interesting typology to differentiate West from East. "In the West it is the individual that is all-important: in the East the mass" and from this it is possible to trace more than one noticeable difference. First, and most obviously, "democracy...prevalent in Europe" whereas in Asia absolute despotism must be not only prevalent but preferable and necessary. Secondly, the oriental idea in the primacy of "the belief of the unity of the deity" carries "the theory of the mass as opposed to the individual to its logical conclusion" to consider "the whole human race as a single body under one Supreme Being. In contrast, the West investing earthly authority in a number of individuals, equally naturally drifted to a pantheon." Thirdly, "from this trampling down of the personality of individual [in the East] we may trace that lack of humanity and that abominable cruelty, which flashes out at intervals from the normal oriental stagnation." Fourthly,

> the oriental individual...is heavily oppressed by the greatness of the deity and his own personal insignificance...'Allah is Great' is a noble rule of life, unrelieved by the freedom of Christianity, overwhelms and checks originality and causes that lack of progress which is characteristic of Eastern affairs.

For Keynes this last is perhaps the most important reason why "the East formed the great civilisations of the past and why it is incapable of further advance...it is altogether lacking in that initiative and invention which can emanate only from individuals and without which further progress is impossible" (p.2). Keynes concedes that "the West has learnt much from the East" but goes on to consider some critical counterfactuals. "Had Persia overwhelmed Greece freedom would have been crushed throughout Europe; if the victorious Turk had not been stayed the East would have swept away Christianity...if the Indian mutiny had been successful, India would have become the home of anarchy and bloodshed" (p.2). It is significant that Keynes excludes Russia and Slavonic Europe from the ambit of the West because for him, as explained much later (1922), "the Russian, who oscillates between a reckless egotism and a vague universalism, is not comfortable with the organised individualism of Western Europe" (CW, XVII: 436), which, for Keynes, is the defining and enduring characteristic of the West.

How well does Keynes's evaluation of the East-West divide stand up in the light of history and critical scholarship? Certainly, history bears ample testimony to what he called the "abominable cruelty which flows out at intervals from the normal oriental stagnation." A perfect example of this are the periodic unprovoked invasions of Europe by the Turks or those of the Central Asian despots which led the distinguished American historian, Will Durant, to label the Mohammedan conquest of India as the 'most barbarous in the annals of mankind'. Equally, Keynes was right in his counterfactuals about the Indian mutiny (1857), which failed because there was no coherent and viable Indian polity ready to assume power from the British: only a congeries of warring principalities and factions. Similarly, Eastern civilisations like Moorish Spain and the Islamic caliphates and imperial China became fossilised after reaching a certain apogee.

Likewise, in validation of Keynes's distinction of West and East, one could invoke the philosopher Karl Popper's dichotomy of open and closed societies. The West, by and large, represents open society marked by a belief in individual initiative and moral responsibility and the affirmation of individualism in all forms moral and methodological. Open societies are abstract and impersonal entities that, by their very nature, "set free the critical powers of man" (Popper, 1984, vol. I: 1). In contrast, closed societies are of a semi-organic nature and place submission to authority among the highest values. They connote primacy of the collective over the individual and the denial of individualism in all forms. Historically, individual rights have never had institutional recognition in the East which has had no counterparts to the Magna Carta, the Bill of Rights, or the Federalist Papers. The West has been the domain of democracy since the establishment of Icelandic Commonwealth in year 930 of the Christian era, whereas the East has been the habitat of despotism. Although Islam provides for *ijtehad* (independent judgement) this has been virtually a dead letter because the scriptures (the *Quran* and the *Hadith*) are regarded as the final and definitive statements on matters of faith, worship and status. There is no Islamic counterpart to the exegesis of the Bible and the Talmud; it would be tantamount to apostasy. Even authoritative scholars of Islam like Bernard Lewis have failed to explain the lapse of *ijtehad*. The Islamic doctrine of the organic unity of religion (*Deen*) and state (*D'awa*) also precludes public debate and secular democracy. Likewise, the concept of *Jahiyiliyah* interdicts pre-Islamic and non-Islamic knowledge and learning, an egregious manifestation of which is the tragic destruction of the ancient Indian universities of Takshila, Nalanda, Udantapura, and Vikramshila—older than Oxbridge and the Sorbonne—by the Muslim rulers of India.

All these factors together explain why the Enlightenment never took root in the Islamic world and its consequent fossilisation and regression. Concomitantly, another anti-modernist influence is the Andalus syndrome, and its variant the Taj syndrome, a vacuous societal nostalgia among Muslims for the vanished glories of Moorish Spain and the Delhi sultanate. Contemporary Muslim scholars attest to this and the failure of the modernist Aligarh model in Muslim societies as against the mystic and eclectic Sufi and the triumphalist Deobandi and Wahabi models which today undergird Islamic extremism (Akbar Ahmed, 2007). Interestingly, the mature Keynes too reverted to this theme in a letter to Bernard Shaw (1934): "My feelings about *Das Kapital* are the same as about the *Koran*...its dreary, out-of-date, academic controversialising seems so extraordinarily unsuitable as material for the purpose. How could either of these books carry fire and sword round half the world?" (CW, XXVIII: 38).

Characteristically, Keynes's acute analysis leads him to ask the lead question: whether "the two branches of the human race will continue to live side by side, or whether the one will succeed in absorbing the other"? (p.2). He addresses this by

> taking into consideration the characteristics of two oriental races, which seem to have little in common either in their physique or in habits—*viz.*, the Chinese and the Jews who have done their utmost to make themselves indistinguishable, and they have signally failed. It is not that the Jews are traditionally the accursed race that makes anti-semites; it is because they have in them deep-rooted instincts that are antagonistic and therefore repulsive to the European, and their presence amongst us is a living example of the insurmountable difficulties in merging race characteristics in making cats love dogs.' (p.2).

Years later (1939), E.M. Forster worried that "Jew-consciousness is in the air…anti-semitism is now the most shocking of all things" (1974: 30-31). These are highly provocative statements that merit very careful analysis. To begin with, Keynes perpetrates an empirical fallacy by lumping together European Jews (Ashkenazim) and the oriental Jews (Sephardim). On the other hand, he was more right than he knew in a cultural sense in light of contemporary scholarship. Thus, Jeremy Adler calls Franz Steiner, the noted Jewish Czech anthropologist and German poet 'an Oriental in the West' (1999: 16), which was confirmed by Steiner, who would always refer to Jews as "we orientals" and dilate on the affinity of Hebrews and Hindus (Chandavarkar, 1994: 15). But Keynes displayed a raw indefensible genetic and cultural anti-semitism when he called them the 'accursed race', a prejudice not uncommon among the British intelligentsia in those days and which was bred even in the best public schools. European Jews have always been well assimilated in their host countries, a fact which did not save them ultimately from the German holocaust.

Keynes's remarks on the Chinese, too, smack of typical European prejudice despite his recognition of their 'unequalled and unparalleled antiquity'. "For morality they are saints, for cruelty they are fiends. Devoid of the finer virtues [they are] unrestrained by respect for human life…the European can no more hope to transform the Chinese than to tame the race of tigers" (p.2). For all that, Keynes assuredly did not subscribe to the popular bogey of the Yellow Peril and conceded that "there is no reason to fear that the Chinese will ever swarm over Europe." He concluded: judging by history, "it is difficult to find reasonable grounds for hoping that the differences between the East and West will be erased by agency of space or time" and concurred with the Psalmist

> as far as the East is from the West. Nature is dual in all her functions; every property has its converse; every value its complement...the two branches of the human race, distinct and antagonistic, have existed, exist, and shall exist until that day when history shall cease to repeat itself. (ibid.).

A pessimistic but wholly realistic assessment. True, the East has always been mysterious to the West. But is the converse not equally true?

As a counterpoint it is interesting to juxtapose the sentiments of a Cambridge contemporary of Keynes, the philosopher Lowes Dickinson, who thought the "Chinese the most civilised of nations...in manners, feelings and art they have a higher achievement...only their 'civilisation' is decadent" (1973: 184). On Japan he wrote: "It's so pleasant to find an Eastern civilization holding its head up...everything seems capable, and efficient and self-respecting. No decay, no squalor, and yet not all Westernized" (ibid.), an assessment well echoed by the noted Japanese economist, Michio Morishima, who wrote about Japanese ethos and Western technology, a successful synthesis. Interestingly, Dickinson felt that "Indian art, Indian religion, Indian society is alien and unsympathetic. What indeed is there or can be in common between the tradition of Greece and that of India?" (ibid.: 181). It would be hard to fault Dickinson's well-measured appraisal of the East-West question but then they are the thoughts of a mature philosopher in contrast to the unbuttoned effusions of a callow Keynes. In sum, this early compilation of Keynes is a fascinating outlier in the Keynes canon, a grand theme which he never revisited.

This piece, however, merits a qualifying postscript by Keynes who himself, for all his merited endorsement of the criticality of individualism for human progress also endorsed the view, much later (1922) invoking Tolstoy, to also recognise that the real cause of epoch-making historical events and change is not particular persons or leaders, whether monarchs, politicians or intellectuals, but the conjoined activity of the masses. "The greatest of Russians has himself taught us how to judge the great movements of history. They are not produced through the execution of power by a few, nor by the intellectual activity of a few but by the activity of all men taking part in the event" (CW, XVII: 438). This, once again, is one of those perennial issues on which the jury can rest. In turn, it also poses the great conundrum: Is it possible, or even conceivable, for the masses to act in unison without a prime leader, like Charlemagne, Napoleon, Lenin, Churchill, or Mao Zedong? The Great Men theory of history is not without merit. For all that, Keynes's endorsement of Tolstoy is yet one more proof of his perennial eclecticism.

NOTES

1 KCKP (King's College Keynes Papers): JMK/PP/31/7, no date.

2 KCKP: JMK/UA/21, November 1904.

3 KCKP: UA/37/1-4.

4 KCKP: JMK/UA/22/1-10, 28 October 1905.

5 KCKP: JMK/PP/34/4, November 1900, Eton College.

REFERENCES

Ahmed, Akbar (2007). *Journey into Islam: The Crisis of Globalization.* Washington, DC: The Brookings Institution Press.

Backhouse, Roger E. and Bradley W. Bateman (2006). *The Cambridge Companion to Economics.* Cambridge: Cambridge University Press.

Bateman, Bradley W. and John B. Davis (1991). *Keynes and Philosophy (Essays on the Origins of Keynes's Thought).* Aldershot: Edward Elgar.

Chandavarkar, Anand (1994). "Franz Steiner", *The Times Literary Supplement*, 25 November, p.15.

Davis, John B. (1994). *Keynes' Philosophical Development.* Cambridge: Cambridge University Press.

Dirk, Nicholas B. (2006). *The Scandal of the Empire: India and the Creation of Imperial Britain.* Cambridge, Mass.: Harvard University Press.

Forster, E.M. (1976). *Two Cheers for Democracy.* Harmondsworth: Penguin.

Keynes, John Maynard (1972). *Essays in Biography, The Collected Writings of John Maynard Keynes.* Vol. X. London: Macmillan.

————. (1977). *Activities 1920–22 (Treaty Revision and Reconstruction).* Elizabeth Johnson (ed.). London: Macmillan.

Lowes Dickinson, Goldsworthy (1973). "Autobiography", Dennis Proctor (ed.). London: Duckworth.

Moggridge, D.E. (1992). *Maynard Keynes: (An Economist's Biography).* London: Routledge.

O'Donnell, R.M. (ed.) (1989). *Keynes: Philosophy, Economics and Politics.* New York: St Martin's Press.

————. (1991). *Keynes as Philosopher-Economist.* The Ninth Keynes Seminar held at the University of Kent, Canterbury. New York: St Martin's Press.

Popper, Karl (1984). *The Open Society and its Enemies.* Vol. I, London: Routledge.

11 Was Keynes Anti-Semitic?

He is like quicksilver on a sloping board—a little inhuman but very kindly, as inhuman people are.

—Virginia Woolf on Keynes,
Diary Vol. 1, 1915-1919

John Maynard Keynes once gently admonished his future wife, Lydia Lopokova, to do her best to compose her quarrel with her beloved friend Vera, daughter of a wealthy Jewish Ukrainian landowner (later wife of Harold Bowen, a British diplomat and oriental scholar) "So far as I am concerned, I don't quarrel. Why should one quarrel about racial characteristics? It is no good" (Hill and R. Keynes, 1989: 107). Having delivered this homily, Keynes himself lapsed within a few months of it when he wrote to Lydia: "Oh, what a Jew Vera is with her tirelessness. I see why you and she get on together. You are so very uncircumcised, that the two of you make a good average and are equal when you added up to two Christians?" (ibid.: 31).

Judging alike by his unpublished writings (at King's College, Cambridge) and his *Collected Writings*, Keynes would appear to have been peculiarly conscious—even in his dreams—of what he thought were the typical racial characteristics of Jews. Recounting a dream to Lydia he said: "But there was one man who took no notice of the tiger. When I asked him how this was, he replied, 'Oh, I am not all tasty—look at my hands, and then I saw that he was a Jew'" (ibid. 25). Keynes seems to have shared the commonly accepted anti-semitism of the British middle and upper classes of his time. In the 1930s, the editor of the American periodical *New Republic* was shocked by one of his milder *obiter dicta* and protested that the readers of his journal could never stand for it (E. Johnson, 1978: 46). Much the same sentiment is echoed years later by Robert Skidelsky (1986: 360): "Klotz [the French minister of finance in the post-World War I negotiations] represented to Keynes, the other face of France's grasping sterility; a view not uninfluenced by the anti-semitism [Klotz was a Jew] which was normal to his class and generation."

Source: Economic and Political Weekly XXXV(19), 6 May 2000.

But before addressing the specific question of Keynes's own prejudices, it is only fair to record that British anti-semitism, like its European counterpart, was by no means a monopoly of the middle and upper classes—a hoary Marxist myth. It was as prevalent among the working classes. As George Orwell rightly reminds us, "It was largely trade union opposition that prevented a big influx of German Jewish refugees. The Blimps were after the refugees because they were largely socialists and the working class line was 'What did they want to come here for'" (Orwell, 1942).

The public perception of Keynes as an anti-semite seems to gain further credence by his published letters to his wife, Lydia Lopokova. David Pryce Jones (1989: 994) while emphasising that these "letters...served an essentially private purpose", pointedly notes that "almost the only attitude the two held in common was anti-semitism, and both go out of their way to indulge in it." Harrod's pioneering biography of Keynes does not even refer to Keynes' attitudes towards Jews, much less discuss it. The devout Harrod was as concerned to overlook Keynes's anti-semitism as he was to suppress any reference to his androgeneity. The icon just could not be besmirched.

What, in fact, is the nature of the evidence to substantiate Keynes's anti-semitism? This question merits careful analysis and appraisal, not only because of the gravity of the charge and Keynes's eminence as a seminal intellect and public figure, but equally because one of the still less researched aspects of Keynes's many-sided personality, despite the fecundity and range of Keynesian scholarship, are his attitudes to Jews as a people and to Zionism as a cause.

The Anti-Semite

Possibly the earliest available manifestation of Keynes's attitude to Jews is to be found in a provocative essay he wrote as a 17-year old Etonian on 'The Differences between East and West: Will They Ever Disappear?', which is as remarkable for its daring historical insights and almost Toynbeean generalisations as for its quirks and prejudices. The young Keynes asked

> whether these two branches of the human race (European and Oriental) will continue to live side by side, or whether the one will succeed in absorbing the other. We can best discuss this question by taking into consideration the characteristics of two oriental races...*viz.*, the Chinese and the Jews [who]...have done their utmost to make themselves indistinguishable from Europeans and they have signally failed. It is not that the Jews are traditionally the accursed race that makes anti-semites, it is because they have in them deep-rooted instincts that are antagonistic and therefore repulsive to the European, and their presence amongst us is a living example of the insurmountable difficulties that exist in merging race characteristics, in making cats love dogs! (Keynes, 1900: 2)

Although the Jews fared better with the young Keynes than the Chinese who are the subject of apocalyptic pronouncements ('the Europeans can no more hope to transform the Chinese than to tame the race of tigers, and nothing less than a second flood will exterminate them') the stereotype of the Jew, so common in Edwardian and Victorian England as in contemporary Europe, as an Oriental was too readily accepted by Keynes. Popular and even intellectual discourse then as now was also prone to the common fallacy of the racial misaggregation of the European Jew (the Ashkenazi) and the oriental Jew (the Sephardi).

Keynes's youthful sentiments about the Jews were no doubt also reflective of the prevalent anti-semitism in British public schools. Even India's first prime minister, Jawaharlal Nehru, recalls as a student at Harrow (1906-07), that

> There were a few Jews in our house and at other houses, they got on fairly well but there was always a background of anti-semitic feeling. They were the 'damned Jews', and so on, almost unconsciously, I began to think that it was the proper thing to have the feeling. I never really felt anti-semitic in the heart, and in later years, I had many good friends among the Jews. (Nehru, 1988: 18)

The exuberance of Keynes, the public school boy, is understandable but even the adult Keynes never seems to have outgrown the younger Keynes's European perception of the Jew as an oriental. In his published obituary of his mentor, Edwin Montagu, the Jewish Secretary of State for India, Keynes wrote: "That he was an oriental, equipped, nevertheless, with the intellectual technique and atmosphere of the West, drew him naturally to the political problems of India, and allowed an instinctive, natural sympathy between him and its people" (Keynes, 1972: 41). It is noteworthy that although Keynes did not either in this memoir or in any of his other published works ever refer to Montagu as a Jew, he described Montagu in one of his letters to Lydia as "one of the Jews of divided nature—half artist and lover, and half consumed with extravagant desires and ambitions ... an emperor, a tout and a child: also a wit, an actor and a gambler..." (Hill and Keynes, 1989: 256). The subspecies of 'Jews of divided nature' is certainly a novel addition to Jewish typology.

It must be remembered that Keynes's prejudices against Orientals—in this case Jews and Chinese—did not inhibit his spirited defence of another group of Orientals, namely, Indian students at Cambridge following a scurrilous article in *The Cambridge Review* (20 May 1909). Keynes regretted the publication of this article "so lacking in discernment and good feeling" containing "the commonplace of prejudice, which should not have been brought forward anonymously and unsubstantiated" (Chapter X: 405). These admirable sentiments appear to have been submerged later, judging by the evidence of anti-semitism scattered throughout his *Collected Writings*.

Keynes seems to have been prone to varying episodes of anti-semitism and he continued to accept the jaded Jewish stereotypes which are so often the staple of Euro-American demonology. Keynes's writings ring with the all too familiar litany of Jewish physiognomy, Jewish deportment and manners, Jewish traits of character and habits of mind. He used 'Jewish post' as slang for gossip, as when he described his friend Sebastian Sprott as the best 'Jewish Post in town' (Hill and Keynes, 1989: 295, 312).

Even in describing eminent gentiles like the economist Stanley Jevons, Keynes could scarcely refrain bringing in 'Jewishness'. He draws a vivid physical portrait of Jevons with "crinkly beard, curling hair, a broad brow and square face, full nostrils, and full, somewhat protruding lower lip, his countenance was almost, one might say, of Jewish cast..."(CW, IX: 149). Writing to Kingsley Wood, Chancellor of the Exchequer, on 2 June 1941, Keynes found the younger US civil servants and advisors to be "exceptionally capable and vigorous (with the very gritty Jewish type perhaps a little too prominent)" (CW, XXIII: 103). He even branded one of them, Edward Bernstein (later the first director of research of the IMF) as "a ghetto rat, brilliant but unwilling to listen to reason" (Black, 1991: 39). Would Keynes have encountered any of his Jewish types among the bronzed, blue-eyed sabras in the kibbutzim, the Israeli civil service or defence forces, the dons of the Hebrew University, the boffins of the Weizmann Institute, or in the animated sidewalk cafes of the Dizengoff Circle in Tel Aviv?

The *Collected Writings* of Keynes no doubt abound in textbook examples, direct and oblique, of anti-semitism. After describing Bolshevism as a "delirium bred by besotted idealism and intellectual error out of the sufferings and peculiar temperaments of Slavs and Jews", he remarked that the economic and commercial ineptitude of the Russian Slavs had put them, "more than any other Europeans at the mercy of their Jews" (CW, XVIII: 373-374, 436) whose economic acumen is the subject of characteristically allusive references to compound interest. "Perhaps it is not an accident that the race which did most to bring the promise of immortality into the heart and essence of our religion has also done most for the principle of compound interest and particularly loves this most purposive of human institutions" (CW, IX: 330).

Without denying or defending Keynes's anti-semitism, it should also be said for the record that Keynes could be witheringly caustic about organised anti-semitism as well as other national groups like the Americans and the French. Keynes described Poland as "an economic impossibility with no industry but Jew-baiting" (CW, II: 185). Writing to Duncan Grant, Keynes said, "The only really sympathetic and original thing in America is the niggers, who are charming" (Skidelsky, 1936: 342). He complained, too, at having to listen to "...vain, mendacious and interminable French and hateful Yank twang" at the Inter-Allied Council for War Purchase and Finance (ibid.: 343).

But then some of my best friends are Jewish is, of course, the time-worn defence of even the most unreconstructed anti-semites like H.L. Mencken. Keynes's personal relations with Jews too illustrate the ambivalence of his brand of anti-semitism. For Keynes, as for his fellow Apostles and Bloomsberries, friendships were not merely instrumental but the highest of values in keeping with the philosophy of G.E. Moore, which animated the Bloomsbury group, rather like Forster's friendship with Ross Masood. Keynes's coteries, whatever their failings, would not be regarded as anti-semitic, with the solitary exception of Virginia Woolf who, of course, had married Leonard Woolf, a Jewish member of the Bloomsbury group. It was Leonard Woolf and Lytton Strachey who secretly vetted Keynes to be a member of the Apostles. "Though they did not like Keynes, ...they were certain of his intellectual suitability" (Spotts, 1989: 29).

Keynes had three acknowledged mentors of whom the latter two were Jewish. The first of these was Alfred Marshall, the eminent economist, the second was Lionel Abrahams (Financial Secretary and later Under Secretary of State for India), who contributed most to the clarification and development of Keynes's ideas on the complexities of Indian finance. Lastly, and most important, was Edwin Montagu, the Secretary of State for India, who played such a decisive role in advancing the public career of Keynes (Chandavarkar, 1989: 190–191). But very significantly Keynes never referred, at least publicly, to Abrahams and Montagu as Jewish. Keynes, in his early lectures at Cambridge (1909-1910) went out of his way to pay handsome tribute to the percipience and originality of Abrahams (Sayers, 1972: 593). Admittedly, Keynes's public memoir of Edwin Montagu does not convey his deep gratitude and affection for him which found such heartfelt expression in his letter to Lydia (Hill and Keynes, 1989: 256).

> I am a little sad at the death of Edwin Montagu. I owed—rather surprisingly—nearly all my steps in life to him. When I was a freshman at Cambridge in 1902, he was president of the Union (the chief undergraduate society) and picked me out in my first term to give me what is called 'a place on the paper'. The first electioneering I ever did in 1906 was for him. In 1913 when he was at the India Office, it was he who got me put on the Royal Commission

> on Indian Currency, which was my first step into publicity (my name was known to no one outside Cambridge before then). It was he who got me called to the Treasury in 1915 during the war. It was he who got me taken to Paris in February of that year for the first inter-Allied Financial Conference and so established me in my war work. It was he who got me taken to the great ones (I first met Lloyd George in a famous dinner party of four at his house: I first met McKenna through him; I first met Margot (Asquith) sitting next to her at dinner in his house). It was he who got me invited to the dinners of the Inner Secretaries during the early part of the war (private gatherings of the Secretaries of the Cabinet and of the ministers who exchanged the secret news and discussed after dinner the big problems of the war). He was the minister to whom I was responsible during the first part of the Peace Conference. It was he who appointed me Vice-Chairman of the Indian Fiscal Commission in 1921. It was he who invited me to join the Mission to Brazil last year. [Keynes did not go with them on the mission.] Thus for more than 20 years I had reason to be grateful to him; and there was a certain affectionate relationship between us.

How many beneficiaries of Keynes's eminence could be found to express their gratitude to their benefactors? Another prominent Jewish friend of Keynes was Reading (Rufus Isaacs), the Viceroy of India (1921–1926), who was very supportive of Montagu's nomination of Keynes as Vice-Chairman of the Fiscal Commission. Keynes 'liked immensely' both the Readings (Skidelsky, 1986: 342).

As with Montagu, Keynes enjoyed a very special relationship, perhaps even unique, with another distinguished Jew Carl Melchior (1871-1933), a partner in the Hamburg banking firm of M.M. Warburg, and the principal German representative at the Paris Conference. Keynes "was deeply affected by his relationship with the ex-enemy alien, whose Jewishness perhaps attracted him, and he was the subject of his most intimate memoir—*Dr Melchior: a Defeated Enemy...*" (Hill and Keynes, 1989: 350). Keynes wrote of Melchior: "I was to have one of the most curious intimacies in the world and some very strange experience." In this posthumously published memoir, a classic of its kind, Keynes pays a moving tribute to

> this Jew, for such, though not by appearance (note too Keynes' ever-present sensitivity to Jewish physiognomy) I afterwards learnt him to be, and he only upheld the dignity of defeat...He spoke with the passionate pessimism of a Jew...I also understand better than before, what a precisian he was, a strict and upright moralist, a worshipper of the Tablets of the Law, a Rabbi – it was these offences against The Word which so much wounded him...I asked him to my hotel, where a German American Jew, Paul Warburg—was also to be my guest—my book was not then out, and I had with me a manuscript of my chapter on the president [Woodrow Wilson]. After lunch, I read it to them. I noted its effect on the two Jews—Warburg hated the president and felt a chuckling delight at his discomfiture...but Melchior grew ever more solemn, until at the end he appeared almost to be in tears. The Tablets of the Law, it was Melchior's thought at the moment, had perished meanly (CW, X: 395, 415, 428).

Keynes's admiration and esteem for Melchior, the (enemy) German Jew were fully matched by his dislike, bordering on contempt, for the (allied) Jew, Klotz, the French Minister of Finance and a participant in the Paris Peace Conference. Keynes described him as

> a short, plump, heavy-moustached Jew…prating on his 'goold' and how Lloyd George bent forward and with a gesture of his hand indicated to everyone the image of a hideous Jew clutching a money bag...[his] words came out with a contempt so violent that…the anti-semitism, not far below the surface in such an assemblage as that one, was up in the heart of everyone. Everyone looked at Klotz with a momentary contempt and hatred…(CW, X: 422).

Equally memorable in a different key is Keynes's encounter with the most distinguished contemporary Jew—Albert Einstein—

> one of the prophets of the ancient race (Jews)—Marx, Freud, Einstein—who have been tearing at our social, personal and intellectual roots, tearing them with an objectivity which to the healthy mind seems morbid, depriving everything, as it seems, of the warmth of natural feeling—Einstein (is) a symbol of the mind travelling in the cold regions of space, and a symbol of the brave and generous outcast, pure in heart and cheerful in spirit. (CW, XXVIII: 21)
>
> He is a naughty Jew-boy, covered with ink—that kind of Jew—the kind which has its head above water, the sweet, tender imps who have not sublimated immortality into compound interest. He was the nicest, and the only talented person I saw in all Berlin, except perhaps old Fuerstenberg, the banker whom Lydia liked so much, and Kurt Singer, two foot by five, the mystical economist from Hamburg. And he was a Jew and so was Fuerstenberg and so was Singer. And my dear Melchior is a Jew too. Yet if I lived here, I felt I might turn anti-semite. For the poor Prussian is too slow and heavy on his legs for the other kind of Jews, the ones who are not imps but serving devils, with small horns, pitchforks, and oily tails. It is not agreeable to see civilisation so under the ugly thumbs of its impure Jews who have all the money and the power and brains. I vote rather for the plump hausfraus and thick fingered Wandering Birds. But I am not sure that I wouldn't even rather be mixed up with Lloyd George than with the German political Jews. (CW, XXVIII: 317, 382–4)

Keynes's pen portraits of eminent Jews is a revealing amalgam of personal admiration and what Forster called 'Jew-consciousness'.

No account of Keynes's Jewish contacts would be complete without reference to his most outstanding pupil and his lifelong intellectual collaborator, Richard Ferdinand Kahn, the eminent Cambridge economist who played such a crucial role in shaping Keynes's path-breaking contributions to economic theory. Keynes had tremendous respect for Kahn and related to him as an intellectual equal—a status barely accorded to any of Keynes's other contemporaries. Keynes was influential in electing Kahn to a fellowship at King's College, Cambridge. In his letter to Lydia (14 March 1924) he wrote: "...the fellowship election tomorrow is going to be a difficult business...I am busy this evening preparing my case in favour of Richard (Kahn)..." (Hill and Keynes, 1989: 170). Kahn "retained his identity as a Jew with pride and took a positive, if critical, attitude to Israel...and his orthodoxy was a byword at King's College" (Harcourt, 1991: 29). Keynes was also very supportive of other noted Jewish economists, Piero Sraffa, Erwin Rothbarth, Abba Lerner, Hans Singer, and Nicholas Kaldor, but was strangely inhospitable to Michel Kalecki, reportedly, on grounds of intellectual incompatibility with the Cambridge milieu. Keynes sponsored Kaldor for a fellowship at Jesus College, Cambridge, in 1943, but Jesus turned him down, as often conjectured, on anti-semitic grounds. Similarly, Keynes had a special rapport with the Austrian (Jewish) philosopher Wittgenstein, and was instrumental in sending a copy of Wittgenstein's *Tractatus* received from his prison camp at Monte Cassino to Bertrand Russell (Kenny, 1973: 2-3). As with his economist colleagues, Keynes remained oblivious of the Jewishness of Wittgenstein and his fellow Bloomsbury Apostle Leonard Woolf.

Zionist Philo-Semite

One of the more remarkable ironies of the by now voluminous Keynesian scholarship is the fact that while his anti-semitism, based largely on his *obiter dicta*, has been widely noticed, Keynes's support for Zionism has been completely ignored both in his *Collected Writings* and activities and in the biographies of Harrod, Skidelsky and Hession as well as in the numerous symposia on virtually every aspect of Keynes. It is little known that Keynes was the only non-Jewish member of a high-powered advisory committee under the chairmanship of Herbert Samuel which prepared a preliminary draft report for presentation of the Zionist case for a Jewish national home in Palestine, for the Peace Conference in Paris on 23 February 1919. The other members of the committee were Lionel Abrahams of the India Office and James de Rothschild.

Equally remarkable is the fact that although Keynes's membership of this important committee is noted in the autobiography of Chaim Weizmann, the architect and first president of Israel (Weizmann, 1949: 243), it is not recorded in the standard histories of Jews and Zionism (e.g., Laqueur, 1972; Johnson, 1987). Keynes's acceptance of the membership of a high-powered Zionist committee, which prepared the ground for the Balfour Declaration is *prima facie* testimony of his sympathy for the Zionist cause, long before it became fashionable with the advent of institutionalised persecution of Jews in Germany and Austria. Although there is no evidence to substantiate his share in the drafting of the report, it would doubtless have been substantial, given his propensity to dominate the proceedings of any committee on which he served, like the Royal (Chamberlain) Commission in Indian Currency and the Macmillan Committee.

What induced Keynes, the economic and financial expert, to accept membership of a political group committed to a specific and by no means a popular cause in Britain – the creation of a Jewish national home in Palestine? In his only comprehensive political testament, Keynes did not list the Jewish question as one of the questions of the day even as late as 1925 (CW, IX: 301). One can discern several elements in Keynes's support of Zionism. First and foremost, it was eminently congruent with his customary stance of espousing the oppressed and the underprivileged rather than any manifestation of ideological support for Zionism. In fact, Keynes, the arch pluralist 'fox'—to borrow Isaiah Berlin's elegant dichotomy of intellectuals and artists as 'foxes' or 'hedgehogs'—distrusted ideologies, whether political or economic. His was the piecemeal social engineering approach of seeking viable solutions for specific issues of public policy, whether it was refugee relief, stabilising the Indian rupee, creating a central bank for India, designing the gold exchange standard, tariffs, reparations, unemployment, war finance, reform of the international monetary system, and commodity price stabilisation. Keynes, who prided himself on never being afraid of 'being in a minority' always stood for the aggrieved—whether it was a lowly official in the Rangoon Stamp Office, Indian students at Cambridge, women's rights (suffrage and degrees) and conscientious objectors in Britain, or a dependent India's case for an appropriate quota in the International Monetary Fund. But it must have posed an acute quandary, and taken a lot of intellectual and emotional conviction, for Keynes to participate in the preparation of the Zionist case, considering that 'the fiercest opponent of the Zionist' in the British cabinet was none other than his prime benefactor Edwin Montagu, the Secretary of State for India.

But in matters of public policy Keynes never fell prey to the clinical cost-benefit approach of an economist. His dramatic resignation from the Paris Peace Conference after five months of futile attempts to achieve a just settlement was an idealistic gesture of the highest order, as was his campaign against the insensitive and heartless insistence on the delivery of milk cows as partial reparation from a starving Austria. It is on record, according to the British director of relief, that "it was only through Keynes's initiative in the Supreme Economic Council that famine was averted in Austria in 1919" (E. Johnson, 1978: 12). Likewise, during the post-war negotiations with the Germans, Keynes, while never compromising the interests of his own country, insisted on treating the ex-enemy as human beings who too had a case. In light of all this, his support for a Jewish national home in Palestine comes as no surprise. But his participation in the drafting committee of the Zionist group must also have been influenced by his deep personal regard for both his fellow liberal Herbert Samuel and for his mentor Lionel Abrahams.

Much later in the 1930s, at the height of the Nazi persecution of Jews, Keynes, formulating a positive peace programme (*The New Statesman and Nation*, 25 March 1938) said: "there should be an offer of Germany to make organised arrangements for all German and Austrian Jews who wish to emigrate and be naturalised elsewhere" (CW, XXVIII: 100). This was a specific constructive proposal for Jewish relief in contrast to the equivocal stand of the British government on this issue. As noted by the editors of his *Collected Writings*, "Keynes was one of the most active in succouring the Jewish refugees" (CW, X: 382). With the outbreak of World War II Keynes intervened actively with the home secretary and other officials concerned to obtain the release of interned Jewish refugee economists, Piero Sraffa, Erwin Rothbarth, Hans Singer, and Edward Rosenbaum (CW, XII: 190). But he confessed that "there are thousands of more obscure people who cannot be dealt with in this way" and remarked with biting sarcasm, "if there are any Nazi sympathisers at large in this country, look for them in the War Office and our secret service, not in the internment camps" (ibid.: 191).

Eventually, Keynes seemed to have developed doubts not so much about the political or ethical foundations of Zionism, but its feasibility. He, along with other English friends of Weizmann, "tried to say to him that England was too tired and too poor to carry the burden of its incompatible promises to the Jews and the Arabs any longer, and consequently must abandon both parties to their own devices" (Berlin, 1981: 57). Keynes became increasingly conscious of the political costs of Zionism—its conflict with the rights of the Arab inhabitants of Palestine just as he had shown up the incompatibility of reparations and a just peace after World War II. Had Keynes lived to see the birth of Israel, his attitude to it would conceivably have been like Kahn's—positive but critical. Equally, Israel would have acclaimed him as a 'righteous gentile'.

An Appraisal

What, in sum, do the foregoing evidence and analysis of Keynes's attitudes and actions in relation to Jews as a group and Zionism as a cause amount to? It is no exculpation of anti-semitism to say that there are degrees and kinds of anti-semitism and that there is a degree between the gas chamber and the prejudices of the country club or the senior common room. Keynes's attitudinal and selective anti-semitism was certainly not of the monolithic variety like the rabid rancours of Ezra Pound and Richard Wagner, nor did it wear the literary raiments of Chesterton and Belloc or assume the programmatic agenda of T.S. Eliot who believed that "The population should be homogeneous...reasons of race and religion combine to make any large number of free-thinking Jews undesirable... and a spirit of excessive tolerance is deprecated" (Eliot, 1934: 20).

In retrospect, Keynes's anti-semitism will be seen more as a peripheral fringe of an inherently compassionate personality, an unamiable foible rather than a fatal flaw of character, a blind-spot which never blurred the totality of his social and political vision. Quite often, Keynes, the master phrase-smith's puckishness also led him into brisk epigrammatic evaluations of men and matters, 'the wish to *epater* the solemn', as Isaiah Berlin put it. But any disproportionate emphasis on Keynes's private anti-semitism would risk appearing as a familiar stratagem of deconstructionists, who, remarkably, expect public figures, particularly intellectuals, to be paragons of virtue and morality, personal and political, and are then concerned to show the shadowside of genius—their non-intellectual aberrations like the physical ineptitude of Bertrand Russell, the sexual peccadilloes of H.G. Wells and A.J. Ayer, or the domestic tyrannies of Tolstoy. Paul Johnson's *The Intellectuals* is a mint specimen of this stance which, more appropriately, should be directed toward deflating the dogmatism of intellectuals on subjects on which they have no expertise.

Perhaps, the supreme irony is the baffling asymmetry between anti-semitism which, rightly, occasions censure and philo-semitism, which hardly seems to merit any notice, much less support. Richard Crossman once confessed to his pathetic failure—when he was a member of the Palestine Commission in 1945—to convince Chaim Weizmann that he was a pro-semite. All that he could evoke was a curt brush-off:

> My dear Crossman, you are a non-Jew, a gentile, and cannot truly understand or have reliable sympathies. If you could admit to being, as the rest of the world is, anti-semitic then we can talk and negotiate and perhaps even wind up being friends. (Lasky, 1986: 64).

Keynes's private anti-semitism, too, is better known than his public philo-semitism, which is virtually ignored, even as Oswald Mosley's anti-semitic aberrations are better remembered than the pro-Zionist proclivities of Churchill, Macmillan, Crossman, and Orde Wingate, or the activities of the National Council for Civil Liberties and the Council of Christians and Jews in Britain which unlike most European countries, has had a vigorous philo-semitic tradition. Keynes always adhered to the spirit of G.E. Moore's *Principia Ethica*, the bible of the Bloomsbury group, which requires that actions be judged by their consequences (Braithwaite, 1975: 245). Keynes's writings may sound anti-semitic, but his activities were emphatically philo-semitic. His actions in relation to Jews and Zionism may not have immediate consequences, but in the long-run they would certainly be judged as ethical. His anti-semitism exemplifies the ambivalence and banality of prejudice, yet does not diminish his stature as "not merely a very great man, but also a very good man" (James Meade). Nevertheless, one is still left with a nagging question: What indeed impelled a man of Keynes's exquisite sensibilities to notice ever so often the 'Jewishness of Jews' alone among national, racial, or religious groups? The answer is best furnished in an acutely perceptive evaluation of Keynes's anti-semitism in the accompanying comment by Isaiah Berlin, himself an eminent Jewish savant of Britain (Annexure 11.1).

Postscript

Ironically, Keynes and Berlin—two inveterate correspondents—never corresponded with each other, although they had several memorable encounters. Berlin found Keynes "literally fascinating and certainly the cleverest man" he "had ever met in his life" with an intelligence which "seemed uncanny." "He knew how one's sentences would end almost before one began them" (Berlin, 1982: 171). While Berlin strongly approved of Keynes, the liberal internationalist he "remained dubious about Keynes's grasp of American politics" and "his provocative insouciance shocked him" (Ignatieff, 1998: 128). The very traits which irked American delegates and officials most and seriously crippled Keynes as a negotiator in the final stages of the Savannah and Bretton Woods international monetary conferences, Berlin was remarkably perceptive about the downside of Keynes's genius and his tantalisingly short piece 'Maynard and Lydia Keynes' (Berlin, 1982: 171-173) only accentuates one's regret that Keynes does not figure in Berlin's masterly portrait gallery of *Personal Impressions* (1981).

References

Berlin, Isaiah (1981). *Chaim Weizmann, Personal Impressions.* New York: Viking.

————. (1982). "Maynard and Lydia Keynes", in Milo Keynes (ed.), *Lydia Lopokova.* New York: St. Martin's Press.

Black, Stanley (1991). *A Levite among the Priests: Edward M. Bernstein and the Origins of the Bretton Woods System.* Boulder: Westview Press.

Braithwaite, R.B. (1975). "Keynes as Philosopher", in *Essays on John Maynard Keynes.* Cambridge: Cambridge University Press.

Chandavarkar, Anand (1989). *Keynes and India: A Study in Economics.* London: Macmillan.

Eliot, T.S. (1934). *After Strange Gods.* New York: Harcourt Brace.

Harcourt, G.C. (1991). "R.F. Kahn: A Tribute", *Banca Nazionale del Lavaro Quarterly Reivew* 176 (March).

Hill, Polly and Richard Keynes (1989). *Lydia and Maynard.* London: Andre Deutsche.

Ignatieff, Michael (1998). *Isaiah Berlin: A Life.* New York: Henry Holt.

Johnson, Elizabeth (1978). "Keynes and the Man", in Elizabeth Johnson and Harry G. Johnson (eds.), *The Shadow of Keynes.* Oxford: Basil Blackwell.

Johnson, Paul (1987). *A History of the Jews.* New York: Harper and Row.

Kenny, Anthony (1973). *Wittgenstein.* Harmondsworth: Penguin.

Keynes, John Maynard (1900). "The Differences between East and West: Will They Ever Disappear?", *Eton College essay* (JMK/PP/31/4), *Keynes Papers.* Kings College Library, Cambridge.

————. (1971–89). *The Collected Writings of John Maynard Keynes (henceforth CW).* Vols. I–XXX. Editors Austin Robinson, Donald Moggridge, Elizabeth Johnson. London: Macmillan.

————. (1971 [1919]). *CW, II, The Economic Consequences of the Peace.*

————. (1971 [1921]). *CW, III, A Revision of the Treaty.*

————. (1972 [1931]). *CW, IX, Essays in Persuasion.*

————. 1972 [1933]. CW, X, Essays in Biography, 'Edwin Montagu' and 'Dr Melchior'.

————. (1976). *CW, XV, Activities 1906–14: India and Cambridge.*

————. (1972). *CW, XVI, Activities 1920–22: Treaty Revision and Reconstruction.*

————. (1977). *CW, XVII, Activities, 1939–1945: International War Finance.*

————. (1979). *CW, XXIII, Activities 1940–1943: External War Finance.*

————. (1982). *CW, XXVIII, Social, Political and Literary Writings,* 'Einstein'.

Laqueur, Walter (1972). *A History of Zionism.* New York: Harper Bros.

Lasky, Melvin J. (1986). "Richard Crossman", *Encounter* 3.

Nehru, Jawaharlal (1988). *An Autobiography.* Oxford: Oxford University Press.

Orwell, George (1942). "London Letter to Partisan Review (January)", in Sonia Orwell and Ian Angus (eds.), *The Collected Essays, Journalism and Letters of Orwell.* New York: Harcourt Bruce Jovanovich, p.178.

Pryce Jones, David (1989). "Review of Lydia and Maynard", in Polly Hill and Richard Keynes (eds.), *Times Literary Supplement:* 994, (15–21 September).

Sayers, R.S. (1972). "The Young Keynes", *Economic Journal,* 82(326).

Skidelsky, Robert (1986). *John Maynard Keynes (Hopes Betrayed, 1883–1920).* New York: Viking Penguin.

Spotts, Frederic (ed.) (1989). *Letters of Leonard Woolf.* New York: Harcourt Brace Jovanovich.

Weizmann, Chaim (1949). *Trial and Error (The Autobiography of Chaim Weizmann).* New York: Harper Bros.

Annexure 11.1

Comment by Isaiah Berlin

Headington House, Oxford,
18 April 1994.

Dear Mr. Chandavarkar,

Thank you for your clear and admirable piece about Keynes and anti-semitism. I read it with great interest, and indeed instruction—I did not know any of those questions. I did not know Keynes at all well, but I met him two or three times, and I know something about his milieu and outlook. I do not think one can call him an anti-semite, as one can, let us say, Evelyn Waugh, T.S. Eliot, Harold Nicholson, Vita Sackville-West, and even, I think, Virginia Woolf (despite the fact that she was married to a perfectly self-identified Jew). In the case of Keynes, as that of several members of Bloomsbury, it seems to me that they simply did not care for Jews socially, did not like their company; they sometimes rationalised this by picking on certain real or alleged characteristic of Jews as a reason for this, even a justification. But I think in fact that it was not that most of them disliked this or that attribute of the Jews they knew or heard of, so much as simply not liking them; some people in England couldn't and can't, bear Germans, or Frenchmen—as many Americans don't like, say 'Hispanics'—and indeed, Jews too. I mean that if Jews were persecuted anywhere, or an act of grave injustice was done to a Jew (as in the case of Dreyfus), people like Keynes would certainly have signed a note of protest, and felt genuine indignation—quite independently of the fact that they could avoid meeting them, or at any rate feel uncomfortable in their presence, felt them to be unsympathetic or alien or ungentlemanly in some way. This was true of Bertrand Russell, probably true of E.M. Forster (though I am sure he would have denied it – but there is a piece by him on an exhibition in, I think, the Royal Academy, where there was a portrait of the late Sir Philip Sassoon—and he expostulates that this oriental should have had anything to do with the way England was governed). In short, it is a kind of club anti-semitism, but it is not a deep, acute hostility to Jews—as in the case of, say Hilaire Belloc or Chesterton or, some would say, though I have no evidence of it myself, Kipling or Henry James—which went beyond social disdain or looking down ...on Jews as somewhat inferior people, vulgar, obsequious, aggressive, etc., which has been said against them, quite apart from greed, dishonesty, and so on. No doubt all forms of anti-Jewish feeling derive from common roots, but in the case of Keynes it was at once genuine and superficial.

You mention Richard Kahn, who worked with Keynes and was a devoted follower and much admired by Keynes. Kahn was a true friend to him, and promoted his interests in every way; nevertheless. I remember being told at King's College, of which both were Fellows, that he sometimes said (of Kahn) 'my little Jew'—half affectionately but half contemptuously, I fear. You must remember that unfriendly feeling for the Jews is centuries old, whatever the cause (which I suspect to be ultimately the Christian Gospels); that if you ask who, even in the nineteenth century in civilized society, showed a positive attitude towards the Jews they met or wrote or spoke about—very few names come to mind: George Eliot was notorious for liking them; Dickens has a famous Jewish villain, and then to make up for it creates a kind of half-hero in another novel: Trollope has at least one noble Jew and several Jewish villains, and so forth. They are felt to be in some sense outsiders, not quite acceptable—with exceptions: Leonard Woolf and Arthur Waley (the Chinese and Japanese experts) were fully received in Bloomsbury, as real members of the group and personal friends. One or two Jewish judges who went to Eton or some other grand public school were similarly accepted: but these were to some degree exceptions.

So you are basically right. Keynes did suffer from the prejudices and tastes of his milieu. He greatly admired, e.g., Lord Samuel, who served in various Liberal administrations but nevertheless could certainly bring himself to crack some joke about him in what might be thought doubtful taste—but it was no more than that.

Thank you ever so much again for your very interesting piece.

Yours sincerely,

Isaiah Berlin

(The communication with Isaiah Berlin is reproduced by permission of his Literary Trustees, one of whom, Henry Hardy of Wolfson College, Oxford, is currently editing Berlin's letters for publication. The citation is from Keynes's *Eton College Essay* (JMK/PP/31/4) and is reproduced from the Unpublished *Writings of J.M. Keynes*, copyright, The Provost and Scholars of King's College, Cambridge, 1999, located in the King's College Library, Cambridge.)

12 B.P. Adarkar and Keynes

*The Ganges and the Cam**

The following notes, which draw on the unpublished writings of J.M. Keynes (Copyright, the Provost and Scholars of King's College, Cambridge, 1988) at King's College Library, Cambridge, are intended to supplement Deena Khatkhate's insightful and moving obituary of B.P. Adarkar ("An Economist whose Present was in the Past", *Economic and Political Weekly*, 8 October 1988). They reveal a little known aspect of Adarkar's life—the high esteem in which he was held by Keynes, who was not only his supervisor for the Economics Tripos at King's, but even more a most solicitous mentor, a connection which began delightfully, as follows:

> I myself had an interesting experience of his (Keynes's) helpfulness and meticulous care as an editor of (*The Economic*) 'Journal'. I had written a note for the 'journal' in 1931, just in my teens, so to say, after graduation. He (Keynes) spoke in encouraging terms about it and made it part of a symposium allowing me to rub shoulders with two or three senior and quite eminent economists (including Edwin Cannan). He called me for a discussion and suggested some slight amendments, cut a joke about my ability as a typist (said I could earn my living as a typist if I ever failed as an economist!) and handed to me the typescript which I found corrected by him to the smallest comma and prepared for the press. I think that was my first lesson in the preparation of manuscripts for the press. (B.P. Adarkar, "Lord Keynes of Tilton – A Tribute", *Eastern Economist*, 10 May 1946, p. 779.)

This note, entitled "Mr Keynes and the Classics" appeared in the symposium on "Savings and Usury" with Adarkar, Cannan, Keynes, Sandwell and Somerville as contributors (*The Economic Journal*, March 1932). This note was not only Adarkar's first publication but also possibly the very first contribution by an Indian economist to economic theory in a professional journal of repute. It showed that Keynesian theory, i.e., the *Treatise*, does not lend any support to the Canonist doctrines of interest as usury. Keynes in his own contribution to this symposium heartily endorsed Adarkar:

> Mr Adarkar is, of course, perfectly right that the Canonists did not see the point accurately and that the distinction which they drew between interest and profit does not logically coincide—or, at least, would not in a modern community—with the distinction between interest on savings represented by debts and interest on savings represented by assets. For one thing, it is impossible to earmark any particular savings against particular debts or assets. Yet as moralists they were trying to devise general rules which would be applicable to the actual circumstances of experience. (ibid.: 136)

* *Source: Economic and Political Weekly* XXIII(43) (22 October 1988): 2207-2208.

Soon after, Adarkar applied for the professorship of economics at the Benares Hindu University and Keynes as his referee wrote to the authorities:

> King's College, 21st June 1932
>
> To,
>
> The Benares Hindu University
>
> Mr B.P. Adarkar
>
> I should like to support his application [for a Professorship] most warmly. Mr Adarkar was my pupil whilst he was at King's. He took a first in the first part of the Economics Tripos [Exhibition Prizeman] and was rather unlucky in just failing to secure a first class in the second part [1931]. I have, however, seen something of his research work since that time, which has convinced me that he has been developing fast and that he is unquestionably of first class quality. Mr Adarkar is a most learned economist and is extremely well fitted for research work in modern economic theory. More than one small contribution of his has been accepted for publication in learned journals, which is a rare thing for a man of his junior standing. I consider him to be the most promising Indian student of economics, as far as original work is concerned; who has been in this country.
>
> John Maynard Keynes

Characteristically, Adarkar never rested on his undergraduate laurels or on testimonials from the good and the great. Like a true scholar, he went on to higher things and beavered away in Benares at his projected book on federal finance, the first draft of which was "written in a London garret, ...eight hours a day, with the other time spent in the British Museum" (Keynes in his letter to Daniel Macmillan, 30 November 1932). In the same letter, Keynes said

> ...Adarkar is a most promising young economist, especially perhaps on the theoretical side. He has developed extraordinarily since he took the Tripos and this year he wrote what Pigou agreed was the ablest essay for the Adam Smith prize. I saw a good deal of him before he went back to India and have the greatest sympathy for him...I think he is the most promising young Indian economist for quite a little time and his book is better than most of the books by young Indian professors. If you could produce it in India in the rather cheaper style that your Indian house sometimes adopts, I believe that it might be a better solution...I do think Adarkar is more worth getting on your list for the future than other young professors in India.

Macmillan did not accept this book presumably for narrow commercial considerations. It was eventually published as *Principles and Problems of Federal Finance* by P.S. King, London, 1933, with a foreword by Sir Cecil Kisch, who said: "it fills with conspicuous success a distinct gap in the literature of public finance". This—Adarkar's first book—was widely acclaimed by many experts, including Hugh Dalton and Hermann Finer, and even to this day it is highly valid as a pioneering contribution to the subject, which has stood the test of time. It is a masterly synthesis of constitutional law, public administration and the principles of public finance, qualities which were once again demonstrated in Adarkar's note on the "Economic Aspects of the Indian Constitution" (*The Economic Journal*, March 1933). Adarkar also published two very significant articles on "High Wages and International Prices" (*Manchester School* 3(1) 1932) and "The Fundamental Error in Keynes' Treatise" (*American Economic Review*,

March 1933). These were followed by another masterly note in the *EJ*, on "The Pareto Law and Distribution of Incomes in India", which he co-authored with S.N. Sen Gupta of the Indian Statistical Institute.

Having dealt with such varied themes, the restless young Adarkar reverted to his first love—economic theory. This he did in a notably original piece on "Fisher's Real Rate Doctrine" (*EJ*, June 1934) which has an uncanny relevance even today to contemporary concerns. Fisher's real rate doctrine, which is a much older notion, is obtained by correcting both the interest and the principal for price changes. Adarkar also pointed out the similarity between Fisher's reference to there being "as many rates of interest expressed in terms of goods as there are kinds of goods diverging from one another in value" and Sraffa's "commodity rates". Nevertheless, there is a difference between Fisher's real rates and Sraffa's commodity rates: the former refers to the relation between two spot prices of a commodity at two different dates and the latter to the relation between the spot and forward price for the commodity at the same given moment. Adarkar concluded that the application of the real rate theorem to practical banking policy would be rather hazardous for it is not certain that it is the rate which would maintain the stability of prices.

Thereafter, Adarkar produced a steady stream of high-quality publications: *Theory of Monetary Policy* (1935), *Indian Monetary Policy* (1936), *The Indian Constitution* (1938), *If War Comes* (1939), *Indian Fiscal Policy* (1941). All this before he was even 40! In between, Adarkar, who loved an intellectual challenge, engaged in scholarly disputation in the late 1930s and early 40s on matters of moment—with Amiya Das Gupta (*Free Trade vs. Protection*), with B.R. Shenoy (*Rupee Ratio and Gold Exports from India*). This was the golden age of public economic debate in India, so decorous and yet so intense and committed, reminiscent of the celebrated Hicks-Hawtrey exchanges on interest rates.

Adarkar's achievements as an economist were outstanding by any criterion, yet his career in independent India abounds in cruel ironies. It is a sad tale of total lack of recognition of his talents either by academia or by government. None of the usual honours came his way. His work on federal finance did not get him on to the Government of India's Finance Commission even as his work on fiscal policy did not lead to the portals of the Tariff Commission. No one ever proposed him for the presidentship of the Indian Economic Conference. One can easily prolong this list of missed honours and distinctions. What would Keynes, who earned his membership of the

Chamberlain Commission on the strength of his book on Indian currency, have thought of the treatment meted out to one of his star pupils by his own country after Independence? The frustrations of Indian economists in the British days were wholly understandable. We all recall that Sir James Grigg (Finance Member, Viceroy's Executive Council, c. 1935), justifying Theodore Gregory's appointment as Economic Adviser to the government of India, had derisively dismissed Indian economists as mere writers of text books (Adarkar wrote many original works but never a textbook!). The Congress MLAs, who were so critical of Sir James, never cared to recognise Adarkar's legitimate claims when their party came into virtually permanent power after independence. Perhaps, the last laugh will always be with Sir James.

The best part of Adarkar's life in independent India was spent in the pathetic obscurity of fringe postings in the Indian Foreign Service—a retreat into obscurity rather like the sad transformation of the very public and famous T.E. Lawrence into the very private Aircraftsman Shaw. Was it an uneasy suspicion of the powers-that-be that Adarkar would not have made a good court economist—the type that produces the perfect memo but no decisions, as was remarked of Saxon Sydney-Turner, the Treasury official, by his fellow Apostles and Bloomsburys. Adarkar's abilities were matched only by his intellectual integrity and he would not have compromised on crucial issues. But then what could one say of the remissness of the Indian academic establishment? The universities did not offer him a chair—the famous 'Jevons' chair at Allahabad—and even the much touted National Professorships eluded him. Adarkar was perhaps carved out to be an Oxbridge College Fellow—the most ideal position where, as Balogh said, one is neither master nor servant.

Keynes's solicitude and regard for Adarkar will always be a standing rebuke to the Indian establishment's studied unconcern for a distinguished economist. For his part, Adarkar throughout his life gratefully remembered Keynes. He wrote an exquisitely sincere letter of thanks to his *guru* from aboard the ship on the long voyage from Southampton to Bombay:

Piroscafo-SS 'Victoria' Near Naples
27 August 1932
Lloyd Triestino

To John Maynard Keynes,

Dear Sir, This is to thank you most sincerely for the personal interest you took in me during my stay in England, I carry with me happy memories of the brief but stimulating intellectual contact which I was lucky enough to have with you,

Yours sincerely,

B P Adarkar

Adarkar's final *guru dakshina* to Keynes was the beautiful, one of the very best, obituary of Keynes (*Eastern Economist*, 10 May 1946) wherein he wrote: "He achieved that rare and coveted combination of Lakshmi, Saraswati, and added the celestial gift of an Urvashi to it by marrying Lydia Lopokova." Pity, Adarkar never got around to writing what could have been his *magnum opus*, a definitive treatise on Keynesian economics and developing countries. Keynes's relationship with Adarkar was unique among his many Indian students. It was both personal and intellectual, unlike Keynes's contacts with other distinguished Indian students like J.V. Joshi and N.S. Subba Rao, which were largely of a personal nature.

In retrospect, Adarkar's life takes on all the poignancy of a Greek tragedy—the sad regress from *Koros* (excess of resources) to *Ata* (self-destruction) but without the interlude of *Hubris* for he never suffered from pretentious arrogance. The Last Post has sounded for a doughty warrior who retired from the battlefield before his prime, RIP. The loss is ours. Perhaps, the executors of the Adarkar estate will make available to interested readers his unpublished writings and consider where appropriate their publication.

13 A Fresh Look at Keynes

*Robert Skidelsky's Trilogy**

The publication of the final volume of Robert Skidelsky's impressive trilogy—*John Maynard Keynes: Fighting for Britain, 1937-1946*—is an appropriate occasion to evaluate Keynes's life and his legacy as the most creative and influential economist of the twentieth century, even though, as the book's subtitle suggests, it is really about Keynes's part in Britain's struggle for survival during the war years. As Lionel Robbins, the Director of the Economic Section of the War Cabinet, wrote to Keynes's widow, the ballerina Lydia Lopokova: "Maynard had given his life for his country, as surely as if he had fallen on the field of battle." Keynes struggled stoically against an incurable heart condition, first diagnosed in 1937, to become the architect of Britain's wartime economic strategy and the post-war financial order. "His illness did not diminish his prodigious energy, though it may have affected his judgment", Skidelsky observes.

Keynes's role, reminiscent of that of Walter Bagehot in the nineteenth century as the 'Spare Chancellor', was that of an unpaid advisor without portfolio—to three successive Chancellors of the UK Exchequer during 1940-1946 (Kingsley Wood, John Anderson, and Hugh Dalton). As such, he was the architect of successive war budgets that were inspired by his seminal monograph, *How to Pay for the War*, which based war finance on the theory that government absorption of purchasing power through taxes, loans, and compulsory savings, while the government allocates resources through the price system, is vastly more efficient and equitable than price and other controls. This role, in Skidelsky's words, "made him the Churchill of war finance and post-war financial planning." Ironically, despite this stellar contribution, there is only one reference to Keynes in Winston Churchill's five-volume history of World War II, even though Churchill knew Keynes intimately as an active member since 1927 of the Other Club, a dining society that Churchill founded in 1919. This omission was not due to any lack of esteem for Keynes. In fact, Churchill exhorted John Anderson on his appointment as Lord President of

* *Source: Finance and Development*, December 2001, 38(4): 60-63.

the Council to 'summon economists like Keynes to give their views to you personally.' Rather, it reflected, as Skidelsky notes, "Churchill's indifference to the economic and financial aspects—and consequences—of the war."

Contributions

Although Skidelsky's work is, in his words, "about practical applications, not theory" and "much more about the relationship between politics and economics than previous biographies of Keynes have been", it does emphasise the influence of Keynes's main theoretical propositions. Thus, Keynes's liquidity preference theory—that is, the public's demand for excessive cash balances—led him to advocate cheap money, capital controls, and the primacy of creditor country adjustment in his plan for an International Clearing Union. The comprehensive analysis of his *General Theory of Employment, Interest, and Money*, which allows an almost infinite variety of applications, framed his fiscal plans to counter both inflation and depression. His scepticism on the sensitivity of international trade and capital flows to price and exchange rate movements explains his preference for fixed over floating exchange rates. His principal achievements....the first 'Keynesian' budget of Kingsley Wood in 1941, the Full Employment White Paper of May 1944, and the establishment of the International Monetary Fund, were largely the work of others. His distinction is rather in the authority and influence he imparted to policies that would not otherwise have been followed or else would have been followed less assiduously. The Bretton Woods Agreement of July 1944 that led to the foundation of the IMF and the World Bank, Skidelsky notes, "reflected [U.S. Assistant Treasury Secretary] Harry Dexter White's ideas rather than Keynes's, not because they were technically superior but because the Americans had the power." Similarly, Keynes's failure in the Anglo-American loan negotiations of 1945 was "not because he had poor arguments, but because he had poor political weapons."

What was the key to Keynes's achievements and influence? It was the rare combination of genius and talent, of charisma and creativity, and a profoundly bicameral mind, at once conceptual and institutional, strategic and tactical. "There was much of the civil servant in Keynes", Skidelsky writes. "Theory must always be serviceable for policy, even if its echoes went beyond practical requirements." The normative Keynes was the fraternal twin of the analytic Keynes. The thinker and policy guru was also a superb institutional architect whether it was in designing the State Bank for India in 1913, an

International Clearing Union (1941), or the Arts Council of Great Britain and the Cambridge Arts Theatre. His financial acumen surfaced during his terms as Bursar of King's College, Cambridge, and as Chairman of the National Mutual Life Assurance Society.

Lonely Genius

Keynes's 'genius was lonely, as all genius is', but Keynes was also the high priest who recognised the essential role of those who have been called supporting 'Levites', without whom lonely genius can be ineffectual. Keynes acknowledged

> Both the currency scheme and the investment scheme are largely the fruit of the brain, not of Harry [White] but of...[Edward M.] Bernstein [assistant director of monetary research at the U.S. Treasury and later the first Director of Research of the IMF]. It is with him rather than Harry that the pride of authorship lies.

Keynes went on to say, "I have been over the economics, and Bernstein has been over the economics, and we are both convinced that the operations of the [International Monetary] Fund are technically sound." Asked about the repurchase provision under which member countries are required to repay their drawings from the IMF, Keynes said, "Bernstein wrote that, and it's correct." These compliments evoked a modest disclaimer from Bernstein to the effect that "he was just a Levite serving the priests in their holy work, that the ideas were White's: all I did was to dress them in economic clothing." Keynes graciously responded: "we priests need Levites just as the flowers need bees." In fact, it was the perfect understanding between Keynes's Levite (Sir Dennis Robertson, the Cambridge economist) and Harry White's Levite (Bernstein) that resolved many a technical glitch in the tortuous negotiations leading to the Bretton Woods Agreement. According to Skidelsky, Keynes thought Robertson "alone had the intellectual subtlety and patience of mind and tenacity of character to hold on to all details and fight them through Bernstein." But readers might well wonder about Skidelsky's accolade for Robertson as "the most subtle mind in British economics in the first half of this century" in a biography of the greatest economist of the twentieth century. There were other Levites, too, in Keynes's career, notably the Cambridge 'Circus', the sounding board for the *Treatise on Money* and the *General Theory*. Richard Kahn, the inventor of the multiplier, and Erwin Rothbarth, who provided the critical statistical framework for *How to Pay for the War*.

SENSIBILITIES

Genius is not synonymous with infallibility. Keynes, too, had his 'Achilles heel', his lack of political sense, according to Skidelsky. Noel Annan, the intellectual historian who later became Provost of King's College, Cambridge, observed that he "never studied the sources of power, nor how society is affected by social stratification or the forces of social control." Isaiah Berlin, the Oxford philosopher, said he remained dubious about Keynes's grasp of American politics, despite the latter's constant contacts with the renowned American columnist Walter Lippman, and Keynes's 'provocative insouciance' shocked Berlin. US President Franklin Roosevelt's special advisor, Harry Hopkins, described Keynes as "one of those fellows that just knows all the answers." Keynes was even irritated by the American variety of legal English, or Cherokee, as he called it. His 'ill manners' crippled monetary discussions, according to James Meade, the Cambridge economist and Nobel laureate, while Skidelsky comments that "as a negotiator, Keynes was fallible. It was as an advocate that he was supreme." The acute political sensibility characteristic of Keynes's *Economic Consequences of the Peace of 1919* and *A Revision of the Treaty of 1921* is conspicuously missing from his World War II writings and activities.

Nor was Keynes the easiest of colleagues. James Meade recalls from his service in the Economic Section of the Cabinet the times when he had "to meet the whole battery of Keynes's wit, petulance, rudeness, and quick unscrupulousness in argument...and was actually reduced to tears." Keynes's legendary put-downs did not spare even the highest civil servants. He called the objections of Donald Ferguson, Permanent Secretary, Agriculture and Fisheries, to his Buffer Stock Plan of 1942 'barmy'. But Keynes did not always get his way. His proposal to replace the income tax with a contribution to a self-supporting social security fund got a withering response from Richard Hopkins, Permanent Secretary to the UK Treasury: "I do not feel equal to settling between now (21 July 1942) and 15th August Lord Keynes's suggestions for a complete modelling of the system of direct taxation."

There was also an intellectual downside to Keynes, unexplored by Skidelsky, most notably a certain disdain for the scholarly apparatus and the state of the art. The Swedish economist and Nobel laureate Gunnar Myrdal complained that Keynes's work, like that of the Cambridge School, "suffers somewhat from the attractive Anglo-Saxon kind of unnecessary originality." Even Richard Kahn, the British economist who was Keynes's favourite acolyte, conceded that it was unfortunate that Keynes failed in his *General Theory* to refer to Myrdal's book *Monetary Equilibrium*. *The General Theory* would have benefited immeasurably from a judicious leavening of Erik Lindahl and Myrdal's work on expectations even as it would have profited from taking into account Frank Knight's 1921 classic, *Risk, Uncertainty and Profit*, considering that, as Skidelsky notes, "in Keynes's vision uncertainty is the condition of all human life which goes back to his early work on probability." This blind spot led Keynes to startling conclusions, like his opposition around 1911 to India's industrialisation because of the country's static comparative advantage in agriculture, whereas the doctrine of dynamic comparative advantage as the basis of international trade and development had been propagated much earlier, by Alexander Hamilton in the United States in 1791 and by Friedrich List in Germany in 1841.

Legacy

What, in fact, is the enduring legacy of Keynes? Skidelsky addresses but does not fully answer this central question in the section of the epilogue titled "A Man for All Seasons?" A distinguished economist, Sir Alec Cairncross, said Keynes was essentially a man who will be "longest remembered for his ideas" and who "never said the same thing for long." Sir Hubert Henderson, the British economist and Treasury advisor, who was arguably the most perceptive and persistent critic of Keynes, remarked that Keynes's influence was too varied to be captured by a single production like the *General Theory*. Rather, Henderson said, "he was an opportunist and eclectic to the end", who once wrote to Prime Minister Ramsay Macdonald that "The peculiarity of my position lies, perhaps, in the fact that I am in favour of practically all the remedies which have been suggested in any quarter."

Skidelsky concentrates too exclusively on the *General Theory* in assessing Keynes's real legacy, which lies in the totality of his scientific contributions. As the first economist to view the economy as a whole, he can claim to be the inventor of modern macroeconomics. He developed a new apparatus of thought in accordance with his lifelong stance that "economics is a technique of thinking ... not a body of settled conclusions", as he put it in his introduction to the *Cambridge Economic Handbook Series*. His ideas are still the most productive matrix of testable hypotheses, the ultimate test of scientific status. Among his lesser-known pioneering contributions are the seminal concepts of 'the fringe of unsatisfied borrowers' and of financial market imperfections, which he described in his *Treatise on Money* and which are the genesis of the modern analysis of credit rationing: and the theory and organisation of central banks, particularly their developmental role, an idea that he expounded in *Indian Currency and Finance*. Keynes has been aptly described as the 'Einstein of Economic Theory' by the economist Teodoro D. Togati. Keynes provided a defining new paradigm and, as Skidelsky notes, "was the impresario of his own revolution."

Keynes would not claim to be a development economist but, in an unpublished address delivered around 1944 to the Marshall Society (for which the author is indebted to a communication from the distinguished Indian economist I.G. Patel), he made a most profound statement on the economics of development: "In the ultimate analysis, economic prosperity depends not on how brilliant a few people are, but on how large a scale you are able to produce competent people in all walks of life." In short, the mass competence of human capital is the key to development.

Finally, a clinching thought on Keynes's influence. Keynes is unquestionably the most quotable and most discussed economist. The battle lines are still drawn between pre-Keynesian and post-Keynesian economics and the interpretation of his thinking still remains a vigorous subdiscipline. The adjective 'Keynesian' is very much a staple of public discourse. Keynes has even figured in English fiction, albeit in an unflattering role, as Barrally, the "half adventurer, half squire, and wholly amoral, financier", in John Buchan's 1936 novel the *Island of Sheep*, a caricature that reflected "the standard right-wing Tory opinion of Keynes as a man of first-class brains but second-class character." Clearly, the pervasive imprimatur of the marketplace seems so much more decisive than even the most stringent academic peer review. The observer who exclaimed 'we are all Keynesians now' in effect acknowledged that we have all been educated by Keynes, and now Skidelsky has further educated us on Keynes, 'warts and all'. Keynes has found both his James Boswell and his Lytton Strachey in Skidelsky. The impressive scholarly apparatus of the book taps virtually every extant primary source except, surprisingly, E.M. Bernstein's unpublished papers at the University of North Carolina, Chapel Hill and the illuminating monograph of Stanley W. Black (1991), which details the crucial role of Bernstein in the formulation of the Bretton Woods system.

The Keynes phenomenon will not be duplicated, and Skidelsky has now enshrined it in an abiding literary monument "for a successful, not a tragic, hero – an Odysseus rather than an Achilles", a fitting epitaph for Keynes. To date, only about one-third of his papers have been published in the 30-volume edition of the *Collected Writings of John Maynard Keynes*. The only part of Keynes's personal papers to have been published so far are the two memoirs – *Dr. Melchior* and *My Early Beliefs* and the three years of his correspondence with Lydia Lopokova before their marriage. One tantalising question remains: what surprises will Keynes's still unpublished economic papers have for posterity? As Keynes remarked, "The inevitable never happens. It is the unexpected always."*

References

Black, Stanley W. (1991). *A Levite among the Priests: Edward M. Bernstein and the Origins of the Bretton Woods System*. Boulder, CO: Westview Press.

Cairncross, Alec (1996). "Keynes the Man", *The Economist*, 20 April.

Howson, Susan and Donald Moggridge (eds.) (1990a). *The Wartime Diaries of Lionel Robbins and James Meade*, 1943–45. Basingstoke: Macmillan.

———. (1990b). *The Collected Papers of James Meade*.Volume IV: The Cabinet Office Diary 1944–46. London: Unwin Hyman.

Kahn, Lord (Richard) (1975). *On Re-reading Keynes*. London: Published for the British Academy, Oxford University Press.

Skidelsky, Lord Robert (2000). "Ideas and the World", *The Economist*, 25 November.

Tagoti, Teodoro Dario (2001). "Keynes as the Einstein of Economic Theory", *History of Political Economy* 33.

* The third and final volume of Lord Robert Skidelsky's study of Keynes, *John Maynard Keynes: Fighting for Britain, 1937-1946*, has been published by Macmillan, London. A US edition will be published by Viking Press, New York. The first two volumes: *John Maynard Keynes: Hopes Betrayed, 1883-1920*, and *John Maynard Keynes: The Economist as Saviour, 1920-1937*, are published by Viking Press in the United States and by Macmillan in the United Kingdom.

II

A Post-Keynesian Miscellany

14 The Unexplored Richard Kahn

The Reclusive Sage

The seminal contributions of Richard Kahn to economic theory have been overshadowed by excessive emphasis on his substantial role as the closest collaborator in the making of Keynes's *Treatise on Money* and the *General Theory*, and as chair of the famed Cambridge Circus, arguably the most influential coterie in economics, which even led to Joseph Schumpeter's grossly exaggerated view that "Kahn's share in the historic achievement cannot have fallen very far short of co-authorship" (1954: 1172). As against this, Noel Annan, a former Provost of King's College, Cambridge and a distinguished intellectual historian was even provoked to take the quaintly contrarian angle on Kahn as merely "Keynes's adjutant" (1999: 209). But the fact remains that Kahn's achievements have been obscured by the chronic penchant to view him as "that elusive figure who hides in the prefaces of Cambridge books" and "who got acknowledged in Pigou, Keynes and Joan Robinson footnotes as the eminence vert who kept them from error and provided generalized proofs" (Samuelson, 1994: 55). These gaps and misconceptions have no doubt been well redressed by the very authoritative Richard Kahn Memorial Issue of the *Cambridge Journal of Economics* (18(1), February 1994), where distinguished contemporaries analyse and comment on Kahn's varied contributions to the making of the *General Theory*, imperfect competition, economics of the short period, economic dynamics, the multiplier, liquidity preference and monetary policy and buffer stocks. But even this symposium still leaves out some significant aspects of Kahn's writings and activities, notably his views on the nature and teaching of economics, his work as a national and international civil servant, his analysis of post full employment inflationary pressures, development and planning. Harcourt's tribute to Kahn (1991) is still the best single comprehensive review of his contributions. Accordingly, this chapter attempts to explore and extend the less noticed aspects of Kahn's work based on Harcourt, Pasinetti, and the Kahn papers in the King's College archives, Cambridge.

The Teaching of Economics

The only occasion on which Kahn commented on the pedagogics of economics and its political nuances is in his little noticed article on "Political Attitudes Involved in Teaching Economics" (1976a), which takes a strangely contrarian stance. It contends that "far too many students read economics, a difficult subject" and "that if many of the less able read other subjects it would be good for them and for the subject" leading to "an increase in the number of able students reading the subjects as a result of teaching resources being less heavily concentrated on the often remarkably unsuccessful attempt to teach a difficult subject to the unintelligent" and also "as a result of greater ease of establishment of lively and productive discussion groups" (p.91). All these are highly debatable propositions based on a somewhat elitist view of economics. For one thing, given the greater employment potential of an economics degree compared to that of history, law, classics, or philosophy, it is no surprise that enrolment in economics is invariably higher. Was it not Edwin Cannan who said that he never knew of any London School of Economics graduate who had ended up in a workhouse. Even Oxford, the bastion of the Ancient Greats, the traditional reservoir of civil servants, including the Indian Civil Service (thanks to Jowett's Balliol) and of corporate executives, broke the monopoly of classics by adding economics to philosophy and politics (Modern Greats) to its degree examinations. Admissions to intimate discussion groups like the Political Economy Club at Cambridge were no doubt selective, a rule which, ironically, was broken by the Kapitza Club at Trinity College for physics, a far more rigorous subject than economics, which was open to all interested. Kahn had duly enthroned economics as the imperial science. But then a university education serves both as a filter and a ladder, and to say that only the able students—the potential First or Upper Second—should be enrolled does sound rather invidious and arbitrary. Equally, Kahn's contention that economics is a difficult subject exaggerates the purely intellectual rigour of economics which has been better described by Keynes, no less, as "an easy subject at which few excel." Even more relevant is Keynes's observation that even the high priests of economics need Levites, an aspect of which surfaced dramatically during Keynes's talk at the Marshall Library where he referred to his presentation at the Federal Reserve Bank in Washington where the room was 'packed with all economists'. This remark provoked Joan Robinson and Kaldor to laughter, whereupon Keynes

> came down on them like a ton of bricks: Nicky, Joan do not laugh. We think we have done our job if we produce one or two great economists in a generation. The Americans believe in

> creating scores of good economists in a generation; and that is why they succeed economically, and we do not. (Patel, 2002: 15)

How could Kahn, himself a very effective wartime civil servant, have overlooked the impressive role of economists in the war effort and post-war reconstruction which transformed economics from a liberal arts discipline into a profession with a meaningful role for the competent, as distinct from the talented and brilliant, rather like the humble dentist which Keynes himself recognised in another context. There will always be a natural and necessary division of labour in economics between the poets and the plumbers, to use *The Economist's* graphic dichotomy.

On the pedagogics of economics Kahn (1991: 91) makes the telling point that the "student is directly exposed as a result of a very casual acquaintance with the history of thought." Likewise, he refers to "the intrinsic difficulty" of "understanding the subject" and how mathematical methods of teaching are "more apt to conceal the processes of thought than to elucidate them." But the "major consideration" that arises in his mind is the "perils of a political character which beset the path of a student of economics", particularly "the students who are sufficiently mature...but not clever enough to use their economics to reason out the intricacies of political controversy involving economic issues" (ibid.). He underscores the vital importance of intellectual integrity on the part of the teacher, who should convey to students that "examination success will not be achieved by professing views the basis of which the candidate does not understand" (ibid.: 92). All these wholly unexceptionable sentiments are tenable only if economics is viewed as a "body of settled conclusions" rather than as "a technique of analysis", as so often asserted by Keynes. But Kahn's cavalier dismissal of "those universities, of which there are far too many in the United States, in which success in climbing the academic ladder depends on dishonesty in the presentation of ideas" is wholly uncharacteristic of an otherwise sober and taciturn personality. Perhaps, a last lingering trace of an unnecessary Oxbridge insularity, or just another specimen of the common-garden variety of the malady, which the French call *terriblement anglais* ('being terribly English'), an affliction of many an English intellectual or writer, such as Graham Greene.

However, in the same article Kahn comments perceptively:

> The refusal [of economists] to see the obvious is even more marked when it is a question of redistribution of income between rich and poor countries than between rich and poor in a country like Britain, simply because the inequalities are more glaring. But in the exposition of the theory of international trade and free trade, the implications are never faced. (ibid.: 93)

This provides a good rationale for development of poorer countries and generally for the economics of development. But, oddly, Kahn goes on to qualify the case for free trade as mutually beneficial to both poor exporting countries and wealthy importing countries by arguing that the latter should "go one stage further and grant a subsidy on imports from the poor country, thus raising its standard of living at the expense of a lowering of the standard of living of the wealthy importing country. This question is never answered because it is never asked" (ibid.). This is a peculiarly convoluted non-sequitur. For one thing, why should a wealthy country have to lower its standard of living to benefit a poorer country? The latter objective can be better achieved by the abolition of the massive subsidies to agriculture in the rich regions, such as the US and Europe, which indirectly cripple the exports of sugar, cotton, and bananas from poor countries. This abolition could be supplemented, if necessary, by untied multilateral aid from the rich countries to the poor.

Having pronounced on the politics of economics, Kahn does not indicate, at any point here or in his other writings, his precise political creed, which perhaps is best inferred by his revealed preference as a member of the Labour Party, who sat on the cross benches, when he was appointed to the House of Lords in 1965 in recognition of his services to the British Government. This cross bench posture was characteristic of his highly nuanced speeches in the Lords on economic policy, particularly incomes policies and industrial relations, which always took a balanced non-partisan position. He might well have asked:.Am I Labour—somewhat in the spirit of Keynes's famed "Am I a Liberal?" address.

Kahn: The Civil Servant and Commissioner

Like Keynes, Kahn, too, had much of the civil servant in him, as was amply proved by his successful and distinctive tenure as a wartime civil servant from 1939 to 1945 at the Board of Trade, where he ultimately became the Head of the General Division with the administrative grade of Principal Assistant Secretary. In the first two years of the war, he was involved in the problems of cutting down the production and consumption of consumer goods in order to free resources for wartime uses and showed an uncanny talent for seizing upon the heart of a problem and suggesting practical solutions, supported by his formidable powers of persuasion (Harcourt, 1991: 22). In the autumn of 1940, Oliver Lyttleton, who became President of the Board of Trade, was much impressed by Kahn's work. And when he was sent in 1941 as Minister

Resident in the Middle East, he asked for Kahn, who then served him for a year as Economic Adviser in the Middle East Supply Centre at a time of drastic reorganisation of supplies for the Middle East theatre. When Lyttleton returned to London to head the new Ministry or Production, he again asked for Kahn's services in the spring of 1943. For the rest of the war, Kahn was chiefly concerned with problems of post-war reconstruction in the Ministry of Production and Supply, returning to the Board of Trade in 1945. At the Ministry of Supply, he also wrote a number of papers on buffer stock schemes, not published. Kahn was also an effective member of various working parties on post-war plans set up in the Board of Trade for a time after the war. He also served for three years as a part-time member of the National Coal Board in the 1960s while being a very productive member of four groups of experts of UNCTAD (UN Conference on Trade and Development) and of the working group of experts of the Organisation for European Economic Cooperation and Development (OEEC), which drafted the influential report on The Problem of Rising Prices (1961). Kahn was also a member of the Research Unit of the Economic Commission of Europe, which drafted the 1956 Economic Survey of Europe.

Kahn's wartime civil service in tactical allocation of manpower and materials poses an unresolved conundrum. Why was an economist of his distinction not absorbed in the higher echelons of strategic macroeconomic policymaking and management in the Economic Section of the Treasury with the likes of Lionel Robbins, James Meade, Alec Cairncross, Austin Robinson, *et al.*, despite the strong recommendation of Keynes to Sir Frederick Hopkins, an influential senior official in the UK Treasury? Keynes wrote: "Kahn…is in [his] judgment quite exceptionally suited for Treasury work...experienced in all financial matters…, one of the half dozen best people in the country for [Hopkins's] purpose...He is an ideal colleague with judgment, knowledge, industry and reliability, all [Hopkins] could wish" (KPKC File UA9 1.9.39). Harrod, too, corroborates this:

> I came across a little note written by [Keynes] to the Treasury at the outset of the war saying that the only two people he had in mind suitable for employment in the Treasury were Richard Kahn and myself. I never got the summons from the Treasury, nor to the best of my knowledge did Richard Kahn. (1959: 183).

In the event, at least Harrod went into the Statistical Section of the Office of Lord Cherwell (Scientific Adviser to Prime Minister Winston Churchill), "a pantomath within the field of science", who insisted on "putting [problems] into quantitative terms", the type of work done so admirably by Donald McDougall and David Bensusan-Butt. It is hard to surmise the reasons for non-acceptance of Kahn by the Treasury; but very plausibly, and paradoxically, "his close ties to Keynes made him not altogether acceptable to the Treasury officials who were still suspicious of and hostile to Keynes himself" (Harcourt, 1991: 21). Whatever the reasons, it was clearly a glaring example of misdirection of a high-value resource.

Be that as it may more importantly, we have to ask what are the lessons Kahn drew from his wartime experience as a civil servant. Harcourt offers an insightful perspective on this aspect of Kahn. To begin with, he disliked the title of 'Economic Adviser', preferring to think of himself as an administrator.

> But his talents were not those of practical administration. He was not altogether an easy colleague; not always tolerant of disagreement and had strong likes and dislikes. Although loyal to his staff he was not a good delegator. His great value was as a 'think tank' producing original and clear ideas for others to work on and one of his assistants thought her most essential task was that of 'interpreting' him to his colleagues. (Harcourt, 1991: 23)

It is interesting to compare this evaluation with Kahn's own recollections of his wartime service based on the manuscript notes for his lecture to the Marshall Society, Cambridge, 1945, on the 'War-time Experience of the Civil Service, its Operation, and the Role of the Economist in its Ranks' (Kahn Papers, RFK 4/21/2). First, he recalls that

> the pressure on the civil servant becomes greater as one climbs the ladder of seniority and those with whom the major decisions rest, have the least time to think and enjoy conditions of life least propitious to thought for in no field of government is thought more difficult or more necessary than in the formulation and execution of economic policy. A great deal of the work must necessarily be done at a fairly low level so that youth has greater opportunities for moulding the channels in which the course of action lies. Important officials are overworked, which is undesirable when economic policy is at stake. (ibid.)

Although Kahn claims that he was never an important official he was still overworked, and could devote barely five minutes to important discussions such as the implications of multilateral convertibility, the possible integration of the British and American zones of Germany, and an import licensing policy for fruits and vegetables (ibid.: 3-4). Kahn notes, in addition:

> Being a civil servant in an economic department was like permanently sitting for an advanced examination in economics, except that one has to do all the papers at once and not less than three questions must be attempted. Simultaneously, the average calibre of junior members has deteriorated sadly with the enormous increase in their numbers. There are varied and vexing questions all the time. How far cooperation and coordination between departments, divisions, and branches be conducted direct between junior civil servants at their own level and how far the more senior officials have a necessary part to play? To what extent meetings, which occupy so much time, are an efficient substitute for minutes and letters? Whether the foibles of Ministers do not add to the congestion at the higher levels and whether too much time is spent on questions of personnel and accommodation. (ibid.: 5)

Kahn adds, however, that he is not too clear on whether insistence on literary perfection is not overdone.

> Given the complexity of economic policy and its execution, there is continuous pressure at a limited number or points at the higher levels. Adding to the number of senior officials, even if it were practical, would only aggravate problems of coordination, sagacious decisions are even more difficult to achieve under conditions of pressure than the successful execution of agreed policy. Fortunately, the congestion of the parliamentary timetable is the civil servant's salvation! (ibid.: 6).

Interestingly, Kahn is categorical that the civil service

> is anything but a system. It is a series of masterly improvisations...very little is determined by tradition...many of the tasks performed are new and for each new test...something has to be improvised, usually at not more than a month's notice...the art of improvisation...is the main ingredient in the art of government.... The miracle is that the organisation functions as well as it does. [I admire] the very high calibre, intellectual and moral, of the senior permanent civil servants who are in training and aptitude close to those who have chosen the academic way of life (ibid.: 7).

Kahn stresses that responsibility on each separate issue should rest with only one department but also recognises that in the economic sphere the interrelation of interests being wide and complex it is difficult to adhere to this and failure is frequent. Surprisingly, Kahn found in his experience of the nationalised Coal Boards that "the industrial expert put up a very poor show compared with the academic...the most successful academics were not economists...it was the exceptional business man who was a success in dealing with problems of administration and policy."

Kahn pointedly asserts that

> the function of economists, at any rate in conditions of war has been scarcely fulfilled at all. I refer to the use of economic modules. One had to take decisions without data, as when I had to decide in the Middle East Supply Centre whether it was worthwhile taking Ethiopian wheat by lorry to Asmara so as to feed Eritrea or to ship it from overseas without any quantitative formulation of the relative scarcities of rubber tyres and shipping space. (ibid.: 23)

Regrettably, Kahn never expressed his views on how he regarded the Economic Civil Service in the UK—a clone or a mutant? In sum, for him the economist in the civil service could not claim any superiority over an equally competent civil servant.

Kahn, however, posed a crucial question of the economist's role in the international civil service when he reviewed the Third Annual Report of the International Bank for Reconstruction and Development (1947-48) (*The Economic Journal*, September 1949: 445-447). He said:

> Whether the results achieved by the Bank and by the other bodies engaged on regional and international economic questions, justify the absorption of so many eminent and promising economists is a question of the utmost importance on which a Report of this kind cannot be expected to throw much light.

Incredibly, half a century later, Strauss-Kahn, the Managing Director of the International Monetary Fund, confirmed these very apprehensions: "The IMF is a factory to produce paper" (*The Wall Street Journal*, 7 December 2007).

We are never told the causes thereof despite the lip-service of the IMF to transparency.

THE IMPERATIVES OF A STATUTORY PRICES AND INCOMES POLICY

With the years of High Theory behind him, Kahn was increasingly concerned with the problems posed by rising prices at high levels of employment in industrial democracies, particularly the UK, which led him to argue forcefully the case for a statutory incomes and prices policy in the UK beginning with his thoughtful intervention in the House of Lords in the discussions on the White Paper on Prices and Incomes Standstill (Cmnd. 3073, 3 August 1966).* Kahn stressed that

> the major element in the mechanism of inflation – the vicious wage-wage spiral often described as the leap-frogging effect...is the competitive struggle between the different labour groups which is the overwhelming influence ... each is trying to secure that its real wage rises faster than the average...an achievement which only one-half of the wage-earners can secure at the expense or the other half. The leap-frogging is largely between different trade unions and within trade unions, and also within individual companies between the more skilled and better-paid workers and the less skilled and less well-paid. Before long differentials are widened again and resolved to their traditional magnitudes. We have far too many trade unions... the greater the number of groups in the competitive struggle for each to secure bigger increases than the others, the faster will wages rise...trade union leaders naturally want to be seen earning their salaries. Their sole concern is with the level of the real wage in the immediate future as opposed to the rate of increase in the real wage. We are backward in promoting training and mobility of labour...and [there] is the enmity between trade union officials and shop stewards. Our central employer (CBI) and trade union organisations (TUC) are sadly lacking in intelligence...they contrast very unfavourably with those of the Scandinavian countries and Austria. (1976: 1-7)

Thus, Kahn very perceptively diagnosed that the core of industrial relations in the UK was the dysfunctional organisation of trade unions and was also emphatic that incomes policies should not only comprehend wages but also salaries and remuneration of company directors and executives as well as prices. But he also recognised the difficult problem of "defining what is meant by an underpaid worker" (House of Lords, 3 August 1966, p.2). In sum, for Kahn a coherent and purposive statutory incomes and policy, taking account of trends in productivity, was as much of a macroeconomic policy

---

* Robert Skidelsky in his biography of *Oswald Mosley* (London: Macmillan, 1981) provides a most interesting historical perspective on the provenance of the concept of prices and incomes policies in Britain. He remarks: "John Wheatley [a Labour MP] had advocated a planned incomes policy in 1926 ... In the 1920s and 1930s [Mosley] advocated in essence...what he called 'a wage-price mechanism' or, as it would now be called, a compulsory prices and incomes policy. As far as I know, Mosley was the first politician to make this the central instrument of economic planning and certainly the first to think of applying it on a European scale ... In 1957 Mosley distinguished between the 'positive' uses of the wage-price policy to secure even growth in a self-contained system and its 'negative' form of a wage-price freeze to hold down costs in order to compete on world markets (European, September 1957); the economist Dr. Thomas Balogh was the intellectual pioneer of this approach about this time: was Mosley influenced by him?" (p.494)

instrument as exchange rate and monetary-fiscal policy, which would also be congruent with the ends of social justice.

Kahn did not, however, explicate the intrinsic complexities of incomes policies, which cannot be reduced to any single unambiguous criterion or type, as so well analysed by Rupert Pennant Rea, who makes the telling point that although incomes policies, which are, in fact, concerned only with wages, are justified as a way of reducing nominal inflation, also change the distribution of income, usually by squeezing real wages (1987). The successful policies have been those which recognise explicitly that the distribution of real income is at stake and "plan the rate of change of money wages as part of a socio-political deal...and/or implemented when real national income is growing rapidly so that all real wages can increase even as the distribution of real income is changed" (ibid.: 750). The moral: Incomes policies can only be designed as part of a consensual social contract, as borne out by the experience of Scandinavia and Austria among industrial democracies and, even more remarkably, Mauritius among developing countries, which has achieved high sustained development and a welfare state based on a balanced socio-economic and political compact between the French economic elite, a political minority, and the political elite, the majority Indians (Subramanian and Roy, 2001).

Incomes and price policies have, in turn, to be viewed in the context of political business cycles, first identified by Michal Kalecki in his path-breaking analysis of the *Political Aspects of Full Employment* (1943), which afflict all industrial democracies but which have been virtually ignored in post-Keynesian discussions of incomes policies, except in Australia (Harcourt, 2001). Full employment, or high employment, is best regarded as a zone of turbulence rather than a Plimsoll line, a tip-over point. It is unrealistic to conceive of stasis, a Goldilocks economy, as it were. In a second-best world, one does not look for final solutions. Rather, one has to build up the capacity for coping with ever emerging disequilibria.

Development Issues and Policies

The only occasion when Kahn addressed developmental issues was in his article on "Pace of Development" (1972), where he analysed the typical case of an overpopulated underdeveloped country, in which there is surplus labour, i.e., underemployment and imperfect employment in agriculture and the service trades and, consequently, its marginal product tends to be zero or even negative. This is a more nuanced version of the conventional concept of disguised unemployment. The economic benefit or any diversion of surplus labour to more productive employment "is measured roughly by the excess of the wages in industry over the marginal product in labour, whereas the private incentive is measured roughly by the excess of the industrial wage over the agricultural average product" (p.189). He argues that what is involved in forcing a high rate of development is not a reduction in the total consumption but principally a redistribution of consumption between different classes, not only between those who are among the fully employed but also those who are unemployed or underemployed. This is the real challenge of development policy. The

> need to allow a fairly rapid rise in the standard of living of the fully employed is not sufficiently questioned, the same growing volume of consumption, if spread out more evenly, would not only mean less human misery, because the growth of employment would be more rapid, but would actually mean a more rapid growth of development. (p. 160)

Kahn is justifiably critical of the pervasive "neglect of the interests of the unemployed and imperfectly employed" in the developing countries, like India and Pakistan, that "goes hand in hand with neglect of the question how in fact they live" (p.166). This points to the containment of "possible sacrifice to the foregoing of part of the year-by-year improvement in standards of living rather than to call at any point of time for an absolute fall in standards" (p.176). But Kahn is also careful to point out that the case for utilising surplus labour to increase output is not to suggest that "greater employment should be secured at the expense of smaller output" (p.181). He does concede that "the question of the right choice or technique is vast and baffling" (p.182), which involves the complex indeterminate issue of the appropriate social rate of discount. However, he is categorical that "the right technique is a less capital-using one than the technique which is calculated to maximize the rate of accumulation" (p.155). This argues the case for labour-intensive techniques of production not only in rural areas but also in the urban areas which too suffer from disguised unemployment.

It is important to restrain the rise in the standard of living of the affluent rural classes through a progressive land tax, a conspicuous failure of the Indian polity which relies on the antiquated regressive land revenue system, a tax subsidy to rich farmers, who also enjoy benefits of subsidised irrigation and electricity. This only reflects the political power of the Indian *kulak* class, a major vote bank of ruling parties like the Indian Congress, even as organised (Marxist) industrial labour jealously guards the privileges of the fully employed classes as against the interests of the unemployed and imperfectly employed.

In sum, Kahn offers a perceptive analysis of the core problems of a typical overpopulated underdeveloped country like India, which has not figured in the otherwise copious discourse on development economics.

Kahn also addressed the question of aid to less-developed countries (1973), where he argued persuasively against the proposal to issue the Special Drawings Rights of the International Monetary Fund to central banks in order to provide aid to less developed countries. He showed that

> while the operation of the Link could add a fairly substantial proportion to the amount of aid now being provided, it is likely that in absolute terms it would be small, since the volume of aid now given is itself so small. It is very important to increase aid, precisely because its total is today so derisory (p.1).

Kahn did not, however, at any time provide the economic rationale for increasing aid to less-developed countries but he did conclude "that were SDRs allocated more liberally and were their allocation the basis of operation of the Link, the world from most points of view would be in a healthier state."

Kahn: A Self Appraisal

How did Kahn assess his own contributions? Remarkably, his self composed entry in the *Who is Who in Economics*, 1986 (ed. Mark Blaug) reads like an essay in self-abnegation in a publication which abounds in the self-referential contributions of the *Arrivisti*. Thus, he very modestly lists his principal contributions as follows: "I was closely associated with Keynes as pupil, as collaborator and in his stock exchange ventures. As a wartime civil servant (1939-1946) I received administrative experience. After the war [I worked] for the Treasury and was a part-time member of the National Coal Board." Then he goes on to list his work on the European Economic Commission and the Organisation for European Economic Cooperation groups to study the problem of rising prices which introduced the idea of the wage spiral via 'leap-frogging.' But, characteristically, Kahn gave credit to the group although he was the recognised originator of this concept. Nowhere in this entry does he list his seminal contributions to economic theory. Ever the reclusive sage whose lexicon lacked the first-person singular, which perhaps also explains his omission from the masthead of the *Cambridge Journal of Economics* 'founded in the traditions of Marx, Keynes, Kalecki, Joan Robinson, and Kaldor.'

In politics, too, Kahn remained the eternal self-critical sceptic, the Labour MP who sat on the cross benches and the observant Orthodox Jew who was positive but never uncritical of Israel.

References

Annan, Noel (1999). *The Dons (Mentors, Eccentrics and Geniuses.* London: HarperCollins.

Harcourt, Geoffrey (1991). 'R.F. Kahn: A Tribute,' *Banca Nazionale del Lavoro Quarterly Review* 176, March.

Harcourt, G.C. (2001). *Selected Essays on Economic Policy*. London: Palgrave.

Harrod, Roy (1959). *The Prof (A Personal Memoir of Lord Cherwell)*, London.: Macmillan.

Kahn, Richard (1972). "The Pace of Development" [1958], *in Selected Essays on Employment and Growth*. Cambridge: Cambridge University Press.

————. (1976a). "Political Attitudes Involved in Teaching Economics", *Oxford Review of Education* 2(1).

————. (1976b). "Thoughts on the Behaviour of Wages and Monetarism", *Lloyds Bank Review* 119, January.

Kalecki, Michael (1971 [1943]). "Political Aspects or Full Employment", in *Selected Essays on the Dynamics of the Capitalist Economy 1933–1970.* Cambridge: Cambridge University Press.

Pasinetti, Luigi (1987). "Richard Kahn", in John Eatwell (ed.), *The New Palgrave (A Dictionary of Economics)*, Vol. 3. London: Macmillan.

Patel, I.G. (2002). *Glimpses of Indian Economic Policy (An Insider's View).* New Delhi: Oxford University Press.

Pennant-Rea, Rupert (1987). "Incomes Policies", in John Eatwell (ed.), *The New Palgrave (A Dictionary of Economics)*, Vol. 2. London: Macmillan.

Samuelson, P.A. (1994). "Richard Kahn: His Welfare Economics and Lifetime Achievement", *Cambridge Journal of Economics* 18(1) : 55–72, (February).

Schumpeter, J.A. (1954). *History of Economic Analysis*. New York: Oxford University Press.

Subramanian, Arvind and Devesh Roy (n.d.Z). "Who Can Explain the Mauritian Miracle: Meade, Romer, Sachs, or Rodrick", *IMF Working Paper* WP/011116.

15 Elasticity of Demand for Gold in India*

This article is intended as an introduction to I.G. Patel's writings on India's gold problem, following the publication for the first time in this issue of his pioneering International Monetary Fund research paper, "India's Elasticity of Demand for Gold", dated 21 August 1950. The introductory essay evaluates the paper as well as Patel's anonymous article, "On Turning Gold into Base Metals", in *Economic Weekly*, July 1958, which analyses different modes of mobilising India's hoarded gold through incentives, compulsion and sustained propaganda. As a civil servant, Patel was also involved in various issues of gold policy. The article also underscores the contemporary relevance of Patel's pioneering research on gold, taking account of subsequent literature, and outlines a research programme, in consonance with the state of the art, to address the still unresolved problems of the analysis of gold demand and the mobilisation of gold for productive use.

I.G. Patel on India's Gold Problem

India has been famously described as the perennial sink of the precious metals (Stanley Jevons) and the first Indian governor of the Reserve Bank of India (RBI) underscored this theme: "Gold and silver run like twin threads in India's economic destiny and operations in those metals have occupied quite a substantial part of the time and attention of the executive of the Reserve Bank" (Deshmukh, 1997: 26). These observations sum up the analytic and policy aspects of India's perennial gold problem, which consistently engaged Patel's attention in later years as an economic advisor and ranking civil servant. What determines the virtually insatiable appetite of India for gold and how does one mobilise its gold for productive purposes? It was therefore uncannily appropriate that the young I.G. Patel, destined to be Deshmukh's mantle-bearer, began his career in the IMF with a pioneering research paper on "India's Elasticity of Demand for Gold" (21 August 1950). It estimated the responsiveness of India's demand for gold to changes in its relative price

* *Source: Economic and Political Weekly* XVI(6) (11 February 2006): 507-509.

(dependent variable) by attempting to correlate the net flow of gold from or into private hoards during the period 1925-1942 and 1949-50 (April-May) with two independent variables: the relative price of gold and the consumption of refined sugar as a proxy for real national income. The results suggested that the demand for gold was highly responsive to changes in its relative price. Patel argued that, historically, price has been a more important explanatory variable than income, allowing for the fact that the shortcomings of the data used tend to overestimate the price effect and underestimate the income effect and that the effect of a certain increase in income may not be symmetrical to the same decline in income. The assumption of linearity of the underlying relation also implies that over the period considered, no factors other than price and income supervened, assumptions which were recognised to be questionable, particularly the changes in the distribution of income induced by changes in the terms of trade between agriculture and non-agricultural occupations. But apart from this the period 1925-26 to 1941-42 seems to have been reasonably free of random offsetting factors. Patel also recognised that in any analysis of demand for gold, which is both a consumer good and a vehicle of savings, the assumption of a linear functional relation coupled with variations in real income around the subsistence level, complicates matters. Likewise, he rightly cautioned about the perils of extrapolating his results given, among others, the exceptionality of the period 1925-1940 when India had no experience of serious inflation or political instability, which are among the most potent customary factors propelling the demand for gold. He, however, sensed the emergent role of gold as a medium of tax evasion in the post-war era.

Patel's paper, however, poses a statistical question concerning the choice of refined sugar consumption as a proxy for real national income. It was suggested by Polak (Deputy Director of Research, IMF) who had found that "the income elasticity of demand for sugar in Indonesia was unity" (Patel, 2002: 29). Apart from the fallacy of territorial transposition, it overlooked that unrefined sugar accounts for the bulk of sugar consumption in India. Cereal consumption as a more universal wage-good would have been a much closer proxy. This does not in any way detract from the pioneering statistical research presented in a characteristically lean and muscular prose. A prototype of its kind that poses the intriguing question: Why then was the paper not published in the IMF Staff Papers, which subsequently carried Patel's much acclaimed articles on post-war monetary policy and selective credit controls? "Polak was very keen on publishing the paper, but I resisted this as, unlike him, I was sceptical of correlation analysis" (Patel, 2002: 30). An astonishing, almost nihilistic, disclaimer by so ecumenical an economist. Correlation analysis, for all its recognised limitations even after the invention of the Granger causality and other tests of significance, remains the primary tool of economics as a science based on hypothesis testing. In fact, the poverty of economics was rightly attributed by Karl Popper to the neglect of hypothesis testing. In the absence of scientific correlation analysis, economics would lapse into casual or implicit empiricism on a par with the implicit theorising of the Cambridge School rightly castigated by Leontief. Was there a more subtle reason for Patel's reluctance to publish this paper as well as his cutting-edge doctoral dissertation (1949) on international trade and economic development? Was it the last remnant of an eccentric Cambridge tradition in economics, most notably represented by Gerald Shove, Patel's supervisor at King's College, who had a curious, almost moralistic, disdain for publication of research no matter how original. Thus, Shove's two fellowship dissertations at King's College were never published. "In his will he left instructions that all his manuscripts were to be destroyed. His determination not to publish anything until it seemed to say exactly what he means sprang ultimately from a deep, indeed religious, fealty to truth" (Kahn, 1987: 328-329). Shove was, after all, the most formative influence, deriving from the applied ethics of the Cambridge philosopher George Moore, on Patel's mindset and values.

Having fathomed the empirics of the demand for gold in India, the doggedly pragmatic Patel was inevitably led to the core issue. Given the demand for gold, how does one mobilise the stock of hoarded gold and flow of smuggled gold into the 'sinews of India's economic growth', an issue which he addressed in a typically astute anonymous article in *The Economic Weekly*—where else!—aptly titled "On Turning Gold into Base Metals" (1958: 917-919). A picturesque and productive inversion of the 'more familiar search for an alchemy to convert base metals into gold'. The article is a closely reasoned evaluation of alternative modes of transferring private gold to official reserves, *viz.*, open market purchases by the government issue of bonds redeemable in rupees against delivery of gold and/or to be subscribed and redeemed in gold, and acquisition by compulsion. He was, however, emphatic that gold bonds would "either prove a flop" or "make for a stronger entrenchment of tax-evasion and smuggling of gold" (ibid.: 919). He concluded that the solution of the problem must be sought in a "mixture of sustained propaganda, compulsion, incentives affecting people's expectations about the value of gold in future" (ibid.: 917). As it happened, Patel reverted to the theme of gold mobilisation in a private communication on Chandavarkar's article on the economics of gold hoarding (1961).[1] He endorsed its conceptual and analytic framework, including the disconnect between Keynesian liquidity preference and gold hoarding. But he took issue with its proposal for auctioning of import licences against surrender of gold on the ground that it would violate the IMF articles of agreement consequent upon purchases of gold at a higher price than the IMF price (Rs 62.50 per *tola*). The counter-argument would have been to seek a waiver, analogous to the one given to the float of the Canadian dollar, which was also a violation of the par value rule.[2] Additionally, India could have invoked Joseph Gold's (general counsel of the IMF) equity doctrine of giving the overwhelming benefit of doubt to member countries. Significantly, Patel "admitted that the gold control" introduced in the wake of the Chinese war "was misconceived and should never have been attempted" and stressed the moral hazards of any gold bond scheme which would only put a premium on hoarding wealth in bars and biscuits (Patel, 2002: 92-93).

How well have Patel's analysis of gold demand and his gold mobilisation stance stood the test of time and what is their contemporary relevance?

The first analysis, following Patel's pioneering effort, estimated that the price elasticity of gold for India (1952-1959) relative to the consumer index, was 1.6, i.e., the real value of gold in terms of consumer goods rose during the period (Heston, 1961: 216). Madan argued that there probably is a considerable upward income elasticity of demand for gold, as indicated, for instance by the close correlation of gold flows and periods of agricultural prosperity (1961: 524). He also cautioned that if the government were to sell abroad the gold obtained from such bonds, it might erode confidence in the bonds. Madan's article is a masterly analysis of the problem of gold mobilisation in India, particularly the intrinsic limitations of gold certificates and controls (ibid.: 523-525). Hugh Patrick's article being primarily concerned with mobilisation of private gold holdings did not make any statistical estimate of the estimate of the demand and merely surmised that, given the high positive net yield on gold as a durable consumer good, demand for gold is quite price-inelastic (1963: 181). However, it provided a comprehensive analysis of the various possible mobilisation schemes, and opted for a well-designed gold bond with a realistic interest rate as the preferred instrument, conceding that "this is essentially an empirical matter which can be verified only by trying it out" (ibid.: 198).

It is a pity that the Reserve Bank of India's discussion paper on "Gold Mobilisation as an Instrument of External Adjustment" (1992), coming as it did after over thirty years from Patel's paper (1958), is a flimsy effort which hardly reflects the state of the art. It treats demand for gold as a monistic concept whereas it is a portmanteau concept which has to be appropriately unbundled into the different characteristics of gold as a consumer and industrial good, inflation hedge, and vehicle for tax evasion, utilising the 'characteristics approach' to demand theory developed by Lancaster (1971). A good example of this approach is the research paper of Peter Abken (1980) which classifies the demand component of gold into bullion and fabrication with appropriate subsets (carat jewellery, electronics, dentistry, industrial/derivative uses, medals/fake coins, official coins). Given the massive tax evasion in India, an important determining variable is the marginal rate of income and wealth tax, which is conspicuously missing from the RBI analysis. Its bibliography, which even lists unpublished reports of the RBI and a newspaper article by the lead author, does not cite a single relevant scholarly or technical article listed in the bibliography of this essay. It ignores the basic contributions of not only Agarwal, Alan Heston and others, but even those of RBI alumni, including Patel and Madan. Patel's IMF paper was available to the authors from the Bank-Fund section files of the RBI. Altogether, the RBI's paper on gold comes across more as a *swadeshi* mutation of "the attractive Anglo-Saxon kind of unnecessary originality", as so memorably stated by Gunnar Myrdal.

The RBI paper, after admitting past failures of gold bonds, gold auctions and gold control, did not care to analyse their causes, and blithely proposed the creation of a gold policy board, a gold management corporation, a gold bank, together with offer of assorted instruments like gold bonds, scrips, gold term deposits, gold repurchase agreements. One more manifestation of the national malady of institutionalitis—create a new institution to solve every emergent problem (Khatkhate, 1961). Unsurprisingly, all these baroque schemes come to naught without any explanation by the RBI, which earlier did not even think it fit to publish the reports of the Working Group on Gold Policy (1989) and the Task Force on the Proposal to Form a National Gold Bank (1992). The latter was even envisaged by the lead author as an alternative to IMF credit! "But whatever the ultimate solution, the agenda for the dethronement of gold from the position it occupies today in India deserves more serious consideration at the hands of thinking people in the country than it has received so far" (Patel, 1958: 917). Despite the long lapse of time, there has been no serious research and debate on India's gold problem: its correctives have been dreamed up on a ad hoc knee-jerk basis.

What are the contours of a realistic research programme to address the problem of gold hoarding, which is both a conventional and psychological phenomenon, in contrast to Keynes's formulation of the rate of interest as a "highly conventional, rather than a highly psychological, phenomenon" (1973: 203)? What then are the relevant testable hypotheses given that gold hoarding is essentially a demand-driven phenomenon, which has to be disaggregated using Lancaster's 'characteristics' approach to demand for gold: as a durable consumer good (ornaments); store of value (bullion—inflation hedge); vehicle for tax evasion (which would vary with the height of marginal rates of income and wealth tax): and industrial uses?

The following is an illustrative list of promising complementary lines of research, structural as well as conjunctural.

- Nature and efficiency of gold markets in India, on the lines of Agarwal and Soenen (1988), Tschoegl (1980), Mani and Vuyyuri (2003).
- Relative strength of price and income elasticity.
- Time series of gold prices decomposed into trend cycle, seasonal and irregular component (random) factors using adjustment programmes like those of the US Bureau of Census (x-11Q quarterly seasonal adjustment). The seasonal factor is calculated to capture demand as determined by harvest, festival and marriage season.
- Why is India's experience of precious metals a polar contrast to that of the West? For instance, medieval Spain's 'foreign trade was destroyed by the effect on the wage-unit of an excessive abundance of precious metals' (Keynes, 1973: 337), whereas India never experienced a comparable impact. On the other hand, the West never witnessed anything like the massive exports of hoarded gold from India in the wake of the Great Depression in the 1930s.

Gold hoarding and gold mobilisation is a complex socio-economic problem, a reminder that "economic policy is not just about economics. It is about history, sociology, politics and psychology as well" (Patel, 2002: 92). The failure of sumptuary legislation in India (prohibition, anti-usury and gold control) is a salutary warning against a dirigiste approach to gold hoarding whose nature and correctives merit an approach drawing on economics, economic history (Tawney plus cliometrics on the lines of Robert Fogel and Douglas North), economic anthropology (Polly Hill and Mary Douglas), and historical politics. Even an economics Nobel laureate, Robert Solow, wondered how often economic discourse seems to end in 'a blaze of sociology'. How else does one explain that even the IMF, after demonetising gold, continues to hold 103 million fine ounces of gold on its balance sheet? The Indian peasant and the Indian housewife, however, would fully appreciate the supreme paradox of the IMF's gold hoard.

The thesaurisation (absorption of precious metals) of the Indian economy is a rich and challenging theme that awaits collaborative research by Indian economists. It could ideally be sponsored by the RBI following the precedent of its monetary statistics of India. This would be a fitting tribute to the memory and intellectual legacy of Patel, whose writings on gold still retain a strong contemporary relevance.

A postscript. Remarkably, Patel, in a talk to the Bombay Economists' Forum at the RBI (c.1953), had also cogently argued for a rise in the IMF's international price of gold ($35 per fine ounce) long before it was aired in the public domain by R.F. Harrod (1958: 10).

NOTES

1. In this communication Patel also disclosed his authorship of the anonymous article on "Turning Gold into Base Metals" in *The Economic Weekly*, July 1958 (Special Number).

2. Patel, however, overlooked that the International Monetary Fund, while it "strongly deprecates international transactions in gold at premium prices and recommends that all its members take effective transactions in gold with other countries or with nationals of other countries" would not object to domestic transactions above parity "unless they have the effect of establishing new rates of exchange or undermining existing rates of other members, or unless they result in significant weakening of international financial position of a member which might affect its utilisation of the Fund's resources" (Report of External Transactions in Gold at Premium Prices, IMF, Washington, 1950, p.6). It would, therefore, have been open to India to seek a waiver in the event of auctions of import licences against surrender of private gold.

References

Abken, Peter A. (1980). "The Economics of Gold Price Movements", *Economic Review:* 3–13, March-April. Federal Reserve Bank of Richmond.

Agarwal, R. and L. Soenen (1988). "The Nature and Efficiency of Gold Markets", *Journal of Portfolio Management* 14(3): 18–21, Spring.

Chandavarkar, A.G. (1961). "The Nature and Effects of Gold Hoarding in Underdeveloped Economies", *Oxford Economic Papers*: 137–48, June.

Deshmukh, C.D. (1997). "Central Banking in India: A Retrospect", in *50 Years of Central Banking (Governosr Speaking)*. Bombay: Reserve Bank of India. pp.1–34.

Harrod, R.F. (1958). "The Role of Gold Today", *South African Journal of Economics*: 3–13, March.

Heston, Alan (1961). 'An Empirical Study of Indian Gold Prices', *Indian Economic Journal* VIII(3): 210–19, (January):.

Kahn, R.F. (1987). "Gerald Frank Shove", in *The New Palgrave: A Dictionary of Economics*, Vol. 4. London: Macmillan: 327–8.

Keynes, J.M. (1973). *The General Theory of Employment, Interest and Money, The Collected Writings of John Maynard Keynes*. London: Macmillan.

Khatkhate, Deena (1961). "The Economic Adviser", *Economic Times*, 11 April (Op.-Ed).

Lancastei, Kelvin (1971). *Consumer Demand: A New Approach*. New York: Columbia University Press.

Madan, B.K. (1961). "The Role of Monetary Policy in a Developing Economy", *Reserve Bank of India Bulletin*: 518–36, April.

Mani, Ganesh and Srivyal Vuyyuri (2003). "Gold Pricing in India: An Econometric Analysis", *Economic Research* 16(1): 29–44.

Patel, I.G. (1950). "India's Elasticity of Demand for Gold", *International Monetary Fund Research Paper* 27: 1–18.

Patel, I.G. (Anon) (1958). "On Turning Gold into Base Metals", *The Economic Weekly* Special Number: 917–19, July.

————. (2002). *Glimpses of Indian Economic Policy: An Insider's View*. New Delhi: Oxford University Press.

Patrick, Hugh T. (1963). "The Mobilisation of Private Gold Holdings", *Indian Economic Journal*, October–December.

Reserve Bank of India (1992). "Gold Mobilistion as an Instrument of External Adjustment", A Discussion Paper, co-authors Atul Sarma, A. Vasudevan, K. Kanagasabapathy, Mythili Narayan, Mohaua Roy, 21 April, Bombay, pp. 1–70.

Tschoegl, A.E. (1980). "Efficiency of the Gold Market", *Journal of Banking and Finance*: 371–9, December.

16 Legal Tender Currency and Public Debt*

The Radcliffe Committee's statistical treatment of notes and coin as part of the gross and net debt of the public sector in its report[1] raises the issue whether, from the point of analysis, statistics or policy, legal tender currency can be treated on all fours with other obligations of the public sector. It is significant that while the committee treats these two categories of government obligations on a par both in the presentation of the relevant statistics of public debt in the report and in course of the evidence[2] proceedings, the analysis of debt management and demand for the debt in the report proceeds on the assumption that legal tender currency and public debt are dissimilar types of public obligations. This is, of course, not surprising considering the differences in the real nature of legal tender currency and public debt, whether regarded as liabilities of the public sector or as assets of the private sector.

Conceptually, no doubt one could regard notes and coin as a liquid debt of the government which is payable on demand, with the difference that the issue of legal tender currency is a form of government borrowing at a zero rate of interest, which does not create problems of redemption, service and refinance as in the case of borrowing through issue of interest-bearing securities.

The non-marketable segment of public debt, comprising small savings and such other securities which are encashable on demand or at very short notice without loss of capital value, is the nearest among government securities in point of liquidity to legal tender currency. And while it is also possible to monetise and thereby assimilate marketable public debt to legal tender currency within fairly close limits, by a stable bond market policy and making securities eligible for settlement of certain dues of the State such as death duties or other taxes, such an approach can at best be 'asymptotic', since no policies or institutional devices can obliterate the distinction between money, near-money and non-money without at least fundamentally changing economic society as we know it.

---

* *Source: Public Finance* XVII(1) (1962): 82-87.

There is a formal point of partial similarity between legal tender currency and the public debt inasmuch as while legal tender currency functions as a unit and instrument of account for the economy as a whole, public debt to the extent that it is held by the government and its agencies is also an instrument of intra-governmental accounting[3] for mediating and recording payments between different parts of the government sector e.g., between the Treasury and the Central Bank.

To the extent that there is a distinct average minimum level of private sector holdings of notes and coin as part of cash balances, it is conceptually similar to the 'floor' level of the holdings of public debt by the private sector. The floors of idle cash and 'firmly held' debt both represent the limit above which monetary and debt policy are really effective since cash balances and security holdings below this level are comparatively insensitive to changes in rates of interest or other relevant variables. This is the line above which the authorities can operate on the asset-behaviour of the private sector since the sensitive holdings of legal tender currency and of government securities are media for transmission of changes in monetary policy.

II

But apart from these few rather formalistic similarities between legal tender currency and government securities, there are many more substantial differences between them in respect of objectives, mechanics and economic significance.

The treatment of the two categories of obligations of the State as part of public debt would abolish the crucial distinction between legal tender currency as a liquid non-interest bearing asset for the community and interest bearing liabilities of the State, which though part of near-money, are certainly distinct from money. There is not merely a gradation but a gap in the spectrum of assets as between money and near-money, which is defined by whether or not any particular asset bears interest. In fact, the very problem of monetary theory is to explain the demand for money even though it has no positive yield in its own terms. This is, of course, abstracting from any psychic income from holding money, which in any case is not relevant in the present context.

The demand for money arises from a different set of causes than those which govern demand for interest-bearing government securities. Likewise, an important objective of monetary and debt policy is to prevent monetisation of the public debt, that is, to avoid a situation where debt becomes a substitute for money, and generally to regulate asset preferences of the public, including banks, as between money and securities. Thus, neither analysis nor policy can overlook the fundamental distinction between 'money' and 'debt'.

The purpose of issue of legal tender currency and of incurring interest-bearing obligations is qualitatively different. The primary aim of issue of legal tender currency is to provide a medium of exchange to the community whereas the object of issuing interest-bearing obligations is to reduce the liquidity of the private sector and/or to finance formation of real assets in the public sector. Insofar as the objective of incurring or redeeming interest-bearing obligations is to compensate changes in the liquidity of the rest of the economy or of any particular sector in it, government borrowing is really an instrument of stabilisation to counteract fluctuations in the private sector's holdings of legal tender currency and bank deposits. The object of reducing the liquidity of the private sector through issue of securities is really to reduce its consumption and/or investment and release real resources to the public sector. This sequence may not always materialise owing to supervention of other factors but, nevertheless, its mechanics and objectives are clear. If, however, the pattern of liquidity preference in a community is such that even currency is hoarded, as for instance in an underdeveloped economy, then the reduction-of-liquidity motive of issuing government securities is correspondingly attenuated. It is because it is more difficult or less easy for people to sell their securities and use the proceeds for current expenditure that government borrowing through interest-bearing securities is less inflationary than through direct issue of non-interest-bearing notes and coin. This would hold good even if government securities were issued in non-interest-bearing form but without the facility of encashment on demand or at short notice. The economic merits of government borrowing through interest-bearing securities *vis-à-vis* issue of legal tender currency are in direct proportion to the gap between money and securities. The greater this gap, the more effective it is in reducing the liquidity of the economy.

III

In examining the relationship between legal tender currency and public debt, it is also necessary to consider their relative roles as liabilities of the public sector and as assets of the private sector.

In drawing up the balance sheet of the public sector we have first to set off against the interest-bearing obligations the real assets of the State.

Consequently, it is only that part of the public debt which is not covered by any real assets, namely the deadweight debt, and which is held by the private sector, that constitutes a net liability of the public sector. Similarly, that part of legal tender currency which is not backed by any real assets of the government such as gold and foreign securities and is held by the private sector, is a part of the net liability of the public sector. To the extent that legal tender currency is issued against the backing of the government's own securities held in the portfolio of the central bank, it in effect amounts to backing one liability of government (legal tender currency) with another liability of the government (securities). Consequently, the net income of a government-owned central bank derived from the holdings of domestic government securities should be regarded more as an accounting profit rather than a genuine economic surplus. But government securities constitute a substantial part of the asset-backing for not only bank notes and coin but also indirectly for bank money in so far as the government securities held by commercial banks function as the basis of credit creation.

From the point of view of their role in the asset structure of the private sector, legal tender currency and government securities are also significantly different. Thus, the Pigou effect of a rise in the real value of money is not significant in the case of holdings of government securities. A rise in the real value of the nominal capital sum of government securities held by the private sector is not of as much consequence to its propensity to consume or to invest as a rise in the real value of cash balances held as legal tender currency and bank money created against government indebtedness.[4] A partial qualification to this argument is the increase in the real value of the interest yield on government securities which, being a part at current income for the private sector, is more likely to affect its behaviour pattern than a rise in capital value of government securities. This, however, would be very small in comparison with the magnitude of the Pigou effect on money balances.

The reverse of the Pigou effect on the behaviour of the public sector is different in respect of legal tender currency and interest-bearing liabilities. A rise in the real value of the public's holdings of legal tender currency imposes no direct additional burden on the government whereas a rise in the real value of capital and of interest on government securities increases the burden of debt on government and affects the terms of new issues. Similarly, a fall in the real value of money eases the burden of interest-bearing debt, a case of depreciation in the value of one government liability (currency) reducing the commitment on another government liability (securities).

IV

From the point of view of monetary and financial statistics and policy, it is, of course, useful and necessary to have data relating to the public debt held by the public, that is to say, entities other than government and public authorities as well as the money supply with the public. In this respect, it is interesting to note that whereas the concept of money supply with the public has long become an accepted part of monetary statistics, the corresponding concept of government debt held by the public has not yet been accorded the same place in financial statistics. It is only now that it is being better recognised that the really meaningful quantity in regard to public debt is that portion of it which is held by the private sector. From this point of view, the Radcliffe Committee's presentation of the public debt excluding that part of it which is held within the public sector itself is a long overdue innovation in the design of public debt statistics. But it is unfortunate that the committee did not make any estimates of the firmly held segment of public debt and of the floor level of idle cash in the economy, magnitudes which would have been invaluable in demarcating part of the area of effectiveness of monetary and debt policy.

V

Thus, on the whole, in view of the qualitative differences between legal tender currency and interest-bearing debt, there is little justification for treating them on par as part of the public debt, whether from the point of view of analysis or of policy. There is all the difference between legal tender currency and interest-bearing government debt though both are formally obligations of the government. They are really different types of government liabilities and, likewise, different forms of assets of the private sector.

Notes

1 Report of the Committee on the Working of the Monetary System, Her Majesty's Stationery Office, Cmnd 827, Tables 24 and 25, pp.192-193.

2 Though there is no systematic discussion in the Report or Evidence of the theoretical justification for regarding legal tender currency as part of the public debt, some of the observations of the two economist members of the Committee recorded in the minutes of evidence bear this out. Thus, according to Professor Sayers, "cash is that part of the National Debt on which the Government does not pay interest" (Minutes of Evidence, para 486). Professor Cairncross's observation, while implying that cash is a part of the public debt, also admits that its relative share in the public debt is a matter of importance, a qualification which would undermine considerably the case for regarding

it as a public obligation similar to interest-bearing government debt. According to him, "...the major material factor is the size of the public debt, but it makes some difference whether it is held in Treasury bills or cash. If you increase the supply of cash relative to Treasury bills you will tend to reduce short term rates of interest" (Minutes of Evidence, para 368).

3 There is an interesting discussion of this aspect of public debt in E. Nevin (1954). "The Debt and Social Accounting", in *The Problem of the National Debt*. University of Wales Press.

4 Bank money issued against private loans and securities is excluded from consideration here because a rise in the real value of such money is offset by a rise in the real value of the corresponding bank assets (loans and securities), which are liabilities of the public. Consequently, the net worth of the public is not increased by a fall in the price level and the Pigou effect is therefore inoperative. There is no such offsetting element in regard to bank money created against government indebtedness.

17 The Premium for Risk as a Determinant of Interest Rates in Underdeveloped Rural Areas*

Mr. Anthony Bottomley's main conclusion, namely, that 'administration charges, together with the premium for risk, are probably the major determinants of the high level of interest rates which obtain throughout the underdeveloped world'[1] overlooks that the elements of monopoly and oligopoly in the lending business may be even more important as an explanation of high rates of interest in these economies than the risk premium and administration charges. Although he does recognise that "wherever interest rates more than cover these charges, they will contain an element of monopoly profit",[2] he makes allowance, only *en passant*, for the component of monopoly profit in interest.[3] The present note attempts to prove that the degree of monopoly power of the lender may well be the most important single determinant of interest rates.

Moneylenders and indigenous bankers supply the major portion of the credit requirements in the rural areas of underdeveloped economies. These lenders are invariably in a position to exercise a considerable degree of discriminating monopoly in relation to the numerous, widely scattered, and economically weak borrowers.

First, the available evidence at least for India suggests that the 'density' of moneylenders as a professional class is very low and as such highly conducive to monopoly in the business both within and outside the village. While the figures below show that pure monopoly could be said to exist in only 11.5 per cent of Indian villages, i.e., those with one resident moneylender, their number and concentration in the other village groupings in the sample are also more indicative of oligopoly than of competition. It is significant that the category with 'four or more resident moneylenders', which may be regarded as the nearest to being competitive amongst all the five groups, accounts for only 10.3 per cent. Moreover, the socio-economic structure of rural society in India

* *Source: The Quarterly Journal of Economics* LXXIX, May 1965: 322-325.

and other similar economies is such as to restrain competition irrespective of the number of moneylenders.

Secondly, in addition to their fewness in relation to the number of actual and potential borrowers, the moneylender is well placed to function as a monopolist or oligopolist because he is not merely a moneylender—in fact, the proportion of pure moneylenders is very low—but also, in addition, a merchant middleman-cum-landlord or cultivator who controls the marketing of the produce of his borrowers. This places him in a position where he can influence not only the price of credit (or the quantity of credit at a given price), but also the price of the end-product of credit. This combination of occupations naturally implies that the lender's pure rates of interest must necessarily be higher than the transfer earnings of his capital in alternative uses.

The following data on the occupational pattern of rural moneylenders in India bring out the non-specialised character of village moneylending, which is also equally prevalent in other comparable types of economies.[4] The predominance of cultivator or middlemen-cum-moneylenders means that the moneylender is invariably a monopsonistic buyer of the borrower's produce and as such able to dictate the price at which the borrower can sell his output. The moneylender can not only overprice the loan but also underprice the produce of the cultivator-borrower. Thus, both ways he can appropriate monopoly gains.

Within the environment circumscribed by the fewness of moneylenders and the extent of their monopoly power arising from the combination of occupations, there is a whole complex of social and economic factors which together restrain competition among moneylenders. The limited supply of loanable funds under monopolistic or oligopolistic control, in conjunction with the fiercely competitive demand for credit, creates an environment ideal for a highly discriminating monopoly. In particular, the inelastic segment of demand for consumption loans by cultivators makes borrowers peculiarly vulnerable to lenders. Farmers in the rural areas of underdeveloped economies are known to develop varying degrees of customary and traditional dependence on particular moneylenders. The very existence of large outstanding obligations compels borrowers to continue to deal with the same lender. The lender-borrower nexus is strengthened by tenancy agreements, trading and family relations, physical distance, ignorance, social pressures, and sometimes sheer inertia. The unequal economic capacity means unequal bargaining power as between lenders and borrowers and results in interest rates that are frequently "out of proportion to the risk involved in the business and constitute an exploitation of the helplessness, ignorance and the necessity of the borrower."[5] The monopoly profits of moneylending are sustained because of insufficient inter-village mobility of moneylenders, who therefore function virtually as non-competing groups. Moneylending being usually a family business, credit investigation is not delegated to hired hands. But whether or not the cost of this is imputed by the moneylender in his accounts does not detract from the monopolistic character of his profits. Thus, the wide gap between risk and the actual interest charged is largely explained by the monopoly profits of moneylending, which attracts the social odium of usury in these countries.

The discriminating monopoly character of the rural loan market in underdeveloped countries is further evidenced by the prevalence of a multiplicity of customer rates of interest individually negotiated with each borrower, unlike in developed countries where the rates are competitively determined in an impersonal market. Apart from the causal factors already mentioned, the absence or inadequacy of suitable assets which can serve as collateral for loans[6] necessitates a close lender-customer relationship wherein intimate knowledge of the ability and character of the individual borrower becomes a substitute for collateral. The predominance of customer rates of interest in underdeveloped money markets leads to a random cluster of interest rates because of the lack of integration among the different segments of the market as against the more harmonious and consistent structure of rates in maturer financial systems.

Thus, on the whole, it could be maintained that the residual element represented by monopoly profits in the determination of interest rates in rural areas of underdeveloped countries could well exceed the sum of the other components, namely, risk and liquidity premia and administrative charges.

Table 17.1

Resident Moneylender Status in Indian Villages

	Number of Resident Moneylenders per Selected Villages				
	None	*One*	*Two*	*Three*	*Four or more*
All India—Sample of 600 Villages	384 (64.0%)	69 (11.5%)	52 (8.7%)	33 (10.3%)	62 (10.3%)

Note: Figures in parentheses denote percentages to total number of selected villages.

Source: *All-India Rural Credit Survey* Vol. I, *Survey Report*, Part 2. Bombay: Reserve Bank of India, 1957: 465-660.

Table 17.2

Number Answering Questionnaire

		Cultivators	*Non-cultivating Landowners*	*Traders, General Merchants, Brokers, Commission Agents, Goldsmiths, Shopkeepers or Other Occupations*	*Numbers of Moneylenders Who Had No Occupation Other than Moneylending*
All India	613	419	64	235	14

Source: Same as Table 17.1.

NOTES

1 "The Premium for Risk as a Determinant of Interest Rates in Underdeveloped Rural Areas", *The Quarterly Journal of Economics* LXXVII: 646, November 1963.

2 Ibid.: 637.

3 "...the advantage which personal knowledge of borrowers gives to moneylenders may often allow them to appropriate *some* monopoly profit on whatever they may lend" (italics mine). (Ibid.: 642-643). "...a reduction in the monopoly profits component, as well as in the premium for risk, will probably account for the difference in interest charges" (Ibid.: 644).

4 "Local buyer monopolies are characteristic of agricultural areas in underdeveloped countries with poor transport facilities, narrow markets, and meagre supplies of capital." J.C. Abbott (1958). "Marketing Problems and Improvement Programmes", *FAO Marketing Guide* No. 1. Rome: FAO, p.84).

"The middleman-cum-lender in rural Malaya may own the instruments of production and generally controls the sale of produce...he forces the owner into a continuous cycle of indebtedness." C. Gamba (1958). "Poverty and Some Socio-economic Aspects of Hoarding, Saving and Borrowing in Malaya", *Malayan Economic Review* III: 39, October.

5 *All-India Rural Credit Survey—General Report II*, Chaps. 11 and 14. See also p. 171.

6 This explains the predominance of unsecured credit in underdeveloped economies. Thus, according to the *All-India Rural Credit Survey*, four-fifths of the debt to both agricultural and professional moneylenders in India is unsecured (p.169). Likewise, in Libya even in the organised banking sector, the major portion of credit is given without any tangible security such as trade bills, shipping documents, merchandise, mortgages, etc. See A.G. Chandavarkar (1960). "Banking in Libya", *The Banker* (London), September.

18 Arthur Lewis on Economic Growth*

The literature on problems of economic growth has hitherto been sharply divided into the strictly theoretical formulation of models, as in the work of Harrod, Domar, Joan Robinson and others, on the one hand and the rather miscellaneous collection of historical and descriptive writing, too amorphous to be specified, on the other. Professor Lewis's work• is, from the methodological point of view, midway between the theoretical and the descriptive. Its purpose is, according to the author, "not to present original ideas on its subject, but to try to provide an appropriate framework for studying economic development", and what he has done is to give us not a theory but a map. As he says, "so many factors are relevant in studying economic growth that it is easy to be lost unless one has general perspective of the subject. This is also my excuse for superficiality." In view of this very modest disclaimer and the rather pointed reference to 'pedantic reviewers' in the introduction, it might appear both ungracious and presumptuous to evaluate the performance by other, though not irrelevant, criteria. The present reviewer's only justification for adopting such a course is the august intellectual parentage of the book and the fact that it is the first treatise, as distinct from monographs, on the subject. Besides, Lewis is singularly well qualified for his task as an academic economist who has also had first-hand knowledge and experience of conditions in underdeveloped areas.

Lewis has very rightly segregated the basic value judgement involved in the present work, *viz.*, the desirability of economic growth, in an appendix, and has adopted a judiciously pragmatic approach to this vexed issue. According to him, some of the so-called costs of economic growth are not its necessary concomitants at all, as, for instance, the impoverishment of the working classes; nor are some of them intrinsically evil, such as individualism, growth of rational attitudes and the like. Even so, he admits that

---

* *Source*: *Economic Weekly* VII(49) (3 December 1955): 1425-1428.

•: *The Theory of Economic Growth*. London: George Allen and Unwin.

> economic growth is only one good thing among many and we can take it in excess. ...Societies are not necessarily wise to choose to speed up their rate of growth above its current level; if they do, they will enjoy substantial benefits, but they may also incur substantial costs, in social or in spiritual terms, and whether the potential gains exceed the potential losses must be assessed separately in each situation as best as we may. It is because economic growth has both its gains and its losses that we are all, almost without exception, ambivalent in our attitudes towards economic growth.

In view of this rather cautious approach, it is regrettable that Lewis should have in his desire to provide a comprehensive framework for the study of economic growth, included much sociological material which is frankly beyond the competence of the economist. Thus, the earlier chapters on 'The Will to Economise', 'Economic Institutions', and 'Knowledge' discuss the impact on economic growth of diverse social factors such as the attitude to work and innovation, the spirit of adventure, non-material rewards, influence of religion, asceticism, family, and slavery. Of course, economic growth itself is defined in operational terms as the growth of output of goods and services per head of population (and per hour of work done) accruing to a national or regional group, and though the relationship between growth on the one hand, and the distribution and consumption of output on the other is analysed, the analysis abstracts from problems of distribution and consumption, *per se*.

It is not as though the meta-economic issues discussed at length by Lewis are not germane to the problem but it is difficult for an economist qua economist to say anything worthwhile on them. Some of these generalisations, in themselves extremely suggestive, require further substantiation from allied disciplines, as for instance the proposition that 'economic change is pioneered by the few and imitated by the many' or that 'it seems plausible that the rate of change for society as a whole should depend on the willingness of the many to accept the leadership of the enterprising few'. The reasons for associating economic growth with a high degree of vertical mobility are convincingly set out and in the course of this, Lewis emphasises the rather neglected point that a certain element of hierarchy in authority is an organisational necessity for any type of society—whether capitalist, communist or socialist—and as such 'growth would cease in a community if authority ceased'. This is a line of thought which has been already propagated in political theory even by philosophers most sympathetic to collectivism like R.G. Collingwood. It would be hard to deny, for instance, that the rate of economic growth in Soviet Russia would not have been possible without an authoritarian element.

All this, of course, is on a different plane of discourse from the quite different issue of the merits of egalitarianism. This is, however, not unconnected with problems of growth even though Lewis abstracts from the distributional aspects of the growth of output. It has been argued by others that an underdeveloped economy cannot afford a highly egalitarian distribution of income and wealth, a hypothesis which is plausible only if it is assumed that growth is largely a function of the rate of increase in the private sector. While attempting to substantiate that "in some circumstances discrimination against a group may cause that group to show vigorous development in direction other than those which interest the ruling class", Lewis makes the astonishing statement that the Parsees in India "being ineligible, because of their religion, for joining the governing classes, concentrated on economic activity and became more expert at it than their hosts." In dependent India all communities, though in varying degrees, were subject to common disabilities from the point of view of participation in the government of the country and this is hardly an explanation of the commercial success of the Parsee community.

It is difficult to generalise about the sociology of business acumen and the relative prosperity of ethnic and other groups in society. This is equally true of the entire discussion on economic institutions and knowledge, where both the intractability of the material and Lewis's anxiety to be eclectic make it impossible for him to draw any significant conclusions. Thus, it is hardly helpful to be told that 'in sum, institutions may change in ways favourable or unfavourable to growth. The change may be a reaction against what has gone before or it may not. If it is a reaction it may have set in early, or it may be long delayed. This is about all that we can say on the direction change may take.'

The subsequent chapters on capital, population and resources, and the role of government in economic development, will be of primary interest to economists. The analysis of the reasons for the divergence of the marginal capital-income ratios as between different countries exemplifies the limitations both of qualitative methods and of aggregative models in analysing this important problem, as there is no unique corelationship between the relevant variables like the proportion of national income invested, the rate of growth of national income, average life of capital assets, etc. On a priori grounds, it is equally possible to argue for a low as well for a high marginal ratio of capital to income in underdeveloped economies. Thus, factors such as exploitation of large potential resources, rapid growth of population, different relative importance of the primary and secondary sectors, can account for a low ratio, whereas the alternative hypothesis of a high ratio could be sustained with reference to factors which make capital less productive in underdeveloped countries, as for instance the absence of social overhead capital, slower rate of growth of 'know-how', tendency to wasteful methods of using capital, etc. In the absence of empirical verification of the sectorwise capital-output ratios in different economies at different stages of growth, the argument will remain inconclusive.

In the course of developing this thesis, Lewis shows that even he is not immune to the exceptionally tenacious but unwarranted belief held by writers on this subject, *viz.*, that

> in the less developed countries it is economical to use capital more sparingly, than in the developed. Thus, if it is possible to use a process which required heavy capital investment associated with low running costs, or alternatively to choose methods associating lower initial investment with higher annual cost, the latter methods are often more appropriate.

Capital intensity cannot be regarded as an investment criterion for the simple reason that there is no unique correlation between factor proportions and maximum net product of a factor combination. In fact, a high rate of investment is indicated precisely on account of the fact that it is the only corrective to the unemployment that arises on account of a serious disproportion between the existing stock of capital and the existing supply of labour. Lewis is also inclined to exaggerate the role of the rate of interest in determining the choice between less capital-intensive and more capital-intensive methods of production.

From the point of view of the professional economist, the most significant portion of the present work is the section entitled "Point of Departure" in the chapter on 'Capital'. This section analyses one of the basic problems of economic growth, *viz.*, the stage at which the process becomes more or less self-reinforcing and cumulative, i.e., the 'take-off' point of the developmental process. Here Lewis propounds the interesting hypothesis that "at low levels of economic activity, production for the foreign market is usually the turning point which sets a country on the road of economic growth." This argument relies on the deficiency of expenditure out of marginal income in a stagnant economy. To quote Lewis,

> Unless some innovation is involved, merely to produce more for the home market is unprofitable, since extra receipts will not equal extra outgoings unless some demand is captured from some other producer and this requires innovation. At low levels innovation for the home market is unusual. Not only does innovation require new techniques, which at these levels usually come from abroad, but more important is the fact that the social atmosphere is usually at these levels not very favourable towards some people trying to grow rich by 'stealing' some part of the markets of their fellow producers. Innovation comes, therefore, usually first of all in foreign trade, partly because it is foreigners who bring the new ideas and partly because the community would not be well disposed towards a struggle for markets at home. (pp. 275-276)

This line of thought is extremely suggestive and one can only regret that it has not been developed at some length. It may, of course, be readily accepted that given differential price-and-income elasticities of demand, consumer responses would be asymmetrical. But then, this problem would arise equally in foreign as well as in domestic markets. Much would also depend upon the composition of exports. In the case of underdeveloped countries, the nature of exports is usually such that they do not afford much scope for innovations or product differentiation.

Lewis also refers to the crucial position of maintaining balance between the rates of growth of the different sectors in the economy. According to him "innovation in one sector of the economy is checked unless other sectors expand appropriately." It is, however, difficult to accept his contention that since the income elasticity of demand for services is higher than for manufactures, economic growth is consequently associated with a higher rate of increase in 'services' and manufactures (in that order) relatively to agriculture. As the investigations of Bauer and Yamey into the occupational patterns of West Africa have shown, the service component can be quite high even at low levels of income and activity.

The analysis of the problem of assigning primacy in development to agriculture or to manufactures is rather inconclusive. While conceding that expansion of the output of manufactures in overpopulated countries does not presuppose increase in agricultural production provided there is a growing export of manufactures, a caveat is also entered that these countries should increase agricultural output since thereby the necessity of relying on exports of manufactures is mitigated. Further, we are told that 'in practice in most backward countries the sector which usually responds least well to growth in other sectors, and which therefore acts as a brake on all economic growth, is the agricultural sector producing food for home consumption'. This is because when agriculture is in the hands of small farmers, introduction of innovations is difficult. But Lewis does not give us the answer to the really important question involved here, whether there is a 'food constraint' on the rate of development of backward areas.

Reference is also made to the fact that while the real cost of using surplus labour in industry is negligible, the money cost is considerable. This is because wages in industry have to be maintained at a level much above the average earnings of farm labour in order to offset higher cost of living in urban areas and also to attract and retain labour in industry. Institutional factors such as unionisation and official policy also keep industrial wages above average earnings in agriculture.

In the concluding chapter on 'Government', the analysis leads to the conclusion that the primary role of the public sector is to step up development through an accelerated rate of investment and "in the absence of government intervention, the rate of domestic saving is determined principally by the ratio of profits to national income."

Perhaps one may conclude this review with the hope that Lewis will give us a more rigorous analytical and empirical proof of some of the very suggestive hypotheses he has advanced in his all too brief section on 'Point of Departure'. *The Theory of Economic Growth* may be said to mark the saturation point of the taxonomic approach to problems of development.

19 Money and Economic Growth*

One of the paradoxical features of the economics of development is that despite the immense proliferation of literature on the subject, the monetary and financial aspects of the growth process and the role of money in development and planning are among its most neglected branches. Apart from the contributions of Gurley and Shaw,[1] it is difficult to think of any recent systematic treatment of these aspects. Curiously, after the classic elaboration by Schumpeter of the theme that credit creation is the monetary counterpart of innovation, there has been no follow up. It is not surprising, therefore, that economic practitioners should likewise, following their theoretical brethren, relegate money and monetary policy to the 'second order of smalls', a good example of which is the treatment of money and finance in the numerous Economic Survey Mission Reports of the World Bank or in the blueprints of planned development in emergent states.

The neglect of the monetary and financial aspects of development is attributable to a variety of influences. First, it is due to the planner's assumption that money is not a limiting factor in economic development, a standpoint rendered plausible by the tendency of economic theory to regard money as a passive variable since it does not absorb real resources, is infinitely elastic in supply and can be always adapted to the requirements of the real variables of the economic system. It is a by-product of the 'physicalist' or 'scientistic' approach to economic planning which would virtually abolish the distinction between the 'economic' and the 'technical' and interpret economic quantities as physical balances. This approach is understandable, even if not wholly justifiable, in a centrally planned economy where savings and investment are centralised in one authority. Consequently, the role of money in a collectivist society is reduced basically to that of a 'numeraire', i.e., unit of account and a medium of exchange; the demand for money takes the form exclusively of 'transactions balances' since there is no need for cash balances to satisfy the precautionary and speculative motives which do not operate in an economy where individual units (firms and households) cease to

---

* *Source: Economia Internazionale* Genoa, XVIII(1) (February 1965): 85-93.

be autonomous decision-makers. Thus, the Keynesian liquidity function in a centrally planned economy would shed the precautionary motive part of M_1 (transactions and precautionary motives) and the whole of M_2 (the speculative motive). But it would be more realistic to disaggregate the Keynesian M_1 so that the transactions motive is differentiated from the precautionary motive, which is more akin to M_2 (the speculative motive). This would mean that M_1 = transactions and M_2 = precautionary and speculative motives. Then M_2 would be the component of which to meet risk and uncertainty for the holder, i.e., the genuine 'monetary' cash balance. In proportion as the magnitude of M_2, as we have redefined it, becomes smaller or is equal to zero as in a centrally planned economy, the more nearly does money become a passive variable and hence of no relevance to economic planning. A fully planned economy, therefore, represents a very good approximation to Say's Law. The real fallacy of Say's Law, after all, lay not in the assertion of the Saving-Investment Identity as in the denial of the influence of money on economic behaviour. A collective economy analytically has a great similarity to a ' barter' economy defined as one where money balances (i.e., non-numeraire balances) are zero and which, therefore, implies the absence of a real-balance effect.[2] But this is far from being the case in a partially planned economy as any mixed economy is, where the demand for money is determined by its use not only as a medium of exchange but as a store of value for precautionary and speculative purposes, which gives rise to a monetary problem, i.e., liquidity preference for reasons other than mediation of transactions. In fact, one of the important dividing lines between a centrally planned and an individualist or a mixed economy is the absence of liquidity preference proper (the Keynesian M_2) in the former and, hence, of a monetary problem in the strict sense. This accounts for the fact that monetary policy is supplanted by fiscal policy in collectivist economies as an instrument for regulation of disposable incomes in relation to the current flow of goods and services. This is well exemplified by the use of the Turnover Tax in Soviet Russia and East European countries. It is, therefore, not surprising if economists now associated with planning in collectivist economies should propagate the view that "even in other economies the problem of avoiding inflationary pressures in economic development is not 'monetary'. It is solved by assuring, by a variety of methods, a correct structure of national expenditure."[3] But in any mixed economy, where there are autonomous spending and saving units, the liquidity-preference of the private sector does affect the saving investment process and variations in it are an important datum for policy, which has to seek to regulate it appropriately.

Secondly, there are some analytical grounds advanced for the neglect of money as an operative influence in growth models. Thus, it has been argued that "apart from the notorious intricacy of theory about it, the chief obstacle to insinuating money into secular growth models is that to do so one must make a dynamic assumption about the way it develops as an institution".[4] A different justification may be that, as Pigou observed, the role of money is important only in the short run. But then, even short period models of growth abstract from monetary factors whether for heuristic or other reasons. There is no reason why, if the entire growth process can be subjected to a schematic treatment, e.g., the Rostovian model, the same procedures cannot be adopted to accommodate money and finance. Even if money is regarded as a short period influence it cannot be disregarded as a causal factor insofar as the long run is a summation of a series of short runs. The ultimate equilibrium may well be determined by the 'path' which, in its turn, is also conditioned by money, among other factors.

Thirdly, and perhaps more plausibly, the real reasons for the neglect of money in the growth process may be attributable to the lack of uniformity or stability, both in monetary relationships like velocity of circulation as well as in that of money to other variables. There is, thus, no direct invariant relationship between money supply and the amount of money spent on goods and services during a given period of time. Nor is there any systematic relationship in the ratio of money supply to gross national product or national wealth.[5] But it could equally well be maintained that the very absence of stability or uniformity in the statistical relationship of money to other variables creates the case for a purposive and vigilant monetary policy.

But the fact that the ultimate determinants of economic development are 'real' does not, however, prove that monetary factors cease to be important or relevant for the growth process. Although money is not a constraint on development in the same sense as food, foreign exchange, technical skill and know-how, this is more valid in the aggregative sense for the economy as a whole than for sectors within the economy. Analytically, there is a threefold relationship of money to growth; namely (a) money as a necessary and sufficient condition,[6] (b) a necessary but not sufficient condition, and (c) money as a completely passive variable. The first and the last are more in the nature of 'limiting' cases; the second is, perhaps, the most realistic formulation and yet it has been less influential than the last one. Somehow, the view that money is a mere 'numeraire' persists even if it is not always clearly articulated.

The adequacy of the total quantity of money for overall growth does not necessarily ensure its availability to particular sectors.

The role of monetary and financial policy in a developing economy is broadly: (a) to provide for the optimum supply of money in consonance with the requirements of economic growth; (b) to ensure that finance is available at reasonable cost to essential and strategic sectors in the economy; and (c) to create and maintain an adequate institutional framework to fulfil these objectives. A developing economy means rising output over time, and this, in turn, necessitates expansion in money supply, first because, as national income increases, the demand for money (transactions balances) increases; secondly, the monetisation of the subsistence sector in the economy also requires additional money; and thirdly, as per capita real income rises, the demand for precautionary and speculative cash balances also tends to increase, although not necessarily in proportion.

The relative significance of these aspects of money and finance in the developmental process may now be examined in somewhat greater detail.[7] To begin with, it would be pertinent to examine the bearing of the non-monetised sector (barter and subsistence) of the demand for money and on economic development generally.[8] Its precise size is always difficult to determine, but available estimates[9] put it at a little over a third of the economy in India and between 60 and 82 per cent in Tropical Africa. But, whatever the rate of monetisation, one would expect the non-monetised sector to shrivel under the impulse of planned economic development. Since monetisation is a finite process, the conversion of non-monetary savings into monetary savings is in the nature of a once-for-all contribution, which would not be available with the complete (maximum) monetisation of the economy. Its pace would also, among other things, be determined by the availability of incentive goods from the exchange to the subsistence sector. The extension of the money economy requires an addition to the stock of money to meet largely the transactions demand of the new units of production since their other cash balances would be negligible. The addition to the total demand for money arising from monetisation would, obviously, be less than from the increase in the volume of transactions in the existing exchange economy, because the average productivity of the subsistence sector being generally low, the magnitude of its contribution to the rise in national income would also be comparatively small. But as long as the process lasts the growth of money supply has to allow for the 'monetisation' component of the demand for money.

Monetisation is often regarded as a process which must be accelerated to achieve a higher rate of economic growth.[10] The consequent commercialisation of agriculture would, it is claimed, facilitate the working of the price and profit mechanism and thereby promote higher output and better allocation of resources. This has, however, to be suitably qualified to take into account the well-known limitations of the price mechanism in agriculture, notably the rigidity of inputs (agriculture in underdeveloped areas is more a way of life than a business) and the operation of 'cobweb' type of economic fluctuations, etc. The peasant's non-commercial morality may even be a safeguard against capital consumption in agriculture under a strict operation of the economic calculus and business ethos.[11] Moreover, for many an underdeveloped economy, the existence of a substantial non-monetised sector acts as a hedge against the ravages of inflation. Generally, the subsistence sector acts as a sheltered hinterland to the exchange economy, which explains the economic miracle of countries with acute inflation and monetary chaos managing to survive without any untoward effects. The supply of food from the subsistence sector is an insurance against erosion of the purchasing power of money. The non-monetised sector partly accounts for the 'low-level equilibrium trap' regarded as characteristic of underdeveloped economies.[12] All this is only to emphasise that monetisation of an underdeveloped economy is not necessarily an unmixed blessing.

While the monetary authority of an underdeveloped economy need not concern itself with the desirability of monetisation, *per se*, it has to allow for its inevitability and, therefore, for accretion to the money supply on this account. But what is more relevant to the authority is the distribution of this addition to the stock of money as between currency and bank deposits. The higher the proportion of deposits, the greater is the scope for monetary policy inasmuch as accretions to the deposit component of money supply help to enlarge the credit base of the banking system, which the central bank is in a position to regulate more effectively than if the increase were wholly or largely in the form of currency. However, since monetisation takes place on the fringes of the economy, it would express itself more through a rise in the currency component, although with the spread of institutional banking the proportion of bank deposits may rise subsequently.

It is evident that within the monetary sector itself, as population and national income increase, the demand for money for transactions would have to rise so as to support the higher level of economic activity. It is, also, important to appreciate the implications of a change in the composition of money, as distinct from a rise in its magnitude, under certain conditions for economic development. For instance, to the extent that coins and currency backed by foreign assets (both absorb real resources) are replaced with a fiduciary currency and bank money a corresponding amount of real savings is available to the economy for investment but this accretion of savings is in the nature of a once-for-all addition. Although this is not of much significance in economies wherein there is a predominance of the fiduciary issue in the legal tender currency, it is a material factor in economies where the currency is wholly or largely backed by foreign assets, e.g., under the Currency Board system in certain British colonies.

There would also be an increase in the demand for precautionary and speculative cash balances, alongside the transactions balances, consequent upon a growth in per capita incomes, and with the gradual financial sophistication a process of asset differentiation, analogous to product differentiation in the goods market, also sets in, leading to a growth of quasi-money and other financial assets. In a sense, asset differentiation is implicit in the growth process because once the limits of self-finance are reached the (net) investing units have to raise funds through sale of financial instruments (debt and equity) to the (net) saving units. But from the point of view of the efficacy of monetary and debt policy, what is relevant is not only the diversification of the financial asset structure but also the extent to which the ownership of these assets is diffused. Liquidity is as much a pattern as a quantity and its ownership is a major datum of financial analysis, an aspect which is perhaps overlooked in the Gurley-Shaw analysis. The wider the dispersion of such assets, the greater is the scope for monetary policy, since thereby the changes in capital values (interest rates) affect the portfolios of a larger section of the community than if the same volume of assets were to be held in more concentrated groups. The significance of the Pigou effect on the 'real balance' effect depends in a considerable measure on the distribution of cash balances among and between different income and economic groups.

Alongside the diversification of assets, appropriate financial institutions also emerge or else have to be created as a matter of public policy. This dual process can be viewed from two angles. First, insofar as there is a multiplicity of financial assets and savings media it helps to increase net saving, although beyond a point this may merely divert savings from one form to another.

Secondly, the development of adequate and efficient financial institutions, including a widely ramified banking system, is an integral part of investment in social overhead capital since the financial system is more akin to a public utility. The economic rationale of a public sector in the financial sphere in an underdeveloped economy can be answered on the basis of its external economies and its effectiveness as an instrument of mobilisation of savings.

Although 'finance' is not a constraint on overall growth, it can be a bottleneck to individual units and sectors, and it is, therefore, a major objective of financial and monetary policy to ensure adequate capital and credit at reasonable cost for essential purposes, while regulating the overall supply of money to hold the price line. Since the size and flow of the agricultural surplus is a major determinant of economic development and bank finance plays an important part in inventory fluctuations, the relevance of credit policy in this context is evident.

Thus, the role of money and finance and of an effective and purposive financial policy is that of a necessary but not a sufficient condition of economic growth. This is admittedly not a very positive statement, but then it only reflects the general position of growth economics, wherein it is easier to categorise the necessary but not the sufficient conditions of growth. This means that perhaps the ultimate determinants of growth cannot be built into even the most ambitious theoretical models.

NOTES

1 "Financial Aspects of Economic Development", *American Economic Review*, September 1955; and *Money in a Theory of Finance*, Washington DC: Brookings Institution, 1960.

2 D. Patinkin. *Money, Interest, and Prices.* pp.119–121.

3 M. Kalecki (1960). "Financial Problems of the Third Plan", *The Economic Weekly:* 1122, 9 July.

4 D.M. Bensusan-But. *On Economic Growth.* p.193.

5 "...the ratio of the money supply (currency plus deposits money) to the gross national product varied in the latest available year (1957 or 1956) from 54 per cent in Switzerland, 46 per cent in Belgium, 38 per cent in Brazil and 36 per cent in France to 30 per cent in the USA, 27.5 per cent in the UK, 18 per cent in Germany and 13 per cent in Mexico. In the period since 1951 this ratio fell in some countries, and rose in others, but there was no systematic connection between these movements and the rate of increase in the money value of the GNP or that and the initial magnitude of this ratio". N. Kaldor, *Memorandum to Radcliffe Committee* Vol. 3: 146.

The average ratio of money supply with the public to net national income in India during the period 1949-1962 has been 19.5 per cent. See A.G. Chandavarkar (1963). "Liquidity in the Indian Economy 1949-62", *Reserve Bank of India Bulletin*, November. p.1400.

6 Cf. J. Exter, in his Report on the Establishment of a Central Bank for Ceylon (Colombo: Government Printer).

7 See J.G. Gurley and E.S. Shaw (1967). "The Growth of Debt and Money in the United States, 1800–1950", *Review of Economics and Statistics*, August.

8 For an application of these ideas to the Indian economy see the present writer's "Some Financial and Monetary Aspects of Development in India" in *Konjunkturpolitik*, Berlin, 1964.

9 According to the *National Sample Survey* (*Fourth Round, April-September 1952*, no.18, p.13, 1959) the proportion of imputed value of consumption in kind to the value of total consumption of households in India is placed at 36.8 per cent for rural and urban areas. The proportions for rural and urban areas separately are estimated at 44.3 per cent and 11.4 per cent respectively. The estimates for Africa are derived from K.C. Abercrombie (1961). "Transition from Subsistence to Market Agriculture", *Monthly Bulletin of Agricultural Statistics*, FAO, February.

10 "The structure of agricultural costs must become monetised because without a monetisation of the inputs it is difficult to expect the normal profit mechanism to work. Monetary input in a great many areas of Latin America does not reach 30 per cent of the total selling value. Labour is not, in the main, paid in money but in kind. Thus price does not regulate production because in the extreme case, that of sharecropping, the receipts of the landlord represent a surplus. Even the use of the pricing system to deflect people from one crop to another under these conditions is extraordinarily difficult. The traditional adherence to certain cropping patterns will be very much higher because there is only a positive incentive for changing production but no negative incentive through creation of losses. Positive incentives will work much less forcefully when there is no risk of losses. Unless there are marginal monetary inputs such as you have in industry, the price mechanism cannot function with flexibility". T. Balogh (1961). *Some Aspects of Economic Growth of Under-developed Areas.* New Delhi: National Council of Applied Economic Research, April. pp.30–1.

11 Cf. Joan Robinson (1958). *Accumulation of Capital.* Macmillan. p.297.

12 C.P. Kindleberger (*Economic Development*, p.189) cites the example of Iran in a non-inflationary context. "When oil royalty and tax payments by the Anglo-Iranian Oil Company to the Iranian government ceased, the western world waited breathless for the ensuing collapse. Nothing happened. The impact of the throughput of oil, foreign exchange and imported consumer goods had affected only a small layer of the economy. Their collapse when payments were cut off, went virtually unnoticed as the modernised sector returned to the ways of its forebears and contemporaries in the subsistence economy."

20 Of Finance and Development*

Neglected and Unsettled Questions

> Whether other things being given, as climate, soil, etc. the wealth be not proportioned to the industry: and this to the circulation of credit.
>
> —Bishop Berkeley, Query 21, *The Querist*, 1735

> Circulation. This word serves as an account of everything. I have not yet been able to discover its meaning. What possible advantage is there which the nation can reap by the transference of checks, notes and India bonds...But what production we owe to Change-alley...though this term had never been explained by those who insist on the advantages that result from a circulation, there seems, however, to be some benefit...
>
> —David Hume, Of Public Credit, *Political Discourses*, 1752

Prologue

The questions on 'circulation' (read finance) which engaged two leading philosophers in the eighteenth century still seem unresolved despite the immense proliferation of the literature since the path-breaking contributions of McKinnon and Shaw. We seem still unclear how to assess the true significance of finance. Is it a passive follower of the real sector, or a causally significant sector in its own right? What are the possible interrelationships between finance and development? Is financial liberalisation an unambiguous policy recipe? The publication of two very representative books in their respective genres of informal and formal finance in developing countries by Jagannathan (1987) and Fry (1988) offers an appropriate occasion for some stock taking on these and related themes.

Fry's competent and useful survey, in addition to presenting his own extensive research, analyses the principal theoretical models of financial development (Tobin, McKinnon, Shaw, Kapur, Mathieson, Van Wijnbergen, Taylor, and Galbis); reviews the econometric evidence on the effects of financial conditions in the developing countries; examines the microeconomic and institutional aspects of financial development and the monetary and financial policies pursued in Hong Kong, South Korea, Singapore, and Taiwan. There is, however, a distinct Asian bias in its empirical material, which is further accentuated by a somewhat exclusive emphasis on these four high-

* *Source: World Development* 20(1) (1992): 133-142.

growth 'super-exporter' countries, and inadequately balanced by the sketchy section on interest rate policies in the Philippines and Thailand. This slant could have been usefully redressed by representative evidence from low- or medium-growth Asian countries as well as Latin America and Africa. Fry's book, which has a small section on indigenous financial institutions and the curb market, is well supplemented by Jagannathan's elegant and insightful analysis of informal markets in developing countries, based on the state of the art in law, anthropology, institutional and development economics, as well as on his own long field experience as an official in the Indian Administrative Service. Given the analytical approach of this study, the evidence presented is of an illustrative character. Although primarily concerned with the economic rationale of all informal markets (urban, rural, commodity, labour and credit), informal contracts, property rights and social assets, it also addresses issues such as rural-urban migration, corruption systems, and policy interventions in a rent-seeking society. This approach illuminates the multiple-interest linkages between financial and non-financial markets—a salutary reminder that informal finance is an integral part of a complex socio-economic milieu, which is the concern of both Durkheim's *Homo Sociologicus* and Smith's *Homo Economicus*.

This essay seeks answers to several neglected and unresolved issues in the literature, somewhat in the spirit of that admirably unique publication, *The Encyclopedia of Ignorance* (Duncan and Weston-Smith, 1977) which, regrettably, omits economics in its quest for "What we do not know, on matters which lie on the edge of knowledge" in the biological and physical sciences. It is hoped that such an 'inverted' state-of-the-art survey might contribute to the researcher's agenda as well as to the policymaker's handbook.

Finance: Still a Follower?

The literature leaves one overwhelming impression: finance still remains very much the poor relation of mainstream development economics. A magisterial history of the idea of economic development is bare of any references to the role of finance in development, a reflection of the state of the art rather than of any bias on the part of a studiously eclectic economist (Arndt, 1987). The theme of the litany "By and large, it seems to be the case that where enterprise leads finance follows" (Robinson, 1952: 86) is faithfully echoed in the literature. Thus, none of the pioneers of development economics, including three Nobel Laureates (Bauer, Colin Clark, Hirschman, Lewis, Myrdal, Prebisch,

Rosenstein-Rodan, Rostow, Singer, and Tinbergen), even lists finance as a factor in development (Meier and Seers, 1984). Successive surveys of the economics of development, down to the latest (Stern, 1989), seem to focus on all aspects except the financial. Neither Stern's inventory of 'the grand issues of the subject' nor, even more significantly, his list of omissions and the suggested research agenda, makes even an oblique reference to financial factors. The nearest that this survey comes to finance is a passing reference to informal credit markets in a random sample survey of 240 villages in South India! Fry reviews monetary and financial policies in economic development (1988, part IV) and the policies for financial development (chapter 17), but ignores the linkages between finance and development. The studied neglect of finance is only matched by the bland eclecticism that "development involves finance as well as goods" (Gurley and Shaw, 1955: 515). The tantalising conclusion of a recent study that "financial factors are important only when financial instability becomes a dominant force in the economy" (Dornbusch and Reynoso, 1989: 204) relies heavily on high-inflation Latin American experience and does not throw light on the role of finance under steady-state conditions. The more suggestive finding that "the empirical support for the growth effects of a liberalised financial system is episodic" (Dornbusch and Reynoso, 1989: 206) merits systematic testing on a countrywide basis over sufficiently long periods. The state of the art is too well reflected in the candid admission of one of its leading protagonists: Although a higher rate of financial growth is positively correlated with successful real growth, Patrick's (1966), the problem remains unresolved: What is the cause and what is the effect? Is finance a leading sector in economic development, or does it simply follow growth in real output which is generated elsewhere (McKinnon, 1989: 390).

The analytic neglect of financial factors in development is also faithfully mirrored on the empirical side. Thus, financial ratios do not figure in a pioneering list of 'great ratios in economics' (savings to income; labour's share of output; the capital-output ratio: the capital-labour ratio: the transactions velocity of money), which constitute a system of equations that might serve to explain trend growth for an economy (Klein, 1962). The latest listing of "the Great and almost Great Magnitudes in Economics" (Simon, 1990) adds the following: the real riskless rate of interest in various eras; the rate of return on common stocks: the price-earnings ratio for common stocks; and the income velocity of money, but still leaves out the significant ratios of monetisation and financial intermediation. Even empirical studies (e.g., Goldsmith, 1969) have not attempted anything akin to a comprehensive Divisia-type of index to capture the full extent of financial intermediation. Altogether, the literature points to yet one more addition, *viz.*, the 'great divide' between finance and development, to Streeten's suggestive list of development dichotomies (1984). The two dwell in an uneasy intellectual apartheid, perhaps equal, but still very much separate.

In contrast to the neglect of finance in mainstream development economics, international financial institutions take the positive stand that "efficient financial systems help to grow, partly by mobilising additional financial resources and partly by attracting those resources to the best uses" (World Bank, 1989: 40). The *World Development Report* devotes an entire Chapter (3) to "illustrate the *central role* of finance in development by reviewing the evolution of financial systems since pre-industrial times" (World Bank, 1989: 40, emphasis added). While it may be excessive to assign centrality to finance in the development process, the World Bank's substantial ongoing interest in financial sector studies and financial sector loans is adequate assurance that the lapses of theory are no bar to effective practice and that finance does matter for development. But finance, too, has several unresolved issues which merit attention.

The Dichotomy of Formal and Informal Finance

There is now an extensive body of literature on informal finance and its significance is, paradoxically, now better recognised by intergovernmental institutions (World Bank, 1989: 112-121; ADB, 1990: 187-211) than by domestic authorities. Nevertheless, the discussion tends to be muddled in some respects and remiss in others. For instance, economists who consistently emphasise the fungibility of finance seem to regard informal finance as a virtual enclave, overlooking that the "unorganised sector is at best a loose way to describe a wide range of activities by small firms, households, and individuals, which are to varying degrees integrated with organised sector markets" (Jagannathan, 1987: 4). There are, in fact, close borrowing and lending links, not always explicit or visible, between formal and informal finance notably through concurrent participation of different economic entities. Likewise, much of the discussion on informal finance blurs the critical distinction between its two constituents, the 'autonomous' and 'reactive' sectors, which raise wholly different policy issues. The core of informal finance is the spontaneous sector comprising mutual and proprietary units like ROSCAS (rotating savings and credit associations), indigenous bankers, pawnbrokers, which historically predates formal finance. The ROSCAS are a textbook example of 'clubs' which, surprisingly, have been so completely bypassed by the economic theory of clubs (Buchanan, 1965; Sandler and Tschirhart, 1980). The other constituent of informal finance is 'reactive', since it develops primarily as a reaction to deficiencies in and controls over formal finance and typically assumes the form of urban kerb markets, private finance companies, and such other fringe entities. In contrast to the autonomous sector whose size is unrelated to the degree of control over formal finance, the reactive sector expands and contracts contra-cyclically to repression and liberalisation of formal finance and serves as a conduit for financial disintermediation, as well substantiated in the case of post-war South Korea (Cole and Park, 1983). Because of the linkages between formal and informal finance, monetary policy, as shown by South Korean and Indian experience, also affects informal finance, albeit with varying time-lags and, consequently, the overall cost and availability of credit, with the exception that informal finance is not amenable to selective credit controls (Acharya and Srinivasa, 1983, 1984). This effect well exemplifies Goodhart's Law, so often noticed in developed countries, that controls over monetary aggregates and banking institutions tend to breed substitutes (Goodhart, 1984: 96). But even with the utmost feasible liberalisation, a hard core of informal finance will always remain at one end of the financial continuum which, however, has also some inherent limitations. These limitations stem, most importantly, from its small average size and operating characteristics, which preclude efficient financial intermediation beyond a recognisably low-scale threshold. It is therefore, primarily a vehicle of small-scale savings and small-scale credit, which also suggests that "the organised sector is more efficient as an intermediator than is the unorganised sector if we believe that the market evolves toward the more efficient system" (Cho, 1990: 480).

What then are the elements of a coherent policy towards informal finance, which is currently a muddled amalgam of benign neglect and outright prejudice? Its advocates among academics and international agencies do not recognise the constraints on informal finance imposed by official policies such as the failure of the Reserve Bank of India since its inception (1935) to rediscount bills of exchange from the informal sector and to generally develop a positive attitude in place of legalistic formalism toward informal finance. A positive policy would, among others, require a drastic reorientation of central bank attitudes, creation of special cells, as in the Bank of Thailand, to study and monitor informal finance, the strengthening of links between informal and formal finance, creative adaptation of informal financial technology based on group lending and peer review by banks, and the transformation of selected groups of ROSCAS into small-scale units in the formal sector. Oddly, the discourse has not posed the question: Why retain anti-usury laws aimed principally at informal finance when it is recognised that it has flourished precisely because of its proven ability to circumvent them?

Financial Reform and Liberalisation: Agenda and Issues

Financial reform is the overarching issue of formal finance, but its discussion has been overly aggregative considering that it involves three distinct constituents, each with different policy implications. There is, first, the negative aspect of eliminating financial repression and restructuring of institutions with substantial non-performing assets. Second, there is the positive element of reform in the regulatory and institutional framework, and finally, the post-liberalisation agenda of how to maintain and monitor a viable competitive financial system and cope with the problems generated by liberalisation. Reform and liberalisation are emphatically not a 'once over' exercise but a continuing essay in flexible public policy.

There is now an emerging consensus that the scope, modality, design and sequencing of financial reform and liberalisation in an increasingly globalised financial system are the really critical issues. Full liberalisation does not appear to be the first-best policy until the macroeconomic climate is relatively stable and an effective regulatory and prudential framework is in place. "Latin American experience suggests the undesirability of simultaneous liberalisation of exchange and trade controls and capital movements, although in the end internal and external liberalisation will be complementary. The latter should await internal reform and establishment of domestic macroeconomic stability." (World Bank, 1989: 128)

Concomitantly, with the development of an adequate non-bank capital market and structural adjustments in trade, industry, and the legal system, a second-best policy might be a phased diminishing degree of official intervention in the financial system deriving guidance from market-related indicators (Cho and Khatkhate, 1989; Villanueva and Mirakhor, 1990).

The consensus, however, conceals significant policy nuances. Most important, financial repression, although an established term, needs to be appropriately disaggregated. It "means a situation in which the repressive effect of usury laws, bank reserve requirements, credit controls and price inflation interact to reduce and distort the flow of domestic savings" (McKinnon, 1984: 3). More generally, it connotes "indiscriminate distortions of financial prices, including interest rates and exchange rates, which reduce the real rate of growth and the real size of the financial system relative to non-financial magnitudes" (Shaw, 1973: 3-4). But not all the elements of financial repression are repressive in substance and intent, and consequently the blanket elimination of financial repression can be a misleading recipe for policy. Thus, while interest rate ceilings, selective credit controls, and portfolio targets are repressive, bank reserve requirements do not constitute a "discriminatory tax on financial intermediation because they incur an opportunity cost in the form of forgone interest that could otherwise be earned on those assets" (Fry, 1988: 436). But is it really valid to invoke the criterion of opportunity costs for reserve requirements which are essentially an instrument of prudential and monetary policy, and can optionally serve even developmental objectives? The hypothetical alternative to bank reserve requirements is a starkly Hayekian monetary system bereft of a central bank.

Liberalisation, too, brings its own problems, recognised by even its leading intellectual progenitor:

> Finance and trade liberalisation with borrowing and lending at substantial real rates of interest made possible by a stable price level is not easy and is full of potential pitfalls. Nevertheless, it remains the only game in town so far as successful economic development is concerned. That, of course, was the main message of my 1963 book, *Money and Capital in Economic Development*. It is perhaps a sign of advancing age, however, that I am now more inclined to emphasize the pitfalls. (McKinnon, 1989: 45)

It is not hard to conjecture the nature of the pitfalls of liberalisation.

First, some of its expected beneficial consequences have not materialised. For instance, it has not led to a splurge of market-induced financial innovation in the developing countries comparable to the creation of new instruments in the developed countries such as variable interest rate securities, the securitisation of credit, etc. Is this a case of 'supply' or 'demand' failure, and what accounts for it? The literature throws no light on this issue. On the other hand, liberalisation may have even accentuated the urban bias of financial systems in developing countries which, typically, siphon rural savings into urban credit, as manifested in the dichotomy of commercial bank branches into the mostly rural net deposit centres, whose deposits are in excess of local credit, and the largely urban credit centres, with credit in excess of local deposits. The urban bias, no doubt reflects the working of market forces as well as intra-bank procedures such as the imputed rate of interest for inter-branch transfer of funds, which, incidentally, has not inspired any attempts to apply the theory of transfer pricing to banks. But is it feasible to devise wholly market-oriented procedures to remedy financial urban bias given the known ineffectiveness of dirigiste prescriptions of targets for credit-deposit ratios of rural branches? One alternative might be to adapt a version of the US Federal Community Reinvestment Act, in terms of which the Federal Deposit Insurance Corporation requires a bank to pay due regard to the credit requirements of the local community in which it operates.

The more difficult but equally neglected problem is how to maintain the competitiveness of oligopolistic financial systems in developing countries, with a few large banks, some or most of which may also be government owned and managed. There are no easy answers to this question even allowing for maximum autonomy of government-owned banks, which is not meaningful unless they are debarred from access to the government budget to meet operating losses. The contestability of the banking industry, although necessary, is not a sufficient condition for ensuring effective competition given the risk of collusive interest rate cartels even in apparently liberalised markets. Would developing countries be willing to permit free entry of foreign financial enterprise to competition? Financial competition itself is, however, an ambiguous concept. Even competitive interest rates may fall short of market-clearing levels, or may rise to risky levels, with adverse consequences for financial institutions and the economy at large (Villanueva and Mirakhor, 1990: 515-519 and appendix). Moreover, bank credit as a vector of price and varied non-price elements such as availability, collateral, lending criteria, competitive positive real rates will not suffice to clear credit markets. There will always be a Keynesian 'fringe of unsatisfied borrowers', i.e., who are unable to obtain credit despite their willingness to pay the going rate of interest. Credit rationing is pervasive as a screen and filter at different rates of interest, which means that quantity adjustments are as influential as interest rate movements in equalising credit supply and demand. It is therefore, not feasible to equalise the 'playing field' for non-price competition. But the phenomenon of credit rationing in developing countries has hardly evoked any analytic or empirical investigation, in contrast to the wealth of research on the interest-elasticity of savings and investment, as so well exemplified in Fry (1988), which in reviewing the literature on credit rationing (Arndt, 1982; Stiglitz and Weiss, 1981), is unable to cite any studies of credit rationing in developing countries.

THE CHANGING ROLE OF CENTRAL BANKS: AUTONOMY AND FUNCTIONS

Clearly, the tasks of financial reform and liberalisation point to a drastic reorientation of the status, organisation and powers of central banks as the principal operating agency. Are central banks properly equipped to cope with post-liberalisation problems? What is the extent of necessary and desirable autonomy for central banks that should, arguably, also be subject to the self-same liberalisation process as other financial institutions? How would liberalisation affect the relative balance of regulatory, monetary, prudential and developmental roles? The literature has been surprisingly sparse on the organisational aspects of central banking in developing countries, including the interesting experience of multinational central banks and currency areas in Francophone Africa and the Eastern Caribbean. For instance, Fry's otherwise exhaustive Part III on microeconomic and institutional aspects of financial development has no section on central banks. The case for autonomy of central banks derives essentially from the technocratic argument for insulating monetary policy by entrusting it to organisations that "will not be tempted by the sirens of partisan politics" (Nordhaus, 1975: 118; Lindbeck, 1976: 18).

> The central bank can be seen as the repository of reason against the short-term claim of passion: an argument...developed...by Francis Sejersted in the context of Norway.... For classical liberalist policy, the exchange rate and the price level were seen as effective parameters that under no circumstances should be transformed into political control variables. Other institutions that have been accorded a similar autonomy for similar reasons include the Foreign Ministries of many countries and the BBC model of broadcasting. The removal of monetary policy, foreign policy or broadcasting from the political sphere is itself a political act. (Elster, 1988: 90–91)[1]

There is, perhaps, an even stronger case for autonomous central banks in the developing countries, given the greater frequency and arbitrariness of political changes coupled with the politicisation of finance and misplaced populism.[2] But would politicians respect the autonomy of central banks, even though it might not compromise their ultimate accountability to governments? Would central banks have the capacity and will to resist fiscal importunities of governments? Even in democratic regimes the necessary minimal autonomy of central banks has been steadily eroded, as in the case of the Reserve Bank of India, which now also has to contend with the overtly parallel Banking Department of the Ministry of Finance.

An added reason for central bank autonomy in a developing country is its value as a source of independent macroeconomic advice to the government. Central banks have considerable comparative cost advantages as technocratic think tanks—of which there are not many in the developing countries—by virtue of their expertise and direct contacts with financial markets. As Paul Volcker aptly remarked,

> in assessing the role of central banks today, one more subtle point seems relevant. In a good many countries, those institutions have long been an important center for independent policy analysis and professional training, sometimes reaching beyond their immediate operational responsibilities. To take just two examples from different hemispheres, think of the role played for decades by the Bank of Italy or the Bank of Mexico in developing talent and in fostering a high degree of intellectual independence in their countries. That kind of performance could well provide an attractive model for other nations at an early stage of development or undertaking the transition to a market economy. (Volcker, 1990: 7)

Other central banks, too, have played a comparable role in their respective countries, notably the Reserve Banks of Australia and New Zealand, the Central Banks of Indonesia, Malaysia, Sri Lanka, Thailand, and the Monetary Authority of Singapore. There is impressive evidence to refute the contrapuntal view that "not often have important ideas on economics entered a government by way of its central bank. Nor should anyone be disturbed. There is not the slightest indication that it will ever happen again" (Galbraith, 1975: 36-37).

The relative mix of a central bank's monetary, regulatory, prudential and developmental functions also merits reassessment in the context of liberalisation. Can a central bank act concurrently as a controller of money supply, supervisor of the financial system and as a developmental agency? There is a clear conflict of interest between its primary monetary and prudential role and its secondary and acquired developmental role through techniques such as participation in capital of development banks, preferential interest and rediscount rates, guarantee schemes, portfolio targets and credit subsidies. This set of contradictions argues the case for divestiture in the developmental activities of a central bank, the government, to specialised institutions, or private entities, an issue which has been discussed publicly since the early 1970s in Latin America but does not seem to have entered the public forum in other regions.[3]

The question of credit subsidies for developmental and distributive objectives raises some special problems. Such subsidies through the central bank are typically invisible, are not subject to review, and can impair credit controls and distort the efficient allocation of financial resources. There is therefore, a strong case for transfer of credit subsidies from the central bank to the government budget where, however, they are not necessarily more transparent, since even in developed countries such as the United States, the budget is known to carry many implicit credit subsidies. Consequently, even after their transfer to the government budget, credit subsidies would need to be subject to periodic cost-benefit review by autonomous agencies such as the Auditor General. Judicious divestiture by central banks, however, need not preclude a catalytic and corrective as opposed to a participatory role in development.

Concomitantly, the regulatory and prudential role of central banks will need to be revamped to meet the vastly changed requirements of a liberalised, high-risk competitive environment. While this need is recognised, much of the discussion has been of a homiletic character, not sufficiently focused on specific reforms such as adequacy of capital and reserves, limits on domestic and foreign exchange exposure to staff, shareholders, large customers, off-balance sheet risks, the optimal mix and periodicity of off-site surveillance and on-site examination, updating of inspection manuals, merits of unified supervisory jurisdiction over bank and non-bank financial intermediaries, creation of a credit information bureau and, above all, adequate quality, motivation and remuneration of supervisory personnel. There is also a tendency to rely uncritically, without creative adaptation, on models of capital adequacy such as the Basle Accord, which really seeks to standardise for the first time minimum capital standards for internationally active banks, or on the US Federal Reserve's CAMEL (Capital, Asset, Management, Earnings, and Liquidity) prototype for on-site inspections. But even the most comprehensive prudential procedures will be ineffective unless financial institutions "recognise that the initial and primary responsibility for the prudent yet profitable conduct of their trade rests squarely with them—not with their governments, not with their regulators, and certainly not with their central banks" (Corrigan, 1990: 7). The widely held supposition of the moral hazard of insurance mistakenly assumes that it is a prudential measure whereas it is avowedly an insurance for the small depositor, hence the relatively moderate limits of coverage. The prudential aspect of deposit insurance really stems from the associated central bank supervisory and lender-of-last-resort functions and obligations and not from insurance *per se*. The moral hazards of banking could be ascribed more properly to an 'implicit contract' that the central bank is ever ready to act as a lender of last resort to bail out any troubled institution.

This issue also raises the interesting question whether "a central bank might be able to exercise its monetary policy responsibilities better if it is independent of primary supervisory and regulatory responsibilities" (Heller,

1991: 11) based on the evidence that central banks—mostly in developed countries—without a shared supervisory authority have had lower average annual inflation rates (1980-1987). Yet, since "the management of the nation's liquidity and money supply is a primary monetary policy function, it makes sense to give the central bank limited supervisory functions in the liquidity area...pertaining to reserve requirements and liquidity ratios" (Heller, 1991). But for central banks in developing countries, it would be more economical and efficient to unify all supervisory functions.

The scope and limitations of monetary policy instruments in fully liberalised systems too await systematic analysis. The abolition of interest rate and selective credit controls and credit ceilings puts the onus on market-based monetary instruments such as open market operations and rediscount rate mechanisms. But the efficacy of market-related monetary policy instruments assumes wide and active dealers' markets which are not artefacts that can be created by fiat but are the result of a process of gradual evolution of open market operations from net purchases to fully reversible net sale transactions. The direct issue of central bank securities can add materially to the breadth and competitiveness of security markets, as in Indonesia and the Philippines. In the absence of effective open market operations, the single most potent instrument of monetary policy would be the variation of commercial bank reserve requirements. Their efficacy depends on the appropriateness of the base for calculation of reserves and the fine-tuning of primary and secondary reserves as well as on the extent of compliance with such provisions since lapses in compliance are far more common than imagined. The monetary effects of open market operations and variable reserve ratios can also be supplemented by the periodic shifting of government balances between the central and commercial banks and between commercial banks, as in the Bank of Canada's shifts of government deposits between itself and the chartered banks, or the German technique of *Einlagenpolitik*. The potential of this technique has scarcely attracted any serious attention in the central banks of developing countries. Does the fact that these banks are modelled predominantly on the Bank of England and the US Federal Reserve account partly for this omission? Paradoxically, the oligopolistic nature of financial systems in developing countries may have the advantage of facilitating moral suasion as a monetary policy instrument since the central bank has fewer entities to deal with.

In the final analysis, the effective autonomy and efficiency of central banks will be determined not so much by statutory provisions as by their integrity and professionalism. Central banks which incur losses and are themselves in serious arrears of accounts, audit, and implementation, as in several instances in Africa and Latin America, are unlikely to command any credibility. This problem only underscores the critical, and yet the most neglected, role of human capital in financial systems. Typically, developing countries find it

> much easier to staff a central planning commission [add central and commercial banks] with the handful of Ph.Ds [and MBAs] which most countries can supply, than to acquire the mass of persons with intermediate skills, technical and administrative competence and so on without whom any modern economy risks grinding into inefficiency. (Hobsbawm, 1969: 61-62)

Financial labour planning might also help forestall the opposite predicament of the industrial countries, who "are throwing more and more resources, including the cream of our youth, into financial activities, remote from the production of goods and services, into activities that generate high private rewards disproportionate to their social productivity" (Tobin, 1984: 14).[4] It is, however, only realistic to recognise that central bank failures too have the same probability as the better known government and market failures!

The foregoing discussion suggests some fruitful application of public choice and bureaucratic theory to developing countries. Bureaucratic theory has been applied extensively to central banks in the industrial countries using rnaximands such as prestige and self-preservation (Chant and Acheson, 1972) and expense preference (Boyes, Mounts and Sowell, 1988). There are several variables that can enter a bureau's utility function such as salary, perquisites, public reputation, power, patronage, on-the-job leisure, output of the bureau, ease of management, fiscal residuum, i.e., the surplus over and above the emoluments payable to administrative staff (Niskanen, 1975; Rowley and Elgin, 1985). But a central bank is a *sui generis* Weberian (1947) public interest bureau whose behaviour has to be explained in terms of a maxim and that can capture output variables such as efficacy of monetary, exchange rate and prudential policies. The input variables, however interesting, are subsidiary to public interest.

Conclusion

This essay has attempted to pinpoint some of the major gaps in the literature on the analytic, institutional, operational, and policy aspects of finance in developing countries. Clearly, the subject has been too long on theory and too short on fact. It would not be amiss to remind financial economists that

"Monetary theory is in 'history'...Monetary economics, try as economists will to reduce it to a pure theory, is in fact the study of a particular social institution...which has inevitably developed in different ways in different milieux" (Hicks, 1982: 132-133). All this points to a rich agenda of country-specific, issues oriented research invoking the techniques and insights of analytic and institutional economics, as well as economic history to draw up an appropriate policy menu to address the many pressing financial problems of developing countries.

Notes

1 Francis Sejersted's writings on this subject are available only in Norwegian. (See Elster's review of Sejersted's work in Elster 1975.)

2 Some developed countries provide explicitly for the central bank's independence. "In the Netherlands, the legislature has opted for a central bank highly independent of the government. This...gives rise to the question whether this might lead to an uncontrolled...power...this dilemma has been solved by investing the Minister of Finance with the power—to be used only as a measure of last resort and, hence, subjected to very strict conditions — to give the bank's governing board directions for the coordination of the bank's monetary policy and the budgetary policy pursued by the government (a power which...has never yet been used after). In Germany, the Bundesbank enjoys an even higher degree of independence as it is not subject to any instructions from the government. However, the Bundesbankgesetz provides that "the Federal Bank shall, without prejudice to the fulfilment of its functions, support the general economic policies of the Federal Government." The reason for this arrangement was the fear that politicians might be tempted to subordinate monetary policy to other policy objectives. It was the legislature itself which—with past experience (such as the pre-war hyperinflation...) in mind—chose to limit the government's as well as its own scope for action in the monetary field. However by amending legislation, it may...remove this self restraint" (Wellink 1989: 152).

3 Colombian experience in the 1970s is especially instructive. "The Banco de la Republica acted as both a central bank to control money supply and as a development bank. The Junta Monetaria and its advisors emphasised its role as a development bank...and urged 'selective credit controls' and 'productive credit' for working capital. The commercial loan theory of central banking, therefore, was as alive in Colombia at this time as it had been forty years earlier in the United States when Currie first wrote of its fallacies and dangers... On February 18, 1974, the President [of the Republic] ...frankly admitted the mistakes that had led to serious inflation, that there was a need to distinguish between the different roles of a central bank and a development bank. Thereafter the President took much more decisive action, overruling the Junta Monetaria, to control the money supply and fiscal deficit. As a result inflation fell to a very low level in the final months of his administration" (Sandilands, 1990: 254-255).

4 "Most developing countries do not possess or cannot attract sufficient expertise to staff an effective bank supervision office, much less a securities commission" (Fry, 1988: 43). The *World Development Report* (1989) recognised the importance of timely and accurate accounts and financial information and of "'good compensation and career prospects" to bank supervisors (World Bank, 1989: 94) but did not analyse financial staffing problems. Hence its candid acknowledgement that it "has treated in a perfunctory way the human and political dimensions of the subject, both in discussing the origins of the financial problem and in offering prescriptions for change" (ibid.: 132).

References

Acharya, Shankar and Madhur Srinivasa (1984). "Informal Credit Markets and Monetary Policy", *Economic and Political Weekly* XIX(36): 1593–8, (8 September).

———. (1983). "Informal Credit Markets and Black Money: Do they Frustrate Monetary Policy", *Economic and Political Weekly*, XVIII(40): 1751–6, (8 October).

Arndt, Heinz W. (1987). *Economic Development: The History of an Idea.* Chicago and London: University of Chicago Press.

———. (1982). "Two Kinds of Credit Rationing", *Banco Nazionale del Lavoro Quarterly Review* 143: 417–25, December.

ADB (Asian Development Bank) (1990). *Asian Development Outlook.* Manila: ADB.

Boyes, William J., William Stewart Mounts, Clifford Sowell (1988). "The Federal Reserve as a Bureaucracy: An Examination of Expense Preference Behavior", *Journal of Money, Credit and Banking* 20(2): 181–90, May.

Buchanan, James M. (1965). "An Economic Theory of Clubs", *Economica* XXXII(125): 11–17, February.

Chant, John F. and Keith Acheson (1972). "The Choice of Monetary Instruments and the Theory of Bureaucracy", *Public Choice* XII: 13–33, Spring.

Cho, Yoon Je. (1990). "McKinnon-Shaw versus the Neostructuralists on Financial Liberalisation: A Conceptual Note", *World Development* 18(3): 477–80.

——— and Deena Khatkhate (1989). "Financial Liberalisation: Issues and Evidence", *Economic and Political Weekly*: 1105–14, 20 May.

———. (1989). "Lessons of Financial Liberalisation: A Comparative Study", *Disscussion Paper* No. 50 (Washington, DC: World Bank. April).

Cole, David and Yung Chul Park (1983). *Financial Development in Korea, 1945–1978.* Cambridge, MA: Harvard University Press.

Corrigan, E. Gerald (1990). "New Challenges for Central Banking", Remarks before the Bank of Korea Fortieth Anniversary Symposium (Seoul: 29 October). Printed in *Discount and Finance* III(3): 4–8, 15 December, Bombay.

Dornbusch, Rudiger and Alejundern Reynoso (1989). "Financial Factors in Economic Development", *American Economic Review, Papers and Proceedings* 79(2): 204–9, May.

Duncan, Ronald and Miranda Weston-Smith (eds.) (1977). *The Encyclopedia of Ignorance.* New York: Pocket Books.

Elster, Jon (1975). "Review", *Economic History Review* 28(2): 360–1.

———. (1988). *Ulysses and the Sirens: Studies in Rationality and Irrationality.* Cambridge: Cambridge University Press.

Fry, Maxwell J. (1988). *Money, Interest and Banking in Economic Development.* Baltimore, MD: Johns Hopkins University Press.

Galbraith, John K. (1975). "How Keynes Came to America", in *Economics, Peace and Laughter.* Harmondsworth: Penguin.

Goldsmith, Raymond W. (1969). *Financial Structure and Development.* New Haven, CT: Yale University Press.

Goodhart, C.A.E. (1984). *Monetary Theory and Practice.* London: Macmillan.

Gurley, J.G. and E.S. Shaw (1955). "Financial Aspects of Economic Development", *American Economic Review* XLV(4): 515–38, September.

Heller, H. Robert (1991). "Prudential Supervision and Monetary Policy", Conference in honor of Jacques J. Polak, Netherlands Bank (13–15 January), Washington, DC: IMF: 1–12.

Hicks, John R. (1982). "A French View of Money (1943)", in *Money, Interest and Wages: Collected Essays of Economic Theory*, Vol. 2. Cambridge, MA: Harvard University Press.

Hobsbawm, F.J. (1969). *Industry and Empire*. Harmondsworth: Penguin.

Jagannathan, N. Vijay (1987). *Informal Markets in Developing Countries*. New York: Oxford University Press.

Klein, Lawrence R. (1962). *Introduction to Econometrics*. Englewood Cliffs, NJ: Prentice Hall.

Lindbeck, Assar (1976). "Stabilisation Policy in Open Economies with Endogenous Politicians", *American Economic Review, Papers and Proceedings* 66: 1–19, May.

McKinnon, Ronald (1984). *Financial Repression and Economic Development.* Taipei: Academia Sinica.

————. (1989). *Financial Liberalizationa nd Economic Development: A Rreassessment of InterestRratePpolicies in Asia and Latin America*. San Francisco: International Center for Economic Growth.

Meier, Gerald M. and Dudley Seers (1984). *Pioneers in Development*. New York: Oxford University Press.

Niskanen, William A. (1975). *Bureaucracy and Representative Government*. Chicago and New York: Aldine-Atherton.

Nordhaus, W.D. (1975). "The Political Business Cycle", *Review of Economic Studies* 42: 169–90.

Patrick, Hugh T. (1966). "Financial Development and Economic Growth in Underdeveloped Countries", *Economic Development and Cultural Change*, XIV(2): 174–89, January.

Robinson, Joan (1952). "The Generalisation of the General Theory", in *The Rate of Interest and Other Essays*. London: Macmillan.

Rowley, Charles and Robert Elgin (1985). "Towards a Theory of Bureaucratic Behavior", in D. Greenaway and G.K. Shaw (eds.), *Public Choice, Public Finance and Public Policy (Essays in Honuor of Alan Peacock)*. Oxford: Basil Black: 31–50.

Sandilands, Roger J. (1990). *The Life and Political Economy of Lauchlin Currie: New Dealer, Presidential Advisor and Development Economist*. Durham, NC: Duke University Press.

Sandler, Todd and John T. Tschirhart (1980). "The Economic Theory of Clubs: An Evaluation Survey", *Journal of Economic Literature* 18(4): 1481–1521, December.

Shaw, Edward S. (1973). *Financial Deepening in Economic Development*. New York: Oxford University Press.

Simon, Julian L. (1990). "Great and Almost-Great Magnitudes in Economics", *Journal of Economic Perspectives* 4(1): 149–56, Winter.

Stern, Nicholas (1989). "The Economics of Development: A Survey", *The Economic Journal* 99: 597–685, September.

Stiglitz, Joseph E. and Andrew Weiss (1981). "Credit Rationing in Markets with Imperfect Information", *American Economic Review* 73(5): 393–410, June.

Streeten, Paul (1984). "Development Dichotomies", in Gerald M. Meier and Dudley Seers (eds.), *Pioneers in Development*. New York: Oxford University Press.

Tobin, James (1984). "On the Efficiency of the Financial System", *Lloyds Bank Review* 153: 1–16, July.

Vilanueva, Delano and Abbas Mirakhor (1990). "Strategies for Financial Reforms", *IMF Staff Papers* 37(3): 509–36, September.

Volcker, Paul A., (1990). *The Triumph of Central Banking: The 1990 Per Jacobsson Lecture.* Washington, DC: IMF, 23 September.

Weber, Max (1947). *The Theory of Social and Economic Organisation.* Edinburgh: W. Hodge.

Welink, A.H.E.M. (1989). "Comments 5", in Joseph E. Stiglitz *et al.* (eds.), *The Economic Role of the State.* Oxford: Basil Blackwell.

World Bank (1989). *World Development Report.* New York: Oxford University Press

21 Towards an Independent Federal Reserve Bank of India

A Political Economy Agenda for Reconstitution

INTRODUCTION

Why and how the Reserve Bank of India (RBI) alone has remained immune to India's critically acclaimed economic reforms, and to the worldwide trend of radical reform and legal independence of central banks, is a baffling conundrum that has hardly attracted any attention. Nor has it figured on the agenda of any political party. This pervasive silence on a major public issue seems a strange aberration in a land of the species aptly described by the poet Iqbal as *guftar kay ghazi* (warriors of discourse), and now the protagonists of Amartya Sen's *The Argumentative Indian* (2005). The lone voice has been the RBI historian: "while the government has set up all kinds of commissions and committees, including a review of the Constitution", there has not "been a comprehensive one on the country's central bank all these many years" (Simha, 2001: 1561). The RBI itself remained inexplicably outside the purview of even the Chakravarty Committee (1985) on the monetary system. Governor Venkitaramanan alluded to the 'vexed question of financial sector reform' without even a reference to the RBI (1997: 377). The omission of the RBI from the reform agenda may, charitably, well represent the judgement that "the Indian Central Bank has relatively little legal independence from the government but has consistently delivered low inflation in response to political pressure" (Stiglitz, 1998: 221). More importantly, perhaps, it reflects Venkitaramanan's belief that "the Reserve Bank has a high degree of independence, in the sense of functional autonomy" and *"that government respects the autonomy of the Reserve Bank"* (emphasis provided). An implausibly Panglossian perception, flatly controverted by another Governor's view that "in a democracy the central bank cannot be totally independent of the government...this does not mean that the bank has to be as subservient as it is today" (Patel, 2002: 184-185).

Source: Economic and Political Weekly XL(35) (27 August 2005): 3837-3845.

Perhaps, the neglect of RBI reform also reflects the views of another Governor (Manmohan Singh), who believed that the autonomy of the bank is a state of mind "which depends on the vision, knowledge and experience of the Governor" and while "the bank must have as much autonomy as possible in the sense that it must be free to give advice to the government" one cannot "legislate the autonomy of the Reserve Bank" (2001: 94). Thus, Manmohan Singh visualised an essentially advisory role for the RBI and implicitly rejected its operational autonomy. Governor Rangarajan was more concerned with the phase-out of the automatic monetisation of the fiscal deficit by the RBI and did not grapple with the core issue of how the RBI could be made genuinely autonomous (1997: 389-395).

Meanwhile, we are also led to believe that in its relationship with the government "the RBI emphasises autonomy in operations: harmony with government policies...and coordination with the government in bringing about structural changes, particularly in respect of public ownership and legislative framework" (Reddy, 2004a: 651). The strident cognitive dissonance of RBI Governors on such a crucial issue as the independence of the RBI is, if anything, a clamorous reminder that the pioneering report of the Indian Central Banking Enquiry Committee (1931) deserves a worthy successor now that the RBI has completed the biblical span of three score years and ten and a former Governor of the RBI has assumed the mantle of Prime Minister and a former member of the Central Board of Directors has been elected President of the republic. Accordingly, this essay presents the case for a radical reconstitution and reform of the RBI to be entrusted to a high-powered commission of enquiry. The enquiry will have to be set in the context of the tectonic shift of paradigm in modern central banking, initiated by the epoch-making reform of the Reserve Bank of New Zealand (1989-90), and manifested in the global trend towards legal independence, governance by committee, accountability, and transparency of central banks (Blinder, 1998, 2004; Kenen, 2000). Equally, any reform agenda of the RBI has to be viewed in light of its relations with the Government of India (GoI) and the requirements of a functioning federal parliamentary democracy now increasingly governed by coalitions with strong regional roots.

Accordingly, the paper is organised as follows: Part II reviews the relations between the GoI and the RBI, and the attrition of the RBI to a quasi-fiscal agency; Part III expounds the rationale for legal independence and accountability of the RBI; Part IV examines the transparency of the RBI; Part V presents the case for transforming the RBI into a Federal Reserve Bank; Part

VI argues for a restructuring of governance involving its management, and the creation of a Monetary Policy Committee (MPC) along with a flattening of its overly hierarchical organisation; and Part VII outlines the modalities of a prospective RBI Commission of Inquiry.

THE GOI AND RBI—THE 'HINDOO MARRIAGE'

On the eve of setting up the RBI, Montague Norman, the legendary Governor of Bank of England, contemplated " "a Hindoo marriage" between the Bank of England (the dominant spouse) and the RBI (the subservient wife), whereby in return for formal advisory services, the RBI was to yield to the Bank of England the right to determine the disposition of its funds and generally cooperate with it in matters affecting the good management of sterling" (Balachandran, 1994: 638-639). Norman's graphic simile is even more expressive of the RBI's real status after its creation. The GoI became the male chauvinist husband and the RBI the ever docile traditional Hindu wife who had forfeited even the minimum right of nagging the husband—the supreme prerogative of a central bank, as memorably stated by Norman himself (1926).[1] The pre-1934 sacramental marriage was formalised by the RBI Act of 1934, which ensured that all the critical initiating and overriding discretionary monetary powers were vested with the GoI. The dependent status of the RBI as embedded in Section 30 (powers of GoI to supersede the Central Board) and Section 58 (the power of the Central Board to make regulations is subject to the previous sanction of the central government) is fully corroborated by a former consultant to the GoI: "a faithful implementor of the wishes of the Finance Ministry...almost all its practices can be traced to the orders of the Finance Ministry" (Desai, 1994: 133).

Ironically, the only time the RBI enjoyed functional autonomy was during World War II, which happened only because of the rare understanding shown by then Finance Member of the GoI, Jeremy Raisman, a trait not always shared by the Finance Ministers of independent India, who have always regarded the RBI as 'a section of the Finance Ministry', as was made abundantly clear by Krishnamachari to Governor Rama Rau, which led to Rama Rau's spirited resignation over the proposed stamp duty on bills, and in protest against Krishnamachari's *ad hominem* attacks on him and public criticism of the RBI. As the RBI historian noted, "Rama Rau's resignation proved that no Governor could hope any longer to defend the autonomy of the Bank by unfurling banners announcing its independence" (Balachandran, 1998:

725). An assessment confirmed by independent observers like B.K. Nehru, who remarked that the day Prime Minister Nehru chose to back Krishnamachari against the RBI, it lost "even such autonomy as it till then exercised and started becoming another subordinate office of the Government of India" (1997: 272). Yet, barely a year after Rama Rau's resignation his successor, H.V.R. Iengar, in his anodyne memorandum to the Radcliffe Committee (UK) proclaimed that the RBI "had all the trappings of an independent central bank..." and that "even after nationalisation the more or less independent functioning of the Bank has not been interfered by the government" (Radcliffe Committee, 1958: 255). Was the use of the term 'trappings', defined by the dictionary as 'superficial and trifling decorations', a Freudian slip? The rare occasions when the Finance Minister did respect the functional autonomy of the RBI, as during Venkitaramanan's tenure, only proves that this so-called autonomy is purely a dispensation of the GoI, a privilege rather than a right. The pathetically subordinate position of the Governor was underscored by the cavalier observation of H.M. Patel, then Finance Minister (c. 1977) when he was on the verge of summarily terminating the tenure of Governor K.R. Puri: "The Governor of the RBI held office at the pleasure of the government and there should be no problem in removing him" (Narasimham, 2002: 93).[2] Likewise, the GoI kept Iengar in the dark on critical policy issues like Plan finance.[3] Small wonder, the GoI never observed even the minimum niceties of protocol with the RBI; deputy secretaries and joint secretaries thought nothing of addressing Governors.[4] Ironically, the first breach of RBI autonomy after Independence was made with the raising of the bank rate in 1951 from 3 to 3.5 per cent by the iconic Finance Minister, Deshmukh, the former Governor and stout paladin of RBI autonomy. He enjoyed a wonderful rapport with then Governor the impeccably suave Rama Rau, who could scarcely be expected to say 'Thou too, Brutus!' The reduction of the bank rate during Governor Jha's tenure (1967-1970) was also made by then Finance Minister Morarji Desai. Although now bank rate changes are made and announced by the RBI it has not been involved in major issues in its own bailiwick like the change in foreign exchange cover for the Indian currency, from the proportional reserve to an absolute amount which was wholly the initiative of I.G. Patel, then Secretary, Economic Affairs (Patel, 2002: 50-51). Likewise, the RBI's involvement in the repatriation of Persian Gulf rupee notes was peripheral at best and it was completely ignored in the nationalisation of commercial banks.

Perhaps "the Bank would have been better off in the longer run had it chosen to offer to the government a brand of economic advice which was distinct from that available, say, from the Planning Commission...the Bank did not have an objective function" (Balachandran, 1998: 729). In sum, the RBI's role in basic policy issues has been reactive at best and rarely, if at all, proactive, barring the inspired Churchillian leadership of Venkitaramanan in mobilising India's gold reserves during the 1991 foreign exchange crisis, which also underscores the striking disjuncture between the acclaimed professionalism of the RBI and the erosion of its status and influence.[5] The RBI has pioneered significant research on a wide range of basic projects a substantial part of which has been published in refereed periodicals of repute.

The history of the RBI bears witness to yet another type of paradox. The attrition of core central banking and the proliferation of its quasi-fiscal activities in agricultural, industrial, and housing finance, which have transformed it into an emasculated fiscal agency. The historical justification for the developmental and supervisory functions of the RBI is no longer valid despite the high authority of Goodhart: "I do not believe that the case for separation which has become stronger in the developed countries, should be transformed also to the developing countries" (cited by Reddy, 2004b: 652). Admittedly, there is no consensus on this issue. The US Federal Reserve has rejected proposals to divest its bank supervision arguing that it is inherently a central banking function. All central banks have their own particular traditions and circumstances but there is always a potential conflict of interest between the monetary policy and supervisory roles of central bank which is also the lender of last resort. A central bank could be tempted to ease monetary policy in order to lighten its supervisory tasks which usually make heavy demands on central bank resources. The present Board for Financial Supervision in India, which is said to be independent within the RBI, should rather be regarded as the nucleus of a separate autonomous entity on the lines of the Financial Services Authority in the UK or the Federal Banking Commission in Switzerland.

The RBI should concentrate on the core central banking function of monetary policy aimed at growth, price stability and financial stability, and the resolution of their trade-offs (Reddy, 2004c: 305). Equally, the ad hoc statement of objectives is no substitute for a statutory formulation, but without a hierarchical ordering, or a quantification of objectives which is the current fad of reformed central banks with their obsessive focus on price stability, as in the case of the European Central Bank, the UK, and New Zealand. This caveat against any ranking of objectives is necessary in view of the RBI doctrine that "consensus could be sought on a medium-term horizon, with a view to evolving a hierarchy of objectives that could be transparently communicated" (RBI, 2004, Table 21.2, Sr. No. 2). It is neither desirable nor feasible to have a hierarchy of objectives which are intrinsically overlapping and whose relative emphasis can change from time to time, a problem well exemplified by the US Federal Reserve Act which commits it to potentially conflicting goals of 'maximum employment, stable prices, and moderate long-term interest rates', or by the legal commitment of the Reserve Bank of Australia to aim for 'the maintenance of full employment'. The objective of price stability itself is by no means as novel as commonly thought of when one recalls that the Riksbank adopted it as early as 1931 when Sweden went off the gold standard. The RBI statute has also several critical lacunae like the absence of a clear statement of its obligations as a lender of last resort (LLR) as in Article 31 of the Reserve Bank of New Zealand Act 1981 (amended as of 20 August 2003) allowing for some constructive ambiguity in regard to LLR obligations in order to obviate the risks of moral hazard. The fostering and proper functioning of the payments system and the advisory role of the RBI to the GoI also merits specific mention as in the central bank legislation of Mexico, Norway and Switzerland. The, 'Hindoo Marriage', of the RBI is now overdue for dissolution and ripe for a new contractual relationship with the GoI, based on a modern statute in supersession of the RBI Act 1934, a dinosaur frozen in a time warp.

An Independent and Accountable RBI

The RBI Act 1934 (Article 2) defines the RBI as a 'body corporate' but does not define its *de jure* status *vis-à-vis* the executive and the legislature. It is said that "a firm view is yet to be taken in RBI/GoI" on amendment to the RBI Act to provide for autonomy, accountability and transparency for which "appropriate conditions need to be created" and "its implementation in the immediate future is difficult since structural transformation is still under way" (RBI, 2004: Table 2, S. No. 1). What are these appropriate conditions? Who creates them? What is 'structural transformation' and who determines when this process is over and a firm view emerges? The case for an autonomous RBI does not depend on any preconditions or on the structure of the financial system, which is a perennially evolving process.

The concept of an independent central bank for India was first formulated by Keynes (1926) in his evidence to the Royal Commission on Indian Currency and Finance: "I conceive a central bank as independent of the government in the sense that it is an organ of the government on a level of authority with the treasury" (1981: 512–13). In fact, the RBI was envisaged as an "independent authority which can act with continuity" (George Schuster, Finance Member, c. 1933, cited in Simha, 1970: 39) but in the event emerged as a subservient entity. The case for an independent RBI has to be argued, taking account of all the conceptual and institutional issues.

Central Bank Independence (CBI) is a multidimensional concept, essentially qualitative, and therefore, hard to quantify and correlate with economic performance. There are not only types but also degrees of independence within each type. The following overlapping collateral typologies well illustrate the intractable problems of defining CBI: Legal—constitutional or statutory; Behavioural—strategic and tactical; Goal independence and instrument independence; Independence as an instrumental good for a central bank and an intrinsic value in a democracy.

This can be supplemented by the following taxonomy which really is a sub-classification of the legal approach (Amtenbrink, 1999:17-23).

- Institutional independence, i.e., central bank separate from the executive and the legislature.
- Functional independence, i.e., when a central bank can decide freely on the application of its instruments (this coincides with instrumental independence) and to decide whether and under what conditions to extend credit to government. The absence of functional independence implies subordination of monetary to fiscal policy.
- Organisational independence (i.e., personnel composition and modalities of appointment and dismissal of central bank officials) implies exclusion of government participation or restricts it to non-voting participation.
- Financial independence (i.e., the role which the government and/or legislature plays in the determination of the budget of the central bank, including distribution of profits'). A hotly debated point is the role of central bank capital, considering that some central banks (Czech Republic, France, Hungary, Iceland, South Korea, Mexico, New Zealand, Norway, Spain) operate without any capital while others (like the RBI, UK, etc.) provide for a fixed sum of capital. The proposed RBI Commission would need to enquire into the rationale of the RBI's capital in light of the experience of no-capital banks and the analysis of those who argue that the impairment of the central bank's capital can

erode its operational and policy effectiveness (Beckerman, 1997; Stella, 1997, 2002).

The foregoing typologies suggest that CBI is akin to a portmanteau concept or a fuzzy set which accounts for the use of reductionist proxies like the turnover rate of Governors. They also indicate that the RBI totally lacks legal and institutional independence and has very limited organisational and financial independence. The goals of a central bank in a democracy are necessarily determined by the legislature while instrument independence appertains to the central bank, except in regard to the exchange rate where government authority is necessarily supreme even though the management of reserves is vested in the central bank. The RBI enjoys instrument independence only by inference. There is, however, an overwhelming case for constitutional rather than statutory independence for the RBI, as in Mexico, South Korea, Switzerland, given the potential for political pressures and the perils of economic populism even under statutory independence with its scope for frequency of amendments. The actual degree of behavioural independence would, however, be determined by a variety of factors such as the size of government debt, the natural rate of unemployment, political conditions, supervision of financial institutions and, above all, public sentiment against inflation as in Germany (Eijffinger and Schaling ,1995).

It is equally important to evaluate the respective merits of the economic and political arguments for CBI to meet the strangely contrarian objections like those raised by Milton Friedman: "I am not in favour of independent central banks, primarily for political rather than economic reasons ... money is too important to be left in the hands of unelected people who are not accountable to the representatives of the public" (2002: 17). For one thing, no advocate of CBI has ever denied the case for accountability, as a concomitant of independence, to elected representatives of the public. Also, while there is an unequivocal political case for CBI the economic case is highly ambiguous, even indeterminate. Thus, the negative correlation between the CBI and average macroeconomic performance (1961-1990) is not very robust and does not hold up when a larger sample of countries—including developing nations—is considered using multivariate analysis (Blinder, 1998: 56-57). Likewise, the post-war experience of advanced industrial democracies (1961-1983) shows that none of the mechanisms that would explain the counter-inflationary effects of CBI hold and that the explanation of the apparent association between CBI and inflation rates must therefore be found elsewhere, i.e., in politics (Posen, 1993: 41-65). This interpretation is also supported by a survey of European

Community members (1976-1993), which corroborates that CBI may be more interconnected with a consensual public anti-inflation culture through a historical feedback process (Hayo, 1998: 241-263). The evidence for the benefit of CBI is still not definitive: it does not take account of unquantified costs associated with CBI, and to date falls short of a convincing case for CBI (Forder, 1998). Another study denies the case for CBI because "the explanatory power of time-inconsistency as a positive theory of monetary policy and inflation lacks any credibility" (Bibow, 2004: 517). One commentator even asserts that an independent central bank "is not a sufficient and/or a necessary condition for price stability" (Eijffinger, 1997: xxv).

Yet another intriguing conundrum is why the IMF, after forcefully arguing 'in favour of a high degree of central bank independence' (Southard, Jr. 1968: 19), allowed this now fashionable doctrine to lapse into oblivion. It does not figure as an element of conditionality in the IMF's adjustment programmes, whose success seems unrelated to the degree of CBI. Does this suggest that policy conditionality is more critical than institutional conditionality? But even the rationale of the instrument-target approach has to recognise that instruments are operated by and through institutions even as policies too are formulated and implemented by institutions. Thus, institutions matter for successful economic performance and the dichotomy between institutions and policies is therefore misplaced.

In contrast to the disarray on the economics of CBI, there is unanimous endorsement of the accountability of central banks to the executive and/or legislature and coordination with the treasury since monetary policy is not a stand-alone instrument. Accordingly, the RBI's statute should provide for government's rights to consultation, to defer or delay the bank's decisions, and the right to veto or instruct (Pringle and Courtis, 1999: xxv-xxix). The statute could require the Governor to report biannually to a joint parliamentary committee and specify the override mechanism.

CBI, however, is no guarantee of central bank infallibility. Even the iconic Alan Greenspan, chairman of the US Federal Reserve, has now been documented as one who "tailored his positions time and again to remain at the helm" and "usually changed his views with a changing of the guard at the White House" (Batra, 2005: 74). The impeccably professional Bank of England is embroiled in a marathon legal battle over a decade, with the liquidators and depositors of the Bank for Credit and Commerce International. The RBI historians, however, do not reveal the state of virtue of the Old Lady of Mint

Road. Oddly, economists who have studied in-depth government and market failures have been strangely coy in analysing central bank failures. Even Blinder does not substantiate his tantalising reference to 'many monetary authorities who have failed to acquit themselves with distinction' (1998: 38). It will be up to the RBI commission to analyse both the successes and failures of the RBI in all its functions (for a detailed evaluation see Chandavarkar, 1996: 218-240).

In the final analysis, the case for CBI rests not so much on the achievement of specific economic objectives but on the insulation of monetary policy from partisan politics, which has been persuasively presented, long before the contemporary vogue, by Montague Norman, Kisch and Elkin (1932), Plumptre (1947), Nordhaus (1975) and Lindbeck (1976). In fact, the arguments for CBI are not basically different from those in support of an objective non-political civil service. Politics influences economics in a variety of ways in India, notably through lobbies like farmer vote banks and the political budget cycles which have been identified both at the centre and in the states. One study found a distinct increase in both the central budget deficit and in its monetisation in the years leading to an election but no evidence of an electoral cycle in output (Sen and Vaidya, 1996: 2023-2027). Another found "a pattern of policy manipulation that points to election-year targeting of special interest groups possibly in return for campaign support, as opposed to populist spending sprees to sway the mass of voters" (Khemani, 2004: 125–54). An independent RBI could play both a pre-emptive advisory as well as a countervailing monetary role to the political budget cycles. A constitutionally independent RBI would also be a deterrent to the perils of rampant judicial activism in economic affairs, like wage determination, which is such a strong feature of the Indian polity.

The conceptual rationale for CBI derives from the accepted doctrine of the Separation of Powers in a democracy:

> Monetary regulation is a major function of government...if it is to be exercised decisively, it needs to be separated in...the constitutional sense from other functions...the judicial function...is recognised to be a function of government, but a function that is better separated. So it is with the monetary function. (Hicks, 1977: 132)

But 'separation of powers' is, properly speaking, also a separation of authorities (Oakeshott, 1985: 145), with the central bank classified as a monetary authority, alongside the executive, an independent judiciary and a democratically elected legislature.

How Transparent Is the RBI?

Transparency, defined as the absence of asymmetric information between monetary policymakers and other economic agents, is a necessary corollary of an independent central bank insofar as it reflects the accountability of the central bank to the democratic electorate at large and from that angle it is also a logical extension of the freedom of information legislation which is a growing feature of functioning liberal democracies. Transparency safeguards the democratic legitimacy of independent central banks but this does not address the economic case for transparency which, given its pluralistic character, requires a taxonomy that reflects the five aspects of transparency corresponding to the different aspects of policy formulation, as follows (Geraats, 2002: 540):

(1) Political transparency refers to clarity of objectives of monetary policy like explicit inflation targets.

(2) Economic transparency highlights the information used for monetary policy, including data, policy models, forecasts and anticipated disturbances.

(3) Operational transparency concerns the execution of monetary policy actions including a discussion of control errors for operating instruments, macroeconomic transmission disturbances and pertains to unanticipated shocks.

(4) Procedural transparency describes the mode of policy strategy and an account of policy deliberations typically through minutes and voting records of MPCs.

The RBI is wholly opaque on all these counts. This classification, however, does not distinguish between *ex-ante* and *ex-post* transparency and omits organisational transparency. In terms of *ex-post* transparency, as evidenced by published accounts, reports and websites, India is now presumably compliant with the *ex-post* disclosures required by the IMF's template on special data dissemination standards (SDDS), but is virtually opaque in terms of *ex-ante* transparency. But we do not know how the RBI website compares with the most effective and user-friendly central bank websites – Canada and the St Louis Fed (Central Banking, 2003: 93-94). Even the IMF's SDDS is in the nature of an interim standard for central banking reporting which requires a uniform accountancy standard for the presentation of on- and off-balance sheet items, including derivatives, defined as forward-looking information. Likewise, the RBI conspicuously lacks organisational transparency which, among others, requires total clarity of the criteria for selection of the top management. The selection process of the RBI Governor remains even more opaque than a papal election.

The criterion for central bank transparency is the provision of adequate information to the markets as a means of overall market stability and symmetry of information (Kurtzig, 2001). However, the conjecture that transparency simply derives from accountability of independent central banks is not supported by the evidence. Rather, central bank transparency has been adopted for economic reasons (Geraats, 2002: 563). It enlarges the impact of monetary policy on expectations, asset prices and interest rates; enhances clarity of objectives; and reduces the costs of unanticipated policy changes. The transparency improves public understanding, and support for monetary policy, as proved by the experience of the Swedish Riksbank (Svensson, 2001: 93).

However, the economic case for central bank transparency is by no means unambiguous. It may actually be distortionary "if the central bank enjoys low-inflation credibility and there is a need for active monetary stabilization" (Jensen, 2002: 399). Uncertainty about central bankers' preferences may be even beneficial if it leads to more wage discipline (Sorenson, 1991), and even from the objective of low inflation uncertainty, "it may not always be optimal to improve the public's information about the central bank's future objectives ...as in the case where there is an upper bound on the degree of information of the public" (Grüner, 2002: 198). Nevertheless, full transparency in the policy conduct of a politically independent bank is an imperative in a democracy, which in the Indian context would be fully congruent with the Right to Information Act of 2005. The enlargement of the RBI's *ex-ante* transparency, however, is critically contingent on adequate disclosures of its monetary policy procedures.

The case for optimal rather than maximum central bank transparency, however, rests on the information paradox. Information is a commodity, an excess of which may conceivably reduce its scarcity and hence economic value. In any event, the RBI is far below the optimal threshold of transparency in all its aspects.

A Federal RBI

There is a striking contrast between the operative political and fiscal federalism in India and the complete absence of monetary federalism as manifested in the architecture of the RBI whose legislation and organisation have essentially a unitary character, which hardly reflect the letter and spirit of India as a federal polity with its concomitant diversity. The contrast is also replicated in other federations such as Canada, Australia, Malaysia, Nigeria, Brazil whose central banks lack the federal architecture of the US Federal Reserve or the German Bundesbank prior to its membership of the European Central Bank. This contrast is, in a sense, true of the economics of central banking, which has neglected the relationship between the design of central banks and the political constitution of a state, whether federal or unitary. There is, therefore, no sure analytic basis for designing the constitution of a central bank in conformity with the political constitution of the state. "A systematic comparative analysis of the relationship between federalism and central bank independence clearly remains an important topic for future research" (Lohmann, 1998: 446).

Monetary federalism has hardly figured in Indian discourse despite the wealth of literature on political and fiscal federalism. The case for a federal RBI can be argued both on political and economic grounds. The political case is best exemplified by the history of the Bundesbank, which shows that "the formal independence of the system is protected by its embeddedness in...German federalism and by the federalist components of its decentralised organisational structure" (Lohmann, 1998: 401). There is also some evidence that the Lohmann hypothesis generalises to other countries which show a positive cross-country relation between federalism and CBI. Federations are characterised by stronger horizontal and vertical checks and balances (Moser, 1999: 1589). Although any sweeping generalisations about the link between federalism and CBI are rightly suspect, it is no accident that in developed countries the most independent central banks are found in federations: Germany, Switzerland and the US, whereas some of the least independent central banks are found in developing countries with federal systems: Argentina, Brazil, India, Malaysia and Nigeria.

The economic case for a federal RBI rests, among others, on the differential impact of monetary policy shocks on status depending upon state-wise differences in the mix of interest-sensitive industries, the distribution of large and small firms, and variations in financial depth (Nachane *et al.,* 2002). Based on this seminal analysis, states seem to fall into two categories as measured by the proportion of state-wise output variance explained by monetary shocks: (i) those significantly affected by monetary policy shocks (Andhra Pradesh, Gujarat, Karnataka, Maharashtra and Rajasthan); (ii) those less significantly affected by monetary policy shocks (Bihar, Haryana, Kerala, Madhya Pradesh, Orissa, Punjab, Tamil Nadu and West Bengal). Broadly, states with a heavy concentration of manufacturing enterprises and greater financial depth tend to be more sensitive to monetary policy impulses than relatively under-banked/less industrialised states. This suggests that if regional asymmetries are indeed significant, the Indian federation may well fall short of an optimum currency area. There is, however, enough evidence to suggest that monetary policy would need to take due account of its regional impact which, in turn, points to the creation of a federal RBI with, say, four regional banks (eastern, western, northern and southern) who would provide valuable inputs into the formulation and evaluation of monetary policy. The degree of involvement of the regional reserve banks in advisory and substantive matters like monetary policy and the payments mechanism with overall coordination resting in the federal RBI is, however, an issue for detailed examination by the prospective commission. A federal RBI would, in fact, strengthen coherence of the transmission mechanism and of monetary policy and act as a bulwark of its independence. Thus monetary federalism would be a valuable adjunct to political and fiscal federalism and help make India a genuine federal democracy.

Governance of the RBI

The two key governance issues, *viz.*, security of tenure for the Governor and the constitution of an executive MPC have not been addressed so far. The former would require amendment of the RBI Act but the latter could be accomplished without any amendment (RBI, 2004: Table 21.2) and yet, this has not been done for reasons undisclosed.

An independent RBI is inconceivable without security of tenure for the Governor, which should be defined by statute specifying the terms and conditions of office, and the qualifications for the job. Oddly, the RBI Act, in common with most central bank legislation, specifies the disqualifications of the Governor, Directors and members of local boards (Article 10) without stipulating their qualifications as in the South African Reserve Bank Act of 1989 (amended 2000), which states: "that the Governor shall be a person of tested banking experience" (4/2a), a provision that recalls Keynes's recommendation (1912) for an Indian state bank that "the Governor and Deputy Governor... should invariably be persons of commercial or banking, not administrative or official, experience" (1971: 161). This stipulation should be incorporated in the new RBI statute.[6] The search and selection process of the Governor should be vested in a composite Cabinet Committee inclusive of representative(s) of the RBI Central Board. The period of office is best restricted to one non-renewable term (six to seven years), as in the case of the European Central Bank (eight years) and Spain (six years). Termination should be subject to due process by the legislature, a valuable safeguard against the vagaries of personal and coalition politics, which have led to arbitrary terminations of Governors in the past. Admittedly, non-renewable terms are very much the exception among central banks but would be the right prescription for India's national malaise of gerontophilia and revolving doors and help infuse the spirit of Hadyn's Farewell Symphony—where each musician departs after playing his part—in our public life.

The Governor of the RBI has sole authority for monetary policy but given the sheer complexity of the task, there is an overwhelming case for a MPC as in most central banks today. There is, however, no necessary correlation between CBI and the formation of MPCs, as proven by the case of New Zealand where the Governor still formulates monetary policy. There are several reasons why a committee is preferable to a single Governor, as cogently stated by Alan Blinder, who speaks with unique authority as an eminent economist and former vice-chairman of the Federal Reserve System (2004: 48). Briefly, they are:

- 'Policy made by a committee is likely to be less volatile.
- Committees are less likely than individuals to adopt extreme positions.
- A committee pools the knowledge of its members, which may be very useful in an uncertain world.
- Committee members bring different decision heuristics to the table, which can be very helpful in solving ill-defined or inordinately difficult problems.'

The newly appointed RBI's Technical Advisory Committee on Monetary Policy (8 July 2005) is a purely advisory and opaque entity, unlike the transparent executive MPCs of the reformed central banks, and will serve no substantive purpose unless speedily morphed into an empowered Executive Committee whose proceedings and voting records should eventually be made public. The RBI's policy process would also greatly benefit by creation of an organised system of regional and sectoral agents, on the lines of the Bank of England, to provide field intelligence in support of its macroeconomic analysis and forecasts.[7] The Bank of England's MPC uses the reports compiled by its agents following discussions with around 1700 businesses in different regions and sectors, including the labour market and services, to assist its assessment of current economic conditions. A summary of the agents' reports is published in the Bank's Quarterly Bulletin, which further enhances the transparency of the policy process. The RBI, like the central banks of South Korea, Turkey, Indonesia, Singapore, and Malaysia, should also consider opening of representative offices in overseas centres like London, New York, Tokyo and Frankfurt to serve, among others, as sources of external intelligence. The closure of the RBI branch in London was a case of misplaced economy.

There is also a pressing need for a drastic reform of the size and structure of the RBI, which is in a state of acute institutional elephantiasis as the second-largest central bank in the world despite the reduction in the staff from 33,168 (1992) to 28,884 (2003) (Pringle, 2004: 89), an instructive contrast to the People's Bank of China with its staff of 1979 (September 2001). There is a strong case for a drastic flattening of its still overly hierarchical organisational chart, singularly inappropriate for a technocratic organisation. The RBI needs to be a lean and muscular knowledge-based bureau, perennially on the learning curve, bearing in mind that "if we think of education as the primary source of information (knowledge) then it is introduced into an organization by its youngest and newest members" but "the prime need in organizational design is increasing capacity to handle a large agenda" (Arrow, 1974: 59).

An independent RBI would also be a potent force for effective governance insofar as a strong sense of staff identity is an important supplement to monetary compensation which as a sole motivator can be both costly and ineffective. A strong staff identity is the ideal motivator, as in the armed forces, which has now led to the academic recognition of the links between identity and the economics of organisation (Akerlof and Kranton, 2005: 28). Despite the RBI's attractive monetary compensation, staff morale has always been eroded by its sense of inferiority *vis-à-vis* the GoI staff. There is a noticeable lack of the *esprit de corps* so characteristic of the Bank of England, the Federal Reserve or the Bundesbank. Strengthening RBI identity would help achieve Max Weber's idea of successful bureaucracies where "an office is a vocation" and "entrance into an office is considered an acceptance of a specific duty of fealty to the purpose of the office" (1978: 958-959).

An RBI Commission

The overdue modernisation of the RBI requires a clear-cut legislative formulation of its non-hierarchical objectives, constitutional independence, coordination with the GoI, accountability, transparency, and governance reforms. This would also close India's democratic deficit and incorporate monetary federalism. The benign neglect of these long-standing issues reflects a discredited Fabianism of the inevitability of gradualness. The complexity of the issues warrants appointment of a high-powered non-official Commission of Inquiry reporting to the Prime Minister within an expeditious time-frame. One can only hope that 'the draft law already pending' to 'sanctify the kind of autonomy being practised by the RBI' will not prejudice the appointment of the proposed commission (Reddy, 2004c: 24). The size and composition of the commission would depend on the range of expertise relevant for its terms of reference—legal, academic, operational, corporate, agricultural and industrial relations. It should permit induction of expert non-nationals in the commission and its secretariat. The chairman would require the talents of an accomplished public intellectual in the mould of what Alexander Hamilton and James Madison (in the US, Federalist Papers) sought in their legislators – 'masters of public business'. The statute should also provide for an expert external evaluation by a non-national of the RBI's performance at convenient intervals on the lines of the instructive evaluation of the Reserve Bank of New Zealand by the Swedish academic Lars Svensson (Princeton). There is no template for central bank reform, which is necessarily a highly country-specific enterprise, and even a synthesis of the best international practice may not necessarily be the answer to the RBI's requirements. Indian reformers could do worse than remember the very Confucian Retort Courteous of the Chinese Premier Zhou Enlai to the fulsome compliment of the visiting Pakistani economist Mahbub-ul-Huq ('We have a lot to learn from China'). "Dr Huq, you disappoint me. China has nothing to teach other countries. Each country has to solve its problems in its own way." Caveat reformer!

Notes

1 "I took upon the Bank as having the unique right to offer advice and to press such advice even to the point of nagging; but always of course subject to the supreme authority of the government", Montague Norman in response to non-parliamentary question 14597 of the Royal Commission (Hilton Young) on *Indian Currency and Finance* (1926).

2 Narasimham, the then Secretary in the Banking Department, records: "I called Puri... and said that it was government's desire that he send in his resignation at an early date" which he did eventually, albeit with some delay (ibid.: 94). Iengar also confessed to a staffer how he was completely trumped by the searching question of a visiting central bank Governor. "Mr. Governor, you preside over an admirable institution but do you feel comfortable in your office, given your bank statute?" (Ali Aneizi, Libya).

3 Iengar was reduced to requesting a visiting Australian economist, H.W. Arndt, not known to him, to "convey to the Planning Commission...his anxiety about a recent decision of the Congress Executive about credit cooperatives" and "to find out a bit more about Delhi thinking on the Third Plan", an odd procedure for the Governor of the central bank to have to use (1987: 32).

4 A textbook example is the following: "Towards the end of 1963, C.S. Krishna Moorthi, who was joint secretary...Ministry of Finance, asked Governor Bhattacharya to spare my services for a few months to help the government prepare a status paper on the Indian economy...for the forthcoming consortium meeting of 1964" (Narasimham, 2002: 34).

5 The following examples are typical. At an India House reception in London for the Indian Sterling Balances Delegation (c. 1949) Krishna Menon, the High Commissioner, after being introduced to the two RBI delegates, P.J. Jeejeebhoy and P.S.N. Prasad, asked an aide to "keep an eye on these two Reserve Bank characters, they are Bank of England agents" (related to the author by Prasad). It hardly mattered for Menon that Jeejeebhoy was the most knowledgeable Indian expert on foreign exchange or that the position paper for the Indian delegation was based on J.V. Joshi's (Executive Director, RBI) classic *Memorandum on India's Sterling Balances*. By the early 1960s, the RBI even lost its privilege of nominating the Executive Director for India on the IMF Board: since then the GoI nominates the Executive Director for both the IMF and the World Bank. Typically, RBI officers on deputation with the GoI never enjoy parity of status with their GoI counterparts. A research officer deputed from the RBI to the Bank Awards Commission (1954) was given Class II status whereas the research officer from the GoI whose emoluments were lower was designated Class I. It took the personal intervention of the Chairman, Justice Gajendragadkar, to redress this disparity in the teeth of GoI's (Labour Ministry) opposition over six months.

6 Keynes even went so far as to suggest that "it might increase public confidence in the... Bank's management...if it were definitely laid down that members of the English or the Indian Civil Service wee ineligible for appointment as officers of the Bank" (ibid.: 161). In the same vein it has been suggested, "some conventions should also be followed to making the appointment of RBI Governors as non-political or non-personal as possible. There is no reason why this important post should be the preserve of senior Finance Ministry officials as it has tended to be for some years now" (Patel, 1994: 50). Given the complexity of central banking there is a good case for an incoming Governor to understudy the incumbent for a convenient period, as was done by Rama Rau before taking over from Deshmukh as Governor, a convention which could be revived. Even Gordon Richardson, one-time Governor of the Bank of England, despite his background as a merchant banker, "took two years to settle into the saddle" as "he didn't have any idea of economic policy" (Fay, 1988: 70).

7 The nearest that the RBI got to market intelligence was the well-intentioned but an ill-conceived experiment initiated in the 1950s by J.V. Joshi, then Executive Director, to

depute research officers to gather information from the commodity markets in Bombay. These officers, given their total ignorance of Gujarati, the market language, and the lack of any briefing, among others, predictably failed to collect any meaningful data relevant to credit policy and the project was abandoned after the first round. In contrast, the Bank of England's agents, who are seasoned participant observers, provide actionable market intelligence.

References

Akerlof, George A. and Rachel E. Kranton (2005). "Identity and the Economics of Organisation", *Journal of Economic Perspectives*: 9–32, Winter.

Amtenbrink, Fabian (1999). *The Democratic Accountability of Central Banks: A Comparative Study of the European Central Bank.* Oxford: Hart.

Arndt, H.W. (1987). *Asian Diaries. Asian Pacific Monograph* No 2. Singapore: Chopman.

Arrow, Kenneth I. (1974). *The Limits of Organisation*. New York: Norton.

Balachandran, G. (1994). "Towards a "Hindoo Marriage": Anglo-Indian Monetary Relations in Interwar India. 1917–35", *Modern Asian Studies* 28(3): 615–47.

———. (1998). *The Reserve Bank of India. 1951–1967*. New Delhi: Oxford University Press.

Batra, Ravi (2005). *Greenspan's Fraud*. New York: Palgrave Macmillan.

Beckerman, Paul (1997). "Central Bank Decapitalization in Developing Economies", *World Development* 25(2): 167–78.

Bibow, Jorg (2004). "Reflections on the Current Fashion for Central Bank Independence", *Cambridge Journal of Economics*: 549–76, July.

Blinder, Alan S. (1998). *Central Banking in Theory and Practice.* Cambridge, Mass.: The MIT Press.

———. (2004). *The Quiet Revolution (Central Banking Goes Modern)*. New Haven: Yale University Press.

Chandavarkar, Anand (1996). *Central Banking in Developing Countries.* Basingstoke: Macmillan; New York: St Martin's Press.

Central Banking (2003). *Website of the Year: Bank of Canada.* May: 93–9.

Desai, Ashok (1994). *My Economic Affair*, 2nd edn. New York: Wiley Eastern.

Eijffinger, S.C.W. (1997). *Independent Central Bank and Economic Performance.* Cheltenham: Elgar Reference Collection.

——— and E.Schaling (1995). *The Ultimate Determinants of Central Bank Independence. Centre for Economic Research Discussion* Paper. No 9505. Tilburg University.

Fay, S. (1988). *Portrait of an Old Lady: Turmoil at the Bank of England*. Harmondsworth: Viking.

Forder, James (1998). "Central Bank Independence: Conceptual Clarification, and Interim Assessment", *Oxford Economic Papers*: 307–34, July.

Friedman, Milton (2002). "Interview", *Central Banking*: 15–23, August.

Geraats, P.M. (2002). "Central Bank Transparency", *Economic Journal*: 532–65, November.

Grüner, Hans Peter (2002). "How Much Should Central Banks Talk: A New Argument", *Economic Letters*: 195–8, October.

Hayo, B. (1998). "Inflation Culture, Central Bank Independence and Price Stability", *European Journal of Political Economy* 14: 241–64.

Hicks, J.R. (1977). *Economic Perspectives*. New York: Oxford University Press.

Jensen, Hendrik (2002). "Optimal Degrees of Transparency in Monetary Policy-Making", *Scandinavian Journal of Economics* 104(3): 399–422.

Kenen, Peter B. (2000). "Key Trends in Central Banking", *Central Banking*: 57–62, August.

Keynes, J.M. (1971). "Activities 1906–1914, India and Cambridge", Elizabeth Johnson (ed.), *The Collected Writings of John Maynard Keynes* Vol. XV. London: Macmillan.

———. (1981). "Minutes of Evidence: Royal Commission on Indian Currency and Finance 1926", *The Collected Writings of John Maynard Keynes.* Vol. XIX, Vol. XXIX, Part III. Edited by Donald Moggridge. London: Macmillan.

Khemani, Stuti (2004). "Political Cycles in a Developing Economy: Effect of Elections in the Indian States", *Journal of Development Economics*, 73: 125–54.

Kurtzig, Joshua (2001). "Coping with Accounting Standards and Central Bank Transparency", *Central Banking*: 76–81, November.

Lindbeck, A. (1976). "Stabilisation Policy in Open Economies with Endogenous Politicians", *American Economic Review* 66: 1–19.

Lohmann, Susanne (1998). "Federalism and Central Bank Independence (The Politics of German Monetary Policy, 1957–92)", *World Politics*: 401–46, April.

Moser, Peter (1999). "Checks and Balances and the Supply of Central Bank Independence", *European Economic Review* 43: 1569–93.

Nachane, D.M., Partha Ray and Saibal Ghosh (2002). "Does Monetary Policy Have Differential State-Level Effects: An Empirical Evaluation", *Economic and Political Weekly*: 4723–8, 23 November.

Narasimham, M. (2002). *From Reserve Bank to Ministry of Finance and Beyond (Some Reminiscences).* New Delhi: UBSPD.

Nehru, B.K. (1997). *Nice Guys Finish Second. Memoirs.* New Delhi: Viking Penguin.

Nordhaus, W.D. (1975). "The Political Business Cycle", *Review of Economic Studies* 42: 169–90.

Norman, Montague (1932). 'Foreword' in Kisch and Elkin (eds.), *Central Banks*. London: Macmillan.

Oakeshott, M. (1985). 'The Rule of Law' in *History and Other Essays.* London: Basil Blackwell

Patel, I.G. (1994). "Some Reflections on Financial Liberalisation", *International Journal of Development Banking* 12: 39–52.

———. (2002). *Glimpses of Indian Economic Policy (An Insider's View).* New Delhi: Oxford University Press.

Plumptre, A.F.W. (1947). *Central Banking in the British Dominions*. Toronto: The University of Toronto Press.

Posen, Adam S. (1993). "Why Central Bank Independence does not Cause Low Inflation: There is no Institutional Fix for Politics", in Richard O'Brien (ed.), *Finance and the International Economy: The Amex Bank Review, Prize Essays.* Chapter 3. Oxford: Oxford University Press, pp. 41–65.

Pringle, Robert (2004). *The Morgan Stanley Central Bank Directory*. London: Central Banking Publications.

——— and Neil Courtis (1999). *Objectives, Governance, and Profits of Central Banks.* London: Central Banking Publications.

Radcliffe Committee on the Working of the Monetary System (1959). *Report cmnd 827*. Memoranda of Evidence, July 1958. London: HM Stationery Office, pp.255–60.

Rangarajan, C. (1997). "Autonomy of Central Banks", in *50 Years of Central Banking (Governors Speak).* Mumbai: The Reserve Bank of India.

Reddy, Y.V. (2004a). "Credit Policy, Systems and Culture", *Reserve Bank of India Bulletin*: 303–11, March.

———. (2004b). "Financial Stability: Indian Experience", *Reserve Bank of India Bulletin*: 651–2, July.

———. (2004c). "Interview", *Central Banking*: 18–26, August.

Reserve Bank of India (2004). *Review of the Recommendations of the Advisory Group Constituted by the Standing Committee on International Financial Standards and Codes: Report on the Progress and Agenda Ahead*, Mumbai.

Sen, Kunal and Rajendra R. Vaidya (1996). "Political Budget Cycles in India", *Economic and Political Weekly*: 2023–7, 27 July.

Simha, S.L.N. (1970). *History of the Reserve Bank of India (1935–1951)*. Bombay: The Reserve Bank of India.

————. (2001). "Resignation of the First Governor of RBI", *Economic and Political Weekly:* 559–64, 5–11 May.

Singh, Manmohan (2001). "Interview:, in V.N. Balasubramanyam, *Conversations with Indian Economists*. Basingstoke: Palgrave.

Sorenson, J.R. (1991). "Political Uncertainty and Macroeconomic Performance", *Economic Letters*: 377–81, December.

Southard Jr, Frank (1968). "The Central Bank in the Policy-Making Process", *Finance and Development* 5(2): 17–19, (June).

Stella, Peter (1997). "Do Central Banks Need Capital", *IMF Working Paper* No 97/83. Washington, DC.

————. (2002). "Central Bank Financial Strength, Transparency and Policy Credibility", *IMF Working Paper* No 021137. Washington, DC.

Stiglitz, Joseph (1998). "Central Banking in a Democratic Society", *De Economist* 146: 199–226.

Svensson, Lars (2001). "Comment", in Alan Blinder, Charles Goodhart. Philipp Hildebrand, David Lipton and Charles Wyplosz (eds.), *How Do Central Banks Talk*. Geneva: International Centre for Monetary and Banking Studies.

Venkitaramanan, S. (1992). "Central Bank Independence", *Central Banking*: 20–2. Summer.

————. (1997). "Current Status of Economic Reforms in India", in *50 Years of Central Banking (Governors Speak)*. Mumbai: Reserve Bank of India.

Weber, Max (1978; 1914). *Economy and Society: An Outline on Interpretative Sociology*, Vol 2. Guenther Roth and O. Claus Wittich (eds.). Berkeley: University of California Press.

22 Modern India's Pioneer Economic Adviser

*Ralph Whitenack**

India can justifiably claim to be the birthplace of economics and the economic adviser in the person of Vishnugupta Kautilya (Chanakya) the minister-adviser of the emperor Chandragupta Maurya and author of the classic *Arthashastra* (The Science of Economics) in the fourth century BC (Rangarajan, 1992; Kangle, 2000), a work unparalleled in the annals of Europe and the Orient. Machiavelli's medieval treatise *The Prince* was essentially a manual of realpolitik devoid of economic content. But Kautilya's work fully measures up to the critical standards of modern analytic economics, as strikingly demonstrated by the researches of Balbir Sihag into the relevance of the *Arthashastra* for public goods, taxation, and the principal-agent problem(2005, 2007).

Kautilya had a worthy successor in the Scottish economist James Steuart, the author of the seminal two-volume book on *An Inquiry into Principles of Political Economy* (1767), who became an adviser to the East India Company (1772) and for whom he wrote the *Principles of Money Applied to the State of the Coin in Bengal* (Sen, 1957). Sen rightly regards Steuart as the first economic adviser to the Government of India and commended his case for detailed intervention into every aspect of economic life. He even remarked that "it would not be any great exaggeration to say that A.P. Lerner's chapter on functional finance seems almost a paraphrase of Steuart" (ibid.: 122). As the author of a 'dirigiste' treatise on economics, Steuart was singularly well qualified to advise a corporation like the East India Company which progressively exercised governmental powers over steadily widening territories in India till 1857 when finally the British crown assumed full sovereignty. It is not known why the office of economic adviser to the East India Company was abolished after Steuart's tenure, although the company did appoint Thomas Malthus as a professor of political economy (1805) at its Haileybury College for training its cadets. John Stuart Mill too worked for the East India

* *Source*: *Economic and Political Weekly* XLII(51) (22 December 2007): 65-68.

My grateful thanks to the late Manu Shroff, who cheerfully accessed the Baroda State archives for the data in this article, which is dedicated to his memory.

Company in its final years (1856-57) and opposed its transfer to the British crown. Thus, the American Ralph Whitenack had distinguished precursors when he took office in 1906 as the economic adviser to a princely ruler, the Gaekwar of Baroda, Sayajirao III, which puts him more in line with Kautilya than with Steuart.

Sayajirao III, the Gaekwar of Baroda, under the tutorship of English teachers like F.A.H. Elliot, and his Indian preceptors like the *diwan* of Baroda, T. Madhavrao and Dadabhai Naoroji, as well as role models like Maharaja Chamarajendra Wodeyar (r. 1863-1894) of Mysore developed an intense interest in the modernisation of his state, based on a voracious appetite for books and new ideas since his younger days, as attested by his English biographers Stanley Rice (1913) and Edward St Clair Weeden (1913).

This intellectual passion for the modernisation of Baroda state, so akin to the spirit of the Meiji rulers of Japan, was the prime motive for his travels to Europe and the US, which further deepened his interest in education, art, and architecture. On his visits to the US, Sayajirao travelled extensively throughout the country, visiting Washington DC, Philadelphia, Chicago, Denver and San Francisco, meeting academics as well as frequenting museums, art galleries, and libraries. On his first visit there in 1906, Sayajirao met the distinguished African-American scientist social reformer, Booker T. Washington, founder of the Tuskegee Institute in Alabama, as well as Ralph Cahoon Whitenack, an economics graduate of the Ivy League Brown University (Providence, Rhode Island) and a Fellow at Wisconsin University, who had also practical experience in industry, manual training, carpentry, machine shop and foundry before serving as private secretary to the treasurer of the American Bridge Company, Philadelphia. Struck by his talent and background as well as his typical Yankee importunity, Sayajirao invited him, at the age of 30, to join his service as Adviser, Industrial Development and to report directly to him.

Predictably, the British Resident in Baroda; Major Pritchard, strongly demurred to this proposal, 'wanting to know more about Whitenack's family and background, being primarily concerned about possible meddling by him in the political affairs of the state'. But Pritchard was confounded when, even before the finalisation of the appointment, he found that Whitenack had landed in Baroda in November 1906 along with Sayajirao, who had deftly bypassed the Government of India and managed to get the approval of the Secretary of State for the employment of Whitenack for a period of six months. His appointment order, dated 27 November 1906, was issued by the 'amatya' (dewan), R.C. Dutt, the noted economist historian, designating him 'as expert adviser in matters relating to the industrial development of the state' at a salary equivalent of $250 per month effective from 3 November 1906. On appointment, however, Whitenack wrote a lengthy four-page letter specifying his requirements requesting a change in his title to Economic Adviser to the Government and an extension of his term for not less than two years and not more than four years. The terms as approved were as follows:

- Salary of Rs 1000 per month; Rs. 1250 in the second year, subject to all state taxes.
- *Bhatta* (travelling expenses) and mileage as per rules. Provision of a tent while travelling on duty as necessary.
- First class return passage to New York at the end of service which in the event was extended till 3 September 1909.

In accepting the offer, Whitenack was actuated 'by a desire...to know India and to carry back to my own nation the unbiased truth concerning India and its people.' For his part, Dutt, although an economist, very commendably did not feel threatened by the appointment of Whitenack.

What prompted Sayajirao to opt for an American economic adviser despite the accepted primacy and ready availability of British economists? He was aware that in fields like engineering and architecture there was no question of conflict of interests, Indian against British, as evidenced by his ready employment of the British engineers R.F. Chisholm and Major Mant as state architects, whose work included the Laxmi Villas Palace, Kamathi Bagh and the British Residency. But in matters economic he shrewdly sensed that there was an ever-present potential of conflict between Indian and British interests as in banking and industry. Equally, Whitenack unlike the common run of ivory-tower British economists, had a unique blend of hands-on industrial experience and a sound knowledge of economic fundamentals. Whitenack too was perceptive enough to insist on a change of title to economic adviser because he realised that industrial development required a congenial macroeconomic environment. For his part, Sayajirao had the vision to accede to Whitenack's very professional plea for a broad-based role to be fully effective as a practical economist in an alien environment. Whitenack was also the first American academic to be employed in India in a non-teaching position in contrast to the essentially commercial and consular relations between India and the US in the nineteenth century (Bhagat, 1970). In the event Whitenack amply justified his appointment, as well documented in the excellent history of the

Bank of Baroda by Tripathi and Misra (1985), which shows the critical role of Whitenack in the foundation and successful working of the Bank of Baroda against very heavy odds, a noteworthy achievement in contrast to the short-lived Bank of Rohilkhand founded in 1862 by the Nawab of Rampur state. Doubtless, the well-clued Sayajirao was only too mindful of the Rohilkhand episode and the sad discomfiture of a fellow princely ruler.

Sayajirao, realising that his state was a woefully under-banked region despite its considerable industrial development as evidenced by textile mills and the pioneering Alembic Chemical Works (1905), showed himself highly receptive to the draft constitution of Whitenack's projected 'The People's Bank of Baroda' the nucleus for the Bank of Baroda, which was finally registered under the Baroda Companies Act of 1897. Whitenack readily sensed the apprehensions of the Baroda financial and business community that the proposed opening of branches of the Bank of Bombay and the Specie Bank in Baroda would only serve to siphon Baroda deposits into metropolitan Bombay credit channels and therefore, worked strenuously to set up an independent Bank of Baroda.. He rapidly built up a consensus between the *shroffs* (those who ran private credit societies), the government and other interested parties to provide for: a state deposit of three-fourths of the paid-up capital of the bank or Rs. 7.5 lakh, whichever was lower, at 4 per cent interest per annum; the amount of the interest-free government fixed deposit was reduced from Rs. 3 lakh to Rs. 2.5 lakh, since the initial paid-up capital was to remain limited to Rs. 10 lakh. The net effect of the preceding two concessions was that during the first five years, i.e., the period of concessions, the fixed deposits with or without interest would equal its paid-up capital. After much controversy, a compromise formula was evolved under which the Baroda government agreed to give a loan of up to Rs. 7.5 lakh at 4 per cent interest for fifteen years. This was over and above the state's interest-free deposit of Rs. 2.5 lakh already agreed upon. In his note to the maharaja, who gave his approval on 16 December 1907, Whitenack emphasised: "The bank is not designed to assist the Baroda government in financial transactions by providing loans, since government has ample funds of its own but to help the people in their industrial pursuits." He added that the "scheme should be fully expounded and discussed in the state before the company is registered."

Accordingly, Whitenack proposed to convene a public meeting, very much on the lines of American town hall meetings, to educate the people on the objectives and usefulness of the proposed bank, which was duly held on 19 July 1908 in the presence of Sayajirao himself. The very next day, 20 July, the Bank of Baroda was registered under the Baroda Companies Act of 1897 under the patronage and support of the Baroda government and was authorised to operate throughout Baroda, Gujarat, Kathiawad, and Bombay, with the subjects of Baroda being given preference in the allotment of shares. The board of directors included four promoters, prominent *shroffs* and financiers in the state, the Accountant General of Baroda, a member of the royal family Sampatrao Gaekwad, Whitenack in his personal capacity, and Vithaldas Thackersey as the first Chairman. The bank also took over from the treasury the task of receiving and paying money on behalf of the state and began to operate as the state bank with effect from 15 June 1910. It was thus, founded on a unique blend of private enterprise and state patronage based on an astute consensus well crafted by Whitenack.

Whitenack's Baroda service as Economic Adviser terminated on 3 September 1909 when he returned to the US to become a Fellow at Harvard University and also spent a year each at the universities of Paris and Munich before ending up at Keio University in Tokyo, Japan. But the India bug continued to bite Whitenack and he expressed renewed interest in re-employment in Baroda for a term of two to three years at a salary of Rs. 1500 per month with first-class fare from America and back. There was an opening for a Director of Education but as Seldon, the British Resident observed, Whitenack 'would not be half as valuable as a junior Bombay civilian and he would cost fully as much'. A state official, B.L. Gupta (title not indicated) advised against Whitenack's re-employment, as 'his administration of the Education Department is not likely to be more efficient than it is at present'. But the dogged Whitenack was undeterred and wrote (15 February 1916) to the Dewan, Manubhai Mehta, asking for re-employment at a lower salary of Rs. 1250 per month and also expressing his desire to write a book on the social and economic life of India, with reference to the reforms in Baroda state. Mehta responded on 1 January 1917 asking Whitenack whether he would like to work as his private secretary or 'in some similar capacity'. Later in a note to Sayajirao dated 13 April 1917, Manubhai Mehta, the dewan posed the following points for determination by Sayajirao.

1. Is it desirable that Whitenack's services should be re-engaged?
2. Should he be paid Rs. 1250 per month with a certain tenure of three years to begin, with his future prospects and terms being left for settlement by mutual agreement hereafter?

3. Should he be appointed to do the work of the general secretary in charge of local self-government, industries, commerce and agriculture?
4. May he be allowed to join any time after July next?

   Mehta added: "It depends on the pleasure of *Huzur*, 2, 3, and 4, if he is to be re-engaged, Yes."

On the same date, Sayajirao noted: "I generally approve of the Minister's recommendation. I think a European or American knowing English thoroughly well is very necessary for the expanding needs of the administration. I prefer Whitenack, though we have to pay him a bit high as he already knows the state." Mehta, presumably after consulting Sayajirao, appended a postscript to the above note before passing it down: "Whitenack will be expected to learn Gujarati and the revenue rules of the state, so as to augment his own usefulness to the state."

Finally, Whitenack was appointed (1918) as a joint revenue commissioner with direct jurisdiction over the Departments of the Excise, Customs, Agriculture, Cooperative Credit. On 14 April 1919 he also functioned as Price Controller and Director of Civil Supplies in the difficult post-war years. Thus, in his second assignment Whitenack functioned like a broad-based economic civil servant with primarily executive responsibilities in contrast to his mostly advisory functions in his first assignment. But in both capacities, his work was fully effective and highly regarded although, surprisingly, he left behind a mass of unpaid bills, judging by the numerous complaints against him by suppliers of goods, including an amount of Rs. 301 from Alpin and Huggat Co., Bombay and an advance of Rs. 667 to Whitenack for his wife's travel from Tokyo.

After his death, the Baroda government received a letter dated 3 June 1919, from a close friend of Whitenack, one Homer of the College of Liberal Arts, Department of Economics, Southwestern University, Evanston, Illinois, asking for information about his career for an obituary in the *American Economic Review*, December 1919. The letter was duly forwarded under the orders of the Dewan by the Political Secretary to Whitenack's wife, who at that point was companion to the Maharani of Vijayanagar. Thus, ended the unusual saga of the lone American economist who served with distinction in India as a pioneering economic adviser, civil servant, and institutional architect. His most enduring monument will always be the hugely successful Bank of Baroda and its impressive branch network, national as well as overseas. The freewheeling Gujarati-speaking Yankee was a natural who was completely attuned to the exuberant entrepreneurial and social ethos of Gujarati Baroda and yet could read the mind of the Gaekwar. Equally, it is only fair to recognise that Whitenack's achievements were rendered possible only because of the perspicacity of Sayajirao, whose creative modernity has been oddly caricatured as mimicked modernity (Bhagavan, 2001: 1).

The appointment of Whitenack as an economic adviser was a singular event at a time when even Keynes had not contemplated a similar functionary, when recommending an economist (George Findlay Shirras) to fill the post of Director of Statistics in India (1914-1921). Amazingly, even Britain did not have an Economic Adviser at the time of Whitenack's appointment. Keynes, even when he proposed the establishment of an economic general staff to serve under the economic advisory council in 1929 (of which he was a member), envisaged a collegial approach to economic advice rather than vesting it in a single ranking functionary. British India, too, did not have an Economic Adviser till the appointment of B.K. Madan to the Punjab Government (c. 1935) and of Theodore Gregory (London School of Economics) to the Government of India (c. 1937). The appointment of Madan was largely the imaginative initiative of Fazli Hussain, the unionist minister, under dyarchy before the advent of Provincial Autonomy (1937), who was quick to recognise the talents of the young Madan, fresh from his laurels as a Ph.D. for his ground-breaking dissertation, published later as *India and Imperial Preference*, and his very productive tenure as secretary, Punjab Board of Economic Inquiry. No Congress ministry under Provincial Autonomy followed this example. Gregory, an avowed *laissez faire* economist, was appointed primarily at the instance of the then Finance Minister, James Grigg, for whom Indian economists were essentially writers of textbooks unfit for high office.

Independent India saw the appointment of Gyan Chand as the first Economic Adviser to the Cabinet, which did not last too long as the spirited Chand submitted his resignation soon enough when he found that Nehru ignored not only his advice but even his bare presence even though Gyan Chand, an avowed Maoist economist like Joan Robinson, had no ideological differences with Nehru the arch planner. Eventually, Gyan Chand found congenial employment as Adviser to the equally socialist Prime Minister of newly independent British Guyana, the charismatic Cheddi Jagan, and lasted out his full contractual term. But then economics and economists in general were a blind spot of Nehru, judging by the experience of B.P. Adarkar* and

* Reportedly, when flying out of Bonn with B.P. Adarkar, an economist of repute, then the Indian Trade Commissioner to West Germany, Nehru asked Adarkar: "What is the secret of Germany's phenomenal economic recovery?" Adarkar forthrightly responded: "Prime minister, I know the answer but you will not like it. It is free enterprise." An impassive Nehru merely looked out of the plane window.

the resignations of three expert finance ministers, Shanmukham Chetty, John Matthai, and C.D. Deshmukh from his Cabinet.

Nehru never really saw the point of economic expertise the way he lionised scientists like Homi Bhabha and Mahalanobis, the mathematical statistician, and dumbed down dissenting economists like B.R. Shenoy regardless of the cogency of their dissent. Nehru's acclaimed political and cultural pluralism was perversely matched by an unreconstructed economic dogmatism, deriving from a peculiarly jaded brand of Fabian post-office socialism, that simply refused to recognise the market economy as the prime engine of growth and the ultimate matrix of equity and social justice. Thus, Nehru was also the progenitor of the Hindu rate of growth—an ironic euphemism for socialist stagnation (1947-1991) in a massive institutionalised rent-seeking society of licences and permits, a truly Faustian pact between a cossetted business community and a kleptocratic bureaucracy.

Clearly, a supposedly feudal ruler like Sayajirao showed greater acumen and statesmanship than the hyper-modernist first Prime Minister of India in using the services of an Economic Adviser. Whitenack's experience is also a stern cautionary tale. No technocrat can be effective without the understanding and endorsement of the chief executive. In fact, the success of the Whitenack-Sayajirao nexus validates the varied criteria of effective economic advice formulated by no less an authority than the economist Lauchlin Currie, the architect of President Roosevelt's New Deal Economic Recovery Programme, and much later Economic Adviser to the Republic of Colombia (1981).

This essay is in the nature of a prolegomenon, based as it is exclusively on the personal file of Whitenack (Section 47, No. 70) in the Baroda state archives. The relevant quotations in the text are all from this file. The fascinating theme of the adventurous Yankee at the Court of the Gaekwar still awaits an exhaustive monograph by a committed scholar drawing on all available records in the Baroda state archives and the Bank of Baroda.

REFERENCES

Bhagat, G. (1970). *Americans in India, 1784–1860.* New York: New York University Press.

Bhagavan, Manu (2001). "Demystifying the "Ideal Progressive" Resistance through Mimicked Modernity in Princely Baroda, 1900–1913", *Modern Asian Studies* 35(2): 385–409.

Currie, Lauchlin (1981). *The Role of Economic Advisers in Developing Countries.* Westport, Conn.: Greenwood Press.

Kangle, R.P. (2000). *The Kautilya Arthashastra,* 3 parts English translation with critical and explanatory notes. Delhi: Motilal Banarsidass.

Rangarajan, L.N. (1992). *The Arthashastra.* Edited, rearranged, and translated. New Delhi: Penguin.

Rice, Stanley (1913). *Life of Sayajirao III, Maharaja of Baroda,* 2 Vols. London: Oxford University Press.

Sen, S.R. (1957). *The Economics of Sir James Steuart.* London: Bell.

Sihag, Balbir S. (2005). "Kautilya on Public Goods and Taxation", *History of Political Economy* 37(4): 723–53.

———. (2007). "Kautilya on Moral and Material Incentives and Effort", *History of Political Economy* 39(2): 263–92.

Tripathi, Dwijendra and Priti Misra (1985). *Towards a New Frontier: History of the Bank of Baroda, 1908–83.* New Delhi: Manohar.

Weeden, Edward St Clair (1913). *A Year with the Gaekwar of Baroda.* Boston: Dana Estes.

23 A Life in Political Economy

*I.G. Patel**

In this refreshingly candid and richly anecdotal monograph,• the author draws on his varied experiences as a don, mandarin, economic diplomat and central banker, and offers revealing glimpses from the unique vantage point of a participant observer, who was involved in some of the most seminal episodes in recent Indian economic history like the Second Five Year Plan, the drift into foreign aid and a regime of controls, the response to the Chinese War and Gold Control, the 1966 devaluation of the rupee, the nationalisation of banks in 1969, the Bangladesh War of 1971, and the response to the second oil crisis about which the author can claim to 'speak from experience not available to many'. The period covered is from the author's student days (1944-1949) to his relinquishing charge as Governor of the Reserve Bank of India (RBI) in 1982. Its organising themes are the economics of politics (rent-seeking and systemic corruption) and the politicisation of economic life and institutions.

There is a wealth of detail and finely nuanced commentary in this richly revelatory and insightful work, which will be an invaluable sourcebook to future economic and even political historians. One can only pinpoint its most salient and instructive features. To begin with, the author's inborn aptitude and confessed vocation for teaching, as against research, have been parlayed into his matchless expository skills in a lifetime of persuasion in economic policy and economic diplomacy. His only regret was his failure, for reasons beyond control, to follow Dennis Robertson's exhortation to 'practise thinking, writing and teaching economics in Gujarati'. Remarkably for an economist, he is more than cognisant of the influential role of non-economic variables and recalls that his

> study of Japan for my thesis led me to emphasize social and cultural factors in development... nowadays it is not politically correct to speak of national or group characteristics...work habits and consumption remained culture specific...we in India can certainly gain by more introspection about our history and about the present state of our national culture.

---

* *Source:* *Economic and Political Weekly* XXXVII(17) (27 April 2002): 1655-1657.

• *Glimpses of Indian Economic Policy: An Insider's View* by I.G. Patel. New Delhi: Oxford University Press, 2002.

Shades of the 'Culture Matters' school which is now challenging mainstream economics. Equally noteworthy is Patel's rapport with diverse and often difficult political masters like Nehru, Lal Bahadur Shastri, Indira Gandhi, Morarji Desai and T.T. Krishnamachari (TTK), while maintaining his professional integrity. An object lesson in the ideal relation of civil servants to the elected elements. Not surprisingly, Shastri emerges a clear deserving political favourite of the author:

> Shastriji had a mind of his own...he was shrewd, had an iron will, a clear view of where the country should be going, particularly in economic policy, and a personal style which was decisive as well as participatory and indeed conciliatory...his views on economic policy have not received enough attention...his untimely death changed our recent economic history and delayed economic reform by some decades.

No less remarkable is his exquisite tribute to TTK's successor as Finance Minister. Sachin Chaudhuri, the proverbial dark horse, a prominent Calcutta lawyer but little known outside Calcutta, who "was neither a politician nor an expert in economics or business ... a very warm and decent minister" who "in the short period that he was in the North Block, left his mark on Indian economic history."

Regrettably, Patel does not touch on an important related issue. The relative roles of the 'generalist' and the 'technocrat' in civil governance, in particular the ambiguous role of technocratic civil servants as embodied in the Indian Economic Service, a poor relation of the IAS at best and doomed to fall eternally between the two stools of bureaucrat and technocrat. Even an economist of Patel's stature had to mark time before he 'gained sufficient acceptability in all echelons of the Civil Service'. Likewise, we are not told about the art and craft of economic policymaking. Is the adviser's role proactive or reactive? What is the relative scope of these roles and of quantitative and qualitative inputs in policy advice? How often does the adviser become the proverbial 'kibitzer' purveying unwanted advice to impervious political masters, as when Indira Gandhi told the author: "For political reasons, it has been decided to nationalise the banks. You have to prepare within twenty-four hours the bill, a note for the cabinet and a speech for me to make to the nation on the radio tomorrow evening." To his lasting credit Patel was at least able to persuade the Iron Lady to nationalise only the major banks and leave the foreign banks alone, which she did with a vengeance by granting a licence to the BCCI against his express advice as Governor. It was D.R. Gadgil's intrepid and principled opposition to the nationalisation of banks, other than the Imperial Bank of India, "merely as an expedient tactic" that was the prime cause of Indira Gandhi's "abominable treatment of Gadgil...a dark spot on Mrs

Gandhi's career...Gadgil was too honest a person for Mrs Gandhi's liking." But then Indira Gandhi never quite grasped the relevance of economic expertise in the way she respected the military expertise of Manekshaw, Arora and Jacob in the Bangladesh War. Small wonder, her regime also spawned the pernicious concept of a 'committed' civil service.

In contrast, while TTK respected economic expertise and had high regard for Patel and J.J. Anjaria, he was guilty of egregious breach of constitutional convention in implicating trusted, honest and competent civil servants like H.M. Patel and G.R. Kamat through the Star Chamber of the Chagla Inquiry into the Life Insurance Corporation of India (LIC). The Inquiry resembled nothing so much as a Roman saturnalia, with Christians being fed to the lions to the infinite glee of the many class IV employees of the Secretariat and RBI, who took casual leave to watch the discomfiture of the 'sahib lok'. But TTK had invested "too much personal pride and ambition...and was unwilling to let it go. To the utter shame of the prime minister...he too did nothing to ease out one of his favourite ministers." The book well substantiates the fatal mutual admiration society of TTK and Nehru. Altogether, the LIC Inquiry and the Mundra affair rank as one of the most squalid episodes which diminished the quality of Indian public life and undermined civil service morale.

However, Patel's argument that "there was some merit" in the notion that the LIC "could buy up shares when prices were tumbling" and "this would stabilise the market" and "could also be profitable for the LIC" is questionable. The LIC is primarily a fiduciary trustee solely concerned to protect policyholder interests and cannot be used as a market stabiliser on the mistaken analogy of central bank intervention in the gilt-edged market. The LIC's transactions in this case violated all the relevant sections of the Indian Trusts Act and insurance legislation. They were a fig leaf to cover the clandestine purchases of the Mundra concerns. The economic rationale of the nationalisation of life insurance has always remained even more dubious than that of commercial banks. If anything, the nationalisation of insurance in the monolithic LIC made the capital market more skewed and oligopolistic by reducing the number of traders and increasing the average size of trades, which consequently accentuate the amplitude of stock price variation.

Patel's views on India's core economic strategy are particularly instructive in the context of the contemporary liberalisation agenda. "India would have developed faster and better if we had given greater attention to exports and obtained our capital goods as fully paid items on the basis of our own export earnings; we would have had a more favourable capital-output ratio as well as a higher savings ratio." It follows that "international trade is beneficial all round and that it makes sense to make it as free as possible." These ideas pose an interesting counter factual. If only Patel, who broke with the Cambridge tradition of the economics of the short period in a closed economy, by choosing the theme 'Foreign Trade and Economic Development' for his doctoral dissertation, had been as vocal and persuasive on policy as he was on aid for India! He would have been an apt pupil of another civil servant, in fact a Commissioner of Customs (Adam Smith), who provided pioneering rationale for free trade as basis of the wealth of nations. Equally noteworthy is Patel's sage prescription to ban restrictive practices of not only management but also labour and government. But India seems to be afflicted with an atavistic dirigisme deriving ironically from the *Raj*. It was "the only part of the British Empire to which *laissez faire* never applied' (Eric Hobsbawm), a sentiment echoed by a visiting Italian economist, Travagliani, who asked the redoubtable socialist Ram Manohar Lohia, "Why are you Indians so critical of *laissez faire* when you have not even tried it?" The nimble-witted Lohia for once was speechless.

A prime example of the dirigiste syndrome is the Gold Control Order, an important by-product of the Chinese War. Surprisingly, Patel confesses he does "not know who originated the idea" but he was to begin with "one of its most ardent proponents." But in the light of its subsequent failure, he "admitted that the Gold Control was misconceived and should never have been attempted." The moral: "Economic policy is not just about economics. It is about history, sociology, politics, and psychology as well." The Gold Control fiasco only underscores the futility of sumptuary and regulatory legislation like the prohibition of alcohol and the interdiction of usury. Gold hoarding reflects the stubborn reality that the gold market is arguably the most completely demand-driven market whose workings are best explained by the unique composite demand for gold as a durable consumer good, including conspicuous consumption, and a store of value invoking the analytic apparatus of Kelvin Lancaster's *Consumer Demand: A New Approach* (1971) rather than the familiar Keynesian liquidity preference, whose elements (except for the precautionary motive) of the transactions and speculative motives are not relevant. The mobilising of gold hoards for productive uses is the problem of 'turning gold into base metal', the very obverse of medieval alchemy. The Indian authorities might even have considered heterodox stratagems like auctions of the much-prized import licences against surrender of gold, even if it meant one more restrictive practice under the IMF Articles of Agreement. Even lily-white Canada got away with floating its dollar when floats were not strictly kosher according to the IMF rabbis. India had never hesitated to add to its then Byzantine exchange control regime down to the Kafkaesque P Form of hallowed memory.

The price and income elasticity of demand for gold in India was researched by Patel at the IMF (c. 1950) but never published because he was 'sceptical of correlation analysis'. Surely, an excessive *dakshina* to his perfectionist Cambridge guru, Gerald Shove, reputed for his "determination not to publish anything until it seemed exactly what he meant" (R.F. Kahn). Patel's study would have been an enduring contribution to understanding the empirics of a problem which still remains unresearched.

Patel also argues the case for qualified independence of the RBI with a single-term (six to seven years) non-official governor 'free to organize the work of the Bank as best as he sees fit' enjoying tactical autonomy in matters like interest rates, reserve requirements, open market operations in gilt-edged and foreign exchange but with a shared responsibility on strategic issues like choice of exchange rate regime, and coordination of monetary and fiscal policy. By inference he concedes the virtually total loss of even the minimal operational autonomy of the RBI but does not discuss the steady erosion of the RBI's status and influence, beginning with the wholly gratuitous and intemperate public criticism of Governor Rama Rau by TTK leading to Rau's resignation, a major episode not even referred to in the book. This marked the subsequent transformation of the RBI into an emasculated fiscal agency and the loss of its institutional gravitas. The RBI was not involved even in major issues in its own bailiwick like the change in foreign exchange cover for the Indian currency from the proportional reserve requirement to an absolute reserve, which was wholly the initiative of Patel in the Department of Economic Affairs. Likewise, the involvement of the RBI in the repatriation of Indian rupee notes from the Persian Gulf was peripheral.

But central bank independence, regardless of its connotation and denotation, is not an intrinsic but a purely instrumental good whose relevance and efficacy have to be determined primarily by the overriding criterion: How does it contribute to the efficacy of monetary policy and other essential central banking functions? A question not addressed by Patel in this book which, surprisingly, carries no evaluation of Indian monetary policy. A disappointing lacuna, as his assessment would have been invaluable, given, among others, his pioneering published research in the IMF on selective credit controls, the traditional workhorse of Indian monetary policy. Sadly, a full-term Governor had to spend more time on the labour problems of an institution manned by singularly unreconstructed Luddites. The only Governor who earned the twin distinction of being 'gheraoed' both by his class IV employees and by the 'politicals' in Delhi.

On the human side, Patel emerges as a most gracious and modest being ever ready to acknowledge debts of gratitude to mentors beginning with Professor Ghosh (Baroda College) 'his first inspiration, *Adiguru* and lifelong well wisher'; Gerald Shove, his Cambridge supervisor, master of the tutorial technique; Anjaria, who led him into economic advice; H.M. Patel, who trained him in economic administration; TTK, who made "no secret of preparing me for higher responsibilities"; and, above all, B.K. Nehru "a most gifted and noble civil servant" who gave "unfailing support, encouragement, guidance and affection." Among his many accomplishments, Patel singles out Nehru's annual foreign exchange budgeting, ably assisted by his deputy, Ezra Kolet, which has provided an invaluable sheet anchor for India's high international credit. How many high achievers in public life even remember the benefactors? In fact, the book is not only the intellectual testament of a distinguished economist civil servant but, equally, the heart-warming saga of a meritorious scholarship lad from a modest middle-class home who made it to the corridors of power and influence, unaided by the customary crutches of affinity networks of family, caste, ethnicity and political patronage. It exudes a judicial quality allied to a fine sensibility, whether it is filial piety to an understanding and supportive set of parents, a love of "my students" and a rare empathy for "rich children" who also have "their cross to bear" like his "loyal and loveable colleague", the late V.K. Ramaswami, the gifted analytical economist, who is the subject of a moving eulogy (pp. 138-139).

After such a magisterial review of India's economic policy, readers would naturally be curious if the author, a non-committed technocratic civil servant, has a personal ideology, a question posed to him at the London School of Economics by a journalist. "I would call myself an old-fashioned socialist" but "not a Marxist opposed to markets and private property...an old-fashioned liberal but not a card-carrying capitalist either...and supportive of certain values like compassion and justice in all social and economic arrangements." He might have more aptly described himself like Henry Martin, the professional protagonist in the philosopher Lowes Dickinson's *Modern Symposium*: "I am by vocation a sceptic, and the vocation I hold to be a noble one...If it were necessary to choose between reason and passion, I would choose reason. But I find no such necessity; for reason to me herself is a passion." Patel's persona, too, recalls the memorable thumbnail sketch of Frank Ramsey, the Cambridge economist philosopher, by Lowes Dickinson:

> ...unworldly without being saintly, unambitious without being sentimental. Through good report and will such men work on, following the light of truth as they see it; able to be sceptical without being paralysed; content to know what is noble, and to reserve judgment on what is not. The world could never be driven by such men, for the springs of action lie deep in ignorance and madness. But it is they who are the beacon in the tempest, and they are more, not less, needed now than ever before.

24 Joan Robinson on 'Economic Philosophy'*

In this provocative little tract# Joan Robinson, perhaps the most dextrous wielder of Occam's Razor among professional economists, attempts a critique of economic philosophy aimed at analysing the many problems and exposing the contradictions that arise owing to the historical evolution of economics, "which has always been partly a vehicle for the ruling ideology of each period as well as partly a method of scientific investigation" (p.7). Perhaps, this is inherent in the very nature of the discipline, although one would not go so far as to imply that the very concepts of the economist are 'value-loaded'.[1] It all boils down to the distinction between science and ideology, between judgements of fact and judgements of value, between testable hypotheses and metaphysical propositions. All this is very much the stuff of received doctrine on the subject, but her elucidation of the bearing of Ideology on Science is particularly refreshing.

> Metaphysical propositions also provide a quarry from which hypotheses can be drawn that do not belong to the realm of science and yet they are necessary to it. Without them we would not know what it is that we want to know. Perhaps the position is different in the respectable sciences, but so far as the investigations of psychological and social problems is concerned metaphysics has played an important, perhaps an indispensable, role. Take an example—the slogan 'All men are equal' provides a programme for research. Let us find out whether class or colour is correlated with the statistical distribution of innate ability. It is not an easy task, for ideology has soaked right into material we are to deal with. What is ability? How can we devise measurements that separate what is innate from what is due to environment? We shall have a hard struggle to eliminate ideology from the answer, but the point is that without ideology we would never have thought of the question. (p. 9)

One may, however, add that it is not merely ideology but the search for solutions of specific problems which often leads to the formulation of hypotheses. It is a case where social technology may precede social hypotheses. The passion for social justice led to the Marxian analysis of the mechanics and end-product of the class struggle and the explanation of all change as the epiphenomenon of economic causes. But then, equally, the Corn Law crisis in nineteenth century England led to free trade doctrines and the analytical

---

* *Source: Indian Journal of Economics* XII(3) (January-March 1965).

\# *Economic Philosophy*, by Joan Robinson, Harmondsworth: Pelican Books, 1964 (Based on the Josiah Mason Lectures for 1959 endowed by the Rationalist Press Association).

framework of the comparative cost doctrines. The Ricardian system has been aptly described as a piece of model-building in the face of a specific problem. The currency disorder in the same period led to the search for an ideal monetary system and gave rise to the Banking and Currency Schools.

But the interdependence of Ideology and Science is so complex in economics that one would hesitate to lay down a sequence. It may be that the search for ideal solutions can lead to system building. But action, ideology and knowledge are all interdependent. To adapt Oakeshott's thesis in regard to political philosophy, we may say that economic activity comes first and an ideology follows later. What he says of political thought and action is equally pertinent in economics, namely,

> just as a scientific hypothesis springs from a knowledge of how to conduct a scientific investigation, and separated from that knowledge is powerless to set empiricism to work, so a political ideology must be understood, not as an independently premeditated beginning for political activity but as knowledge (in an abstracted and generalized form) of a traditional manner of attending to the arrangements of a society. The catechism which sets out the purposes to be pursued merely abridges a concrete manner of behaviour in which those purposes are already hidden.[2]

All this would be conceded by social scientists irrespective of ideology. But Robinson is on more debatable ground when she maintains,

> whether or not ideology can be eliminated from the world of thought in the social sciences, it is certainly indispensable in the world of action in social life. A society cannot exist unless its members have common feelings about what is the proper way of conducting its affairs, and these common feelings are expressed in ideology.

The need for a social ethic in any society is incontrovertible but it is not possible to argue from this that a society must also have an ideology in the sense of a teleological view of social purpose. This is an issue of considerable significance to developing countries.

It is undoubtedly true that like technology "the evolution of society has grown self-conscious" (p.110). But does it follow that an 'underdeveloped country has to take a view about what kind of society it wants to develop'? This raises a number of questions. Is society an artefact to be moulded and fashioned according to a given set of values which may not be acceptable to all? At this stage, it may be pertinent to point out a certain contradiction in Robinson's thinking. Thus, at one point, she also recognises that it is "far easier to build machines than to reorganise society." This is precisely because there is a basic qualitative difference between machines and society. Historically, social arrangements like the price mechanism, money as distinct from monetary system, or language, have never emerged from blueprints or drawing-boards. They are undesigned effects of conscious individual actions, a point of view so ably and persuasively elaborated in the writings of Hayek. A large part of economic behaviour ultimately falls in this category. The point to emphasise is that a backward economy can develop without adopting a teleological view of social purpose. In this, Robinson's attitude betrays what may be called the inarticulate major premise of leftist intellectuals—that it is necessary for society to have a central purpose. But this pertains to a different universe of discourse, of ideology rather than of science and logic, a distinction well elaborated in the first chapter but overlooked later! The need of emergent societies is for Faith rather than Ideology. This is derivable from the corpus of economic analysis itself.[3]

II

Robinson's quest for an adequate theory to explain the origins and rise of industrial capitalism leads her to invoke some promising hypotheses advanced by Ayers,[4] who seeks the mainsprings of economic and technical progress in conditions wherein the ceremonial patterns of behaviour put up a weaker resistance than in the older civilisations to the spread of new inventions. But is this vastly different from Weber's theory of the Protestant Ethic as a liberating force as Robinson seems to imply? Even so, it is interesting to see the uses to which Robinson puts this hypothesis of Ayres, in particular the inferences which she draws for the application of the theory to contemporary emergent societies. According to her, and she may well prove prophetic, "in Black Africa...the most modern technology is coming to the notice of peoples very little encumbered by ancient traditions; if Professor Ayers' theory is correct they are destined, in due course, to outstrip us all."[5] To this one may also add the other differential advantages of tropical Africa over other underdeveloped areas, namely, the absence of the food and foreign exchange bottleneck as well as of population pressure. Non-traditional societies (Tropical Africa) and non-metaphysical and authoritarian societies (China) may have some advantages over traditional and democratic societies (India) purely from the point of view of the pace of development. A 'frontier' society and a non-traditional society have doubtless many similarities. There is the same uninhibited search for and response to opportunity. The simplicity and standardisation of wants, too, is an advantage, although not decisive because in any case the market is relatively small to take advantage of economies of scale. The existence of an expansible virgin land frontier, so important in the context of American economic history, is another favourable factor in African economies.

III

Robinson is incisive on the contemporary relevance of the Malthusian doctrine. Its manifestations and effects in underdeveloped economies are well known. The limitations of bare numbers as a source of capital formation are succinctly brought out by Robinson. "There is still a limit to the amount of investment that can be carried out by any given labour force" and this is set by "the surplus per man employed in producing the mere necessities of consumption over his own consumption" (p.108). Even so, the fact remains that the investment potential, such as it is, of disguised unemployment has been barely tapped in most overpopulated agrarian economies. One can even conceive of 'overpopulation' (excess supply of labour) as one of the 'frontiers' of the social production possibility curve analogous to, although not as expansible, as the geographical (unexploited natural resources) and the technological (innovation) frontiers.

More interesting is her attempt not only to expose the ambivalence of the Marxists[6] on the population question, but also to demonstrate how a Malthusian situation can arise even in the most advanced economies.[7] The most conspicuous effect of rising population in advanced economies is the accentuation of external diseconomies of consumption. This much would, of course, be conceded. But are not these diseconomies a by-product of planless conurbations and hence of *laissez faire* in an unwarranted sphere, rather than of growth *per se*, an aspect which Robinson may well have brought in to complete the argument? Even so, it is salutary to be reminded that the Malthusian devil, far from being chained, can coexist with different levels of development and in vastly dissimilar societies. It is one more proof that the economic problem is basically the same in all societies, feudal, capitalist or collectivist. But, here one can only regret Robinson's refusal to follow her hunches into spheres other than population.

Thus, the basic distinction between the ethical and the economic aspects of investible surplus[8] is independent of the form of society or the nature of the State. Similarly, inflation in its widest sense of the excess of Aggregate Demand in relation to Aggregate Output is unrelated to the skewness of distribution of incomes and property, although a prolonged inflation does aggravate economic inequalities. It manifests itself, even with constant prices under a centrally planned egalitarian economy, in the form of lengthening queues and commodity shortages or, more subtly, in deterioration of quality and service (Socialist Inflation?). An assiduous econometrician may well detect cobweb-type commodity cycles in centrally planned economies. Even problems supposed to be wholly peculiar to individualist or mixed economies like the phenomenon of U-sector consumption[9] have an awkward knack or turning up in collectivist economies (dachas for party bureaucrats, ballerinas and intellectuals). The point, after all, is that one group, not necessarily the most deserving, may stake out higher claims for current consumption even if property is collectively owned. Or, more perversely, could one say that some species of U-consumption is a necessary 'incentive good' to the creative elite in all societies? This is, of course, not to deny the relevance of incentives to the 'maintenance elites' as well. What then is the significance of U-sector consumption for developing economies? According to Robinson,

> the pre-existing surplus of unnecessary consumption is small, however, in relation to the accumulation required. The main advantage of wiping out unearned income is that it makes it easier, socially and politically, to prevent real wages from rising too fast. Moreover, collective consumption contributes more per unit of national expenditure, to the general welfare...than a rise of wages spread over individual families. (p.11)

This analysis can be further extended by taking account not merely of the magnitude of U-sector consumption of the gross national product that goes into such consumption, which further limits the significance of the phenomena. The point surely is its effect on the willingness of labour to accept cuts in real wages. This shows how the interdependence of individual consumption functions and the demonstration effect can work both ways—upward in stimulating consumption and downward in creating greater willingness to accept reduction provided it affects every one's consumption in equal measure. But in addition to the suppression of unearned incomes, the disappearance of private property, domestic and foreign owned, through expropriation can contribute to some rapid economic growth under certain conditions, despite its apparent character as a once-for-all source of development finance.[10]

But all this will appear in perspective if only economists, who are prone to treat the problem of development primarily as one of 'resources' rather than of 'incentives', were to rehabilitate the latter as one of the prime movers of development. One may then realise, adapting Paretian terminology, that the lack of 'tastes' may itself be an 'obstacle'. Even the most egalitarian society runs up against the awkward problem of incentives. There is no need to run the entire gamut of economic problems common to all societies. Suffice it to say that the economist has to recognise, along with the political philosopher, that if the distinction between the rulers and ruled, and hence the problem of political obligation, exists in all states and societies (pace Collingwood), it is no less true of the Economic Problem, which can no longer be regarded, as Keynes once thought, as "nothing but a frightful, a transitory and an unnecessary muddle."

IV

One of the conspicuous gaps of Robinson's analysis of the economic fallacies of the Left is lack of even a bare reference to the crucial question—why collectivists, whether economists or ideologues, are more obsessed with the problem of inter-group equity rather than of intergeneration equity. Philosophers of collectivism have always been more than anxious to diagnose and prescribe the ills which arise from economic inequalities between classes but have been hardly mindful of the equally critical problem of reconciling the interests of the present generation with those of generations yet unborn. This is evidenced, among other things, by the obsession of collectivism with 'investment goods industrialisation'. But Robinson scarcely sheds any light on the investment bias of collectivism.

One could, however, venture a few hypotheses to account for the tendency of collectivist philosophers to emphasise investment as against consumption. There is, first, the non-economic case for investment on grounds of power, defence and the general build-up of the collectivist states as against the capitalist private enterprise world. From the organisational point of view, decision-making and control are easier in investment industries which have necessarily to be operated on a scale and in a manner that lends itself more easily to centralised control than consumption goods industries. On the other hand, the need for decentralisation of decision is greater as well as easier in consumption industries. A good example is the failure of collectivist society generally to control and discipline the vast mass of the peasantry. It is also possible to make a purely economic case on familiar lines for the investment bias of collectivism on the ground that investment results in a greater magnitude of backward and forward linkages compared to consumer goods industry. But this is seldom spelt out in a way that sets out clearly the economic rationale of the investment bias of collectivism. Even so, it still remains a puzzle why and how long can the claims of the present generation be sacrificed indefinitely to the hypothetical interests of future generations. It is easy for an authoritarian state to slide from the position of investment for the sake of future prosperity into a situation wherein there is no visible improvement in the standard of living over several generations. In fairness to the collectivist states, it should also be stressed that they are not the only ones to be bemused by the charms of building up heavy industry for future increments of welfare.[11] Witness the blueprints of economic development of almost all emergent countries, irrespective of their form of social and economic organisations.

The investment bias of collectivism is perhaps an outstanding example of 'misplaced concreteness'. Of course, even otherwise the tendency of modern economic thought and organisation is increasingly blurring the distinction between the 'physical' and the 'economic' with the result that economic science is virtually becoming an extension of operations research and production engineering. Possibly, the obsession with physical quantities as a technique of development planning makes it easier to lapse into an acceptance of the superior merits of investment for its own sake.

On the whole, both political philosophers and economists have perhaps slurred over the vital problem of the role of the state as the custodian of different generations. To the extent there has been any discussion of this crucial problem it has been more to emphasise the interests of future generations as against the present. For instance, even a comparatively orthodox economist like Pigou emphasised, inferentially, the role of the State as a protector of the wasting assets of society and based part of his argument for state intervention on the superior telescopic faculty of the State *vis-à-vis* the individual. Similarly, Burke envisages the State as a bridge between the generations. Curiously enough, there appears to be a basic contradiction in the Marxist theory of the State. If, on the one hand, the Marxist desires and foresees the withering of the State at the stage of full socialism, who would then act as the bridge between generations and who would fulfil the role of the State as the arbitrator of different interests? But if the State is regarded as an arbiter of intergeneration equity, it cannot be allowed to wither!

V

But whatever the gaps in the structure of the book, one cannot but be impressed by the vigour and insight of her observations. The summing up is magistral.

To some, perhaps, it even recommends the old doctrines, since it offers no 'better 'ole' to go to. The contention of this essay is precisely that there is no 'better 'ole'. The moral problem is a conflict that can never be settled. Social life will always present mankind with a choice of evils. No metaphysical solution that can ever be formulated will seem satisfactory for long. The solutions offered by economists were no less delusory than those of the theologians that they displaced. All the same we must not abandon the hope that economics can make an advance towards science, or the faith that enlightenment is not useless. It is necessary to clear the decaying remnants of obsolete metaphysics out of the way before we can go forward. The first essential for economists, arguing among themselves, is to "try very seriously", as Professor Popper says that natural scientists do, "to avoid talking at cross purposes" and, addressing the world, reading their own doctrines aright, to combat, not foster, the ideology which pretends that values which can be measured in terms of money are the only ones that ought to count.

All this is wholly in character. After all, the essay is not merely the testament of an agnostic. It is even more an affirmation of faith by a high-minded social scientist. One can discern in it a parallelism to the tenor of her earlier observations on 'Indeterminacy in Economics'. As in economic analysis so in economic philosophy, there are no final categories or moral absolutes. It is like the Aristotelian proposition, "Of things which are indeterminate, the rule also needs to be indeterminate." But then, would Robinson's agnosticism accommodate Poppersque 'Social Engineering' or Hirschman's compulsive reform mongering to the exclusion of a monistic fundamentalist Marxism as the philosophy of social change?

All in all, a stimulating little volume which, perhaps, poses even more questions than it answers. In its own sphere its scheme and purpose are comparable to her *Exercises in Economic Analysis*. If the one is the economic analyst's toolkit, this may well be the economic philosopher's guidebook.

Notes

1 Cf. G. Myrdal, *An Internal Economy: Problems and Prospects.* New York: Harper and Brother, 1956, p. 337.

2 Michael Oakeshott, *Political Education.* Cambridge: Bowes and Bowes, 1951.

3 "...There is a subtle reason drawn from economic analysis why...faith may work. For if we consistently act on the optimistic hypothesis, this hypothesis will tend to be realised; while by acting on the pessimistic hypothesis we can keep ourselves forever in the pit of want". J.M. Keynes, *Essays in Persuasion, Collected Writings of John Maynard Keynes*, Vol. IX, London: Macmillan, 1972, pp.vii-viii.

4 cf. Ayers, *The Theory of Economic Progress.* Carolina: University of North Carolina Press, 1944.

5 It is interesting to note a similar view expressed by a percipient modern African writer. "All this should be a warning to those Africans who think of culture as an anthropological thing that belongs in the past and must be reconstructed as a mere landmark or a monument; the here and now of its struggle to come to terms with modern technology, with the confrontation of other ways of life, must give as valid a definition to our culture as its historical past. When one sees the granite monument that Indian culture and civilization are, and what a barricade against change they have been through the years, one begins to wonder if after all the African is not at a greater advantage for being able to absorb and contain the shock of change." Ezekiel Mphalele, "The Fabric of African Cultures", *Foreign Affairs*: 618-619, July 1964.

6 "Orthodox Catholicism and orthodox Marxism agree in protesting that there is no such thing as a population problem (although both seem to be softening their attitude a little in recent times)...with every mouth God sends a pair of hands. True enough but he does not send a combine-harvester. As for the Marxists, one cannot but suspect that they know better and have some reason for not saying so" (p.108).

7 "There is a population problem also in the advanced industrial section of the world ... The rise in population in the Western world (especially the United States) has set in at a time when technical progress is also rapid. The natural rate of growth in Harrod's sense is evidently running ahead of accumulation and the US seems to be drifting into a kind of high-level underdevelopment with employment opportunities falling short of the available labour force. This is mitigated to some extent by a kind of high-level disguised unemployment in small scale service trades" (p.109).

"The most noticeable effect of a growth in numbers when it occurs at a high standard of life is the way human beings destroy amenities for one another though cluttering up the country with their bodies, their houses and their motor cars" (ibid.).

8 Robinson's analysis of the similarity of profit margins and indirect taxes is a good case in point. "The difference between profit margins and indirect taxes, in terms of their economic functioning is not at all clear-cut; one is no more and no less 'a burden' than the other ... The idea that one is necessarily more 'economic' than the other has no foundation except in ideological prejudice" (p.185).

Cf. "The pattern of the capitalist development is fairly well known. So also is the performance of socialism in the Soviet Union. But what has perhaps not been noticed or, at least, not emphasised, is the basic similarities between the two. The proletarianisation of the peasantry by land-enclosures, the creation of wage labour by making it impossible for handicrafts to survive, the indirect exploitation of even the existing peasantry by cheaper bread and dearer manufactured goods, the increasing capitalisation of agriculture, the intensive use of labour and even forced labour in certain areas—in short all the diverse ways and means to appropriate surplus value from those who create it." Daya, "Profit Exploitation and Surplus Value". *Review of Economic Studies* 58: 101, 1954-55.

9 This is a term which we owe to Dr. B.V. Krishnamurthy, who first analysed the phenomenon in an article on this subject in the *Economic Weekly*, Bombay.

According to Robinson, "the overall savings ratio ... distracts attention from the distribution of income between individual families. It helps to disguise the awkward problem of what the Indians have begun to call the "growth of the U-sector" which takes place when private wealth is swollen by the overflow from public investment. The need to restrain consumption in order to permit the rate of accumulation to increase gives an advantage to the economies carrying out development under socialist institutions. A revolution which nationalises property without compensation makes available resources that formerly fed U-consumption available for investment" (p.111).

10 On this see M. Bronfenbrenner, "Appeal of Confiscation in Economic Development", *Economic Development and Cultural Change* (Chicago, 1955). But this type of argument, apart from its other limitations, does not sufficiently recognise that 'confiscation' may also affect prospects of foreign aid and capital inflows, a strategic variable for all developing economies, whatever their ideologies.

11 A. Gerschenkron, on the basis of his researches in nineteenth-century European industrialisation, adduces the proposition that "the more backward was a country's economy, the more pronounced in its industrialization was the stress on bigness of both plant and enterprise...and on producer goods as against consumer goods." "The Early Phase of Industrialization in Russia", in W.W. Rostow (ed.), *Economics of Take-off.* London: Macmillan, 1963, p.152.

25 Economics and Philosophy

*Interface and Agenda**

Prologue

There is an unsuspected commonality between philosophy and economics. Both disciplines are not amenable to an unambiguous monolithic definition. Thus, Isaiah Berlin claimed that "there is no universally accepted answer to the question: What is the subject matter of philosophy?" (Berlin, 2000: 24). He sought to define philosophy with reference to its purpose. "It is to try to answer...questions of general importance for which no technique either empirical or logical can provide solutions" (Berlin and Jahanbegloo, 1991: 136). As against this, Karl Popper argued that "all life is problem solving" and that "error correction is the most important method in technology and learning" (Popper, 1999: 99-100).

There is, however, a more positive commonality between economics and philosophy as well expressed by the two towering giants of modern economics and philosophy—Keynes and Wittgenstein. Keynes viewed economics as a technique of analysis even as Wittgenstein insisted that philosophy was an activity and not a body of doctrine (Magee, 2001: 13). In fact, for Keynes, "Philosophy came before economics; and the philosophy of ends came before the philosophy of means" (Skidelsky, 1983: 133). The dominant philosophical influence on Keynes was Moore's *Principia Ethica* (1903) and Keynes essentially formulated the basic idea of his *Treatise on Probability* (1921) as a result of grappling with the applications of the *Principia Ethica*. Keynes's exposure to philosophy through Moore is strikingly paralleled by the critically important influence of the distinguished Italian economist Piero Sraffa in bringing about Wittgenstein's momentous movement from his early position in *Tractatus Logico-Philosophicus* (1921) to the later *Philosophical Investigations* (1951)

---

* *Source: Economic and Political Weekly* XLII(3) (20 January 2007): 221-230.

This is a revised version of an article on "Philosophy and Economics: Issues and Questions" in Daniel Kolak and Raymond Martin (eds.) (2006), *Experience of Philosophy* (6th edn.), New York: Oxford University Press, based on an invited presentation to the Annual Meeting of the American Philosophical Association (Eastern Division), 27-30 December 2003.

(Sen, 2003: 1240). According to Wittgenstein, "the most important thing that Sraffa taught him was an anthropological way of seeing philosophical problems...While the *Tractatus* tries to see language in isolation from the social circumstances in which it is used, the *Philosophical Investigations* emphasises the conventions and rules that give the utterances particular meaning" (ibid.: 1242). Likewise, Sen stresses that Sraffa's economic contributions cannot in general be divorced from his philosophical understanding, particularly in altering and broadening the nature of the inquiries in mainstream economics. For instance, Sraffa found that the use of counterfactuals involved problems that purely observational propositions did not; there was a big methodological divide between factual descriptions and counterfactual magnitudes.

The very roots of modern economics go back to philosophy and the great economic thinkers (Adam Smith, Malthus, John Stuart Mill, Karl Marx, Henry George, and John Maynard Keynes) have been rightly acclaimed as the worldly philosophers (Heilbroner, 1980). Yet economists have posed the question: "should economists pay attention to philosophers? The answer is...not much...the economist *qua* economist, need not pay much attention to philosophy, good or bad, but the philosopher of science had better pay attention to economics, good and bad" (Gordon, 1978: 728). While this point of view may not necessarily be shared by the majority of economists, it merits attention as a core issue of the discourse between philosophers and economists. If anything, it is economics that raises serious philosophic issues which have to be squarely faced by its practitioners. For instance, given the character of economics as pre-eminently a subject of cognitive dissonances, can it claim to be a science? If it is a science is it deductive or inductive, positive or normative? While its explanatory power is considerable, its predictive power is virtually nil. Paradoxically, despite its flaws as a science, economics has emerged as an imperial science among the social sciences. There is also the question whether given its character as a problem-solving and policy discipline, it confers a superior role to the economist as an expert adviser and source of value judgements in a functioning liberal democracy.

Economics: Cognitive Dissonance

There is not even an agreed definition of economics and economists are notorious for their perennial propensity to disagree on matters of analysis and policy, a situation without parallel in the physical sciences. The most representative definitions cover some but not all aspects of what economists study and prescribe, but there is no single comprehensive and logical definition of economics. According to Keynes's classic definition in his preface to the *Cambridge Economic Handbook Series* (Nisbet, 1928): "Economics does not furnish a body of settled conclusions immediately applicable to policy. It is a method rather than a doctrine, an apparatus of the mind, a technique of thinking, which helps its possessor to draw correct conclusions." Keynes's definition is eminently congruent with Karl Popper's definition of scientific method—the generation and testing of hypotheses. Keynes's definition, while scientific, does not convey any notion of the subject matter of economics. It could well apply to any of the other social sciences. Alfred Marshall defined economics as

> a study of men as they live and move and think in the ordinary business of life. But it concerns itself chiefly with those motives which affect, most powerfully and most steadily, man's conduct in the business part of his life...the motive is supplied by a definite amount of money, and it is this definite and exact money measurement of the steadiest motives in business life, which has enabled economics far to outrun any other branch of the study of man...But economics cannot be compared with the exact physical sciences; for it deals with the ever changing and subtle forces of human nature. (Marshall, 1920:14)

While Marshall's balanced definition conveys the substance of economics, it omits its techniques of investigation. The celebrated definition of economics as a "science which studies human behaviour as a relation between given ends and scarce means which have alternative uses" captures the core concept of economics, namely, opportunity cost, i.e., the price which one pays for forgone alternatives (Robbins, 1962: 15). But what happens to Robbins's definition and to opportunity cost when there is sustained unemployment? It also overlooks the techniques of analysis employed by economists.

The cognitive dissonance manifested in the definitions of economics is paralleled in the subject matter of economics, which shows up the polar divergences between equally reputed economists on matters of substance and policy, despite the widespread "feeling that modern economics has established itself as a science enjoying a high degree of consensus" (Frey *et al.,* 1984: 985). Jurg Niehans states: "In fact, the economic doctrines taught in Nairobi, Sao Paulo, New Delhi, Tel Aviv, Geneva, Harvard, and Bowling Green State...have a large common core" (Niehans, 1981: 170). This, however, is a pedagogic rather than an epistemic consensus. The results of a stratified random sample survey of 2072 economists with respect to country, position, and occupation who were asked to respond to 27 propositions about economic problems are instructive (Frey *et al.,* 1984: 994). The answers by the over 900 economists in five countries (the US, Germany, Austria, France, and Switzerland) showed the highest degree of consensus in respect of the market price system as an effective and desirable social-choice mechanism, as well as the most disagreement about normative propositions relating to income distribution and government spending and issues such as monetarism and supply-side economics. The major cause for dissension was the different views of economists, attributable to differences in history, politics, and culture. In general, it could not be confirmed that positive and micro-propositions showed a greater consensus than normative and macro-propositions.

The persistence of cognitive dissonance is glaring in both analysis and policy. For instance, the Nobel Prize for Economics in 1978 was shared between Arthur Lewis and Theodore Schultz for their contributions to development economics despite their diametrically opposite findings regarding the marginal productivity of peasant farmers in poor countries, which was zero according to Lewis and positive according to Schultz. This would be the figurative equivalent of dividing the Nobel Prize for Physics between Ptolemy and Copernicus. Similarly, the effects of globalisation have been hotly debated between Joseph Stiglitz (Nobel Laureate, 2001), who argues its downside in his *Globalization and its Discontents* (2002), and Jagdish Bhagwati, who is equally articulate on its net benefits in his *In Defense of Globalization* (2004). In fact, the acrimony of debate between economists on just about every issue recalls the memorable verdict of an eminent archaeologist, Mortimer Wheeler, that saw his own discipline 'as more of a vendetta than a science'. This may well reflect the sheer complexity of economic phenomena and its pervasive anomalies and paradoxes, regularly featured in the *Journal of Economic Perspectives*, which pose a challenge to economists and philosophers alike. There are those who explain "Why Economics Is Not Yet a Science" (Eichner, 1983); that it is essentially a positive science (Milton Friedman, Nobel Laureate, 1976); and that it can never be a value-free science (Gunnar Myrdal, Nobel Laureate, 1974). The jury will always be out on *Is There an Economic Consensus?* (Brittan, 1973). Is the term 'economic science' then an oxymoron?

Epistemology: Is Economics a Science?

Economics is regarded by its practitioners as the imperial social science, but its regalia will be seen to be ersatz if one examines its major epistemic features and contrasts them with those of the exact sciences.

To begin with, the basic concepts and magnitudes of economics, such as gross national product, balance of payments, and money supply are portmanteau concepts which are composites of disparate elements subject to errors and ambiguities, unlike the monistic concepts of the physical sciences, like atoms and molecules. Economic concepts need to be further disaggregated into nominal and real elements as well as stock and flow magnitudes. Similarly, economic variables can be classified into exogenous and endogenous, depending upon whether they are governed by influences external or internal to the economic system. Econometrics is classified into explanatory and instrumental variables. Some variables are akin to fuzzy sets, with differences of degree rather than of kind, as for instance, the concept of central bank independence, which may be *de jure* or *de facto*, constitutional or statutory, strategic or tactical, and of goals or instruments. The 'money illusion', which occurs because economic agents often overlook the real variables, distorts both behaviour and policy. More importantly, economic agents are cognitive and subject to autonomous and feedback influences. As Hicks (Nobel Laureate, 1972) remarked, "there are few economic laws which can be regarded as all firmly based. Economics is a leading example of uncertain knowledge" (Hicks, 1983: 2). Economic laws are at best statements of tendencies, subject to 'other things being equal', and there are no identifiable determining influences, like gravitation in the movement of the tides, which also explains why economic policy cannot claim triumphs comparable to those of applied scientists or engineers. Economics lies on the edge of both science and history, since the economist is "concerned with the present and for the sake of the present with the past" (ibid.: 4). It is "specially concerned with the making of decisions and with the consequences that follow from the decisions" (ibid.: 5). This makes economics a prescriptive policy science, in addition to its descriptive and analytic functions, which has to cope with the phenomena of contemporaneous as well as sequential causality.

Paradoxically, while economics does not qualify as an exact science, it does adhere to the scientific method and the criteria of falsifiability, say, as defined by Karl Popper, whose formula of objective knowledge is used in practice by economists (Popper, 1975: 145).

$$P_1 \rightarrow TS \rightarrow EE \rightarrow P_2$$

where P_1 is the initial problem, *TS* the trial solution proposed, *EE* the process of error elimination applied to the trial solution, and P_2 the resulting situation with new problems. This is essentially a feedback process, which is neither cyclical nor dialectical, and validates the objective theory of essentially conjectural knowledge. Unfortunately, falsifiability in economics is too uncritically associated with econometrics, and "no piece of research in economics seems now to be regarded as respectable unless it is decorated with least squares and confidence intervals" (Hicks, 1983: xi–xii). Econometrics, too, is often bedevilled by a failure to distinguish between statistical significance and economic significance (McCloskey and Ziliak, 1996). Likewise, falsifiability is as much a test of patterns and trends in economic events as embodied in history as is orthodox regression analysis of time-series. The use of statistical techniques to quantify causality (Robert Engle and Clive Granger, Nobel Laureates, 2003) poses the basic philosophic issue: Is it legitimate to quantify causality, which is an amalgam of varied factors, qualitative and quantitative? Economic decisions affect and are affected both by the sign as well as the magnitude of change. Also, causality can be contemporaneous or sequential.

Economics as a social science is afflicted with peculiar foibles which do not affect the exact sciences. Thus, George Stigler (Nobel Laureate, 1982) observed that "there is a simply enormous amount of unprogressive publication, articles which certainly add nothing to the accumulation of rigorous theory or tested findings", which he substantiates in the case of the literature on the kinked demand curve in oligopoly, where he found that "two-thirds at a minimum made no positive contribution to received knowledge" (Stigler, 1982: 240). This suggests that peer review in publication puts a premium on technical virtuosity as against realism and relevance. Even more disconcerting is the prevalence of interpersonal and institutional bias: "Local faculty receive a perhaps inevitable preference in the student's work and the ideological preferences of the professors are communicated in some degree to the students" (ibid.: 221). The obsessive preoccupation of economists with methodological issues has no counterpart among natural and physical scientists or even in the other social sciences.

Allied to the premium on technical virtuosity is the 'attractive Anglo-Saxon kind of unnecessary originality' (Myrdal, 1965: 8) which now afflicts the economics profession as a whole, where the claims to originality also rest on a studied neglect of past contributions, as for instance, the Nobel Laureate (1992) Gary Becker's *Treatise on the Family* (1991), which takes no account of Philip Wicksted's profound analysis of family behaviour in his *Commonsense of Political Economy* (1910). Likewise, the copious literature on credit rationing scarcely mentions its provenance in Keynes's seminal concept of 'the fringe of unsatisfied borrowers' in his *Treatise on Money* (Volume II). The cavalier attitude "I have no interest in the history of my subject. What the dead had to say, when of value, has long since been absorbed" (Hahn, 1992: 165) is all too typical of the profession. In physics, even Newton proudly confessed that he 'stood on the shoulders of giants', a sentiment totally bereft among economists thanks to the virtually total omission of the history of economic thought in the standard economics syllabus. No wonder, in economics neophilia can pass muster as originality.

The power and utility of a scientific theory are often judged by its ability to explain and to make predictions that can then be tested by observation or experiment. Prediction, however, is not an imperative condition for scientific status if one takes the case of a major theory like evolution in biology, which fully explains evolution but is unable to predict the future course of evolution. On the other hand, Ptolemaic astronomy had predictive capability but lacked an adequate explanatory apparatus. How central is prediction to economics considering that prediction is not the only exercise with which economics is concerned as a descriptive, analytic, and prescriptive science? Prescription in a policy science like economics has to go well beyond pure prediction, because no prescription can be made without a careful assessment of all its implications, good and bad. Of course, some of economics is concerned with description and analysis without being explicitly involved with either prescription or prediction. For instance, in examining the trends of population or economic growth, the object of enquiry is researching actual facts without being directly concerned with prediction or prescription. Description does involve choice, but that does not make the act of description necessarily predictive or prescriptive (Sen, 1980).

Economists are sharply divided on the centrality or even the relevance of predictability for economics theory. Thus, according to Milton Friedman, the worth of a theory "is to be judged by the precision, scope, and conformity with experience that it yields...The ultimate goal of a positive science is the development of a 'theory' a hypothesis that yields valid and meaningful... predictions about phenomena not yet observed" (Friedman, 1953: 3, 4, 7). In stark contrast, Ronald Coase (Nobel Laureate, 1991) argues that "the view that the worth of a theory is to be judged solely by the extent and accuracy of its predictions seems to me wrong...We are not interested simply in the accuracy of its predictions. A theory also serves as a base for thinking" (Coase, 1982: 6). Furthermore, Coase argues that "testable predictions are not all that matters. Realism in an assumption is needed if our theories are ever to help us understand why the system works in the way it does" (ibid.: 7). A more balanced and realistic assessment of the role of prediction in economics has been presented by Sen, who develops the theme that "not all of economics is concerned with predicting but the crucial role of prediction in economics can scarcely be denied" (Sen, 1986: 4) and attempts to answer the following critical questions: Why are economic predictions so difficult? What techniques does economic theory use to cope with these difficulties?

The proverbial difficulties of making accurate economic predictions are aptly exemplified by the fact that to date no Nobel Prize has been awarded for the most predictive economic model even though the work of Lawrence Klein on the creation of econometric models and their application to the analysis of economic fluctuations and economic policies was recognised by the Nobel Committee in 1980. This is also borne out by the track record of major economic predictions like the failure to anticipate post-World War II inflation. The classic prediction of Milton Friedman that eventually the oil cartel will collapse has yet to materialise. Why are predictions more difficult in economics than in the natural and physical sciences? There are two specific sources of difficulties in making economic predictions: (i) difficulties in predicting human behaviour and choice, which can be influenced by a complex collection of social, political, psychological, biological, and other factors ('the choice problem'), and (ii) difficulties in predicting the results of interactions of countless different entities encountering each other in a wide variety of ways ('the interaction problem'). The traditional techniques of dealing with complexities which involve a reductionist use of the concepts of equilibrium, rationality, and maximisation are not entirely realistic, and their 'reductionist' usefulness may be outweighed by the extent to which they mislead and misdirect' (Sen, 1982: 18). Any economic theory that does not recognise the variations of social norms between societies and enterprises is unlikely to serve as a basis for economic predictions with an acceptable measure of success. The task of prediction must be seen as necessarily more modest than often conceived; it must be a matter of estimating possible variations of parameters that indicate the predicted values of outcomes within specifiable ranges, rather than predicting that the outcome will be a particular point. "However, the nature of economics leaves us with no other intellectually satisfactory options. The impressions of economic predictions have to go hand in hand with a precise recognition of these imprecisions" (ibid.: 201). There is also one overriding constraint on economic predictions arising from the nature of uncertainty defined as unique uninsurable risks in dynamic non-linear systems. As Keynes famously remarked, "The inevitable never happens. It is the unexpected always" (Keynes, 1982: 1117).

The discussion shows up the fundamental difference between economics and the physical sciences. In the physical sciences, the basic equations can generate their own 'observations', whereas in economic models the equations are derived empirically from the economic data. Likewise, weather forecasts have no effect on the weather, whereas economic forecasts often affect the economy and may sometimes be even self-fulfilling. The past is more directly relevant for economic prediction because of the influence of memory and learning than it is, say, for meteorological predictions, in which the influence of the past is largely confined to the currently observable variables.

Given the intrinsic limitations of economic predictions, is the obsession of economists with the predictive powers of their science justified, or is it a subliminal and none too subtle mimesis of the physical sciences? One may well ponder the reasoned scepticism of Ronald Coase, who boldly asserts: "faced with a choice between a theory which predicts well but gives us little insight into how the system works and one which gives us this insight but predicts badly, I would choose the latter" (Coase, 1982: 6). This approach rightly emphasises the priority of the explanatory power of economic theory, deriving from its relevance and realism, over its predictive properties in any research programme.

The ambiguities of economics lend credence to the memorable summation of economics as "a discipline not a science" (Hicks, 1983: 365), a discipline that has evoked starkly opposite reactions from eminent physicists and mathematical philosophers. Thus, Max Planck, the originator of Quantum Theory, remarked to Keynes that he had once thought of studying economics "but had found it too difficult" (Keynes, 1972: 186), whereas Bertrand Russell intended to study economics but gave it up, as he found it too easy! This paradox is best explained by Keynes, a mathematician who contributed to both economics and philosophy:

> The study of economics does not seem to require any specialized gifts of an unusually high order. Is it not, intellectually regarded, a very easy subject compared with the higher branches of philosophy and pure science? Yet good, or even competent, economists are the rarest of birds. An easy subject, at which very few excel! The paradox finds its explanation, perhaps. in that the master-economist must possess a rare combination of gifts. He must reach a high standard in several different directions, and must combine talents not often found together. He must be mathematician, historian, statesman, philosopher – in some degree. He must understand symbols and speak in words. He must contemplate the particular in terms of the general, and touch abstract and concrete in the same flight of thought. He must study the present in the light of the past for the purposes of the future. No part of man's nature or his institutions, must lie entirely outside his regard. He must be as aloof and incorruptible as an artist, yet sometimes as near the earth as a politician (1972: 173-174).

However, Keynes's explanation has to be suitably qualified, keeping in mind that since World War II, which witnessed the impressive mobilisation of economists in the war effort, economics has been transformed from a liberal arts discipline into a profession with a meaningful role for the competent—as distinct from the talented and the brilliant—rather like the humble dentist, as Keynes himself recognised in another context.

Economics: The Imperial Social Science

Paradoxically, the dissonance of economics has not inhibited the steady enlargement of its intellectual domain to other fields of social inquiry, such as the economics of law, pioneered by Aaron Director, with Ronald Coase and Richard Posner: the 'new' economic history, which combines economic theory and quantitative methods to explain economic and institutional change (Robert Fogel and Douglas North, Nobel Laureates, 1993); the economic analysis of social structure and non-market behaviour, such as crime, hatred, racial discrimination, marriage, divorce, fertility, and the family (pioneered by Gary Becker); and the economic analysis of constitutional design, politics, and bureaucracy by James Buchanan (Nobel Laureate, 1986), Gordon Tullock, and Anthony Downs, the founders of the 'Public Choice' school. Economics has therefore been aptly christened the 'Imperial Science' by George Stigler. But the label goes back much earlier, as pointed out by Harcourt in a characteristically clarion address: "By social science imperialist...I mean that leading species of the large genus social scientists...the economists...the late 1970s are the age of economic imperialism" as well described by Lester Thurow (Harcourt, 1979: 379). Unsurprisingly, the economic profession is divided even over the imperialism of economics. The senior members have not been too enthusiastic about the 'extension of their domain, and not one of the leading exponents of this movement, such as Coase, Buchanan and Becker, has been elected president of the American Economic Association, even though each one of them won the Nobel Prize. But this disapproval, judging by citations, is not shared by the younger economists, who support Schumpeter's view that "a science progresses through the dying off of its old professors" (Stigler, 1984: 311). The emerging heterodoxy is ably argued by Edward Lazear (2000), who adduces the extension of economics to the valuation of non-monetary attributes of goods, services, jobs, and even linguistics, as additional proof of the scientific character of economics and the success of economics as an imperial science. Equally, within its own domain, "descriptive economics has suffered from the imperialism of predictive economics" (Sen, 1980: 363).

Economists: Imperial Advisers

The advisory role of economists, which derives from the prescriptive function of economics, is one more dimension of economics as the imperial social science. There are economic advisers of all stripes but hardly any sociological or political advisers. The advisory role of economists, however, is far from being purely advisory. It "is close to being participatory" and "also closer to that of an insider or player rather than that of a detached expert" (Dixit, 1997: 226). It is also closer to what most economists who give policy advice actively perform, like those who work or consult for the ruling government, the opposition, labour unions, business associations, lobbies, etc., and thereby become direct participants. Even think tanks and many policy institutes who profess expertise or objectivity barely disguise their partisanship as well exemplified by the published work of prominent Washington think tanks like the Brookings Institution, the Cato Institute, the American Enterprise Institute, and the Institute for Policy Studies, each representing a particular shade of the political spectrum. "For the vast majority of economists, giving policy advice entails accepting a participatory role, at least to some extent. And to play that role effectively, economists must include politics and the strategic games of policy-making in the analysis" (ibid.: 229). This stance, while unexceptionable, encounters daunting complexities in the case of coalition democracies. Is there also not a critical threshold at which economic advisers turn into mere kibitzers, given their Scheherazade complex to 'tell them something'? Be that as it may, economists have turned a dissonant imperial science into a highly marketable commodity through sheer product differentiation. The participatory role of economists is an added factor that blurs the distinction between judgements of fact and judgements of value.

In sum, the cognitive dissonance of economics, coupled with the imperialism of economics, poses issues for the philosopher which far transcend the philosophy of economics, whose remit is conventionally restricted to the study of methodological issues facing positive economic theory and normative problems of the interface of welfare economics with political and moral philosophy. It involves a comprehensive evaluation of the interaction of economics and the various branches of philosophy, notably religion, ethics, psychology, epistemology, and even rhetoric, and the role of the philosopher in public policy. Given the generic character of philosophy and the complexity of economics, the analyst has to necessarily seek the Aristotelian path of 'illumination through disaggregation', beginning with the most universal form of organisation, *viz.*, institutional religion. Every economic agent is born and raised in a specific religion, which can influence his conduct and behaviour in varying degrees.

The Economics of Religion

Religion has a two-way interaction with political economy, both as a dependent and as an independent variable (MaCleary and Barro, 2006). As a dependent variable, a central question is how economic development and institutions affect religious participation and beliefs. As an independent variable, a key issue is how religiosity affects individual characteristics such as work ethic, honesty, trust, and thrift and thereby influences economic performance. Religion, which is usually regarded by economists as a directly unproductive activity, has not attracted much professional attention, even though economic historians and sociologists like Richard Tawney (*Religion and the Rise of Capitalism*, 1926) and Max Weber (*The Protestant Ethic and the Spirit of Capitalism*, 1930) made it their central theme. According to Tawney, the economic categories of modern society have their roots in the economic expansion and social convulsions in the age of the Renaissance and the Reformation. One can also identify various religious and quasi-religious elements which have had an economic outcome, like the economic doctrines of Calvin, the teachings of Jesus on usury and allied topics, and the attitudes of English non-conformists (Wesleyans and Quakers). Weber's theme of the Protestant ethic as the engine of capitalism is subject to the strictures of all monocausal theories, like the Marxist interpretation of history derived from economic factors, and lacks any empirical support. Even historically, Weber's thesis is flawed as it fails to take account of economic success stories like those of the Catholic city states of Antwerp, Florence and Venice. Surprisingly, the positive contributions of Christian missionaries to the infrastructure of many African and Asian countries, principally in education and health services, have not been systematically analysed in the literature, although some British historians, like Keith Hancock, refer to the role of the 'missionary frontier' in the economic development of West Africa.

A prime example of the interface between religion and economics is the injunction against usury in the Abrahamic religions—Judaism, Christianity and Islam—which is based upon the fallacious notion of money and capital as unproductive assets, whereas in point of fact it embodies the core element of exponential economic growth and the concept of compound interest, hailed by Einstein as the greatest invention outside of the natural sciences. Even the notion of usury as exploitation overlooks that it reflects the high-risk premium attached to particular categories of loan transactions. The interest-free Islamic financial systems of Saudi Arabia, Iran and Pakistan also exhibit the familiar phenomenon of evasion of interest through surrogate categories variously named as fees and commissions. A more fundamental criticism of the Islamic ban on interest is that it strictly applies to fixed rates of interest but not to variable rates of interest, a point often overlooked by advocates of Islamiç finance. Variable interest rates make loan transactions as risky as profit-oriented activities which are approved by Islamic law. Yet Islamic states impose a blanket ban on all interest. The application of Islamic economics, too, is highly selective; it is confined to the interdiction of interest but does not pay due regard to equally important elements like *Zakat*, the capital levy on affluent Muslims as a transfer payment to the needy and poor. Islamic redistribution schemes have had no perceptible effects on poverty or destitution. The negative economic aspects of religion emerge in Muslim countries like Indonesia, where the highly productive Chinese minority (Buddhist and Christian) is subject to periodic discrimination.

The eastern religions like Hinduism, Buddhism, Sikhism, Jainism, Confucianism, Taoism and Shintoism do not have a specific economic content in their teachings, and the differential economic performance of their respective societies can be confidently attributed to more influential non-religious factors. For instance, Taiwan, the only country where Confucianism is a state religion, has achieved a phenomenal combination of growth and equity owing to a favourable conjuncture of policies like timely and effective land reforms, meaningful economic incentives, and realistic exchange, interest rate, and fiscal policies. Japan, a Shintoist country by religion, is an example of the application of the Confucian work ethic and values while absorbing the best of western technology. In a sense, Confucian values are universal and hardly merit a doctrinal label, as when some analysts argue that "Confucianism has room for survival as a synthesis of distinctive social practices and a competitive identity" (Rozman, 2002: 37).

This discussion poses the question: How significant is the economics of religion, given the growing secularisation and globalisation of the world economy? Some would argue:

> Like religious economics, economics of religion is likely to be an expanding pursuit for the foreseeable future. It has largely explored the norms why religion exists and the functions it serves...Important contributions may well grow out of the expanding interdisciplinary literature on the role of trust and morality in social systems. Though this literature has not yet focused on religion per se, many of its insights carry implications for issues that the economics of religion will sooner or later begin analysing in depth. (Kuran, 1995: 774)

One can discern a response to this agenda in the pioneering empirical research of Robert Barro and Rachel MaCleary (2003), which analyses 'Religion and Economic Growth across Countries' using six international survey data sets on religiosity for a broad panel of countries between 1981 and 1999. The estimation, which relies on instrumental variables (presence of state religion, regulation of the religious market, and an indicator of religious pluralism) and dependent variables (church attendance and religious beliefs), shows that economic growth responds positively to religious beliefs but negatively to church attendance, i.e., growth depends on the extent of believing relative to belonging. These results also accord with a model in which religious beliefs influence individual habits that embrace economic performance. The authors recognise that it would be valuable to extend the analysis of religiosity at a countrywide level to individual behaviour and to political and social variables, including democracy, the rule of law, fertility, and health. Their results, while interesting and suggestive, do not throw light on the more basic question: How influential is religiosity compared to non-religious variables like economic incentives, appropriate state policies, and rule of law?

Even religious extremists seem to obey economic laws in some cases, when radical religious militias like Hamas provide public goods such as education and health services in failed or weak states such as Palestine, Algeria, Somalia and Chechnya (Berman, 2003). This is an apt example of rational fanatics, who are conceptually akin to the category of a rational fool, defined as "the thoroughly methodical person who chooses with impeccable consistency but does not distinguish between different issues...the rational fool is invoked a great deal in economic theory" (Sen, 1982: 9). There are, of course, notable exceptions to Berman's theory, such as Saudi Arabia, where despite generous state provision of public services, extremists flourish: the al Qaida terrorists are neither illiterate nor impoverished. In contrast, the Jewish extremist group Gush Emunim has failed to evoke public support in Israel, a functioning welfare democracy, where it is not the sole or major supplier of public goods to its members.

The real challenge of religion to economics lies in the fact that every religion's tradition and sacred literature "contains enough ambiguity to justify any number of economic positions...religion seems to matter, but its impact is far from uniform" (Iannaccone, 1998: 1478). It affects some behavioural outcomes—such as earnings, education, and economic attitudes—much less than others. Religious effects do not reduce to a single unobserved factor.

Economics as Applied Ethics

Contemporary economics, with its clear-cut distinction between judgements of fact and judgements of value, would appear at first blush to be a self-consciously non-ethical subject, as categorically stated in the 1930s by Lionel Robbins in his influential book *An Essay on the Nature and Significance of Economic Science*, where he argued that "it does not seem logically possible to associate the two studies (economics and ethics) in any form but mere juxtaposition" (Robbins, 1962: 148). But the historical evolution of modern economics has been largely as an offshoot of ethics. In fact, economics has had two rather different ways, concerned respectively with ethics, on the one hand, and with what may be called the logistic and engineering task of identifying means to attain given ends in the most efficient way. The ethical tradition goes back to Aristotle's *Nichomachean Ethics*, which relates economics to human ends, and to his *Politics*, where he argues that the end of the state is the common promotion of a good quality life. The engineering and logistical approach has been developed, as it happens, by actual engineers, like the French economist Leon Walras, the Italian economist Vilfredo Pareto, and the Englishman Sir William Petty who had a strong interest in the natural and mechanical sciences and is justly regarded as a pioneer of numerical economics. The engineering approach also connects with the technique-oriented approach to statecraft pioneered by Kautilya (the adviser and minister of the Indian emperor Chandragupta), a contemporary of Aristotle. Kautilya wrote in the fourth century BCE his classic treatise on economic statecraft, *Arthashastra* (in Sanskrit), which distinguishes between metaphysics, ethics (knowledge of right and wrong), the science of government, and the science of wealth. However, ethical considerations do not figure too prominently in Kautilya's analysis of human behaviour, which makes Kautilya with his emphasis on economic realpolitik, an economic forerunner of Machiavelli.

Historically, economics, with its origins in moral philosophy, has been an offshoot of ethics, and the influential Cambridge School of Marshall and Pigou has always regarded economics as a branch of applied ethics. The father of modern economics, Adam Smith, was a professor of moral philosophy at the University of Glasgow who authored his *Theory of Moral Sentiments* (1759) long before his classic *Wealth of Nations* (1776). In fact, modern economics shows a varying mix of ethics and economics, with a greater emphasis on ethics in the writings of Adam Smith, John Stuart Mill, Karl Marx, and Francis Edgeworth, whereas the contributions of William Petty, Francois Quesnay, David Ricardo,

Augustino Cournot, and Leon Walras are more focused on the logistic and engineering problems within economics. This, in turn, poses the classic core question of economic methodology: Is economics essentially a positive science, as argued most notably by Milton Friedman, or a normative science, which can never be neutral or objective in the positive sense, as maintained by Gunnar Myrdal (1973: vi)? These polar attitudes have only served to impoverish modern economics, as cogently argued by Amartya Sen:

> Economics can be made more productive by paying greater and more explicit attention to the ethical considerations that shape human behaviour and judgement...the methods used in economics, related, inter alia, with its engineering aspects...can be of use to modern ethics as well and the distance that has grown between economics and ethics has also been... unfortunate for the latter. (Sen, 1980: 9)

The intermixture of motives and incentives complicates both economic analysis and policy, as is well illustrated in the case of Japan, where there is strong empirical evidence to suggest that systematic deviations from self-interested behaviour in the direction of duty, group loyalty, and goodwill account for Japan's economic performance, a blend of the best practice of western technology and the Japanese ethos. Similarly, the Confucian explanation for the industrial success of South Korea, Taiwan, and Singapore shows that ethical factors can be as influential as profit-centred motivation. 'The jettisoning of all motivations and valuations other than the extremely narrow one of self-interest is hard to justify on grounds of predictive usefulness, and it also seems to have rather dubious empirical support' (ibid.: 79). In taking account of non-market motivation and behaviour, the distinction between 'deontological' and 'consequentialist approaches' is highly relevant. The deontological approach assigns the concept of duty a primary position, whereas the consequentialist approach, which derives duty and right actions on the basis of their respective consequences, is more pertinent to the concerns of economics. Deliberate human actions and policies pose some of the most intractable problems for economic analysis and policies, which have unforeseen and unintended consequences. "The significant goes well beyond the proximate" (Sen, 1993: 227).

The complexities of the interface between economics and ethics are typified by the variety of ways in which the criteria of justice can be interpreted and applied. One source of variation is the metric or unit of measurement in terms of which a person's advantage is to be evaluated in assessing equity and justice. The various metrics analysed in the literature include utility, primary goods index (as in the Rawlsian theory of justice), capabilities index (Sen), and statistical measures of poverty. Secondly, there are different ways of aggregating the diverse information regarding the advantages of different individuals. For instance, utilitarianism is only concerned with the aggregate of the overall utilities of different people. Other approaches are more concerned with the distributional properties of the relative positions of different individuals *vis-à-vis* each other. There is also the issue concerning the priority of some particular person's valuation (e.g., Rawls's insistence on the priority of liberty), or the non-consequentialist priority of processes over results (e.g., Nozick's view of rights as unreliable constraints). One can also argue about the relevant dimensions of justice—horizontal, vertical, and intergenerational—and their relative weight in policy. What, for instance, is the optimal social rate of discount and who determines it? What weight should we give to the interests of future generations? How do we respond to the person who asks, 'What has posterity done for me?'. At least one philosopher has argued, "the social discount rate is indefensible" (Parfit, 1987: 357).

In sum, as Amartya Sen argues:

> Welfare economics can be substantially enriched by paying more attention to ethics, and...the study of economics can also benefit from a closer contact with ethics...Even predictive and descriptive economics can be helped by making more room for welfare economic considerations in the determination of behaviour. These exercises involve deep-seated ambiguities, and many of the problems are inherently complex. But although the case for bringing economics closer to ethics does not rest on this being an easy thing to do...the rewards can be expected to be rather large. (Sen, 1980: 89)

As the citation for the Nobel Prize awarded to Sen in 1998 stated: "By combining tools from economics and philosophy, he has restored an ethical dimension to the discussion of vital economic problems."

There is, however, another neglected aspect of this debate which poses important epistemic problems. It has been argued that "many so-called 'value-judgements' are not value judgements at all, but subjective judgements of fact" (Ng, 1972: 1014). While value judgements are admittedly untestable, not all untestable judgements are value judgements. Economists are often more qualified than non-economists to make subjective judgements of fact related to their expertise, but many subjective judgements of fact are subjective only because the interrelationships are too complex to be identified precisely. The advisory role of economists derives from their capacity to make subjective statements of fact which do not have the same validity as well-established scientific propositions, but they are necessary and unavoidable in making important policy decisions. Positive welfare economics exists, but non-native welfare economics involves value judgements which are actually subjective statements of fact. It also involves trade-offs between different aspects of policy, most importantly between economic efficiency, and non-economic objectives such as equity and justice, in which the ultimate decisions rest not on expertise *per se* but on social values and objectives as formulated by legislators and policymakers in a democracy.

Ethical variables affect not only issues of economic efficiency and equity but also economic growth and development, as demonstrated by the sociologist Edward Banfield in his seminal work *The Moral Basis of a Backward Society* (1958), which explained the poverty of southern Italy as being due not to government neglect or poor education but to a peculiar kind of 'amoral familism' manifested in the reluctance of people to cooperate outside their families (Wilson, 2003: 64). This finding is corroborated on a global scale by contemporary research, which shows that economic development (GNP per capita) is significantly correlated with levels of interpersonal trust transcending family groupings (Inglehart, 2000: 90-91).

Relevance of Psychology

Traditionally, economics as a behavioural science has relied largely on the assumption of a 'homo-economicus' actuated by self-interest aimed at the maximisation of utility, income, or wealth, and capable of rational decision-making. This was modified by Herbert Simon (Nobel Laureate, 1978), who proposed that decision-makers should be viewed as boundedly rational and developed a model in which utility maximisation was replaced by 'satisficing'. Subsequently, Daniel Kahneman (Nobel Laureate, 2002) integrated the insights of cognitive psychology into economic science, especially those concerning human agents and decision-making under uncertainty. He has demonstrated how human decisions may systematically depart from those predicted by standard economic theory and how human judgement may take heuristic shortcuts that systematically depart from basic principles of probability. The researches of Kahneman and Amos Tversky (1937-1996) draw a map of bounded rationality by exploring the systematic biases "that separate the beliefs that people have and the choices they make from the optimal beliefs and choices assumed in rational-agent models" (Kahneman, 2003: 1449). Their researches are particularly noteworthy for their provenance and interdisciplinary discourse. They viewed their research primarily as a contribution to psychology, 'with a possible contribution to economics as a secondary benefit' (ibid.). The collaborative research of Kahneman, Tversky, and others comprised three separate programmes of research which explored, respectively, the heuristics that people use and the biases to which they are prone in various tasks of judgement under uncertainty, including predictions and evaluations of evidence; prospect theory, a model of choice under risk and with loss evasion in riskless choice; and framing effects, with their implications for rational-agent models. Kahneman develops a unified treatment of intuitive judgement and choice, whose guiding ideas are that most judgements and most choices are made intuitively and that the rules underlying intuition are generally similar to the rules of perception. This implies that the discussion of the rules of intuitive judgements and choices relies exclusively on visual analogies, which also shows up its limitation.

Kahneman's framework helps explain why the effects of incentives are neither large nor robust and why cognitive effort expended in bolstering a decision already made will not improve its quality. Does this throw light on the Hamlet syndrome? It is not that economic agents reason poorly but that they often act intuitively and on what they often happen to see at a given moment. Kahneman's approach highlights several features of the cognitive system; that intuition and reasoning are alternative ways to solve problems; that intuition resembles perception; and that categories are represented by stereotypes. More importantly, Kahneman's findings have restored a central role to emotion, which is incorporated in his view of intuition, and thus substantially respond to the criticisms of Jon Elster (1998)[+] that economists have not been able to incorporate emotions into the toolkit of economics. On the other hand, Elster also makes several valid points, particularly the central issue, *viz.*, how emotions combine with other motivations such as self-interest to affect behaviour. There is an extensive spectrum of emotions, personal and social, which allows for innumerable variations and nuances, some of which are universal while others are culture-specific. According to Elster, emotions have a dual role in shaping choices as well as rewards, and there is a trade-off between emotional and other rewards.

The insights of social and cognitive psychology have also been harnessed by Timur Kuran in his ground-breaking work on the social consequences of preference falsification (1990, 1995), which seriously undermine the core concept of revealed preference underlying neo-classical economic methodology.

+ This article analyses the psychology of the emotions and its bearing on economic theory and behaviour and thus, supplements Matthew Rabin's survey (1998), which deals with cognitive psychology. Its main focus is on 'How can emotions help us explain behaviour for which good explanations seem to be lacking?'

This concept asserts that people's preference orderings are revealed by their actions, which, according to Kuran, produce either useless tautologies or serious errors of interpretation. His framework accords explicit recognition to the multiplicity of human motivations using three sources of individual utility: the available options; the social consequences evoked by an individual's decisions; and an individual's decisional autonomy. These potentially conflicting determinants generate for each individual two distinct preferences: a private preference known only to him, and a public preference he reveals to others. Kuran argues that the divergence between private and public preferences throws light on important contradictory social phenomena: why, despite substantial and growing opposition, as reflected in confidential opinion polls, vocal support for affirmative action remains strong in the US; why even the victims of India's caste system do not always speak against it in public; why, despite contrary evidence, welfare economics continues to be grounded on the assumption that welfare depends on absolute, not relative, income; why, despite growing income inequality, the US has the least progressive tax system of any industrial nation. The conventional rational-choice model of the economist simply cannot answer many of these questions. Kuran blends the insights of psychology and sociology into a behavioural model which explores the causes and consequences of holding one set of opinions privately while expressing another in public—the pathology of private truths and public lies, a phenomenon more usually associated with the world of politics and diplomacy.

Since economics abounds in cognitive dissonance, it would be appropriate to examine the consequences of cognitive dissonance to which psychologists have devoted considerable attention. Akerlof (Nobel Laureate, 2001) and Dickens have incorporated cognitive dissonance theory into a decision model that is a modification of the standard model of rational decision-making but closely follows it insofar as persons are completely informed about the potential consequences of their actions and make their decisions to maximise their own utility or welfare. Akerlof and Dicken's results (1982) differ from the standard analysis and provide a better explanation for several phenomena that are a puzzle according to the standard approach, as for instance, why non-informational advertising is effective; why safety legislation and social security legislation are popular; why persons fail to purchase actuarially beneficial hazard insurance for flood and earthquake; and why workers tend to underestimate the dangers of hazardous jobs. The explanations do not rely on the assumption of misinformation; if people believe something other than the truth, they do so by their own choice. The theory of cognitive dissonance can thus, be expressed in economic terms in three propositions: persons have both preferences and beliefs about the state of the world; they have some control over beliefs; and they can manipulate their own beliefs by selecting sources of information and knowledge which are likely to confirm 'desired' beliefs. Studies in social psychology show that people in certain circumstances behave according to each of these propositions. The Akerlof-Dickens model formulates an economic theory of the choice of beliefs which, initially, are only adopted if the net economic and psychic benefits are positive. But once adopted, beliefs are persistent because of cognitive dissonance, which explains why persons tend to resist or avoid new information that contradicts already established beliefs. This is borne out by the history of science as well by the experience of industrial organisation, which shows that the major innovations mainly come from outside.

While psychological research has been fruitful and suggestive, it is equally important to bear in mind that "not all psychological research will be both confirmed by field data and proven to be of great importance...We can confront plausible hypotheses about human behaviour with both healthy scepticism and genuine curiosity, empirically test their validity, and carefully draw out their implications" (Rabin, 1998: 41). A particularly intractable problem in the application of psychology to economics is the admixture of motivation, like the combination of self-interest with altruism, reciprocity, and social conformity. What is the relative weight of different motives and emotions in the decisions of economic agents? Psychological economics has yet to be extended to agents other than individuals and households. How do firms, clubs, bureaucrats, central bankers, politicians, and institutions think and act? How does the psychology of institutional traders on the stock exchange differ from that of individual operators?

Economics as Rhetoric

Rhetoric, the art of using language for persuasion in speaking, writing, and oratory, is a necessary adjunct to economics as a prescriptive discipline, and every economist seeks to propagate his doctrines as well as his policy prescriptions with literary devices. Yet it did not figure in the otherwise prolific methodological discussions on economics until the publication of Deirdre McCloskey's provocative work *The Rhetoric of Economics* (1985) and its revised edition (1998). McCloskey's work is part of a wider intellectual trend towards rhetorical inquiry which occurs in an interdisciplinary matrix that touches not only on such fields as philosophy, cognitive science, psychology, sociology, anthropology, political theory, and accounting but even on mathematics, physics, and biology (Bender and Wellbery, 1990). McCloskey's principal argument is that economics is essentially literary, and relies, in addition to facts and logic, on literary devices like stories and figures of speech—metaphors, analogies, and appeals to authority, which 'are not mere frills. They think for us' (McCloskey, 1998: xix). The most important example of economic rhetoric is metaphor, which economists call 'models'. A prime example of the metaphorical character of even the most quantitative and technical contributions, cited by McCloskey, is the famous 1957 essay by Robert Solow (Nobel Laureate, 1987) on the production function and productivity change. Solow's production function takes the special form $Q = A(t)f(K,L)$ and the multiplicative factor $A(t)$ measures the cumulative effects of shifts over time. It will be seen that four master literary tropes are at work here: metaphor, metonymy, synecdoche, and irony.

The aggregate production function says that the making of our daily bread is like a mathematical function, i.e., a metaphor: the K and L in the equation are metonymies, symbols standing for other things. The L reduces the human attentiveness in making bread to an hour of work. 'The K reduces the material inheritance of the work place to a pile of shmoos' (ibid.: 50). The identification of $A(t)$ with technical change is a synecdoche, taking a part for the whole, since technical change is an umbrella concept which includes a vast variety of inventions and improvements. One can concede that 'economists make more appeals to their audience than simply their appeals to the Facts or the Logic' (ibid.: 51), but it only reminds us that rhetoric is just one more instrument in the toolkit of the economist, like logic, mathematics, econometrics, and history, which scarcely warrants the wholly disproportionate controversy generated by McCloskey's work. Rhetoric accentuates the persuasiveness of a new theory or a policy, as demonstrated by the triumphalism of Keynes's *General Theory of Employment, Interest and Money* (1935) or his classic *Economic Consequences of the Peace* (1919), a magisterial indictment of the inequity and the irrationality of the Treaty of Versailles. The *General Theory* would not have had its vogue but for the richness and eloquence of its fastidious prose and the consummate use of Mandeville's *The Fable of the Bees*; or, *Private Vices, Public Benefits* (1714), a mint specimen of an organising metaphor used to illustrate its central theme. Keynes, the master theorist, was also the master rhetorician.

Adam Smith's 'invisible hand', too, is arguably the most visible and effective metaphor of economics.

Economics and Philosophy: Agenda

The scope and mechanics of cooperation between economics and philosophy are perhaps best summed up in the masthead of the journal *Economics and Philosophy*.

> It aims to bridge the increasingly artificial disciplinary boundaries that divide economics and philosophy. Economists more and more acknowledge that their work in both positive and normative economics depends on methodological and ethical commitments that demand philosophical study and justification. Philosophers increasingly insist that philosophy of science must be informed by and test against studies of current science and of its history, while ethics and political philosophy must depend on what we know about human aims and interest and about the principles, benefits, and drawbacks of different forms of social organisation. Articles in Economics and Philosophy will explore the foundations of economics as both a predictive/explanatory enterprise and a normative one and will examine the relevance of economic techniques, methods, and conclusions to philosophical questions in ethics and social theory.

The collaboration of Amartya Sen with the philosophers Bernard Williams and W.C. Runciman and Sraffa's with Wittgenstein typifies the potentialities of interchange between economists and philosophers. But given the plurality of avenues these are best approached on strictly pragmatic grounds as argued by Robert Solow in the following comment on the author's original article.

> I am a minimalist on matters of scope and method, i.e., I don't feel any need to take a position on big, general questions; it is enough to look for a pragmatic answer to small questions as they come along. I don't really care if economics is a science, or what it would mean if it were. But I do think economics should be scientific, not in any complex or grandiose way, but in the sense that it should respect logic and facts. I realize that 'fact' is a concept with many layers, but there too I am happy to come to a decision in any concrete case, on pragmatic grounds.
>
> ...my pulse rate does not budge in either direction when McCloskey tells me that some formulation of mine embodies this or that rhetorical trope. The only interesting question to me is whether this metaphor or metonymy, or whatever, is a good one or a bad one, i.e., whether it fits the known facts reasonably well, leads one to look for other interesting facts or ideas, whether it contains any logical contradiction, and so on.
>
> I don't have to decide whether 'economics' should cooperate with 'philosophy'. My view is: if this philosopher wants to cooperate with that economist in the investigation of this particular question, let them try: if it works out usefully, so much the better. If it does not, well, they have probably learned something any way. Ditto for psychology, and *ditto for sociology, which strikes me as more relevant than psychology, and more often neglected* (emphasis provided).

To this agenda, one could add the Economics and Law movement, whose relevance is even more enhanced with the advent of economic liberalisation and the need for a strong regulatory apparatus to make markets efficient and to reconcile growth with equity. However, the realm of economics as a policy discipline is also the world of the second best and perennial trade-offs for which there are no final solutions. This only reflects that economic space is habited by asymmetries, anomalies, and indeterminacy which together account for the unintended and unforeseen consequences of purposive actions. Given the sheer complexity and limitations of their discipline, and its interface with philosophy and the social sciences to which one could add that the economist innocent of the history of economic ideas is likely to be an incomplete economist. Economists might do worse than heed John Stuart Mill: "A person is not likely to be a good economist who is nothing else" (Marshall, 1920: 771).

It is only fitting to conclude this essay with a most judicious summation by an Economics Nobel laureate (1972):

3 December 2007
Department of Economics
Stanford University

Dear Dr. Chandavarkar:

I am afraid that my in-box fills up. This is the first chance I have had to read your article, "Philosophy and Economics: Issues and Questions," in the volume, *The Experience of Philosophy*, edited by Kolak and Martin.

It is indeed an excellent and provocative survey, raising many questions beyond the familiar ones of epistemology and of Hume's Law.

I have one reservation on the epistemological side, a reservation motivated by my own experience as a meteorologist (during World War II). You ask (p.694, first column, second paragraph), "why are predictions more difficult in economics than in the natural and physical sciences?". Part of my job was statistical verification of weather forecasts; they were then simply useless beyond 72 hours. I believe the limit is now 120 hours at the most. (You yourself noted earlier that the theory of evolution is not predictive.) You give two answers to your question. Both really reduce to complexity. Complex systems can be difficult to predict because the non-linearities imply explosive behavior, so small deviations have large consequences. This is true even when the act of analysis does not transform behavior, a point you make about the social sciences. I returned to my studies in economics with less of an inferiority complex with respect to the natural sciences.

Sincerely yours,
Kenneth J. Arrow

REFERENCES

Akerlof, George A. and William T. Dicken (1982). "The Economic Consequences of Cognitive Dissonance", *American Economic Review* 72(3): 307–19.

Altman, B.M. (2001). "Disability Definitions, Models. Classification Schemes and Applications", in G.L. Albrecht, K.D. Seelman, M. Bury (eds.), *Handbook of Disability Studies*. Sage.

Barro, Robert J. and Rachel McCleary (2003). "Religion and Economic Growth across Countries", *American Sociological Review* 68: 760–81.

Bender, John and David Wellbery (eds.) (1990). *The Ends of Rhetoric: History, Theory, Practice.* Stanford: Stanford University Press.

Berlin, Isaiah (2000). *The Power of Ideas.* Princeton, NJ: Princeton University Press.

Berlin, Isaiah and Ramin Jahanbegloo (1991). *Conversations with Isaiah Berlin.* New York: Charles Scribner's Sons.

Berman. Eli (2003). "Hamas, Taliban and the Jewish Underground: An Economist's View of Radical Religions Militias", *Working Paper* 100004. Cambridge, Mass.: National Bureau of Economic Research.

Bhagwati, Jagdish (2004). *In Defense of Globalisation.* New York: Oxford University Press.

Blaug, Mark (1992). *The Methodology of Economics*, 2nd edn.Cambridge: Cambridge University Press.

Brittan, Samuel (1973). *Is There an Economic Consensus*? London: Macmillan.

Coase, Ronald H. (1982). *How Should Economists Choose*. Washington, DC: American Enterprise Institute.

Dixit, Avinash (1997). "Economists as Advisers to Politicians and to Society", *Economics and Politics* 9(3), November.

Eichner, Alfred S. (1983). "Why Economics is not yet a Science", *Journal of Economic Issues* XVII(2): 507–19.

Elster, Jon (1998). "Emotions and Economic Theory", *Journal of Economic Literature* XXXVI: 47–74.

Frey, Bruno S, Werner W. Pommerechene, Friedrich Schneider and Guy Gilbert (1984). "Consensus and Dissension among Economists: An Empirical Inquiry", *American Economic* Review 7(5): 986–94.

Friedman, Milton (1953). *Essays in Positive Economics.* Chicago: Chicago University Press.

Gordon. Scott (1978). "Should Economists Pay Attention to Philosophers?", *Journal of Political Economy* 86(4): 717–28.

Hahn, Frank (1992). "Autobiographical Notes with Reflections", in Michael Szenberg (ed.), *Eminent Economists: Their Life Philosophies*. New York: Cambridge University Press.

Harcourt, G.C. (1979). "Conclusion: The Social Science Imperialists", *Politics* XVI(2): 2431–51.

Hausman, Daniel M. (1994). *The Philosophy of Economics*, 2nd edn. Cambridge: Cambridge University Press.

Helibroner, Robert L. (1980). *The Worldly Philosophers: Lives, Times and Ideas of the Great Economic Thinkers*. New York: Simon and Schuster.

Hicks, J.R. (1983). "Discipline, Not a Science", in *Classics and Moderns: Collected Essays* 3. Oxford: Basil Blackwell.

Iannacone, Laurence R. (1998). "An Introduction to the Economics of Religion", *Journal of Economic Literature* XXXVI: 1465–96.

Inglehart, Ronald (2000). "Culture and Democracy", in Lawrence E. Harrison and Samuel P. Huntington (eds.), *Culture Matters: How Values Shape Human Progress*. New York: Basic Books.

Kahneman, Daniel (2003). "Maps of Bounded Rationality: Psychology for Behavioral Economics", *American Economic Review* 93(5): 1449–75.

Keynes, John Maynard (1972). "Alfred Marshall", in *Essays in Biography: Collected Writings of J.M. Keynes.* Vol. X, London: Macmillan.

———. (1982). *Social, Political, and Literary Writings. Collected Writings of J.M. Keynes.* Vol. XXVIII . London: Macmillan.

Kuran, Timur (1990). "Private and Public Preferences", *Economics and Philosophy* 6: 1–26.

———. (1995). *Private Truths, Public Lies: The Social Consequences of Preference Falsification*. Cambridge, Mass.: Harvard University Press.

Lazear, Edward P. (2000). "Economic Imperialism", *Quarterly Journal of Economics* 115: 99–145.

Magee, Bryan (1978). *Popper*. London: Fontana Collins.

———. (2001). *Talking Philosophy: Dialogues with Fifteen Leading Philosophers*. Oxford: Oxford University Press.

Marshall, Alfred (1920). *Principles of Economics*, 8th edn. London: Macmillan.

MaCleary, Rachel M. and Robert J Barro (eds.) (2006). "Religion and Economy", *The Journal of Economic Perspectives* 20(2).

McCloskey, Deidre N. (1998). *The Rhetoric of Economics*, 2nd revd. Edn. Madison: University of Wisconsin Press.

McCloskey, Deidre N. and Stephen T. Ziliak (1996). "The Standard Error of Regressions", *Journal of Economic Literature* XXIV: 97–114.

Myrdal, Gunnar (1965). *Monetary Equilibrium*. New York: Augustus Kelly.

———. (1973). *Against the Stream*. New York: Pantheon Books.

Ng, Yew-Kwang (1972). "Value Judgments and Economists' Role in Policy Recommendations", *The Economic Journal* 82(327): 1014–18.

Niehans, Jurg (1981). "Economics: History, Doctrine, Science, Art", *Kyklos* 34: 165–77.

Parfit, Derek (1987). *Reasons and Persons*. Oxford, Clarendon Press.

Popper, Karl (1975). *Objective Knowledge: An Evolutionary Approach*, Oxford: Oxford University Press.

———. (1999). *All Life Is Problem Solving*. London: Routledge.

Rabin, Matthew (1998). 'Psychology and Economics', *Journal of Economic Literature*, XXXVI: 11–46.

Robbins, Lionel (1962). *An Essay on the Nature and Significance of Economics Science*, 2nd edn. London: Macmillan.

Rozman, Gilbert (2002). "Can Confucianism Survive in an Age of Universalism and Globalisation?", *Pacific Affairs* 75(1): 11–37.

Sen, A.K. (1980). "Description as Choice", *Oxford Economic Papers* 32: 353–69.

———. (1982). "Rational Fools: A Critique of the Behavioral Foundations of Economic Theory", in *Choice, Welfare and Measurement*. Cambridge, Mass.: MIT Press.

———. (1986). "Prediction and Economic Theory", in *Predictability in Science and Society: A Joint Symposium of the Royal Society and the British Academy*, March 20–21. Organised and edited by Sir John Mason, P. Mathias and J.H. Westcott. London: The Royal Society and the British Academy.

———. (1993). "Money and Value: On the Ethics and Economics of Finance", *Economics and Philosophy* 9: 203–27.

———. (2003). "Sraffa, Wittgenstein and Gramsci", *Journal of Economic Literature* XVI: 1240–53.

Skidelsky, Robert (1983). *John Maynard Keynes: Hopes Betrayed, 1883–1920*. New York: Viking

Stigler, George J. (1982). *The Economist as Preacher and Other Essays*. Chicago: University of Chicago Press.

———. (1984). "Economics: The Imperial Science?", *Scandinavian Journal of Economics* 86(3): 301–13.

Stiglitz, Joseph E. (2002). *Globalisation and its Discontents*. New York: W.W. Norton.

Tawney, Richard H. (1998). *Religion and the Rise of Capitalism*. New Brunswick, NJ and London: Transaction (reprint of the classic 1926 edition with a new introduction by Adam B. Seligman).

Weber, Max (1930). *The Protestant Ethic and the Spirit of Capitalism*. London: Allen and Unwin.

Wilson, James (2003). "The Independent Mind of Edward Banfield", *Public Interest:* 63–68, Winter.

26 The Political Economy of Aid*

This is an exceptional work in its genre, by any criterion, that fills a conspicuous gap in the exponentially voluminous literature on aid, which has been primarily concerned with the economics of aid.• It provides a comprehensive and transparent, yet critical and constructive, narrative of the origin, evolution and the politics of aid by the United Nations, the major donor in the international grants economy. The robust scholarly apparatus, well supported by archival research and instructive tabular material, is robed in lean, muscular prose. The author, a well-credentialled economist, writes with hands-on experience having held several senior positions in the UN, including Director of Development Administration Programme in the Department of Technical Cooperation. Remarkably for a civil servant, he is objective in his evaluation of programmes, free of the self-referential institutional pietas, which often afflicts retired civil servants who venture into print.

The book's emphasis on the politics of aid is well merited insofar as "giving policy advice entails a participatory role, at least to some extent. And to that role effectively, economists must include politics and the strategic games of policymaking in their analysis" (Dixit, 1997). More fundamentally, politics is the inarticulate major premise of economic discourse which explains why there are no economic or political problems but only problems, as memorably stated by Gunnar Myrdal. A textbook example of the invasiveness of politics is afforded by the experience of even the lily-white International Monetary Fund (IMF) whose Evaluation Report (2004) noted that political considerations have influenced prolonged use of Fund resources in some cases as, for instance, Pakistan. The politicisation of the World Bank, too, and the US role in it is in clear violation of its Article IV, Section 10 ('Political Activity Prohibited'),[1] as well documented by Brown (1992). Clearly, the Bretton Woods twins have lost their vestal virginity. Bilateral aid by major donors is more liable to be a continuation of politics by other means which, if anything, strengthens the case for multilateral aid. But as the IMF Evaluation Report

---

* *Source: Economic and Political Weekly* XLIII(1) (5 January 2008): 25-27.

• *United Nations Development Aid (A Study in History and Politics)* by Digambar Bhouraskar (2007), New Delhi: Academic Foundation, pp. 269.

noted, political considerations are bound to enter where ultimate approval rests with shareholder governments, which only strengthens the case for greater transparency and accountability. There is growing conviction that development is all about making politics work for the poor, and that an essentially technocratic approach to aid is insufficient (Armon, 2007).

Foreign aid is best defined as official grants and concessional loans, in currency or in kind, which aims at transferring resources from the developed countries to the less developed countries (LDCs) on developmental and/or income-distributional grounds. There is no endogenous economic rationale for aid, which is to be rather derived from the realm of the Economy of Love and Fear, i.e., one-way transfers arising out of 'love' or 'fear' in the national and international sphere (Boulding, 1973). Exchange, i.e., market, economics cannot grapple with problems involving the distribution of power, wealth and income but any viable international system has to view both grants and exchange as interacting mechanisms. The modern welfare state is the ultimate expression of grants economics in the national sphere. If Adam Smith's *Wealth of Nations* is the progenitor of exchange economics, his *Theory of Moral Sentiments* can be read as the precursor of grants economics.

The cross-country evidence on effectiveness is fragile (Bourguignon and Sundberg, 2007) and the evidence whether aid helps or hinders development is indeterminate (Easterly, 2007). Oddly, the aid literature generally does not differentiate between growth and development, a vital distinction, and also ignores the deleterious consequences of the massive agricultural subsidies in the developed countries on the LDCs which more than offset aid. But even the most vocal critics of aid like Easterly and Bauer (1976) have not pleaded for the elimination of aid. Rather they argue for aid to be selective and targeted towards eliminating the binding constraints on growth and development in the spirit of piecemeal social engineering. Thus, the core issue is how to make aid more effective, a governance rather than an economic problem. This book makes a vital contribution to this debate. In any event, it is ironic to attach the Kiplingesque rubric of the *White Man's Burden* (Easterly) to aid whose proceeds are all spent on the goods and services of the White Man's countries. This is over and above the historically exploitative drain from the colonies to the imperium, not to speak of slavery, as well substantiated by Africanists like Colin Leys, Giovanni Arrighi, Walter Rodney and Indian analysts like Dadabhai Naoroji and R.C. Dutt. Rather, it is the "Black Man certainly[who has had to pay dear for carrying the White Man's burden", as plaintively exclaimed by George Padmore, the West Indian pan-Africanist (Rodney, 1981: 205).

The UN Programme of Technical Assistance, set up in 1948, marked the beginning of unconditional multilateral aid[2] by the UN, which was disbursed till 1970 through three programmes—the UN Regular Programme, the Expanded Programme of Technical Assistance, and the Special Fund. This led to considerable overlaps until the centralisation in the United Nations Development Programme (UNDP). Since the creation of UNDP, there have been major reforms in the conceptualisation and administration of technical assistance, but there are still several important issues on which further progress is desirable, as identified by the author. First, the goal of the centrality of the UNDP for mobilising resources and their programming and coordination has not been achieved. Secondly, the question of coordination at the country level between the UNDP and agencies and between the agencies themselves has never been fully resolved. Thirdly, although the evaluation office of UNDP has done good work, there is a need for an independent office of evaluation on the lines of the IMF. Fourthly, there is the question of effective implementation. The UNDP should cease to implement projects on its own and like the World Bank they should rather be implemented by recipient governments, and thereafter undertake evaluation of project performance. Finally, the extremely complicated decision-making process of the General Assembly of 191 members, which in turn is delegated to several subordinate legislative bodies, merits a drastic overhaul. Technical assistance activities should be vested in the executive board of the UNDP which should then report to the General Assembly for any amendments or comments. Aid, too, is not exempt from the iron law of unintended consequences, as evidenced by the measures announced by the IMF on 6 July 2007 to help member countries to cope with high and volatile aid inflows that can cause inflation and exchange rate volatility, which could make the poor even worse off. It has, therefore, been proposed that the IMF should coordinate with the World Bank and key donors to help use aid effectively.

However, the book raises three overarching questions: Is there any evidence of aid fatigue among donors other than the Netherlands and Scandinavia? Has aid bred an entitlement culture among recipients? Is there not a strong case for graduation of recipient countries from the UN aid roster on the lines of International Development Association (IDA) in the World Bank? Be that as it may, the book will take its rightful place as an indispensable sourcebook and catalyst for further debate on the subject. The handsome get-up and accurate text of the book is also a deserved tribute to the publishers, who are up to the best international standards.

Notes

1 The effort was made to forestall this curse by including two provisions in the Bank's articles. Article I sets forth the purposes of the Bank and ends with the sentence: "The Bank shall be guided in all its decisions by the purposes set forth above." Article IV, Section 10, is headed "Political Activity Prohibited" and provides that "The Bank and its officers shall not interfere in the political affairs of any member; nor shall they be influenced in their decisions by the character of the member or members concerned. Only economic considerations shall be relevant to their decisions, and these considerations shall be weighed impartially in order to achieve the purposes stated in Article I." Article IV reflected the prescient wisdom of Keynes who had exhorted the Boards of Governors of the IMF and the Bank at their inaugural meeting at Savannah, Georgia, on 9 March 1946 to be aware that: "If these institutions are to win the full confidence of the suspicious world, it must not only be, but appear, that their approach to every problem is absolutely oecumenical, without prejudice or favour."

2 For instance, subsidies to about 20,000 American cotton producers (with an average annual income of more than $125,000) are about 72 cents a pound even though the market price of cotton has averaged about 57 cents. According to Oxfam America, reform of the US subsidies would increase the family incomes of about 10 million people in cotton-growing West Africa by 2.3 to 5.7 per cent. The US has retained these subsidies despite the WTO ruling on their illegality.

References

Armon, Jeremy (2007). 'Perspective', *Development Policy Review* 25(5): 653–56.

Boulding, Kenneth (1973). *The Economy of Love and Fear (A Preface to Grants Economics)*. Belmont, California.: Wadsworth.

Bourguignon, Francois and Mark Sundberg (2007). "Aid Effectiveness—Opening the Black Box", *American Economic Review* 97(2): 316–20 (May).

Brown, Bartram S. (1992). *The United States and the Politicisation of the World Bank: Issues of International Law and Practice*. London: Kegan Paul International.

Dixit, Avinash (1997). "Economists as Advisers to Politicians and to Society", *Economics and Politics* 9(3): 225–9 (November).

Easterly, William (2006). *The White Man's Burden (Why the West's Efforts to Aid the Rest have Done So Llittle Good)*. New York: Penguin.

———. (2007). "Was Development Assistance a Mistake", *American Economic Review* 97(2): 328–32.

Rodney, Walter (1981). *How Europe Underdeveloped Africa*. Washington, DC: Howard University Press.

27 Myth of *Laissez faire* in Colonial India*

At a convivial occasion hosted by the late Sachin Chaudhri, founder editor of the *Economic Weekly*, Rammanohar Lohia, the legendary, nimble-witted Indian socialist and a well-credentialled economist, confessed how he was completely trumped by the clarion question of a visiting Italian economist, Travagliani: "Why are you Indians so critical of *laissez faire* when you have never even tried it?" India, after all, "was the only part of the British empire to which *laissez faire* never applied" (Hobsbawm, 1969: 148). The clinching evidence for this is now provided in the revised edition of this beautifully researched book, first published in 1971, which carries an expanded introduction that reviews the state of the art and a new edited imprint of the original text.• Its primary focus is upon ideas and interests, Indian and British, and the contestations, which went into the making of the financial and economic policies of the *Raj* during the intensely formative period following the transfer of the governance of India from the East India Company to the British crown (1858). The period 1858-1872 witnessed revolutionary innovations in financial organisation and policy commencing with the appointment of the first Finance Minister of India (then called the Finance Member) James Wilson, founder editor of *The Economist*. It saw, among other things, the introduction of the budget system, the income tax and paper currency.

The overarching theme of the book is: "Though the *laissez faire* principle was often invoked in defence of a policy of studied inaction in certain policy areas, it did not serve as a guide to practical policy. The policy actually pursued...may be more correctly described as *discriminatory interventionism* than *laissez faire*" (p.40) (emphasis provided). Its chosen instruments were tax and expenditure policies to subserve selected interests and achieve specific objectives. "*Laissez faire* was modified when the industrial and mercantile interests of England so demanded, and the Indian government, pursuing

* *Source:* *Economic and Political Weekly* XLI(35) (2 September 2006): 3772-3773.

• *The Financial Foundations of the British Raj (Ideas and Interests in the Reconstruction of Indian Public finance 1858-1872)* (revised edition) by Sabyasachi Bhattacharya (2005), Hyderabad: Orient Longman.

a policy that was essentially pragmatic, often deviated from *laissez faire* in important segments of public policy" (p.101).

The distinctive feature of the book is the perceptive analysis of the complex interplay of ideas, interests and policies. The ideas, based on a thick underlay of Benthamite utilitarianism, were an amalgam of "general notions derived from the philosophy of economic liberalism and the financial principles associated with the name of Gladstone" and "what one may call a special theory for India", which "derived from the special needs the government had to meet in the Indian empire" (pp. 40-41). These were: first, the need for security; second, the encouragement of capital investment through state guarantees, or some form of subsidy, as in the case of construction of railways and irrigation works, aptly called "private enterprise at public risk", third, to "aid the merchant indirectly, rather than play an entrepreneurial role" (p.43); and finally, "to help India perform her special role as the supplier of raw materials" (p.44).

Ideas, however, do not operate in a vacuum. They involve complex interactions with both the bureaucracy, and groups who have a real community of interests. "This study is confined to those groups which concerned themselves with the economic, particularly the financial policies of the Government of India" (p.4). In attempting to formulate a workable taxonomy of interest groups, the author, rather surprisingly, says: "We have not found in relevant literature a suitable typological scheme" (p.6). This overlooks, among others, Mancur Olson's classical monograph *Public Goods and the Theory of Groups* (1965). If for any reason the author found Olson's framework unsuitable, surely this aspect merited discussion. Nonetheless, his typology has a useful dichotomy of two broad groups. The first type comprises the "highly organised groups, each more or less homogeneous in terms of economic interests and pursuing objectives specific to those interests" (p.6) as exemplified by the chambers of commerce (Calcutta, Bombay, Madras and Karachi), the British Indian Association (Calcutta), the Calcutta Trades Association and the Indigo Planters, which was dominated by Europeans. These groups were interested chiefly in the government's policy concerning tariffs, income tax, inland duties, and land regulations affecting plantation enterprise. The second type of pressure group, although more heterogeneous, was nevertheless united in formal associations and usually offered general policy prescriptions because their heterogeneity precluded special pleading on behalf of a single economic group. These were broad-based coalitions like the East India Association, the India Reform Society and the Bombay Association.

The techniques used by pressure groups were necessarily limited in an authoritarian system. Typically, they involved the petitioning or memorialising the relevant organs of government, but proximity to the apex of the pyramid, India Office and Parliament, gave the pressure groups in England an edge over those in India. Another method was through deputation to the Secretary of State or the top members of the Government of India. A third method was propaganda through publicity organs like the periodical *Cotton Supply Reporter* or newspapers such as the *Hindoo Patriot* run by the British Indian Association, and *The Englishman* and *The Pioneer* representing the European commercial community in India. Similarly, *Rast Goftar*, the leading Parsi journal of Bombay, was used for propaganda by Dadabhai Naoroji and his associates in the East India Association. Lobbying in Parliament was an art, which Indians were gradually beginning to acquire. Not all lobbies were actuated by direct self-interest. There were independent critics of British policies in India like Henry Fawcett, MP for Brighton (1865 and 1868) and professor of political economy at Cambridge (1863-1884), who became notorious for his pro-Indian proclivities. Finally, another channel between a pressure group and the Government of India was through a group's representation in the Legislative Council and official committees. However, "foreign rule placed the indigenous pressure groups under special disabilities. Not the least of these was the social distance between the two races. This gave British interest groups an immense advantage over Indian ones" (p.24). All these varied constitutional techniques of lobbying were beyond the reach of the common people, the 'silent many' as the Viceroy Mayo called them, whose grievances and demands found vent in massive violent upsurges like the Indigo rebellion of Bengal or the Deccan riots. But even the *Raj* did not treat agrarian protest as a law-and-order problem. Is there a moral for contemporary India?

The post-1857 period, under the stewardship of Finance Members Wilson, Laing and Trevelyan, witnessed notable institutional innovations, the most important of which was the budget system that ensured a complete review of the income and expenditure of the coming year and a full scrutiny of the past year. It also ensured that expenditure would not exceed specific sanctions on each head of charge. Concomitantly, the new system of audit and accounts modernised the financial system inherited from the East India Company. Mayo's landmark scheme of financial devolution was implemented in 1871-1872. However, the Government of India Act 1858 concentrated full financial control in the hands of the Secretary of State in Council. The improvements in organisational efficiency were not reflected in the overall budgetary position, which showed deficits in all financial years except for 1862-1864, 1865-1866 and 1870-1872. More importantly, as Walter Bagehot asserted, nineteenth century India remained very much a member of 'a family of arrested civilizations'. Mayo, too, wrote scathingly of "European officials who look on India as a milch cow for themselves"; of English merchants, "who did not pretend to have any other object than the rapid acquirement of as much money as will enable them to live at home in idleness"; and of the native of substance "whose only idea of taxation is to ravish the poor" (p.288). In fact, there was an uncanny commonality of interest between the British mercantile community in India and propertied Indians, who were both united in their opposition to increases in direct taxation, while being very supportive or indirect taxes like the salt tax.

The author rightly cites the Indian opium question as a good instance of "how often questions of ethics and economics became inseparable in public discussions in this period" (p.90). There was no doubt a considerable body of opinion in England as well as India that was against the opium traffic on moral and other grounds. The government monopoly in opium, as Mayo admitted, was "one of the deepest blots on our escutcheon" (p.294). Ironically, Indian public opinion, with rare exceptions, was notably silent on the moral aspect of the opium question, as rightly pointed out by Dadabhai Naoroji, who also noted that many Indian newspapers took the stand that the opium revenue could not be given up for fiscal reasons (p.292). John Bull's self-interest morphed into his economics, and his economics soon became his ethics, but were contemporary Indians any less complicit in this sordid commerce?

This book, apart from its intrinsic contribution, has a corollary. It also exposes the curiously truncated character of the hackneyed and sufficiently vulgarised quotation from Keynes:

> The ideas of economists and political philosophers, both when they are right and when they are wrong, are more powerful than is commonly understood....Practical men, who believe themselves to be quite exempt from any intellectual influences, are usually the slaves of some defunct economist....The power of vested interests is vastly exaggerated, compared with the gradual encroachment of ideas. (1936: 383)

The economic history of India (1858-1872) conclusively demonstrates that ideas *per se* have little influence on events and policies. Rather it is the interplay of ideals, institutions, personalities and pressure groups.

However, this illuminating monograph raises a tantalising question. It does not explain whether the doctrines and policies of the East India Company had any carry-over influence on the successor government, considering that Sir James Steuart (1713-1780), the Scottish political economist, author of the pioneering classic, *An Inquiry into the Principles of Political Economy* (1767), was an adviser to the East India Company. He has been rightly called "the first Economic Adviser to the Government of India" (Sen, 1957), who presented a case for detailed state intervention into every aspect of economic life. "It would not be any great exaggeration to say that A.P. Lerner' s chapter on functional finance [in his *Economics of Control*, 1944] seems almost a paraphrase of Steuart" (Sen, 1957: 122). Is it conceivable that the strong institutional memory of the East India Company that passed through its civil servants trained at the Haileybury College did not also transmit the doctrines of Steuart to the successor Government of India, which surely did not innovate on a *tabula rasa?*

Overall, Bhattacharya's book is a distinctive work of historical scholarship, not least because of its sternly non-ideological stance, a shining contrast to the dogmatism of much of this genre in India. The robust scholarly apparatus too is draped in lapidary prose.

References

Hobsbawm, E.J. (1969). *Industry and Empire.* Harmondsworth: Pelican.

Keynes, John Maynard (1973; 1936). *The General Theory of Employment, Interest and Money*. London: Macmillan.

Olson, Mancur (1965). *The Logic of Collective Action (Public Goods and the Theory of Growth)*. Cambridge, Mass.: Harvard University Press.

Sen, S.R. (1957). *The Economics of Sir James Steuart*. London: Bell.

28 Dharma Kumar: A Pioneer Economic Historian

The passing of Dharma Kumar, the distinguished economic historian, after a harrowing terminal syndrome, evokes fond memories of an unusual personality, a scholar who carried her learning lightly, a *bon vivant* with an infectious zest for life, a splendid *raconteur*, a gracious host and, above all, a being with a gift for human relations that transcended station and nationality.

Our association began as colleagues in the Reserve Bank of India (RBI) which Dharma joined as the very first woman officer by direct entry. Despite her undoubted professionalism, it was clear that she was not cut out to be a central banker or a civil servant though, had she persevered in the RBI, she might well have stormed that male bastion as the first woman governor, a true Lady of Mint Road. She left the RBI for a predictably short stint in the Department of Economic Affairs (GOI) before joining the staff of the Delhi School of Economics where she found her true metier in economic history as an admired unorthodox teacher—who even recommended Edmund Wilson's classic *To the Finland Station*—a researcher, editor of the flagship *Indian Economic and Social History Review*, and editor of the pioneering *Cambridge Economic History of India* Vol. 2.

Who shaped Dharma the economist? Dharma was fortunate in her teachers both at Bombay and Cambridge, beginning with the universally admired N.S. Pardasani of Elphinstone College, Bombay, the proud *alma mater* of the pioneers of Indian economics—Naoroji, Ranade, Gokhale and Telang. From Pardasani, she learnt that economics is essentially a technique of analysis. At Cambridge (Newnham College), she was exposed to Ruth Cohen, "one of the select band of leading professional economists whose importance is measured more by her emphatically common sense influence on colleagues and pupils than by the length of her publications list". Cohen, author of the standard *Economics of Agriculture* was also an important, albeit neglected, contributor to contemporary capital theory. The analytics of rural economics imbibed from Ruth Cohen served Dharma well in her doctoral research on Land and Caste in South India.

Characteristically, Dharma fondly remembered Cambridge over dinner at that most literate eatery in Cambridge—Hobson's Choice—as a 'wonderfully haphazard place', whose real ethos lies in the junior Common Room with its indefinable blend of cerebral conviviality. But she also captured a neglected facet of Cambridge economics in a memorable witticism now happily enshrined in Skidelsky's biography of Keynes (Vol. II). 'There is a famous Cambridge joke. In the 1960s, a group of Cambridge economists were discussing Bergson's aphorism that time was a device to stop everything happening at once, when one of them, Dharma Kumar, quipped, "I suppose space is a device to stop everything happening in Cambridge".' A subtle dig at the insularity of Cambridge economists, on a par with Myrdal's magisterial stricture on the Cambridge School's "attractive Anglo-Saxon kind of unnecessary originality." But for Dharma even academic Cambridge had its lighter side. Her favourite Cambridge anecdote—now confirmed in Noel Annan's *Our Age*—as if to illustrate its haphazardness, was Michael Postan's matrimonial route to the chair of economic history on the retirement of Sir John Clapham. The only other candidate was Postan's better known collaborator, Eileen Power. Postan eliminated his rival by marrying her, a delicious stratagem undreamt of by any novelist of academia—Snow, Amis, Bradbury, or David Lodge.

What transformed Dharma the economist into an economic historian? To begin with, she was powerfully influenced by Michael Postan's inaugural lecture at Cambridge as Professor of Economic History on 'The Historical Method in the Social Sciences', which served her as a constant reminder of the historical method as a potent tool for economics, too. But it was the persuasiveness of M.N. Srinivas, the noted social anthropologist, who first noticed her special aptitude for economic history, that eventually prompted her to do her award-winning (Ellen MacArthur Prize) Cambridge doctoral dissertation subsequently published as *Land and Caste in South India*, also a bridge between economic history and social anthropology. Srinivas held up to her the example of his own teacher at Oxford, the redoubtable Evans-Pritchard, who demonstrated the potentiality or history as the prime tool of social anthropology in his work on the Sanusi, the Nuer, and the Azande.

The Cambridge University's invitation to Dharma to serve as the editor of the Second Volume of the *Cambridge Economic History of India (CEHI)* was a signal recognition of her professional standing. It was a monumental, even arduous, enterprise, which involved shepherding some incredibly wayward *prima donnas* among the contributors. The CEHI brought me into a close, sustained, and most instructive relationship with Dharma. Since her departure from the RBI we had lost contact. I was flattered but also overwhelmed by her invitation to contribute the chapter on "Money and Credit" which was delayed because a RBI jack-in-office informed her that Mr Chandavarkar had left the RBI and his address was not known to them, although I was still on deputation from the RBI to the IMF. Luckily, a common friend gave her my address. I was too diffident to accept her invitation as economic history was not my specialisation. She overcame my hesitations. In the event, she proved a most constructive editor with an unerring instinct for essentials. The only mishap was the Italian post office's failure to deliver her my typescript at her holiday address. I received a plantive cable, "A shameful confession. The Italian PO has not delivered your article. May I please have a replacement copy? Apologies." I cabled, "Will send another copy by courier. The Italian PO is only true to form. Remember the East India Company required its India-bound cadet officers to make an obligatory stop-over in Brindisi (Italy) to acclimatise them to Indian conditions." Dharma thus launched and kept afloat an unreconstructed central banker in the heady waters of Indian economic history. I vividly recall Dharma's scintillating performance as moderator of the conference on the CEHI held at Selwyn College, Cambridge, in the 1980s. She gave a most cogent expose of the framework and spirit of the history and demolished the usual cohorts of critics, ideological and *ad hominem*, rearing to hurl Wittgenstein's Poker. One critic who had a snide remark about the gaps in the reading of a contributor and his institutional affiliation was disarmed by Dharma in private.

Dharma's mindset exemplified the philosopher's Occam's razor—entities should not be multiplied beyond necessity. It could be seen in her thought and language with its unerring instinct for the jugular. The diction was spare but elegant and incisive. I recall her sententious two-line letters on tasteful picture postcards. Conversationally, she was a consummate exponent of the Retort Courteous. She had tremendous sangfroid which surfaced when she emerged unfazed from a committee meeting of a Washington research institute after a gratuitous personal attack on her by a North American academic. She hardly said a word on what had transpired. Dharma never bore grudges but she did not lack for jealous critics even during her terminal condition. As Bernard Shaw said of Joan of Arc she was burned not for any reason except that she was talented. She always liked to look at the lighter side of men and matters. We shared a common interest in collecting bureaucratic foibles at all levels and had agreed on a project, 'Tales of the Abominable No-Man and the Babucracy', which sadly never came to fruition. We had even agreed on the lead epigraph for this irreverent collection ("As this is a matter of the highest importance it should dealt with at the lowest possible level", Graham Greene). A priceless nugget was her own *chaprasi* (peon) in Delhi who persisted in referring her to her callers as Dharam Kumari *Sahib* and her husband as Dharam Kumar *Sahib*—surely decision-making at the lowest possible level.

Dharma was an ardent Indian protective of Indian *amour propre*. She never belonged to the vocal hegemons of the school, "No patriotism, please! We are objective intellectuals of the Left but we are always in the Right." She took a quiet effortless pride in her country and she relished Joan Robinson's memorable quip, "Human nature is the same everywhere but it is more so in India." In a tell-tale encounter following I.G. Patel's stellar performance at Cambridge (starred First in the Economics Tripos, the Wrenbury Scholarship, and Adam Smith Prize), Dharma was accosted by an English undergraduate: "You Indians must be terribly jealous of Patel." "Not half as much as those stunned by a native's achievements" was the cool riposte. Equally, Dharma was an outgoing cosmopolitan with a catholicity of friends and interests, an aspect which surfaced most memorably in the 1980s, during one of the periodic lows in Indo-Pak relations, when she and her husband, Lovraj, at considerable political risk, helped a Pakistani economist Ehtisham Ahmad then at the LSE (now at the IMF) to come out as a visiting fellow at the NIPFP, New Delhi. Ehtisham Ahmad writes, "Dharma and Lavy opened their home to us, with an affectionate warmth that we have always cherished...Dharma took Mahnaz [Mrs Ahmad] under her wing, and gave her counsel and strength, much as a mother would."

Eulogies, like epitaphs, are all too soon forgotten. Dharma's life was an unfinished symphony, whose notes and resonances were muffled well before the finale and died down unheard. What could be more fitting than the endowment in her name of an Oral History Archives and Research Centre at the Delhi School of Economics, to house oral archives based, among others, on structured interviews of significant protagonists in public life. Such a memorial would help perpetuate her memory and remove a glaring deficiency in the research base of Indian historiography which relies so heavily on documentary material.

Her devoted mother-in-law, Mrs Sahai, now in her nineties, gave her unremitting care and affection through the last years of her tragic condition. It was a lonely vigil wholly uninterrupted by visits from "friends" who had enjoyed her generous hospitality. We share with Mrs Sahai and Dharma's daughter, Radha, the loss of a much loved and admired person, a feminine exemplar of Chaucer's 'verray, parfit gentil knyght'. RIP.

29 A Macroeconomic Whodunit*

Keynesian or Monetarist?

At last, economics has entered the world of crime fiction with this murder mystery authored by Murray Wolfson, professor of economics at California State University, Fullerton, and Vincent Buranelli, a professional writer and holder of a doctorate in history from Cambridge University.• It can claim to be possibly the first crime novel authored by an economist with economists as the principal protagonists and macroeconomics as the arena of conflict and crime.

Academic economists, as befits rigorous social scientists, have traditionally disdained the writing of crime fiction unlike literature and history Oxford dons such as J.I.M. Stewart (Michael Innes), J.C. Masterman, and the poet Cecil Day Lewis (Nicholas Blake). The possible exceptions are, first, G.D.H. Cole, the Fabian economist, who held the chair of political and social theory at Oxford, and collaborated with his wife Margaret Postgate in writing detective fiction. The other economist who ventured into crime fiction was Per Jacobsson, one-time managing director of the IMF, who collaborated with Vernon Bartlett, a British journalist and broadcaster, in two thrillers, *The Death of a Diplomat* (1928) and *The Alchemy Murder* (1929), using a shared pseudonym Peter Oldfield. As his biographer daughter Erin Jacobsson says, "The writing of these two books probably gave P.J. more pleasure than all his economic writing...he was always delighted to explain that he owed his membership of the PEN Club to his detective stories: he was touchingly proud of them" (*A Life for Sound Money*, Oxford: Clarendon Press, 1979: 70). This is, indeed, heartening if only to establish, as does this novel, that economics need not be a bar to literary productivity, albeit in the historic treason trial of the poet Ezra Pound, the defence counsel admitted pathetically that his client's poetic fecundity had been rendered sterile by a somewhat excessive addiction to monetary economics. But the unexplained mystery is why the rare economist

---

* *Source:* *Economic and Political Weekly* XXV(33) (18 August 1990): 1833.

• *In the Long Run We Are All Dead (A Macroeconomics Murder Mystery),* by Murray Wolfson and Vincent Buranelli, New York: St Martin's Press, 1990 (second edition); pp. vi+184.

who ventures into crime fiction needs to collaborate with a non-economist—a carryover of professional habits!

All this should not deter the curious reader from this gripping 'whodunit' set in the Washington DC, ambience of the US presidential offices, the Pentagon, the US Navy, and Georgetown. The appropriate but wholly predictable title of the novel is from Keynes's famously unread *A Tract on Monetary Reform* (1923). The whole action is set in the midst of a deepening economic crisis in the US with the twin deficits in the federal budget and foreign trade threatening to destabilise the new order of President Curtin, whose contractionary monetary and fiscal policy plunges the country into a deep recession. The president collapses under the strain and Vice-President Wedik, who takes office in panic, proceeds to appoint Murray Sokolow, a retired Ivy League professor and a traditional Keynesian, as chairman of the Council of Economic Advisors. Sokolow believes that macroeconomic policy can regulate the economy if he can negotiate a social contract between competing interests, but his neo-Keynesian former student and now protégé, Howard Tilson, is insistent that demand management be directed to favour the less privileged. In counterpoise stands the Chicago monetarist Martin Christopherson, a former banker and now chairman, by way of the Federal Reserve Bank of St Louis, of the Board of Governors of the Federal Reserve System. Supply-side economics is represented by Geraldine Anderson of the Commerce Department ("More interesting than her economic theories. She is dazzling"). Then there are an assorted crew of neo-classical economists.

Wedik, pulled in opposite directions by the Keynesians and monetarists, cannot act in the face of a speculative crisis and impending collapse of the dollar and is only three days away from a major policy announcement scheduled for Sunday. The presidential advisor, Admiral Harcourt Green ("every economist I know is mad about something") hopes he will make "some sense out of this four-way rhubarb, Keynesians, monetarists, supply-siders and neo-classical economists." His aide is the attractive Navy Lieutenant Alice Ritter ("Black is beautiful. Even in the Navy"), fully confident of her college (Annapolis Naval Academy) Economics 101 expertise. The other dramatis personae are: Frances Green, the shrewish suspicious wife of the Admiral; Marianne Van Thuys, the sophisticated dulcet-voiced Dutch mistress "at whose Georgetown apartment the good Admiral is often found" working late; Professor Alan Claus of Georgetown University, a specialist in the theory and measurement of expectations; and a business partner of the Admiral holding a balloon mortgage.

In the first chapter Admiral Green, being a non-economist, reaches a decision pretty briskly, but on his way to the fateful Sunday meeting is murdered by an unknown assailant. Who could it be—the fanatical Keynesian adviser; the equally passionate monetarist chairman of the Federal Reserve; the jealous wife; the ambitious mistress Marianne; the attractive aide Alice; the personable supply-sider Geraldin; the business partner; or the consultant Georgetown professor? Each has a motive. But what of the murder weapon (poisoned Occam's razor, laced treble martinis, high-velocity telescopic rifle, James Bondish Biretta with a silencer)?

The text, larded as it is with money illusion, Say's Law, Phillips Curve, balanced-budget theorem, *et al.*, is strong meat for the non-economist. Clearly, this novel is not only about economists by an economist but also for economists to read and enjoy. The two major protagonists, the Keynesian and the monetarist, however, come across as somewhat stylised personalities lacking in flesh and blood unlike the others, notably the female of the species. But the story does not lack in suspense. What more can one ask of a 'whodunit'? The authors, who deserve full kudos for an original type of crime fiction, have also performed the unique literary feat of a second edition (not a reprint) of a crime novel! Certainly, an unresolved mystery for at least one reader.

Index

J

K

L

M

N

Y

Z